KW-742-144

LONGMAN LINGUISTICS LIBRARY

THE ACQUISITION OF SYNTAX

LONGMAN LINGUISTICS LIBRARY

General editors

R. H. ROBINS, *University of London*
GEOFFREY HORROCKS, *University of Cambridge*
DAVID DENISON, *University of Manchester*

For a complete list of books in the series, see pages v and vi.

P118 ACQ

QMW Library

23 1186600 3

DATE DUE FOR RETURN

CANCELLED

NEW ACCESSIONS

- 1 MAY 2009

0 1 MAY 2009

- 4 MAY 2007

0 1 MAY 2009

WITHDRAWN
FROM STOCK
QMUL LIBRARY

The Acquisition of Syntax:

Studies in Comparative Developmental Linguistics

Edited by Marc-Ariel Friedemann and Luigi Rizzi

LONGMAN

An imprint of **PEARSON EDUCATION**

Harlow, England · London · New York · Reading, Massachusetts · San Francisco · Toronto · Don Mills, Ontario · Sydney
Tokyo · Singapore · Hong Kong · Seoul · Taipei · Cape Town · Madrid · Mexico City · Amsterdam · Munich · Paris · Milan

Pearson Education Limited
Edinburgh Gate
Harlow
Essex CM20 2JE
England

and Associated Companies throughout the world.

Visit us on the World Wide Web at:
www.pearsoned-ema.com

First published 2000

© Pearson Education Limited 2000

All rights reserved; no part of this publication may be
reproduced, stored in a retrieval system, or transmitted
in any form or by any means, electronic, mechanical,
photocopying, recording, or otherwise without either the
prior written permission of the Publishers or a licence
permitting restricted copying in the United Kingdom
issued by the Copyright Licensing Agency Ltd.,
90 Tottenham Court Road, London W1P 9HE.

ISBN 0-582-32883-7 CSD
ISBN 0-582-32882-9 PPR

British Library Cataloguing-in-Publication Data

A catalogue record for this book is
available from the British Library

Library of Congress Cataloging-in-Publication Data

The acquisition of syntax : studies in comparative developmental
    linguistics / edited by Marc-Ariel Friedemann and Luigi Rizzi.
        p.   cm. — (Longman linguistics library)
    Includes bibliographical references and index.
    ISBN 0-582-32883-7. — ISBN 0-582-32882-9 (pbk.)
    1. Language acquisition.   2. Grammar, Comparative and general—
Syntax.   I. Friedemann, Marc-Ariel.   II. Rizzi, Luigi, 1952–
III. Series.
P118.A1427   1999
401'.43—dc21   99–27239
                                                      CIP

QUEEN MARY &
WESTFIELD
COLLEGE LIBRARY

Set by 35 in 10/11 pt Times
Produced by Pearson Education Asia Pte Ltd.,
Printed in Singapore

LONGMAN LINGUISTICS LIBRARY

General Editors:

R. H. Robins
University of London

Geoffrey Horrocks
University of Cambridge

David Denison
University of Manchester

Introduction to Text Linguistics
ROBERT DE BEAUGRANDE and
WOLFGANG DRESSLER

Psycholinguistics
Language, Mind and World
DANNY D. STEINBERG

Principles of Pragmatics
GEOFFREY N. LEECH

Generative Grammar
GEOFFREY HORROCKS

The English Verb
Second edition
F. R. PALMER

Pidgin and Creole Languages
SUZANNE ROMAINE

General Linguistics
An Introductory Survey
Fourth edition
R. H. ROBINS

A History of English Phonology
CHARLES JONES

**Generative and Non-linear
Phonology**
JACQUES DURAND

Modality and the English Modals
Second edition
F. R. PALMER

Dialects of English
Studies in Grammatical Variation
PETER TRUDGILL and
J. K. CHAMBERS (eds)

An Introduction to Bilingualism
CHARLOTTE HOFFMANN

Linguistic Theory
The Discourse of Fundamental Works
ROBERT DE BEAUGRANDE

Verb and Noun Number in English
A Functional Explanation
WALLIS REID

A History of American English
J. L. DILLARD

Historical Linguistics
Problems and Perspectives
CHARLES JONES (ed.)

Aspect in the English Verb
Process and Result in Language
YISHAI TOBIN

English Historical Syntax
DAVID DENISON

The Meaning of Syntax
A Study in the Adjectives of English
CONNOR FERRIS

Latin American Spanish
JOHN LIPSKI

A Linguistic History of Italian
MARTIN MAIDEN

The History of Linguistics
All edited by GIULIO LEPSCHY

**Volume I:
The Eastern Traditions of
Linguistics**

**Volume II:
Classical and Medieval Linguistics**

**Volume III:
Renaissance and Early Modern
Linguistics**

**Volume IV:
Nineteenth Century Linguistics**
ANNA MORPURGO DAVIES

To come:
**Volume V:
The Twentieth Century**

Modern Arabic
Structures, Functions and Varieties
CLIVE HOLES

Frontiers of Phonology
Atoms, Structures and Derivations
JACQUES DURAND and
FRANCIS KATAMBA (eds)

**An Introduction to the Celtic
Languages**
PAUL RUSSELL

Causatives and Causation
A Universal-typological Perspective
JAE JUNG SONG

A Short History of Linguistics
Fourth edition
R. H. ROBINS

**Grammar and Grammarians in the
Early Middle Ages**
VIVIEN LAW

Greek
A History of the Language and its
Speakers
GEOFFREY HORROCKS

The New Comparative Syntax
LILIANE HAEGEMAN (ed.)

**The Structure and History of
Japanese**
LONE TAKEUCHI

The Acquisition of Syntax
Studies in Comparative
Developmental Linguistics
MARC-ARIEL FRIEDEMANN and
LUIGI RIZZI (eds)

Contents

Contributors

Sonja Eisenbeiss, MPI für Psycholinguistik, Nijmegen, the Netherlands

Marc-Ariel Friedemann, Département de linguistique générale, Université de Genève, Switzerland

Na'ama Friedmann, Department of Psychology, Tel-Aviv University, Israel

Yosef Grodzinsky, Department of Psychology, Tel-Aviv University, Israel, and Aphasia Research Center, Department of Neurology, Boston University School of Medicine, USA

Maria Teresa Guasti, Facoltà di lettere e filosofia, Università di Siena, Italy

Liliane Haegeman, Département de linguistique générale, Université de Genève, Switzerland

Cornelia Hamann, Département de linguistique générale, Université de Genève, Switzerland

Philippe Prévost, Langues et linguistique, Université Laval, Canada

Lucienne Rasetti, Département de linguistique générale, Université de Genève, Switzerland

Luigi Rizzi, Facoltà di lettere e filosofia, Università di Siena, Italy

Manuela Schönenberger, Institut für Linguistik-Anglistik, Universität Stuttgart, Germany

Lydia White, Department of Linguistics, McGill University, Canada

Editors' acknowledgements

We wish to thank the contributors to this volume for their generous collaboration, which made this work possible: Sonja Eisenbeiss, Na'ama Friedmann, Yosef Grodzinsky, Teresa Guasti, Liliane Haegeman, Cornelia Hamann, Philippe Prévost, Lucienne Rasetti, Manuela Schönenberger and Lydia White. Other colleagues have also been very helpful in providing ideas, comments and criticisms at the various stages we went through in the preparation of this volume and its content: special thanks are due to Adriana Belletti, Harald Clahsen, Zvi Penner, Ur Shlonsky, Tali Siloni, Juergen Weissenborn and Ken Wexler. Finally, we are grateful to the staff at Addison Wesley Longman for their help and support throughout the production of this book, and to Florence Faval, who made the etching especially for the cover of the book. Marc-Ariel Friedemann has been supported by grant N° 8210-042998 of the *Fonds national. suisse de la recherche scientifique* and by the *Programme plurifacultaire 'Langage et communication: acquisition, traitement et pathologie des structures grammaticales et lexicales'* (University of Geneva).

Chapter 1

The acquisition of syntax: introduction
Marc-Ariel Friedemann and Luigi Rizzi

1 Generative grammar and language acquisition

Ever since the fifties, the research program of generative grammar has focused on language acquisition. Chomsky's celebrated review of Skinner's *Verbal Behavior* (Chomsky 1959), one of the milestones of the cognitive revolution, bases its critique of the behaviorist approach on the characteristics of language acquisition: natural languages are extraordinarily rich and complex systems of knowledge; still, children acquire them early in life, with considerable ease and rapidity, without explicit instruction, and on the basis of limited exposure to linguistic data. In order to account for such a remarkable accomplishment, which is well within the cognitive capacity of every normal child, it is necessary to assume a strong innate predisposition to acquire a language, as part of the biological endowment of our species; elementary and unspecific techniques of induction, generalization, reinforcement such as those assumed by the empiricist tradition had no hope of even starting to address the problem.

During the sixties, the problem of language acquisition became so important in generative grammar that a specific notion of explanation was defined which was directly tied to acquisition: an analysis of some element of linguistic knowledge of the adult native speaker was said to reach 'explanatory adequacy' when, in addition to properly expressing the speaker's linguistic intuitions ('descriptive adequacy'), it came with a reasonable account of how the speaker had acquired it. Explanatory adequacy could be reached through the assumption of a rich system of predetermined linguistic knowledge, Universal Grammar, which guided the child in his or her preliminary analysis of the incoming linguistic data by drastically reducing the 'search space' for tacit grammatical constructions, thus enormously facilitating the acquisition of the language he or she was exposed to (see the introduction of Chomsky 1965

for detailed discussion). Given these premises, it comes as no surprise
that Chomsky's article 'Conditions on Transformations', the first large-
scale attempt to structure a theory of Universal Grammar, starts with
the following statement: 'From the point of view that I adopt here, the
fundamental empirical problem of linguistics is to explain how a person
can acquire knowledge of language' (Chomsky 1973).

   In spite of such a strong focus on acquisition, until relatively recently, little attention was paid by theoretical linguists to the actual
course of language development. The problem of language acquisition
was addressed as a logical problem, in the abstract terms sometimes
referred to as 'Plato's problem': how can every human being develop a
rich system of linguistic knowledge on the basis of limited and fragment-
ary empirical evidence? More precisely, given the course of linguistic
experience available to the learner (the sentences he or she hears in early
childhood) and the system of his or her adult linguistic knowledge,
which can be studied and explicitly modeled through the techniques of
modern linguistics, we want to know what internal structure a learning
system must have to ensure the transition from the available experience
to the acquired knowledge. This question, which can be made fully
precise with the techniques of Learnability Theory (Pinker 1979, Wexler
and Culicover 1980), can be asked in its simplest form by abstracting
away from the actual time course, and idealizing the process as instant-
aneous. Such an abstract approach to language acquisition as a particular
subcase of Plato's problem was extraordinarily successful. It uncovered
the massive existence of 'poverty of stimulus' situations, situations in
which all speakers have unerringly converged to share elements of knowledge which are underdetermined by the experience available in childhood. The pervasive poverty of stimulus made it legitimate to ascribe
significant portions of the adult knowledge of language to Universal
Grammar, thus allowing theoretical linguists to make rapid progress in
the study of the human language faculty. So, till relatively recently, a
rather common attitude among theoretical linguists was to think of
language acquisition uniquely in the abstract terms of Plato's problem,
paying little attention to the empirical study of what children actually
know or do with language in the course of development.

2 The new comparative syntax and the study of language acquisition

Things have changed very considerably since the early eighties. It is not
accidental that the change of attitude took place shortly after the introduction of the Principles and Parameters model of Universal Grammar
(Chomsky 1981). The parametric approach introduced technical tools
well suited for the comparison of natural languages, capable of concisely

expressing the points of divergence between grammatical systems while at the same time highlighting the fundamental underlying uniformity. These theoretical advances had important consequences for the study of language acquisition.

On the one hand, the parametric approach offered a very appealing route to address the learnability issues. A particular grammar, an explicit theory of the adult speaker's knowledge of his or her native language, could be conceived of as a particular instantiation of Universal Grammar under a specific set of parametric values: the grammar of French is UG with the headedness parameter fixed on the 'head initial' value, the null subject and V-2 parameters fixed negatively, the clitic parameters fixed positively with the clitic host(s) identified in the inflectional system, and so on. The grammars of Italian and English differ from the grammar of French with respect to the values of the null subject and the clitic parameters, respectively, etc. German and Swedish are alike with respect to V-2, but differ in headedness, etc. Language acquisition could then be modeled in part as the operation of fixing the values of the parameters of the system: the child, equipped with the invariable principles of Universal Grammar, interprets the incoming linguistic data and, on the basis of this linguistic experience, he or she fixes the values of the parameters. The initial cognitive state for language is Universal Grammar before the fixation of parameters (possibly with the parameters preset on an initial, unmarked value). Acquisition involves the fixation of parameters through experience (as well as other tasks, such as the memorization of the arbitrary form–meaning associations that form the lexicon). For instance, the learner of French must figure out from the incoming data that the language he or she is exposed to has a clitic system with the host(s) in the V-related inflectional system; the child learning Swedish must determine that his or her language is V-2, and so on. The stable cognitive state is UG with a stable set of parametric values, a particular grammar which is able to compute linguistic representations over an unlimited domain. So, under the parametric approach, the task of the learner was clearly identified as involving a limited, possibly small, number of operations (and additional progress has been made more recently in this respect with the attempt to limit the format for parameters within the Minimalist Program; see Chomsky 1995). Even under such conditions, the task remained far from trivial, and additional assumptions on unmarked values and the learning procedure were needed to make the task feasible for the learner (Wexler and Manzini 1987, Clark 1992, Gibson and Wexler 1994). Nevertheless, there is little doubt that the theory of principles and parameters represented a major conceptual and formal breakthrough in the approach to Plato's problem for language, with the identification of a much more well-defined set of tasks for the learner than the rather obscure 'induction of a particular rule system' which was assumed in previous approaches.

On the other hand, the theory of principles and parameters provoked new interest in the study of development. The parametric approach is well adapted to compare systems that are essentially uniform but diverge in specific and limited structural respects, in a way that highlights the fundamental underlying uniformity without obliterating the specificity of each system. It is only natural to try out the same approach for the comparison of early and adult grammatical systems. A preliminary question for the study of language development along these lines is the continuity issue: are early grammatical systems UG-constrained systems, systems fundamentally homogeneous to adult systems in their structural properties and in the tools they use? Of course, only a positive answer to the continuity question makes it legitimate and fruitful to use parametric models to compare early and adult systems. To the best of our current understanding, the answer is indeed largely positive: early systems are cast in the same mold as adult grammatical systems. On the one hand, the continuity hypothesis is supported by the observed early sensitivity to UG principles: in a number of cases, children appear to be sensitive to UG principles as early as it is possible to test their grammatical knowledge experimentally (Otsu 1981, Crain and Fodor 1984, Hamburger and Crain 1984, Crain and Nakayama 1987, Crain 1991). On the other hand, the very empirical success of the developmental studies of the last ten years through the UG apparatus is a strong a posteriori confirmation of the validity of continuity assumptions.

3 Parameters and the study of development: the case of early null subjects

In the early eighties, intensive work was devoted to the study of the null subject parameter, the first case addressed in a systematic way within the Principles and Parameters approach. Some natural languages allow the possibility of not overtly expressing the pronominal subject of tensed clauses. A number of other properties (free subject inversion, subject extraction across an overt complementizer, etc.) appear to correlate with the null subject option. It was possible to show that this state of affairs can be made to follow from a single primitive property, the licensing of a null pronominal subject by the verbal inflection, in interaction with the deductive structure of the theory of UG (Chomsky 1981, Rizzi 1982 and much subsequent work). As soon as the field was ready to address the question of how parameter fixation works in the actual course of development, the null subject parameter appeared to be a natural candidate. Earlier work had already noticed that children acquiring English go through a stage, some time around the second birthday, during which subjects appear to be optional (Bloom 1970, Bloom, Lightbown and Hood 1975). Below are some examples from Eve's corpus (Brown 1973), available through the CHILDES database (MacWhinney 1999, MacWhinney and Snow 1985):

(1) a. __ was a green one (1;10)
    b. __ have to drink grape juice first (1;10)
    c. __ falled in the briefcase (1;10)

Hyams (1986) proposed that (1) could be interpreted directly in terms of the null subject parameter. If one thinks of parameters as binary switches which can take one of two values, one could assume that the null subject parameter is always set initially on the positive value; the language learner then starts with a system which allows null subjects. If the language he or she is exposed to is consistent with this value (e.g. Italian), nothing changes; but if the language to be acquired (say, English) is inconsistent with the initial value, the child must reset the parameter on the negative value. This may require time and the processing of a significant amount of data, whence the observable developmental stage characterized by the null subject option. Hyams' proposal was extremely influential among theoretical linguists, as it showed the concrete possibility of applying UG models to the study of development, thus significantly enlarging the empirical basis of the theory. It also caught the attention of developmental psycholinguists, as it offered a promising basis for a theory-guided approach to the description of language development.

Hyams' work (like many recent studies inspired by her proposal) takes up a stand against extragrammatical accounts of early subject omission, accounts that argue that the occurrence of subjectless utterances in the early stages of language development is the result of performance limitations. Early systems, under such approaches, suffer from severe processing limitations that lead to production that does not reflect the grammatical knowledge of the child. Subsequent years have known a controversy between supporters of the extragrammatical option (Bloom 1990, 1993, Valian 1991, among others) and proponents of the grammatical account (Rizzi this volume, and Hyams and Wexler's 1993 comprehensive discussion). By now, we believe, a significant amount of evidence has been accumulated that the early drop of subjects is sensitive to very subtle syntactic properties and cannot be reduced to purely extragrammatical factors such as heavy processing load or other global limitations of the early performance system.

Much work over the last decade has provided robust evidence that the phenomenon of early subject drop is indeed a typical stage in the linguistic development of children across languages. Children acquiring French, German, Dutch, Danish, whose target languages are not null subject languages, pass through a stage of subject omission (Pierce 1992, Weissenborn 1992, Haegeman 1996, Hamann and Plunkett 1998, respectively). On the other hand, the study of the fine structural properties of early null subjects has revealed that the phenomenon obeys configurational constraints which are not at all typical of subject drop in adult null subject languages. First, early null subjects virtually do not occur in post-*wh* environments (Crisma 1992, Levow 1995 for French, Haegeman 1996 for Dutch, or Clahsen, Kursawe and Penke 1996 for German). Second, they are limited to main clauses. Roeper and Weissenborn (1990) and Valian (1991), for example, found no null subjects in the earliest finite subordinate clauses of children acquiring English, at a stage where main clause null subjects are still produced. Early Italian null subjects, in contrast, do not exhibit these structural properties on a par with their adult equivalents. That is, natural production corpora in early Italian typically contain target-consistent sentences such as the following:

(2) Dove vai?
    where (you) go

This difference between early English and early Italian suggests that around the age of two, learners of the two languages have already converged to the correct value of the null subject parameter. This conforms to results of much recent research suggesting that the final fixation of basic parameters of word order or verb movement takes place at a very early age. Often, the correct value is manifested by the earliest relevant outputs (see next section for relevant references). If so, then early subject omission in non null subject languages ought to be accounted for in different terms.

4 Early null subjects and root infinitives

Retaining Hyams' insight that the phenomenon of early subject drop is a genuine grammatical option, Rizzi (1992) suggests that the drop in question instantiates a different grammatical option which is more limited and found only in particular adult registers (Haegeman 1990a, 1990b): the option to omit subjects in the first position of the structure, i.e. in the specifier of the root. The proposal relies on the following background of theoretical assumptions. Early grammars, unlike adult grammars (in the unmarked case), do not require that propositions be full CPs. Early sentences can therefore be cut off or truncated at some lower level. Truncation is constrained to proceed systematically, cutting off external layers without skipping arbitrary intermediate projections. Under the truncation hypothesis, children can produce both full CPs and reduced structures. If the CP layer is truncated, the IP layer becomes the root and the subject position is the specifier of the root, the highest position of the clausal structure. Apparently this position is one which freely allows an empty filler. Why is it so? In general, the possible occurrence of empty positions is governed by restrictive principles: in particular, the content of null elements must be identified in a principled manner by overt elements in the immediate structural environment (for instance, the content of PRO is identified by a controller, the content of a trace is identified by its chain antecedent, etc.). So, how can a null Spec of the root fail to comply with the identification requirement? Suppose that clause-internal identification is compulsory up to virtual satisfiability, i.e. it must be satisfied if it can be satisfied, a mode of application which has been proposed for other grammatical principles as well (Chomsky 1986). The specifier of the root is the highest position of the clause, it is not c-commanded by any other position, so there is no clause-internal potential identifier for it: it can then escape clause-internal identification, under the proposed interpretation of the principle. This accounts for the fact that the distribution of early null subjects is by and large limited to matrix declarative contexts. The question finally arises why root null subjects cease to occur in adult Standard English, French, etc. The possibility that was entertained in the reference quoted is that at a certain stage in the linguistic development, the principle requiring that the canonical realization of propositions be a CP becomes operative, possibly in accordance with an inner maturational schedule (Borer and Wexler 1987), and the conditions making root null subjects possible cease to be met (see Rizzi, this volume, for the discussion of a possible alternative).

The truncation approach has been invoked also in connection with another major property of early child grammars. Children around the age of two typically produce 'root infinitives', matrix declaratives whose main verb is in the infinitival form, as in (3); parallel infinitival constructions do not occur in adult grammars. Wexler's (1992) seminal study on the topic offers a broad crosslinguistic cover of the phenomenon. Below are some examples in early French, German and Dutch, respectively:

(3) a. Dormir tout nu. (Daniel 1;10, from Pierce 1989)
     sleep$_{inf}$ all naked
   b. Ich der Fos hab'n. (Andreas 2;1, from Poeppel and
     I the frog have$_{inf}$ Wexler 1993)
   c. Eerst kleine boekje lezen. (Hein 2;6, from Haegeman 1995)
     first small book read$_{inf}$

It has been suggested that the production of these main clause infinitives results from the lack of functional categories at the early stages of
acquisition (Guilfoyle and Noonan 1991, Lebeaux 1988, Platzack 1990,
Radford 1990). Children use small clauses where adults project the full
functional material. The small clause hypothesis is fully systematized
in Radford's (1990) extensive work on the topic. Children, in this view,
do not master the functional layers from the onset, and therefore use
nonfinite forms. When producing finite forms, children use them as
unanalyzed variants of the nonfinite forms. However, subsequent research
has shown that children at that age syntactically distinguish between
finite verbs and infinitives, and can coherently use functional structure.
Thus, children acquiring French systematically raise finite verbs, but
not infinitives, across negation to I, just like adults do (Pierce 1989,
1992, Weissenborn 1988, among others):

(4) a. Grégoire voit pas voisine. (Grégoire 1;11)
       Grégoire sees not neighbor
    b. Touche pas. (Philippe 2;1)
       touch not
    c. Pas marcher toboggan. (Philippe 2;2)
       not work$_{inf}$ sledge
    d. Pas laisser tout   nu. (Philippe 2;3)
       not leave$_{inf}$ completely naked

                                        (Friedemann 1993–94)

Likewise, children acquiring V2 languages typically show V2 effects in
early stages: they raise finite verbs and place them in the second position, leaving infinitives in clause-final position (de Haan 1986, Verrips
and Weissenborn 1992, among others). German early examples are
given in (5):

(5) a. Ich mach das nich.
       I   do that not
    b. Ich hab ein dossen Ball.
       I   have a   big   ball
    c. Thorsten Caesar haben.
       Thorston Caesar have$_{inf}$
    d. Du das haben.
       you that have$_{inf}$
                (Andreas 2;1, from Poeppel and Wexler 1993)

In light of that, it seems fairly safe to conclude that children project functional layers very early on; their initial syntactic representations cannot be purely lexical nor can they systematically constitute
manifestations of small clauses excluding functional material. It is

however possible that the early grammatical systems do not always project the entire functional structure of adult grammars, as suggested by the truncation hypothesis, which to a certain extent comprises Radford's basic insight with regard to structural reduction. Under the truncation hypothesis, early grammars can generate full CPs alongside reduced structures. The latter give rise to both root null subjects and main clause infinitives. Are there good reasons to believe that early matrix infinitivals are not full CPs? And why would they be licensed in truncated structures?

First, it has been observed that early infinitives, like early null subjects, do not appear in *wh*-questions in French (Crisma 1992), Dutch (Haegeman 1995), or German (Weissenborn 1992). If early matrix infinitivals lack the CP layer (they are truncated lower in the structure), they cannot give rise to *wh*-questions. Second, weak pronominal subjects scarcely ever occur with early French infinitives (Pierce 1989, 1992), which shows that early infinitives are not simple variants of finite verbs. Under the assumption that French weak pronominal subjects intrinsically bear structural nominative Case, which is checked exclusively in the specifier of IP, their (near) absence follows from truncation, if the structures are cut off below SpecIP. Third, early infinitives typically involve lexical verbs and not auxiliaries (Wexler 1992). Assuming that auxiliaries necessarily bear tense features that have to be checked in the inflectional system, one can derive the fact that they do not appear in early infinitivals, proposing that the latter are truncated lower than the specification of tense in the inflectional system. In the absence of the (relevant part of the) IP layer, an early infinitive auxiliary will not be able to check its tense features, and the derivation will not converge due to unchecked features.

As mentioned above, adult grammars do not normally allow declarative root infinitives. They do permit matrix infinitives in a very limited number of constructions involving overt or covert operators and some kind of modal interpretation, as illustrated by Italian examples in (6):

(6) a. Che cosa dire in questi casi?
       what   say$_{inf}$ in such   cases
    b. Io fare questo? Mai!
       me do$_{inf}$ this   never
    c. Partire immediatamente!
       leave$_{inf}$ immediately

On the other hand, infinitives can be used in descriptive statements in embedded context, but not as main clauses in adult grammars:

(7) a. Vedo i   ragazzi giocare al pallone
       (I) see the boys   play$_{inf}$ soccer

IO

THE ACQUISITION OF SYNTAX

b. *Giocare al pallone
   play$_{inf}$ soccer

Why is it so? Assuming that clauses contain a tense variable, which must be fixed somehow to comply with the principle of Full Interpretation (Chomsky 1986), Rizzi 1993–94 suggests that while the tense variable of finite verbs is fixed by the finite morphology, the tense of infinitives must be bound by an external binder. The tense of embedded infinitives such as (7a) is bound by the tense of the matrix clause (see the reference quoted for a proposal concerning the special environments (6)). Adult declarative matrix infinitives such as (7b) are thus excluded because they contain no binder for the tense variable, which gives rise to a violation of Full Interpretation. Suppose now that early infinitivals are truncated below TP, the layer of the inflectional system which contains the tense variable; in such truncated structures there is no unbound tense variable, hence no violation of Full Interpretation arises. The incompatibility of root infinitives with constructions involving higher clausal layers (*wh*, subject clitics, etc.) follows. When the principle stating that any matrix verbal utterance is a CP becomes operative, the free option of root infinitives naturally disappears.

Cipriani, Chilosi, Bottari and Pfanner (1992), Guasti (1993–94) and Schaeffer (1990) report that root infinitives are extremely rare in early Italian (see also Grinstead 1994 for Spanish and the discussion in Hoekstra and Hyams 1998). The different behavior of early Italian versus early French (or early German for that matter) becomes apparent if Italian infinitives obligatorily bear abstract I-features (i.e. they necessarily move to higher layers of the inflectional system such as the subject agreement projection: Belletti 1990), while French infinitives do not have to bear them and can/must remain in the VP or in the lower part of the inflectional system (Pollock 1989). So, the infinitives of early Italian, bearing features to be checked in the (higher) IP layer, cannot function as main verbs of matrix declaratives. If the structure is truncated as suggested above, the infinitival verb will not be able to check its abstract I-features; if the structure is not truncated, the tense variable will remain unbound. Early French does exhibit such main clauses, as it has infinitives that are not marked for these features and can therefore serve as the main verbs of structures truncated lower than TP.

An approach along the lines sketched above illustrates the pervasive effects that a tiny primitive difference between two grammatical systems, the truncation option, may have on the manifested linguistic structures. This is the central insight of modern comparative syntax, an insight that has now been successfully extended to the comparison of early and adult systems, and to the study of developmental phenomena.

5 Contributions

The contributions by Rasetti, Friedemann and Rizzi directly bear on truncation and subject positions in early grammars.

Lucienne RASETTI offers a detailed analysis of the distribution of early null subjects and root infinitives in a large corpus of six two-year-old children acquiring French: Philippe (Suppes, Smith and Léveillé 1973, available in the CHILDES database (see MacWhinney and Snow 1985)), Daniel and Nathalie (Lightbown 1977), and Augustin, Marie and Jean (University of Geneva; see Rasetti's contribution for details). Two major claims are defended in her chapter. First, early grammars employ two distinct types of null subjects in finite and nonfinite contexts, respectively. Second, early null subjects and root infinitives should be derived from a single property of early grammars as their temporal evolution is similar and they disappear around the same age.

It has been claimed by Sano and Hyams (1994) for early English, that early null subjects are to be uniformly analyzed as instances of PRO (the null subject typical of uninflected contexts in the adult grammar). Based on early French data, Rasetti argues that the very high proportion of null subjects appearing with root infinitives (an average of almost 90 percent; see her Table 9.3) might indeed be analyzed as instances of PRO. However, she also finds a significant rate of null subjects in unambiguously finite contexts (over 25 percent), and concludes that these latter instances should not be regarded as an over-generalization of the adult strategy licensing PRO in untensed contexts, but rather involve a different mechanism.

Further, Rasetti provides a meticulous study of the developmental pattern of root infinitives and early null subjects in finite contexts. She shows that both phenomena follow a similar evolution across time and tend to disappear simultaneously. This provides further support to the hypothesis that the two structurally different phenomena of root infinitives and early null subjects of finite sentences have a common origin, the child option of truncating sentential structure, Rasetti argues.

Marc-Ariel FRIEDEMANN is concerned with the extensive use of subject-final structures in early French which are not consistent with the adult grammar. In the relevant files of the CHILDES database they amount to 73 percent out of all lexical nondislocated subjects. Below are a few examples from Grégoire (Champaud) and Philippe (see above):

(8) a. Va   dedans Christian. (Grégoire 2;3)
       goes inside   Christian
    b. Faire   boum sur camion maman. (Philippe 2;1)
       make$_{inf}$ boom on truck   Mummy
    c. Fait   du bruit la voiture. (Philippe 2;2)
       makes noise   the car

The exact position of the subject in such early structures has been debated in the recent literature. Does the final subject occupy its base position within the VP (Pierce 1989, 1992, Déprez and Pierce 1993, Friedemann 1993–94), or is it right-dislocated (Ferdinand 1993, Labelle and Valois 1996)? And if it is VP-internal, what is its precise position?

The chapter surveys the approaches defended in recent studies, and claims that the structures in question cannot all be analyzed as subject right-dislocations: quantitative and crosslinguistic considerations strongly suggest that they involve overt VP-internal subjects. If so, it is further argued, the relative ordering of elements within the VP shows that early (and, under reasonable continuity guidelines, also adult) French merges the subject (the external argument) as a right-branching VP specifer (or, in Kayne's 1994 *Antisymmetry* terms, as a left-branching specifier, which is crossed over by the rest of the VP material).

Independently of the exact position of early postverbal subjects, their availability, Friedemann proposes, follows from the option of truncated structures. Leaving the canonical subject position unpronounced is made possible due to the same apparatus allowing early null subjects, as the position can be occupied by a null expletive licensed at the root, under truncation.

Friedemann's contribution draws from early production a type of evidence which is not available, or is only partially accessible in very special constructions, in the adult linguistic system.

Luigi RIZZI's contribution has two main goals. On the one hand, his chapter surveys recent research on early null subjects, highlighting the various factors at play. On the other hand, it reviews the original formulation of the truncation hypothesis and proposes a refinement of its theoretical basis.

The existence of child-specific null subjects was recently challenged by several researchers. Phillips (1995) has suggested that some structural characteristics of root null subjects discussed above in section 4, in particular their absence in post *wh*-contexts in early French, may be an artifact of the independent lack, or rarity, of null subjects with functional verbs. Kraemer (1993), Sano and Hyams (1994) have argued that all instances of early null subjects are to be reduced to tokens of PRO (but see Rasetti's contribution). Roeper and Rohrbacher (1994) and Bromberg and Wexler (1995), in turn, have observed that early English does show null subjects in post-*wh* environments, but only in uninflected contexts. Taking into consideration various studies on Dutch, English, French and German, Rizzi concludes that two formally distinct types of early null subjects must be admitted: null subjects occurring with infinitives and null subjects licensed in the specifier of the root, the latter being possible in uninflected environments as well.

Further, he examines the type of empty category liable to function as the early root null subject of finite utterances. The original proposal has been that the element in question is a null constant, that is a [−anaphoric, −pronominal] empty category to be bound by an nonquantificational operator, such as the one occurring in appositive relatives (Rizzi 1992). Empirical reasons (null constants appear to be restricted to referential arguments, while early null subjects can be expletives) lead Rizzi to revise the null constant proposal in terms of the approach to empty categories developed in Chomsky (1995).

Finally, the chapter examines the theoretical status of the principle requiring adult root declaratives to be CPs, a question which is at the heart of the truncation approach. Rizzi conjectures that truncated structures result from the interplay between two basic principles of Economy: (a) Structural Economy (use the minimum of structure consistent with well-formedness constraints) and (b) Categorial Uniformity (assume a unique canonical structural realization for a given semantic type). The idea is to exploit the tension between the partially contradictory requirements of these two principles to explain the selective occurrence of truncation in early systems and in abbreviated adult registers.

Liliane HAEGEMAN's contribution investigates a particular adult phenomenon strongly reminiscent of early null subjects. She examines null subjects found in special registers of non pro-drop languages such as English or French. Such null subjects are regularly found in diary registers, where they appear in a significant proportion of main sentences. They are also attested in written short notes and are often used in casual spoken English. Below, we reproduce two examples from English and French diaries, respectively:

(9) a. __ have always wanted to 'make something' (Plath 1983) by hand.

b. Elle est alsacienne. __ paraît intelligente. (Léautaud 1989)
   she is   alsatian   seems intelligent

Haegeman discards the possibility that the empty category under scrutiny is an NP trace or PRO, as the latter are not in complementary distribution with a full DP. *Pro* is not a candidate either, as English and French do not show characteristics of pro-drop languages. We are left with null elements typical of the A'-system.

Indeed, several authors have claimed that initial null subjects of adult languages are best characterized as null topics (Haegeman 1990a, 1990b, Weissenborn 1992, Bromberg and Wexler 1995). Two main arguments lead Haegeman to abandon this hypothesis: first, it erroneously predicts the existence of null object topics in the relevant register; second, nonreferential null subjects are attested although they could not be topicalized.

Adopting the truncation hypothesis, Haegeman analyzes 'diary' null subjects as antecedent-less empty categories licensed in the specifier of the root; this derives their distribution, which is reminiscent of that of early null subjects. Contrary to expectations, however, sentences involving root null subjects do occur in the corpora with a preposed adjunct (but not with a preposed argument). Relying on Rizzi's (1997) articulated CP structure, Haegeman adopts a mechanism allowing the null subject to bypass a preposed adjunct (but not a preposed argument). Truncation thus allows special adult registers to license null subjects at the root, in a way similar to early grammars. Haegeman concludes with evidence based on principle C effects, which shows that the null subjects at stake are located in a structurally higher position than the preposed adjunct.

Of high potential relevance for a theory of first language development is the systematic comparison with the acquisition of a second language. The two domains are sufficiently close to permit a detailed comparison, which should highlight similarities and differences between the two acquisition processes.

As in the domain of first language acquisition, spontaneous production of target inconsistent nonfinite forms has been observed in second language corpora. A number of researchers have argued that this failure follows from relatively low level morphological problems (Epstein, Flynn and Martohardjono 1996, Grondin and White 1996, Lardiere and Schwartz 1997 among others). In other words, the second language learners know all abstract properties of functional categories, but lack the full knowledge of the specific realization of particular morphemes.

Philippe PRÉVOST and Lydia WHITE propose testing this hypothesis (which they refer to as the Missing Inflection hypothesis) against an alternative approach which aims at deriving characteristics of second language acquisition, particularly in the inflectional domain, from structural constraints. This alternative amounts to suggesting that second language learners can (in some cases) employ a slightly underspecified UG to the extent that they can have recourse to the truncation device, for example.

The empirical array of their study is based on two types of corpora: four children ranging from age 5 to age 10, and four adults; two subjects of each group were learners of French as a second language, and two were learners of German. Prévost and White test the predictions made by the truncation hypothesis in the domain of finiteness and missing subjects, investigating phenomena such as uninflected morphology according to clause type, distribution of subject clitics (for French), lexical subjects or phonetically unrealized subjects, and different word ordering.

Both the adults and the children produced in French as well as in German infinitival structures in declarative contexts and unpronounced subjects. Interestingly, the predictions made by the truncation hypothesis are not equally borne out in the two groups of learners. By and large, the early second language learners produced nonfinite verbs as well as null subjects only in main clause declaratives without CP instantiations, basically the same pattern found in first language acquisition. Likewise, for example, they produced subject clitics only with finite verbs. The adult learners, in contrast, did not show such distributional constraints in the production of infinitival forms nor in the omission of subjects: both phenomena occurred, but without obeying clear structural constraints. The following distinction seems to emerge between the two populations: while children may have recourse to truncated structures and hence to structural underspecification, the adult behavior is more in concert with the predictions of the Missing Inflection hypothesis.

Note that these primary results, as the authors themselves emphasize, should be taken with some caution as the learners were not homogeneous with regard to their first language. Still, if the emerging generalization is on the right track, second language acquisition provides interesting evidence for a gradual disappearance of the truncation option in nonabbreviated registers.

The behavior of early interrogatives is addressed in Hamann's and Guasti's contributions, which both extend the descriptive coverage of the truncation hypothesis within the early systems. Both contributions adopt the position that truncation can also apply within the CP layer, thereby allowing additional licensing of null elements.

Cornelia HAMANN investigates the mechanisms of early question formation, concentrating on French corpora (Augustin, Marie and Philippe; see above). First, she shows that children start either with in-situ questions, or by fronting the *wh*-word, which are both strategies employed by the adult (colloquial) grammar. Second, she observes that neither infinitivals nor null subjects are found with overt *wh*-movement, as expected by the truncation approach. In contrast, *wh*-in-situ questions, which are also incompatible with root infinitives, appear to license null subjects:

(10) a. ___ fais quoi? (Marie 2;3)
    b. ___ est où? (Augustin 2;6)

Hamann accounts for the occurrence of null subjects in early *wh*-in-situ questions by adopting (a) truncation within an articulated CP layer (Rizzi 1997), (b) a bypassing device along the lines proposed by Haegeman and (c) an interpretative procedure à la Baker (1970) or Reinhart (1995) for *wh*-in-situ constructions. The *wh*-phrase is interpreted in situ through binding by a null operator in the domain of the CP system. The null subject raises (bypassing the null operator) to the top of the truncated structure, where it is licensed at the root. A fronted *wh*-phrase blocks a parallel raising; hence the absence of null subjects in fronted *wh*-questions. Hamann further suggests that her analysis may carry over to other early question types where null subjects seem to be attested: for example, early yes/no questions, and early German or Dutch interrogatives with omitted *wh*-elements (see Clahsen, Kursawe and Penke 1996, van Kampen 1997).

Hamann derives the asymmetry between *wh*-in-situ and fronted *wh*-questions regarding the licensing of root null subjects from the distinct interpretative procedures employed in each of the interrogative contexts: movement vs. in-situ interpretation. If her analysis is on the right track, it argues against a generalized movement approach to questions, which has been dominant until very recently in the generative literature. Note that both fronted *wh*- and *wh*-in-situ questions employ an adult strategy in early French. Can it be concluded that the principles of question formation are operative from the outset? This is indeed the view explicitly advocated by Guasti in her comparative study of early interrogatives in English and Italian.

Teresa GUASTI argues in favor of the early operativeness of the *wh*-criterion (May 1985, Rizzi 1991), which requires a Spec–head configuration between the *wh*-phrase and a head specified +*wh* (often the finite verb). Two major observations lead her to this conclusion. First, Italian children do not produce target inconsistent questions. Second, a large amount of the questions produced in early English are also well formed. Still, children acquiring English do produce a considerable rate of nontarget consistent questions, which typically lack an auxiliary form, and therefore do not show inversion. They are found with different verbal forms: the -*ing* verbal form occurring without the auxiliary *be* (11a); a bare verbal form occurring without *do* (11b); and a finite verbal form (11c). Can the early operativeness of the *wh*-criterion be defended despite the production of interrogatives such as (11a–c)?

(11) a. What that train doing? (Adam 2;4)
     b. Where ball go? (Adam 2;3)
     c. Where dis goes? (Adam 2;8)

(Brown 1973)

Although the above utterances are not adult-consistent interrogatives, they do satisfy the *wh*-criterion, Guasti argues. In the first two types of utterances, the criterion is satisfied by a null auxiliary, which is licensed at the root in a way that is ultimately traced back to a particular instance of truncation within the CP system. As for noninverted finite questions (11c), Guasti proposes that the criterion is satisfied by the base-generation of the *wh*-feature directly in the complementizer system. This option, although unavailable in adult English, is attested in other adult grammars (e.g. Hebrew) and is therefore part of UG. Guasti speculates that children acquiring English (but not Italian) have recourse to questions unavailable in their target language due to the morphosyntactic complexities of English interrogatives.

Guasti's chapter emphasizes the role of crosslinguistic studies in language acquisition. On the basis of English interrogatives of the type in (11), one could readily conclude that the child does not master basic principles of UG. Italian data shed a different light on the issue, suggesting that the non target consistency in (11a–b) is due to modest inconsistencies with the target grammar rather than to the nonoperativeness of principles of question formation.

Up to now, we have discussed clausal truncation at the level of CP and lower (Friedemann, Guasti, Haegeman, Hamann, Prévast and White, Rasetti, Rizzi). It has been suggested that external sentential layers can be cut off in early grammars. If this is so, the question arises whether a similar device is at work in the nominal domain, too. There are good reasons to believe that there is a functional analogy between CP and DP (Siloni 1995, 1997, Szabolcsi 1989, 1994). Can then DP be cut off in early nominal expressions on a par with its CP analogue? It is well known that children can omit determiners, producing adult inconsistent utterances, as illustrated below with French examples:

(12) a. a   mangé __ œufs (Augustin 2;0)
        has eaten   eggs
     b. est là   __ voisine (Grégoire 1;11)
        is here   neighbor

Sonja EISENBEISS investigates the acquisition of noun phrases in German, focusing on possessive constructions and missing determiners. Eisenbeiss offers an extensive analysis of a set of data from seven monolingual children ranging from age 1;11 to 3;6. Determiners and possessive markers (*'s*) are optionally missing in the corpora under investigation, as illustrated by the following contrasting pair produced by Andreas (Wagner 1985):

(13) a. Hm papas   gürtel (Andreas 2;1)
        daddy's belt
     b. E mama   ticktack is(t) das (Andreas 2;1)
        Mummy watch   is   that

Under closer examination, Eisenbeiss argues, the possessive marker seems to be acquired gradually. It is systematically omitted in the earlier files, marked on specific nouns at an intermediate stage, and finally produced systematically (and sometimes even overgeneralized) in the last files. Moreover, only the unmarked word order possessor–possessee appears in earlier files, while the more marked possessee–possessor order surfaces in the latest files. This state of affairs suggests, according to the author, that the unmarked word order represents the basic ordering, while the marked order is derived by movement of the possessee over the possessor, movement which is unavailable in the early production due to lack of relevant structure.

As for determiners, their initial absence is more debatable. Nevertheless, Eisenbeiss claims that there are reasons to believe that the first occurrences of determiners are unanalyzed parts of formulaic units ('impostors'). This, alongside other phenomena, such as U-shaped developmental curves characterizing the realization of determiners, is argued to provide support in favor of a gradual emergence of determiners, similar to the gradual acquisition of the possessive marker (along the lines proposed by the lexical learning hypothesis; Clahsen, Eisenbeiss and Vainikka 1994, Clahsen, Eisenbeiss and Penke 1996).

Still in the domain of the acquisition of Germanic verb-second languages, some surprising results emerge in Schönenberger's study of verb placement in embedded clauses. Her investigation concerns somewhat later developmental stages, as it examines the production of subordinate clauses. It bears on word order, and raises again the question of the early operativeness of basic principles and parameters of UG.

Manuela SCHÖNENBERGER deals with the acquisition of verb placement in Swiss German. Her study is based on a corpus of spontaneous speech by two children acquiring Lucernese (see Schönenberger 1998 for details on the corpus). This variant of Swiss German, like Standard German, is a verb-second language usually displaying verb-final order in embedded clauses. There is a general consensus in the literature that children acquiring Standard German master verb movement early in their linguistic development, and, in particular, do not encounter problems in the production of verb-final patterns in embedded clauses (Clahsen 1982, 1989, Mills 1985, Rothweiler 1993, etc.). Surprisingly, in her Lucernese corpus, Schönenberger observes that although the children produce adult-like main sentences, correctly raising the verb to the second position, embedded clauses do not look target consistent. Up to the age of 4;11, both children consistently raise the verb in subordinate clauses and very rarely use the adult verb-final pattern. They move the verb in any type of embedded clause, even in clauses introduced by a complementizer:

(14) a. [Wenn hät er Buchweh] cha-n-er nüt   mache
        when has he bellyache can he   nothing make
        bim Elefant. (Eliza 3;11)
        for-the elephant

THE ACQUISITION OF SYNTAX: INTRODUCTION

    b. Ich weiss nur [wo   tuetm'r   abschtelle] (Moira 4;4)
        I   know only where does-one off-turn

To account for these data, Schönenberger proposes that the apparent complementizer does not occupy C (as it does in the adult garmmar), but SpecCP. This frees the C position to host the verb, giving rise to embedded V-to-C movement. Schönenberger points out that the first complementizers used by the children, the relative complementizer *wo* and the complementizer *wenn* ('when/if'), are homophonous with the interrogative operators *wo* ('where') and *wenn* ('when'), respectively. Arguably, then, children assign a uniform analysis to these elements, and accommodate them in SpecCP. Other complementizers such as *dass* ('that') and *öb* ('if') are acquired several months later, and might be initially assimilated to the class of complementizers already in use. Finally, Schönenberger proposes that doubly filled Comp structures, involving a *w*-element and *dass*, trigger the reanalysis of complementizers around the age of 5, with the consequent loss of embedded V movement to C.

    The chapter thus argues that although the Lucernese corpora show drastic word order target inconsistencies in embedded clauses, the children's underlying grammar is in fact minimally different from that of the adult. The target inconsistent generalized verb-movement strategy employed by children in embedded clauses does not stem from unfamiliarity with basic parameters regulating verb placement in Lucernese, but rather from an initial misanalysis of certain complementizers as maximal projections.

    Finally, Na'ama FRIEDMANN and Yosef GRODZINSKY examine yet another extension of structural underspecification in the domain of neuropathology; they study the production of agrammatic patients. It is standardly assumed that damage to Broca's area in the left cerebral hemisphere gives rise to agrammatism, a general impairment of all functional elements (e.g. Goodglass 1976, Grodzinsky 1984, Ouhalla 1993). Focusing on the inflectional domain, Friedmann and Grodzinsky presented completion and repetition tasks to eleven Hebrew-speaking and two Arabic-speaking agrammatic patients in order to test this common claim, which mainly relies on spontaneous production. Their results suggest that the generally adopted description is too crude: the pattern of impairment observed in agrammatism is more selective than previously thought; in particular, properties related to agreement are virtually intact. (15) summarizes some characteristics typical of agrammatism as they emerge from Friedmann and Grodzinsky's study:

    (15) a. Tense, but no agreement errors with main verbs and copulas
        b. Copula omissions
        c. Errors in the placement of negation

    d. Target inconsistent subject omissions
    e. Failure to produce correct *wh*-questions
    f. Severe impairment in the production of embedded sentences

Friedmann and Grodzinsky further corroborate their results by reanalyzing available spontaneous data from Romance or Germanic languages. The characteristics in (15), again, are reminiscent of properties typical of early child language. Friedmann and Grodzinsky suggest that agrammatic patients suffer from a syntactic deficit that results in the unavailability of any syntactic node from TP and up (the Tree Pruning hypothesis, in their terms). They further note that their research on aphasic patients provides neuropsychological evidence for the dissociation of agreement and tense, a claim put forward in theoretical linguistics by Pollock (1989).

Of course, an important difference between the Tree Pruning hypothesis and the truncation hypothesis lies in the fact that the latter refers to an optional mechanism, while the former deals with a rigid structural deficit. Nonetheless, neuropsychological results of this sort are relevant to a better understanding of the functioning of underspecification and the role it plays in language development. The extensions of the truncation hypothesis to the domains of adult registers, second language acquisition and neuropathology bear on the lively debate over the formulation and limits of continuity. Agrammatism, characterized by a rigid (though selective) structural underspecification, if Friedmann and Grodzinsky are correct, involves a more radical departure from full-fledged UG then developing systems and special abbreviated registers; nevertheless, the high structural selectivity of the deficit suggests that grammatical breakdown is still interpretable along the structural guidelines defined by UG.

References

BAKER, C. L. (1970) 'Notes on the Description of English Questions. The Role of an Abstract Question Morpheme', *Foundations of Language* 6, 107–219.
BELLETTI, A. (1990) *Generalized Verb Movement: Aspects of Verb Syntax*, Rosenberg and Sellier, Torino.
BLOOM, L. (1970) *Language Development: Form and Function in Emerging Grammars*, MIT Press, Cambridge, MA.
BLOOM, L., P. LIGHTBOWN and L. HOOD (1975) *Structure and Variation in Child Language*, Monograph of the Society for Research in Child Development, Vol. 40, no. 2.
BLOOM, P. (1990) 'Subjectless Sentences in Child Language', *Linguistic Inquiry* 21, 491–504.
BLOOM, P. (1993) 'Grammatical Continuity in Language Development: The Case of Subjectless Sentences', *Linguistic Inquiry* 24, 721–34.

BORER, H. and K. WEXLER (1987) 'The Maturation of Syntax', in T. Roeper and E. Williams (eds), *Parameter Setting*, Reidel, Dordrecht, 123–72.

BROMBERG, H. and K. WEXLER (1995) 'Null Subjects in *Wh*-Questions', *MIT Working Papers in Linguistics* **26**, 221–47.

BROWN, R. (1973) *A First Language: The Early Stages*, Harvard University Press, Cambridge, MA.

CHOMSKY, N. (1959) 'Review of B. F. Skinner's *Verbal Behavior*', *Language* **35**, 26–58.

CHOMSKY, N. (1965) *Aspects of the Theory of Syntax*, MIT Press, Cambridge, MA.

CHOMSKY, N. (1973) 'Conditions on Transformations', in S. Anderson and P. Kiparsky (eds), *A Festschrift for Morris Halle*, Holt, Rinehart and Winston, New York, 232–86.

CHOMSKY, N. (1981) *Lectures on Government and Binding*, Foris, Dordrecht.

CHOMSKY, N. (1986) *Knowledge of Language, its Nature, Origin, and Use*, Praeger, New York.

CHOMSKY, N. (1995) *The Minimalist Program*, MIT Press, Cambridge, MA.

CIPRIANI, P., A. M. CHILOSI, P. BOTTARI and L. PFANNER (1992) *L'acquisitione della morfosintassi in italiano: fasi e processi*, UniPress, Padova.

CLAHSEN, H. (1982) *Spracherwerb in der Kindheit. Eine Untersuchung zur Entwicklung der Syntax bei Kleinkindern*, Narr, Tübingen.

CLAHSEN, H. (1989) 'Bedingungen der Parameterfixierungen: Zur Analyse einiger Erscheinungen aus der Kindersprache im Rahmen der GB-Theorie', paper presented at the University of Hamburg.

CLAHSEN, H., S. EISENBEISS and M. PENKE (1996) 'Lexical Learning in Early Syntactic Development', in H. Clahsen (ed.), *Generative Perspectives on Language Acquisition*, Amsterdam, Benjamins, 129–60.

CLAHSEN, H., C. EISENBEISS and A. VAINIKKA (1994) 'The Seeds of Structure. A Syntactic Analysis of the Acquisition of Case Marking', in T. Hoekstra and B. Schwartz (eds), *Language Acquisition Studies in Generative Grammar*, Amsterdam, Benjamins, 85–118.

CLAHSEN, H., S. KURSAWE and M. PENKE (1996) 'Introducing CP. The Development of *Wh*-questions and Embedded Clauses in German Child Language', in C. Koster and F. Wijnen (eds), *Proceedings of the Groningen Assembly on Language Acquisition*, 5–22.

CLARK, R. (1992) 'The Selection of Syntactic Knowledge', *Language Acquisition* **2** (2), 83–149.

CRAIN, S. (1991) 'Language Acquisition in the Absence of Experience', *Behavioral and Brain Sciences* **14**.

CRAIN, S. and J. D. FODOR (1984) 'On the Innateness of Subjacency', *Proceedings of the Eastern States Conference on Linguistics* **1**, Ohio State University, Colombus.

CRAIN, S. and M. NAKAYAMA (1987) 'Structure Dependence in Grammar Formation', *Language* **63**, 522–43.

CRISMA, P. (1992) 'On the Acquisition of *Wh*-questions in French', *Geneva Generative Papers* **0.1–2**, 115–22.

DÉPREZ, V. and A. PIERCE (1993) 'Negation and Functional Projections in Early Grammar', *Linguistic Inquiry* **24**, 25–67.

EPSTEIN, S., S. FLYNN and G. MARTOHARDJONO (1996) 'Second Language Acquisition: Theoretical and Experimental Issues in Contemporary Research', *Behavioral and Brain Sciences* **19**, 677–714.

FERDINAND, ASTRID (1993) 'Subject Dislocations in Child Language', *HIL Manuscripts*, 54–64.

FRIEDEMANN, M. A. (1993–94) 'The Underlying Position of External Arguments in French', *Language Acquisition* **3** (3), 209–55.

GIBSON, E. and K. WEXLER (1994) 'Triggers', *Linguistic Inquiry* **25**, 407–54.

GOODGLASS, H. (1976) 'Agrammatism', in H. Whitaker and H. A. Whitaker (eds), *Studies in Neurolinguistics* **1**, Academic Press, New York.

GRINSTEAD, J. (1994) 'Consequences of the Maturation of Number Morphology in Spanish and Catalan', MA thesis, UCLA.

GRODZINSKY, Y. (1984) 'The Syntactic Characterization of Agrammatism', *Cognition* **16**, 99–120.

GRONDIN, N. and L. WHITE (1996) 'Functional Categories in Child L2 Acquisition of French', *Language Acquisition* **5**, 1–34.

GUASTI, M. T. (1993–94) 'Verb Syntax in Italian Child Grammar: Finite and Nonfinite Verbs', *Language Acquisition* **3** (1), 1–40.

GUILFOYLE, E. and M. NOONAN (1991) 'Functional Categories and Language Acquisition', ms., MIT and McGill University.

DE HAAN G. (1986) 'A Theory-bound Approach to the Acquisition of Verb Placement in Early Dutch', in G. de Haan and W. Zonneveld (eds), *Formal Parameters of Generative Grammar* **3**, University of Utrecht.

HAEGEMAN, L. (1990a) 'Non-overt Subjects in Diary Contexts', in J. Mascaro and M. Nespor (eds), *Grammar in Progress*, Foris, Dordrecht.

HAEGEMAN, L. (1990b) 'Understood Subjects in English Diaries', *Multilingua* **9**, 157–99.

HAEGEMAN, L. (1995) 'Root Infinitives, Tense, and Truncated Structures in Dutch', *Language Acquisition* **4**, 205–55.

HAEGEMAN, L. (1996) 'Verb Second, the Split CP and Null Subjects in Early Dutch Finite Clauses', *Geneva Generative Papers* **4**, 133–75.

HAMANN, C. and K. PLUNKETT (1998) 'Subject Omission in Child Danish', to appear in *Cognition*.

HAMBURGER, H. and S. CRAIN (1984) 'Acquisition of Cognitive Compiling', *Cognition* **17**, 85–136.

HOEKSTRA, T. and N. HYAMS (1998) 'Aspects of Root Infinitives', ms., University of Leiden and UCLA.

HYAMS, N. (1986) *Language Acquisition and the Theory of Parameters*, Reidel, Dordrecht.

HYAMS, N. and K. WEXLER (1993) 'On the Grammatical Basis of Null Subjects in Child Language', *Linguistic Inquiry* **24**, 421–59.

VAN KAMPEN, J. (1997) *First Steps in Wh-Movement*, Doctoral dissertation, OTS, University of Utrecht.

KAYNE, R. (1994) *The Antisymmetry of Syntax*, MIT Press, Cambridge, MA.

KRAEMER, I. (1993) 'The Licensing of Subjects in Early Child Language', *MIT Working Papers in Linguistics* **19**, 197–212.

LABELLE, MARIE and DANIEL VALOIS (1996) 'The Status of Post-verbal Subjects in French Child Language', *Probus* **8**, 53–80.

LARDIERE, D. and B. D. SCHWARTZ (1997) 'Feature-marking in the L2 Development of Deverbal Compounds', *Journal of Linguistics* **33**, 327–53.

LÉAUTAUD, P. (1989) *Le fléau. Journal particulier 1917–1939*, Mercure de France, Paris.

LEBEAUX, D. (1988) *Language Acquisition and the Form of the Grammar*, Doctoral dissertation, University of Massachusetts, Amherst.

LEVOW, G. A. (1995) 'Tense and Subject Position in Interrogatives and Negatives in Child French: Evidence for and against Truncated Structure', *MIT Working Papers in Linguistics* **26**, 281–304.

LIGHTBOWN, P. (1977) *Consistency and Variation in the Acquisition of French*, Doctoral dissertation, Columbia University.

MACWHINNEY, B. (1999) *The CHILDES Project: Tools for Analyzing Talk*, second edition, Lawrence Erlbaum Associates, Hillsdale, NJ.

MACWHINNEY, B. and C. SNOW (1985) 'The Child Language Data Exchange System', *Journal of Child Language* **12**, 271–96.

MAY, R. (1985) *Logical Form: Its Structure and Derivation*, MIT Press, Cambridge, MA.

MILLS, A. E. (1985) 'Acquisition of German', in D. I. Slobin (ed.), *The Crosslinguistic Study of Language Acquisition, Vol. 1: The Data*, Erlbaum, Hillsdale, 141–254.

OTSU, Y. (1981) *Universal Grammar and Syntactic Development in Children: Toward a Theory of Syntactic Development*, Doctoral dissertation, MIT, Cambridge, MA.

OUHALLA, J. (1993) 'Functional Categories, Agrammatism and Language Acquisition', *Linguistische Berichte* **143**, 3–36.

PHILLIPS, C. (1995) 'Syntax at Age Two: Cross Linguistic Differences', *MIT Working Papers in Linguistics* **26**, 325–82.

PIERCE, A. (1989) *On the Emergence of Syntax: A Crosslinguistic Study*, Doctoral dissertation, MIT, Cambridge, MA.

PIERCE, A. (1992) *Language Acquisition and Syntactic Theory: A Comparative Analysis of French and English Child Grammars*, Kluwer, Dordrecht.

PINKER, S. (1979) 'Formal Models of Language Learning', *Cognition* **7**, 217–83.

PLATH, S. (1983) *The Journals of Sylvia Plath*, Ted Hughes and Frances McCollough (eds), Ballantine Books, New York.

PLATZACK, C. (1990) 'A Grammar without Functional Categories: A Syntactic Study of Early Swedish Child Language', *Nordic Journal of Linguistics* **13**, 107–26.

POEPPEL, D. and K. WEXLER (1993) 'The Full Competence Hypothesis of Clause Structure in Early German', *Language* **69**, 1–33.

POLLOCK, J. Y. (1989) 'Verb Movement, UG and the Structure of IP', *Linguistic Inquiry* **20**, 365–424.

RADFORD, A. (1990) *Syntactic Theory and the Acquisition of English Syntax: The Nature of Early Child Grammars of English*, Oxford University Press, Oxford.

REINHART, T. (1995) 'Interface Strategies', *OTS Working Papers*, University of Utrecht.

RIZZI, L. (1982) *Issues in Italian Syntax*, Foris Publications, Dordrecht.

RIZZI, L. (1991) 'Residual Verb Second and the *Wh*-criterion', *Technical Reports on Formal and Computational Linguistics* 2, Geneva University.

RIZZI, L. (1992) 'Early Null Subjects and Root Null Subjects', *Geneva Generative Papers* 0, 102–14. [Published in T. Hoekstra and B. Schwartz (1994) (eds), *Language Acquisition Studies in Generative Grammar*, John Benjamins, Amsterdam, 151–76.]

RIZZI, L. (1993–94) 'Some Notes on Linguistic Theory and Language Development: The Case of Root Infinitives', *Language Acquisition* 3.4, 371–93.

RIZZI, L. (1997) 'The Fine Structure of the Left Periphery', in L. Haegeman (ed.), *Elements of Grammar*, Kluwer Academic Publishers, Dordrecht, 281–337.

ROEPER, T. and B. ROHRBACHER (1994) 'True Pro-drop in Child English and the Principle of Economy of Projections', ms., University of Massachusetts, Amherst.

ROEPER, T. and J. WEISSENBORN (1990) 'How to Make Parameters Work', in L. Frazier and J. de Villiers (eds), *Language Processing and Language Acquisition*, Kluwer Academic Publishers, Dordrecht, 147–62.

ROTHWEILER, M. (1993) *Der Erwerb von Nebensätzen im Deutschen*, Niemeyer, Tübingen.

SANO, T. and N. HYAMS (1994) 'Agreement, Finiteness and the Development of Null Arguments', *Proceedings of NELS* 24, 543–58.

SCHAEFFER, J. (1990) 'The Syntax of the Subject in Child Language: Italian Compared to Dutch', MA thesis, University of Utrecht.

SCHÖNENBERGER, M. (1998) *The Acquisition of Verb Placement in Swiss German*, Doctoral dissertation, University of Geneva.

SILONI, T. (1995) 'On Participial Relatives and Complementizer D°: A Case Study in Hebrew and French', *Natural Language and Linguistic Theory* 13.3, 445–87.

SILONI, T. (1997) *Noun Phrases and Nominalizations: The Syntax of DPs*, Kluwer Academic Publishers, Dordrecht.

SUPPES, P., R. SMITH and M. LÉVEILLÉ (1973) 'The French Syntax of a Child's Noun Phrase', *Archives de Psychologie* 42.

SZABOLCSI, A. (1989) 'Noun Phrases and Clauses: Is DP Analogous to IP or CP?', to appear in J. Payne (ed.), *The Structure of Noun Phrases*, Mouton, Amsterdam.

SZABOLCSI, A. (1994) 'The Noun Phrase', in F. Kiefer and E. Kiss (eds), *Syntax and Semantics* 27, 179–274.

VALIAN, V. (1991) 'Syntactic Subjects in Early Speech of American and Italian Children', *Cognition* 40.

VERRIPS, M. and J. WEISSENBORN (1990) 'Finite Verbs in the Acquisition of German, Dutch and French', ms., Max-Planck Institute, Nijmegen.

WAGNER, K. (1985) How Much Do Children Say in a Day?' *Journal of Child Language* 12, 475–87.

WEISSENBORN, J. (1988) 'The Acquisition of Clitic Object Pronouns and Word Order in French: Syntax or Morphology?', ms., Max-Planck Institute, Nijmegen.

WEISSENBORN, J. (1992) 'Null Subjects in Early Grammars: Implications for Parameter Setting Theory', in J. Weissenborn, H. Goodluck and T. Roeper (eds), *Theoretical Issues in Language Acquisition*, Lawrence Erlbaum, Hillsdale, NJ.

WEXLER, K. (1992) 'Optional Infinitives, Head Movement and the Economy of Derivations in Child Grammar', *MIT Occasional Paper* **45**. [Published in D. Lightfoot and N. Hornstein (1994) (eds), *Verb Movement*, Cambridge University Press, Cambridge.]

WEXLER, K. and P. CULICOVER (1980) *Formal Principles of Language Acquisition*, MIT Press, Cambridge, MA.

WEXLER, K. and R. MANZINI (1987) 'Parameters and Learnability in Binding Theory', in T. Roeper and E. Williams (eds), *Parameter Setting*, Reidel, Dordrecht.

Chapter 2

The acquisition of the Determiner Phrase in German child language
Sonja Eisenbeiss

1 Introduction

During the last few years, more and more theoretical linguists and acquisition researchers have come to the conclusion that acquisition data can enrich the data basis for linguistic investigations both quantitatively and qualitatively. On the one hand, experimental data from many languages support the view that the principles of UG are operative from the onset of syntactic development (cf. Crain 1991 for an overview). If this view is correct, child data may broaden the empirical basis for investigations of UG. On the other hand, recent studies on early syntactic development suggest that structural representations in early child grammar may be 'underspecified' compared with the respective structural representations of adult language. If these underspecified structures represented genuine options of UG which are not realized in adult languages, acquisition data would provide a type of evidence which could not be gained through the study of adult linguistic systems. Thus, the study of language development would lead to a qualitative enrichment of the data base for theoretical linguistics.

Such a view is argued for in many recent approaches to early child language. However, there is still a lot of discussion about the exact interpretation of the term 'underspecification'. In the accounts which have been proposed for the acquisition of the Determiner Phrase in German, three concepts of underspecification – which will be discussed in more detail in section 3 – play a central role:

(i)   'Underspecification' might be taken to mean that certain UG parameters have not been set yet – neither to the value of the target language nor to a value chosen by other natural languages (cf. Penner and Weissenborn 1996).

(ii)   The term 'underspecification' might be used to indicate that a specific feature which is obligatorily assigned a value in adult language is left unspecified in certain child utterances (cf. Hoekstra, Hyams and Becker 1996).

(iii) Structural representations might be 'underspecified' in that certain categories or grammatical features of the corresponding adult language are not instantiated in the child's grammar (cf. Clahsen, Eisenbeiss and Vainikka 1994, Clahsen, Eisenbeiss and Penke 1996).

When they are combined with linguistic analyses of the German DP (see section 2) these concepts of underspecification lead to different predictions for DP development (see 5.1 and 6.1). So far, these predictions have been tested only on the basis of the longitudinal Simone-corpus (see Miller 1976) or on the basis of small cross-sectional corpora. In this chapter, I will therefore analyze an extensive corpus of longitudinal and cross-sectional data from seven monolingual German children (age range: 1;11–3;6) with respect to the predictions derived from the three underspecification approaches under discussion (see 5.2 and 6.2). As I will show in 5.3 and 6.3, the results of these analyses can best be captured by the concept of underspecification in (iii), which has been developed on the basis of the Lexical Learning hypothesis (Clahsen, Eisenbeiss and Vainikka 1994, Clahsen, Eisenbeiss and Penke 1996).

2 The DP in German

According to the DP hypothesis, noun phrases are projections of the functional category D. This category contains the nominal agreement features [CASE], [NUMBER], [GENDER], and a feature licensing possessor nouns in SpecDP ([POSS]; see (1)). In German, these features are overtly realized by determiners, pronouns, nominal agreement affixes and the possessive affix -s (see e.g. Haider 1988, Bhatt 1990, Olsen 1991).

(1) *The DP analysis of the German noun phrase*

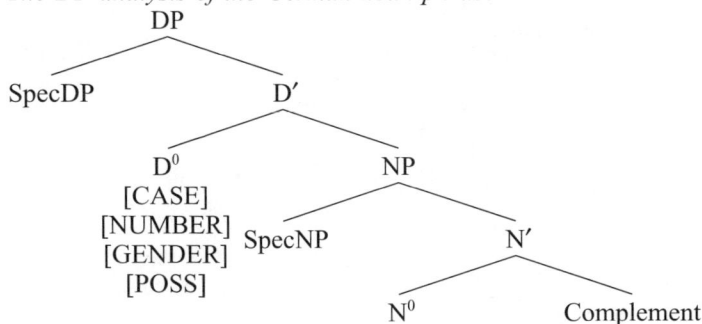

In recent studies, a number of additional nominal functional categories have been postulated (e.g. Q(uantifier), NUM(ber), AGR(eement), C(ase), see e.g. Szabolcsi 1987, Ritter 1991, Siloni 1997, Löbel 1990, Valois 1991), and the categorial status of articles, quantifiers, pronouns and other functional elements within the noun phrase has been discussed controversially. However, these discussions are not relevant for the question whether early grammars are underspecified with respect to DP. It is still generally assumed that determiners, quantifiers, pronouns and the possessive marker -s are realizations of nominal functional projections and their features. Thus, no matter which functional category and structural positions these elements are assigned to, their occurrence in early child language can provide evidence for functional projections in early noun phrases.

For the interpretation of possessive constructions, however, specific linguistic assumptions about the base-position of the possessor are crucial. In German, two linearizations for possessor and possessum are possible (see (2)), the order 'possessor < possessum' (2a) being the unmarked order in spoken language:

(2) a. Svenjas Kenntnisse
       'Svenja's knowledge'
    b. die Kenntnisse Svenjas
       'the knowledge Svenja's'

In order to capture these two variants of the possessive construction, several analyses have been proposed. In all of them it is assumed that the possessor occupies its base-position in possessive constructions with determiners (see (2b), (3a)) and is moved to the SpecDP-position if no determiner is present (see (2a), (3b)). The exact nature of the base-position, however, is currently under debate. Penner and Weissenborn (1996) claim that the possessor is base-generated in the complement position of N^0; cf.:

(3)

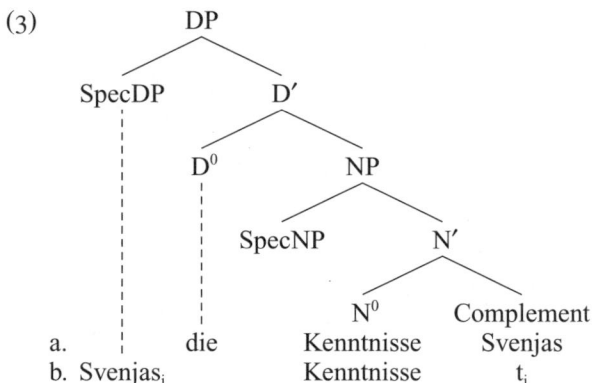

```
(3)                       DP
                       /      \
              SpecDP            D'
                 ¦           /     \
                 ¦         D⁰         NP
                 ¦          ¦       /    \
                 ¦          ¦   SpecNP     N'
                 ¦          ¦            /    \
                 ¦          ¦         N⁰      Complement
    a.           ¦        die      Kenntnisse   Svenjas
    b. Svenjasᵢ          Kenntnisse   tᵢ
```

The drawback of this analysis is that it cannot describe noun phrases with one and two arguments in parallel. In constructions with two arguments (e.g. *Svenjas Kenntnisse des Deutschen*, 'Svenja's knowledge of German'), agent or possessor arguments cannot be base-generated in the complement position of NP, as binding data show (see Lindauer 1995). Their base-position must be higher in the tree than the position of the second argument, which is generally assumed to be the complement position of NP.

In order to capture this observation, Bhatt (1990), Lindauer (1995) and Johnson, *et al.* (1996) argue that possessor phrases are base-generated in SpecNP, both in noun phrases with one argument and in noun phrases with two arguments. These analyses differ in the way they derive the linearization of possessor and possessum in (2). Bhatt (1990) and Lindauer (1995) assume that the specifier-position of NP is projected to the right of the possessum:

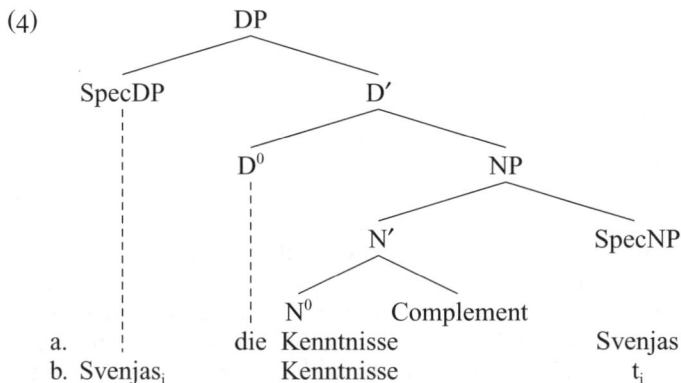

(4)

```
                              DP
                 _____/    \
            SpecDP                 D′
              ¦                ____/   _____
              ¦            D⁰                    NP
              ¦             ¦               ____/    \
              ¦             ¦            N′            SpecNP
              ¦             ¦         __/  \__
              ¦             ¦      N⁰        Complement
      a.      ¦            die  Kenntnisse              Svenjas
      b.  Svenjasᵢ              Kenntnisse              tᵢ
```

This analysis is not compatible with the widely held assumption that specifiers always precede the head (see e.g. Haider 1993, Kayne 1994, Chomsky 1995). This assumption is integrated in the analysis of Johnson *et al.* (1996). These authors propose that the 'possessor < possessum' order in (2a) results from movement of the head noun to the functional head NUM.

(5)

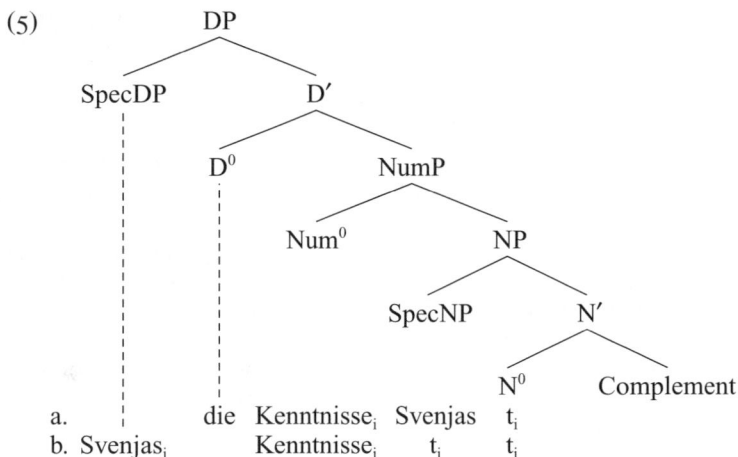

a.		die Kenntnisse$_i$	Svenjas	t$_i$
b.	Svenjas$_j$	Kenntnisse$_i$	t$_j$	t$_i$

Choosing one of these analyses has consequences for the interpretation of possessive constructions in early child language. If the base-position of the possessor is projected to the right of the possessum – as in (3) and (4) – the appearance of the possessor to the left of the possessum provides evidence for the availability of movement to functional positions in the DP. However, if the possessor is base-generated to the left of the possessum as in (5), noun phrases with the order 'possessum < possessor', such as (2b), support the assumption that the DP is operative. Thus, if children use only one of the two possible orders, the interpretation of this order depends on the linguistic analysis one adopts. In contrast, the use of both potential serializations in parallel can be interpreted without reference to a specific variant of the DP analysis. No matter which base-order is postulated, at least one of the two types of possessive constructions deviates from this order. Thus, it can be taken as evidence for the operativeness of a functional projection that can host the moved element(s).

Summarizing so far, the early use of nominal functional elements and the availability of the two types of possessive constructions in (2) would unambiguously support the assumption that early child grammar contains fully specified nominal functional categories. In contrast, it depends on specific linguistic assumptions whether one can take the appearance of one of the two potential possessor–possessum orders as evidence for the operativeness of DP.

3 Approaches to the acquisition of the DP in German

With respect to the development of the DP in German, Clahsen, Eisenbeiss and Vainikka (1994) have distinguished two stages. Initially, the possessive marker -*s* is omitted and determiners are optional. Furthermore, determiners and adjectives occur in complementary distribution and show a high percentage of agreement errors. Finally, determiners are not inflected for case. Later, -*s* is used productively, determiners become obligatory and can be freely combined with adjectives, the percentage of agreement errors drops significantly, and nominative forms are distinguished from accusative and dative forms. These findings have been largely confirmed by other studies on DPs in early German (see Eisenbeiss 1994a, 1994b, Müller 1994, Penner and Weissenborn 1996, Hoekstra, Hyams and Becker 1996). In order to account for them, several approaches have been suggested, which involve the three different concepts of underspecification.

Penner and Weissenborn (1996) argue that the functional category DP is instantiated before the two-word stage, but that early DPs may remain underspecified with respect to certain parameter values of the target language (see also Penner 1993). According to these authors, contrasts between vocative and argument noun phrases enable the child to find out very early that the DP has to be spelled out overtly in German argument DPs – e.g. by a determiner (6b) or a raised possessor (6d).[1]

(6) *Vocative noun phrases*   *Argument noun phrases*
    a. (*der) Hans komm nach   b. der Hans kommt nach
       Hause!   Hause
       '(*the) Hans come-IMP home'   'the Hans comes home'
    c. Maria!   d. Papas kleine Maria
       'Mary!'   'daddy's little Mary'

Acquiring the language-specific implementation of the insertion in D^0, however, requires the analysis of morphological paradigms. These trigger data are not as salient and easily accessible as the contrasts in (6). Thus, there should be a discrepancy between the fixation of the different types of parameters. This may lead to omissions of possessive markers or determiners, and to the use of 'proto-Determiners' such as *de*, which mark the D position but do not spell out any morphological information.

According to Hoekstra, Hyams and Becker (1996), all functional categories are operative at the earliest stage of syntactic development, but certain features which are obligatorily assigned a value in adult language may be left unspecified. Specifically, Hoekstra, Hyams and Becker argue that young children do not have the pragmatic principle that requires the functional category D to be specified for NUM and definiteness. Thus, at this stage of development, children are expected to produce both fully specified noun phrases and noun phrases which are underspecified, and therefore lack determiners and morphological markers.[2]

The Lexical Learning approach claims that functional projections are built up in a stepwise fashion as a result of children's learning of lexical and morphological elements. Thus, early grammars may lack functional categories or grammatical features. The Lexical Learning approach has first been applied to the development of the sentential functional categories INFL and COMP (see e.g. Clahsen 1990, Clahsen and Penke 1992, Clahsen, Penke and Parodi 1993, Clahsen, Eisenbeiss and Penke 1996, Clahsen, Kursawe and Penke 1996). With respect to DP development in German, Clahsen, Eisenbeiss and Vainikka (1994) have claimed that possessors bear structural genitive case and that the acquisition of the genitive affix -*s* forces the child to posit a position for genitive-marked possessors (SpecDP) and a position for the Case-assigner (D^0). Clahsen, Eisenbeiss and Vainikka do not explicitly discuss how the other features of D become syntactically active.

In the following, I will argue that children are equipped with an inventory of potential grammatical features. During language development, these features function as predispositions for the categorization of syntactic and morphological elements. They become active when the child becomes aware of minimal distinctions between elements in the input – e.g. distinctions between bare names such as *Leonie* and possessor nouns such as *Leonies*, 'Leonie's', or between singular and plural forms such as *Auto*, 'car', and *Autos*, 'cars'. Then, the relevant features are instantiated, integrated into lexical entries for individual word forms and projected into syntax according to UG principles. These word-form entries are then strengthened through continued exposure. During this stage, the expression of the respective grammatical element is lexically restricted. Finally, children discover that different word forms sharing a specific affix express the same feature(s), and thus create lexical entries for affixes (e.g. for the possessive marker -*s* and the plural suffix -*s*) and generalized morphological paradigms.[3] Then, the respective grammatical features should be overtly realized in all obligatory contexts.

This view of underspecification ties in very well with recent minimalist concepts of phrase structure. In the Minimalist Program (Chomsky 1995), phrase-structure representations are not based on innate phrase-structure templates but constructed on the basis of the features contained in the lexical elements which are chosen for the construction of the utterance.[4]

4 The data

When combined with the linguistic assumptions outlined in section 2 above, the approaches to the development of the DP in German child language yield predictions for the development of possessive constructions and for the acquisition of nominal functional elements. These

TABLE 2.1   The data

Child	Source	Age	MLU^5	Number of files
Hannah	LEXLERN	2;0–2;7	1.2–2.9	8
Mathias	Clahsen	2;3–3;6	1.3–3.5	18
Leonie	LEXLERN	1;11–2;11	1.6–2.9	15
Annelie	LEXLERN[6]	2;4–2;9	2.0–3.1	6
Svenja	LEXLERN	2;9–3;3	3.3–4.1	15
Andreas	Wagner[7]	2;1	2.4	1
Carsten	Wagner	3;6	4.2	1
Total		1;11–3;6	1.2–4.2	64

predictions will be formulated in 5.1 and 6.1, respectively. They will be tested on the basis of 64 files from five longitudinal and two cross-sectional corpora of monolingual German children. As Table 2.1 shows, these data cover the age period between 1;11 and 3;6, and the MLU values range from 1.2 to 4.2.

5 The development of possessive constructions

In the following, I will first investigate the development of possessive constructions, and I will show that the interpretation of the child language data depends on the linguistic analysis assumed for these constructions.

5.1 Predictions

Penner and Weissenborn's (1996) analysis is based on a specific linguistic assumption: they claim that the possessor is base-generated to the right of the possessum and moved to SpecDP if no determiner occurs (see (3)). As this raising process only occurs in non-vocative contexts, Penner and Weissenborn argue that the relevant trigger data involve a vocative/non-vocative contrast and should therefore be analyzed very early.[8] The overt marking of the possessive relation, however, involves morphological information and should therefore be delayed.

Under the approach advocated by Hoekstra, Hyams and Becker (1996), we should find both fully specified and underspecified noun phrases in early child language. The authors do not explicitly discuss the consequences which the underspecification of NUM might have for possessive constructions. But if one assumes that possessor raising and possessive affixes may only occur in fully specified DPs, one would expect to find a contrast between fully specified and underspecified possessive constructions. In fully specified DPs, the possessive relation should be marked morphologically and both serializations observed in the target language should be allowed. In contrast, underspecified possessive constructions should be characterized by the lack of possessive and number marking and by the restriction to the base-order of possessor and possessum. Thus, if the possessor is base-generated to the **left** of the possessum (see (5)), underspecified DPs should always show the order 'possessor < possessum'. However, if the base-position of the possessor is projected to the **right** of the possessum (see (3) and (4)), possessors in underspecified DPs should always occur at the right periphery of the noun phrase.

Under the Lexical Learning approach, one would expect all early noun phrases to be underspecified with respect to the features of D. Thus, at the beginning of syntactic development, the possessive suffix *-s* should be consistently omitted and there should be no evidence for movement processes in possessive constructions. Only the base-order of possessor and possessum should be observed: 'possessor < possessum' or 'possessum < possessor', depending on the linguistic analysis chosen. Furthermore, in contrast to the other approaches, the Lexical Learning approach explicitly predicts initial distributional restrictions for the occurrence of the possessive marker. Children should first build up lexeme-specific representations for possessors with the possessive marker and the feature [+POSS]. These lexical entries should lead to the projection of full DPs for the respective possessive constructions. Noun phrases with possessor nouns for which the child does not – yet – have a lexical entry with the feature [+POSS], however, should be NPs. Only later, children should be able to generalize over the different possessor nouns with *-s* and create a lexical entry for the possessive marker, which allows them to affix all names used as possessors with *-s* and to project all possessive constructions to the DP level.

In sum, in order to test the predictions derived from the different concepts of underspecification, two sets of questions have to be answered.

(7) *The morphological marking of the possessive relation*
   • Is there an early stage in which the possessive affix *-s* is consistently omitted?
   • Is the morphological realization of the possessive relation subject to distributional restrictions in early child language?

(8) *The serialization of possessor and possessum*
   • How are possessor and possessum linearized in early child language?
   • Does the serialization change in the course of development?
   • Is there a developmental relation between the acquisition of the possessive affix *-s* and the development of the serialization of possessor and possessum?

5.2 Results

In the following, I will compare the predictions developed in 5.1 with the data of Andreas, Annelie, Hannah, Leonie, Mathias and Svenja.[9] Tables 2.2–2.7 in the appendix give an overview of the 121 possessive structures found in the data of these children. The analysis of these structures has lead to the results listed below.

(i) In the first files of Annelie, Leonie and Mathias, the possessive marker -s does not occur (Tables 2.3, 2.5 and 2.6 in the appendix). During this stage, the possessive affix is omitted in all of the 30 obligatory contexts, even in immediate repetitions of correctly inflected forms, as shown in (9).

(9) S.E.:   Und Papas Hose brauchen wir noch.
            'And daddy's pants need we still'
    Leonie: da papa hose (Leonie, file 3)
            'there daddy pant'

(ii) Files 4 to 7 of Leonie's data and the cross-sectional data of Andreas (see Tables 2.5 and 2.2 in the appendix) provide evidence for a subsequent stage which is characterized by the optionality of the possessive marker and by distributional restrictions for -s. During this stage, Leonie produces the possessive marker in 35 of 38 obligatory contexts, but only with the possessor nouns *peters*, *mamis* and *leonies*, which often appear with -s in the input. In possessive constructions with unfamiliar names as possessors, she omits the possessive marker – even if the correct form is presented, as in (10).

(10) S.E.:   Und welches ist Sonjas Auto?
             'And which one is Sonja's car?'
     Leonie: sonja autos (Leonie, file 6)
             'sonja cars'

Andreas combines -s with the possessor noun *papa* ('daddy', see e.g. (11)), but not with the possessor noun *mama* ('mummy', see e.g. (12)). As both nouns are very similar with respect to their phonological structure, there is no phonological factor that could account for the distribution of -s. However, these restrictions could be explained by the assumption that the child first builds up lexeme-specific representations for forms with the possessive marker, which contain the feature [+POSS].

(11) hm papas gürtel (Andreas 2;1)
     'hm daddy's belt'

(12) e mama ticktack is(t) das (Andreas 2;1)
     'e mummy's watch is that'

In late recordings of Leonie (see Tables in the appendix) and in the data of Svenja, -s is sometimes overgeneralized to nouns that cannot be

combined with that affix in the adult language (see (13), (14)).[10] Such
overgeneralizations have also been reported in other studies (see e.g.
Scupin and Scupin 1910: 125, Mills 1985: 185). All of them occur in
later stages of development.

(13) S.E.:   Das is?
                'This is?'
        Leonie: affes banane (Leonie, file 7)
                'monkey's banana'

(14) S.E.:   Und das is?
                'And that is?'
        Svenja: das is junges gürtel (Svenja, file 13)
                'that is boy's belt'

(iii) Before the mastery of -s (Table 2.2; Table 2.3; Table 2.5, files
1–7; Table 2.6, files 9–13), the possessor precedes the possessum in all
of the 56 possessive constructions with possessor and possessum, independently of the morphological marking.

(iv) After the mastery of the possessive marker, we find one possessive construction which deviates from this pattern, as shown in (15a). The
noun phrase in (15a) does not involve an overt possessum noun. Thus,
it is not possible to establish an order for possessor and possessum.
However, this noun phrase contains a determiner, which is characteristic for noun phrases with the order 'possessum < possessor' in the
adult language. Another example of a possessive construction in which
the possessor does not precede the possessum can be found in the data
of Simone (see (15b)).[11] As with Svenja, this type of possessive construction occurs after the mastery of -s (see Clahsen, Eisenbeiss and
Vainikka 1994 for the development of -s in Simone).

(15) a. S.E.:   für den Sascha?
                'for the Sascha?'
        Sven: mhm die sascha die saschas (Svenja, file 15)
                ziehn wer erstmal an
                'mhm the sascha the sascha's [shoes] put we first on'
    b. Mar: Sag mal, was is'n das, Mensch?
                'Tell me, what is this, man?'
        Simone: mones das sind die fisch mones (Simone 2;4)
                'mone's that are the fish mone's'

5.3 Discussion

The finding that there is a stage in which -s is always omitted (see
paragraph (i) above) provides evidence against the approach suggested by Hoekstra, Hyams and Becker (1996), which predicts that

fully specified DPs can be produced in the earliest stages of syntactic development. Finding (i) can either be captured by the approach of Penner and Weissenborn (1996), which allows for a delay of morphological development, or by the Lexical Learning approach, according to which D is not operative in early stages.

The occurrence of a stage in which the possessive marker is optional (finding (ii)) is consistent with all approaches to the development of the German DP, because all of them allow for underspecified DPs without -*s* during early stages of development. However, only the Lexical Learning approach explicitly predicts the observed lexical restrictions of -*s* marking which cannot be attributed to phonological factors. According to this approach, the possessive marker -*s* should first be stored individually for each possessor noun and only later be generalized and applied to all possessors.

As discussed in 5.1, the occurrence of both possible orders of possessor and possessum would provide unambiguous evidence for the operativeness of D. For the stage before the mastery of the possessive marker, such evidence cannot be obtained. 'Possessor < possessum' is the only order to be observed, independently of the morphological marking of the possessive relation (see paragraph (iii)). The interpretation of this finding depends on linguistic assumptions about the base-position of the possessor in possessive constructions. If one adopts the linguistic hypothesis that the possessor is base-generated to the right of the possessum, one can only account for finding (iii) if one assumes that possessors are always moved to SpecDP in early child German, independently of the appearance of -*s*. Such an assumption would be incompatible with a Lexical Learning approach, which assumes that D is not instantiated in early child language. The assumption of early obligatory possessor movement would also cause problems for the approach suggested by Hoekstra, Hyams and Becker (1996), which would predict an alternation between underspecified possessive constructions without -*s* and possessor movement on the one hand and fully specified possessive constructions with -*s* and possessor movement on the other hand. Thus, the assumption of early obligatory possessor movement would be compatible only with the analysis of Penner and Weissenborn (1996), who assume that possessor movement is acquired earlier than -*s*.

However, if one adopts the linguistic assumption that the possessor is base-generated to the left of the possessum (see the discussion in 5.1, which supports this analysis), possessive constructions in which the possessor follows the possessum must necessarily involve movement to nominal functional projections. Under this assumption, the finding that such structures appear only after the mastery of -*s* (see (iii) and (iv)) might suggest that movement to positions in nominal functional projections is not available before the acquisition of the possessive marker and the resulting instantiation of the feature [+POSS]. This would support the Lexical Learning hypothesis.[12]

Taken together, the empirical findings on the development of possessive constructions challenge the underspecification approach of Hoekstra, Hyams and Becker (1996) and provide evidence for the initial lexical restrictions predicted by the Lexical Learning approach. Furthermore, if one assumes that possessors are base-generated to the left of the possessum, the findings also confirm the predictions the Lexical Learning approach makes with respect to word order. In the following, I will provide evidence for this approach which is independent of the particular DP analysis chosen.

6 The acquisition of nominal functional elements

Like possessive markers, determiners are frequently omitted in early child language. In contrast to possessive markers, however, determiners occasionally appear in early child language. This observation has led to a controversy about the status of early determiners. In the following, I will contribute to this controversy by investigating determiners with quantitative methods which take into account developmental changes.

6.1 Predictions

Early determiners can either be analyzed as overt instantiations of nominal functional categories or they can be interpreted as 'impostors', i.e. as elements that have the same form as adult nominal functional elements, but do not involve functional categories or their features (see Radford 1990: 103). Such impostors could be unanalyzed parts of formulae such as *wo's-der*+N ('where's-the+N'), unanalyzed parts of fixed det+N units (e.g. *der*+*papa*, 'the+daddy'), or unanalyzed fillers, which children insert to mimic the prosodic structure of the target language.

According to Hoekstra, Hyams and Becker (1996), even in very early stages of grammatical development, D is syntactically active and can be spelled out by determiners. Thus, we should find determiners which cannot be interpreted as impostors.

In contrast, Penner and Weissenborn (1996) claim that the acquisition of determiners may be delayed because it involves morphological information, which is not easily accessible. Thus, the approach advocated by Penner and Weissenborn is compatible with the assumption that the determiners observed in early stages are impostors. For the Simone-corpus, they argue that this is indeed the case. However, they do not explain their criteria for determining if an utterance is formulaic.

Furthermore, Penner and Weissenborn claim that the first non-formulaic determiners appearing in child language are expletive

definite articles, i.e. definite articles which are combined with inherently definite nouns such as proper names (*die Leonie*, 'the Leonie').
According to these authors, expletive elements are not semantically
motivated and thus children should easily recognize that these elements
are motivated by the syntactic requirement to spell out D overtly. Thus,
expletive definite articles should be more accessible than semantically
motivated determiners and should be acquired earlier. Penner and
Weissenborn claim that this prediction is confirmed by an analysis of
the Simone-corpus. An analysis of the raw data shows, however, that
the early use of expletive determiners is restricted to utterances of the
type *wosde*+N ('where's-the+N'). According to Penner and Weissenborn
(1996) and Clahsen, Kursawe and Penke (1996), this utterance type is a
formula for Simone. The first expletive definite articles which cannot
be attributed to this formula appear at 2;0,26, i.e. when the number
of semantically motivated determiners in clearly non-formulaic utterances increases (cf. Clahsen, Eisenbeiss and Vainikka 1994, Penner and
Weissenborn 1996). Only from 2;1 on, non-formulaic utterances with
expletive articles become more frequent (see Clahsen, Eisenbeiss and
Vainikka 1994: 100). Thus, the data from the Simone-corpus do not
provide clear support for Penner and Weissenborn's assumptions.
Furthermore, in Standard German and in some varieties of colloquial
German, proper names must not appear with determiners. So they cannot function as triggers for all German children.

   Advocates of the Lexical Learning hypothesis claim that D is not operative in early stages of syntactic development. Thus, early determiners
have to be analyzed as impostors. Furthermore, the Lexical Learning
approach involves the assumption that the lexical entries for the different
types of nominal functional elements (definite and indefinite articles,
possessive pronouns, etc.) should be acquired independently. Thus, they
might appear at different times in development.

   In order to test the predictions derived from the underspecification
approaches under discussion, criteria for determining whether determiners
are impostors are required. In the following, I will discuss five criteria.

   (i) One phenomenon which suggests a change from unanalyzed to
analyzed forms is the occurrence of a U-shaped developmental curve.
Such curves have been reported for the acquisition of the English past
tense (see e.g. Marcus *et al.* 1992). It has been shown that English-
speaking children initially use only correct past tense forms such as
walked or *went*. Then, they go through a stage in which they sometimes
overgeneralize the regular past tense affix *-ed* to irregular verbs (e.g.
goed). Finally, they produce target-like forms again. These findings
have been taken as evidence for a transition from stored unanalyzed
forms to target-like representations which allow for the generalization
of *-ed* to verbs which have not been encountered in the past tense.

Thus, if early 'determiners' are impostors, we should observe a U-shaped curve in the realization of determiners in obligatory contexts: In early child language, we should find 'determiners' which are based on unanalyzed structures such as *da-ein*+N, 'there-a+N', or *die+puppe*, 'the+doll'. Later, when children realize that these structures contain elements which cannot be assigned representations (namely the early 'determiners'), they should leave out these elements until they are able to categorize them. After the categorization of the formerly unanalyzed 'determiner' elements, the proportion of overt determiners should rise again.

(ii) If early determiners are impostors, one should be able to account for most of the early utterances with 'determiners' by referring to certain formulae with slots for nouns (e.g. *da-ein*+N, 'there-a+N') or fixed det+N combinations (e.g. *die+puppe*, 'the+doll'). In contrast, later utterances with determiners should show more variation with respect to the elements the determiners are combined with. Thus, in 6.2, I will first determine how many noun phrases with an overt 'determiner' can be accounted for by the assumption that they are based on formulae. My criteria for potentially formulaic utterances with determiners are given in (16).

(16) Criteria for potentially formulaic utterances with Determiners:
   • Only the noun following the determiner in question shows lexical variation (e.g. *wo's de+hund*, 'where's-the+dog', *wo's-de+haus*, 'where's-the+house').
   • The invariant part of the utterance (e.g. *wo's-de*, 'where's-the') occurs at least three times in one file, always combined with a noun.
   • For the longitudinal data, the invariant part of the utterance appears in at least two files.

For those noun phrases with determiners which occur in utterances not fulfilling the criteria in (16), I will calculate the number of different types of det+N combinations.

(iii) If early 'determiners' result from a small set of unanalyzed formulae, they should only occur in a restricted set of syntactic contexts.

(iv) Imposters should not be combined with adjectives. A+N combinations cannot fill the N slots of fomulae such as *wo's-der*+N ('where's-the+N'), fixed det+N units such as *der+papa* ('the+daddy') do not allow for the insertion of adjectives between determiner and noun, and in A+N combinations the presence of the adjective before the noun makes prosodically induced fillers superfluous.

(v) If D, the locus of the nominal Case features, is not instantiated in early stages of syntactic development, early 'determiners' should not express Case distinctions.

In sum, in order to test the predictions made by different approaches to phrase-structure development, two sets of questions have to be answered.

(17) *The status of early determiners*
- Is there a stage in which there are no overt determiners?
- Does the development of determiners show a U-shaped curve of development?
- Can early determiners be attributed to formulaic utterances and unanalyzed det+N units?
- Do early determiners appear in a restricted set of syntactic contexts?
- Can early determiners be combined with adjectives?
- Do early determiners express Case distinctions?

(18) *Developmental relationships*
- Are expletive definite articles acquired before semantically definite articles?
- Do different nominal functional elements appear at different times in development?

6.2 Results

In order to test the predictions developed in 6.1, I analyzed the long-itudinal and cross-sectional corpora under study with respect to the development of nominal functional elements. Figures 2.1–2.4 and Tables 2.8–2.28 in the appendix give an overview of the use of these elements in the data investigated. The curves show the proportion of overt determiners in obligatory contexts. The shaded area under the curves represents the proportion of these overt nominal functional elements

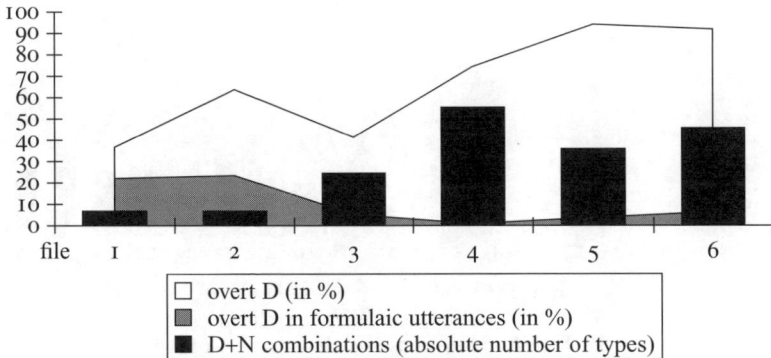

FIGURE 2.1   Overt determiners in obligatory contexts – Annelie

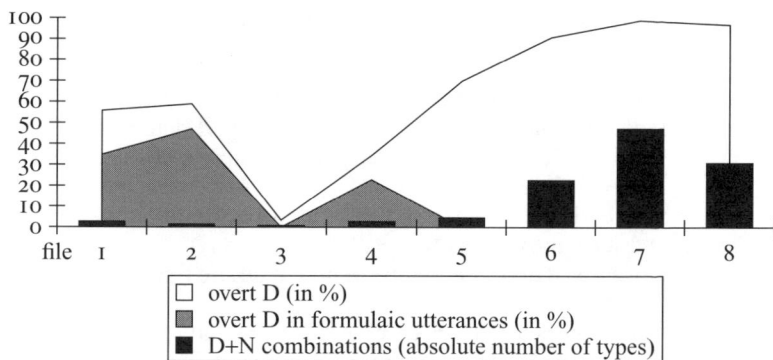

FIGURE 2.2   Overt determiners in obligatory contexts – Hannah

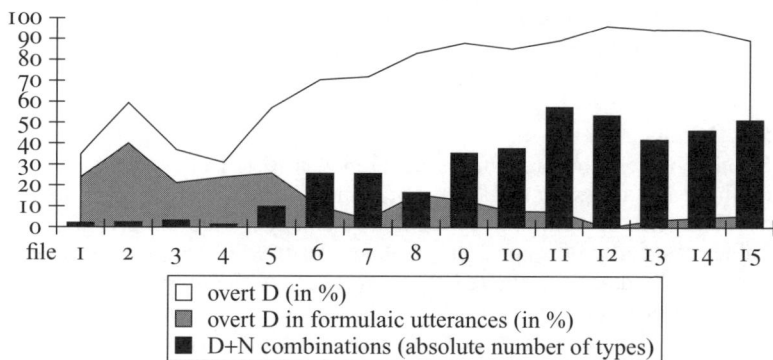

FIGURE 2.3   Overt determiners in obligatory contexts – Leonie

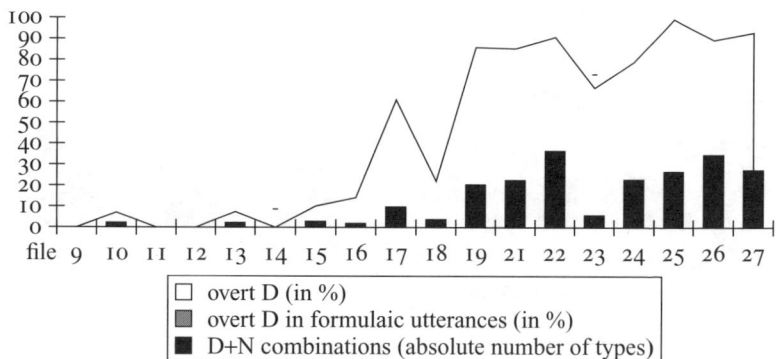

FIGURE 2.4   Overt determiners in obligatory contexts – Mathias

which appear in potentially formulaic utterances (see (16)), and the colums indicate the absolute number of the different types of determiner–noun combinations which do not occur in potentially formulaic utterances. Files with less than 10 obligatory contexts for overt determiners are marked with –.

The analysis of these data leads to the following results:

(i) In the data of Mathias, we can observe an early stage in which he hardly ever produces the required determiner (Figure 2.4, files 9–16; Table 2.13 in the appendix). During this stage, he uses these elements in only 9 of 157 obligatory contexts (= 5,7%). A stage without overt determiners has also been documented for the Bernese child Juval (cf. Penner and Weissenborn 1996), for the English-speaking child Adam (cf. Brown 1973: 392) and the bilingual (English/German) child Hildegard (see Leopold 1949), among others.[13]

(ii) As can be seen in Figures 2.1–2.4, the development of determiners in the longitudinal data of Annelie, Hannah, Leonie and Mathias shows a U-shaped curve of development. After a stage in which the proportions of overt determiners in obligatory contexts range from 35% to 64%, they drop to values between 4% and 42%. Then, they increase again to values of more than 90%.[14]

(iii) For Annelie, Hannah and Leonie there is a close relationship between the omission rate and the proportion of potentially formulaic utterances with determiners (Figures 2.1–2.3). In the early stage before the temporary decrease in the proportion of overt determiners, most of the determiners occur in four types of potentially formulaic utterances: noch+indef.art., 'another', auch+indef.art., 'also a', da+indef.art., 'there a', and wo/da-(i)s(t)+def.art., 'where/there's the'.

The remaining determiners occur in a small number of det+N combinations which frequently appear in children's input (e.g. die+mama, 'the mummy'). When the proportion of overt determiners drops, the rate of potentially formulaic utterances decreases rapidly and remains low. Furthermore, the range of nouns with which determiners are combined increases, and the same noun is produced with various determiners. Similar findings have been reported for the English-speaking child Adam (Brown 1973: 392ff.)

Mathias, Svenja and Carsten do not produce any utterances that meet the criteria for potentially formulaic utterances. For Mathias, the lack of potentially formulaic utterances may be due to a sampling artefact. In the early stage before the temporary drop in the realization rate, there are only very few contexts for determiners so that it is hard to reach the minimum of three instances in one file. However, the observed variation might also reflect an individual strategy for coping with input elements which cannot be analyzed at that point in development. This strategy might also account for the very low proportion of overt nominal functional elements in the early files of Mathias. In contrast to Mathias, Svenja and Carsten use nominal functional elements in 95% and 91% of obligatory contexts (Tables 2.14 and 2.10 in the appendix) and combine them with a broad range of nouns. Thus, their data may be taken to represent a late stage of development in which formulaic utterances do not play an important role anymore. Andreas is a little less advanced. He supplies the required nominal functional elements in 315 of 364 obligatory contexts (= 87%) and produces three utterances that can be derived from the formula *da*+indef.art.+N, 'there+indef.art.+N' (= 1% of obligatory contexts).

(iv) As Tables 2.8–2.14 in the appendix show, early determiners appear in a restricted set of syntactic contexts. In the data of Annelie, Hannah, Mathias and Leonie, we find only one determiner in a prepositional phrase before the temporary drop in the rate of overt nominal functional elements (see Table 2.12, file 2). All other determiners appear in nominative noun phrases or accusative objects. Once the proportion of overt determiners steadily increases, determiners are not restricted to nominative contexts and accusative objects anymore, but also appear in other syntactic contexts. However, the prepositional phrases still show a higher proportion of determiner omissions than noun phrases in nominative contexts and accusative objects.[15] In the data of the children that show a high proportion of overt determiners (Svenja, Carsten and Andreas), determiners appear in all types of syntactic contexts.

(v) The data of Annelie, Hannah, Leonie and Mathias confirm the prediction that there is an early stage in which determiners and adjectives occur in complementary distribution. Before the temporary drop in the rate of overt nominal functional elements, these elements are omitted in all of the 46 noun phrases with adjectives (Tables 2.16, 2.18, 2,19 and 2.20 in the appendix). This observation cannot be attributed to a performance restriction that would allow only noun phrases consisting of two elements. Given such a restriction, we would expect to find det+A combinations, which are possible in adult German. However, such structures do not appear at that time.

Once the proportion of overt nominal functional elements increases steadily and the proportion of formulaic utterances decreases, Annelie, Hannah, Leonie and Mathias start to produce both det+A combinations and det+A+N combinations. Furthermore, Svenja, Carsten and Andreas, who use determiners in nearly all obligatory contexts, show no complementary distribution of determiners and adjectives.

(vi) Early determiners do not express Case distinctions. In the early stage before and during the temporary drop in the proportion of overt determiners, we find 13 prenominal determiners and 6 pronominally used determiners in contexts which require a distinct non-nominative marking (acc.masc.sg. and dat.). In none of these contexts is the required marker supplied. Instead, children use nominative forms (i.e. the default Case in German) or phonologically reduced forms of articles, such as *de* or *e*, which do not bear any Case-marking. This distribution cannot be attributed to the lack of the required morphological accusative and dative forms. Annelie uses the acc.mas.sg. form *den* of the definite article as a demonstrative pronoun 17 times during that stage. However, 15 of these forms appear in nominative contexts and 2 in fem./neut.acc.sg. contexts. Thus, the nominative and non-nominative forms which appear during the earliest stage of DP development do not serve to express Case distinctions. The first non-nominative forms which are used appropriately appear during the stage in which the proportion of overt determiners starts to increase again. Thus, the data investigated in this study confirm the results Clahsen, Eisenbeiss and Vainikka (1994) have obtained for the Simone-corpus.

(vii) As can be seen in Tables 2.23, 2.25, 2.26 and 2.27 in the appendix, expletive definite articles are not acquired before semantically motivated determiners. Rather, the acquisition of semantically motivated determiners seems to precede the use of expletive articles. The more advanced children Svenja, Carsten and Andreas, who produce nominal functional elements in the vast majority of obligatory contexts, freely combine expletive articles and proper names. In the longitudinal data of Hannah and Mathias, expletive definite articles can be found only in a later stage in which the use of determiners in obligatory contexts is almost target-like (Tables 2.25 and 2.27 in the appendix). Leonie starts to use expletive articles more frequently once she produces determiners in about 90% of all obligatory contexts (Table 2.26 in the appendix). Before that time, only 3 of 70 noun phrases with a proper name (= 4%) contain a determiner. In the data of Annelie, expletive articles appear more frequently once the proportion of overt semantically motivated determiners in obligatory contexts increases. Before that time, she combines only 3 of the 35 proper names which she uses with an article.

(viii) The various types of nominal functional elements appear at different times in development. Specifically, indefinite articles are acquired before definite articles, as can be seen in the longitudinal data of Annelie, Hannah, Leonie and Mathias (Tables 2.23, 2.25–2.28 in the appendix). In the early stage before the temporary drop in the proportion of overt determiners, these children use both definite and indefinite articles. Distributional errors with respect to definiteness cannot be observed. However, this does not show that children express the feature [±DEFINITE] in an adult-like fashion. First, it is hard to detect errors with respect to definiteness in spontaneous speech (see Brown 1973). Second, most of the early 'determiners' appear in potentially formulaic utterances, in which the contextually required element seems to be stored together with the predicate (see (iii) above).

During the stage in which the proportion of overt nominal functional elements increases steadily and the proportion of potentially formulaic utterances decreases (file 4 for Annelie, 5 for Hannah, 5–8 for Leonie, 19–21 for Mathias; see Figures 2.1–2.4), the proportion of indefinite articles is higher than the proportion of definite articles in all files. Only later, when determiners are realized in nearly all obligatory contexts, definite articles are the dominant type of determiner in most files.

6.3 Discussion

The finding that – at least for some children – there is a stage in which there are no overt determiners (see finding (i)), provides evidence against the assumption that fully specified determiners may appear even in early stages of syntactic development. Furthermore, findings (ii)–(vi) confirm the assumption that early 'determiners' are not instantiations of nominal functional categories but rather impostors, i.e. unanalyzed elements. The observation that the development of nominal functional elements is characterized by a U-shaped curve (see finding (ii)) suggests that the early determiners are reanalyzed during early language development. This assumption is supported by the observation that determiners before and after the temporary drop in the realization rate of determiners show a different distribution. Early determiners mostly appear in potentially formulaic utterances (see finding (ii)), only in a restricted set of syntactic contexts (see (iv)), and never in det+A combinations (see (v)). Furthermore, early determiners do not express Case distinctions (see (vi)). As soon as the proportion of overt nominal functional elements increases again, the distributional restrictions for these elements disappear and Case distinctions can be observed.

Thus, in sum, the findings in (i)–(vi) provide evidence against the approach developed by Hoekstra, Hyams and Becker (1996), which would lead us to expect fully specified DPs in the earliest stages of syntactic development. These findings can be captured either by the approach of Penner and Weissenborn (1996), which allows for a delay of morphological development, or by the Lexical Learning approach, according to which D is not syntactically active in early developmental stages. However, the finding that expletive definite articles in noun phrases with proper names do not precede substantive definite articles for all children (see (vii)) provides evidence against Penner and Weissenborn's assumption that trigger data involving expletive elements are more easily accessible than semantically motivated elements. In addition, the observation that different nominal functional elements appear at different times in development (see (viii)) confirms the prediction which the Lexical Learning hypothesis makes for the course of development.

7 Conclusion

Taken together, the findings discussed in 5.3 and 6.3 can best be captured by the Lexical Learning approach to underspecification, which assumes that in early stages of syntactic development certain categories or grammatical features of the corresponding adult language may remain unprojected. On the one hand, this approach can account for the observed initial absence of overt nominal functional elements and morphological markings; on the other hand, it explicitly predicts the initial lexical restrictions which have been observed in the distribution of functional elements and affixes.

Adopting the Lexical Learning approach has consequences for linguistic analyses. If early noun phrases do not involve nominal functional projections – as I have tried to motivate independently in section 6 – the 'possessor < possessum' order observed in early stages should reflect the base-order. That is, given the Lexical Learning approach, the child language data suggest that possessors are base-generated to the left of the nominal head. As I have argued in section 2, such an analysis is in accord with minimalist assumptions about phrase structure and thus provides additional support for them.

Appendix

TABLE 2.2   Possessive constructions – Andreas

Nr	n	N+N	Possessor	N's+N	Possessor	N's	Possessor
I	4	2	*mama*	2	*papas*	–	

Nr:	Number of file
n:	Total number of possessive constructions requiring -*s*
N+N:	Possessive constructions without -*s* (e.g. *mama ball, 'mummy ball')
N's+N:	Possessive constructions with -*s* (e.g. *mamas ball*, 'mummy's ball'),
N's:	Possessive constructions with -*s* but without an overt possessum (e.g. *mamas*, 'mummy's')
Possessor:	The types of possessor nouns used in the respective construction. Nouns which often appear with -*s* in the input (kinship terms such as *mama*, the child's own name, and the names of close friends or relatives) are presented in italics. Overgeneralizations of -*s* are indicated by uppercase letters.

TABLE 2.3   Possessive constructions – Annelie

Nr	n	N+N	Possessor	N's+N	Possessor	N's	Possessor
1	–	–		–		–	
2	1	1	annelie	–		–	
3	1	1	annelie	–		–	
4	3	3	benni, mama	–		–	
5–6	–	–		–		–	

TABLE 2.4   Possessive constructions – Hannah

Nr	n	N+N	Possessor	N's+N	Possessor	N's	Possessor
1–4	–	–		–		–	
5	1	–		1	hannahs	–	
6	1	–		1	hannahs	–	
7–8	–	–		–		–	

TABLE 2.5   Possessive constructions – Leonie

Nr	n	N+N	Possessor	N's+N	Possessor	N's	Possessor
1	9	9	omi, papa, mann, peter, mama	–		–	
2	8	8	mama, mami, peter	–		–	
3	5	5	papa, peter, leonie	–		–	
4	5	1	peter	1	peters	3	peters
5	14	–		9	mamis, peters	5	mamis
6	8	1	sonja	6	leonies, mamis, peters	1	leonies
7	11	1	sonja	3	leonies	7	mamas, leonies, omas, sonjas, AFFES
8	3	–		2	leonies, mamas	1	saschas
9	7	–		3	sonjas, peters, leonies	4	sonjas, saschas, BABYS, klaras
10	3	–		–		3	sonjas, peters
11	3	–		1	CLOWNS	2	sonjas
12	2	–		1	peters	1	saschas
13	1	–		1	leonies	–	
14	–	–		–		–	
15	2	–		1	mamas	1	mamas

TABLE 2.6   Possessive constructions – Mathias

Nr	n	N+N	Possessor	N's+N	Possessor	N's	Possessor
9–10	–	–		–		–	
11	1	1	*daniel*	–		–	
12	1	1	*julia*	–		–	
13	1	1	*julia*	–		–	
14–21	–	–		–		–	
22	2	–		2	*daniels, julias*	–	
23–24	–	–		–		–	
25	1	–		1	*daniels*	–	
26	1	–		1	*daniels*	–	
27	1	–		1	*julias*	–	

TABLE 2.7   Possessive constructions – Svenja

Nr	n	N+N	Possessor	N's+N	Possessor	N's	Possessor
2	–	–		–		–	
3	3	–		3	rudis, *papas, mamas*	–	
4	–	–		–		–	
5	2	–		1	*papas*	1	*papas*
6–10	–	–		–		–	
11	2	–		2	*mamas*	–	
12	–	–		–		–	
13	9	–		7	annas, *mamas, papas*, saschas, JUNGES	2	annas
14	–	–		–		–	
15	3	–		2	*mamas*, saschas	1	*mamas*
16	2	–		2	*papas*, saschas	–	

TABLE 2.8   Nominal functional elements in obligatory contexts – Andreas

Nr	Total		NOM		ACC		DAT		PP	
	n	–F%	n	–F%	n	–F%	n	–F%	n	–F%
1	364	13	186	5	127	17	5	0	32	56

Nr: Number of file
n: Total number of obligatory contexts for overt nominal functional
      elements (articles, possessive pronouns, demonstrative pronouns,
      quantifiers and prenominal *wh*-elements such as *welch*-'which'). The
      following types of noun phrases were not taken into account: nominal
      functional elements which are used as pronouns, one-word utterances
      consisting of a single noun, onomatopoetic nouns (e.g. *bumm*, 'bang')
      and noun phrases with combinations of determiners and quantifiers
      (e.g. *meine vielen Katzen*, 'my many cats'). Noun phrases with
      adjectives and noun phrases containing proper names were analyzed
      independently (cf. Tables 2.15–2.21 and Tables 2.22–2.28,
      respectively).
–F%: Proportion of determiner omission in obligatory contexts
The proportions were calculated separately for the following syntactic contexts:
NOM: Subjects, predicative noun phrases and noun phrases in naming
      contexts
ACC: Direct accusative objects
DAT: Dative objects of transitive and bitransitive verbs
PP: Prepositional phrases with and without an overt preposition
Total: NOM, ACC, DAT, PP, and noun phrases with unclear syntactic
      function

TABLE 2.9   Nominal functional elements in obligatory contexts – Annelie

Nr	Total		NOM		ACC		DAT		PP	
	n	–F%	n	–F%	n	–F%	n	–F%	n	–F%
1	46	63	40	63	5	60	0	–	1	100
2	25	36	16	38	5	40	0	–	1	100
3	83	58	57	56	11	73	0	–	12	67
4	93	25	42	24	25	12	0	–	14	57
5	57	5	40	5	11	9	0	–	0	–
6	76	7	36	3	17	12	0	–	13	15

TABLE 2.10 Nominal functional elements in obligatory contexts – Carsten

Nr	Total		NOM		ACC		DAT		PP	
	n	−F%	n	−F%	n	−F%	n	−F%	n	−F%
1	661	9	267	3	212	10	2	0	147	14

TABLE 2.11 Nominal functional elements in obligatory contexts – Hannah

Nr	Total		NOM		ACC		DAT		PP	
	n	−F%	n	−F%	n	−F%	n	−F%	n	−F%
1	16	44	12	33	2	50	0	–	2	100
2	17	41	13	23	3	100	0	–	1	100
3	24	96	5	80	15	100	0	–	3	100
4	26	65	21	57	0	–	0	–	2	100
5	10	30	8	25	1	100	0	–	0	–
6	34	9	20	0	7	0	0	–	2	0
7	67	1	48	2	10	0	0	–	4	0
8	35	3	19	5	4	0	5	0	2	0

TABLE 2.12 Nominal functional elements in obligatory contexts – Leonie

Nr	Total		NOM		ACC		DAT		PP	
	n	−F%	n	−F%	n	−F%	n	−F%	n	−F%
1	17	65	15	60	2	100	0	–	0	–
2	10	40	5	20	4	75	0	–	1	0
3	19	63	11	45	5	80	2	100	1	100
4	13	69	4	50	8	75	0	–	1	100
5	31	42	14	29	14	43	0	–	3	100
6	65	29	26	15	29	31	1	100	3	100
7	56	27	31	23	14	21	1	100	5	60
8	31	16	26	8	3	33	0	–	2	100
9	62	11	29	14	24	0	3	0	5	60
10	72	14	36	19	28	4	1	100	4	25
11	97	10	35	6	48	13	2	0	5	40
12	73	3	37	0	18	0	2	0	14	14
13	76	5	25	8	32	0	1	0	10	10
14	75	5	47	0	16	6	2	0	7	29
15	90	10	37	0	24	4	2	0	20	40

TABLE 2.13   Nominal functional elements in obligatory contexts – Mathias

Nr	Total		NOM		ACC		DAT		PP	
	n	-F%	n	-F%	n	-F%	n	-F%	n	-F%
9	11	100	6	100	2	100	0	–	2	100
10	29	93	13	92	15	93	0	–	0	–
11	17	100	10	100	7	100	0	–	0	–
12	23	100	11	100	8	100	0	–	4	100
13	29	93	17	94	7	100	0	–	0	–
14	3	100	3	100	0	–	0	–	0	–
15	31	90	18	89	8	100	0	–	0	–
16	14	86	6	83	6	83	0	–	2	100
17	21	38	11	27	6	50	0	–	2	100
18	18	78	8	75	6	67	0	–	1	100
19	30	13	27	11	2	50	0	–	0	–
21	37	14	14	14	20	15	0	–	0	–
22	52	8	24	4	21	5	0	–	5	40
23	9	33	4	0	2	50	0	–	3	67
24	33	21	13	15	8	25	0	–	9	33
25	36	0	13	0	11	0	4	0	5	0
26	42	10	20	15	12	0	0	–	8	13
27	32	6	16	0	3	33	0	–	9	11

TABLE 2.14   Nominal functional elements in obligatory contexts – Svenja

Nr	Total		NOM		ACC		DAT		PP	
	n	-F%	n	-F%	n	-F%	n	-F%	n	-F%
2	6	17	4	25	1	0	0	–	0	–
3	41	17	27	4	4	50	0	–	9	44
4	54	4	24	0	17	0	0	–	10	20
5	66	6	35	6	15	7	0	–	12	8
6	26	0	12	0	10	0	0	–	2	0
7	18	6	6	0	7	0	0	–	5	20
8	130	5	44	7	52	0	3	0	19	21
9	28	4	6	0	15	0	0	–	3	33
10	33	3	6	0	13	0	0	–	8	13
11	68	1	28	4	25	0	0	–	13	0
12	27	0	7	0	8	0	0	–	8	0
13	105	7	29	7	50	2	3	0	20	20
14	48	2	12	0	29	3	0	–	3	0
15	122	7	33	3	62	0	1	0	19	37
16	118	3	38	3	54	2	4	0	16	6

TABLE 2.15   Nominal functional elements in noun phrases with adjectives –
Andreas

Nr	Adjective+N		Adjective		Total	
	n	−F%	n	−F%	n	−F%
I	13	38	28	21	41	27

Nr:	Number of file
n:	Total number of noun phrases with adjectives which contain obligatory contexts for overt nominal functional elements (articles, possessive pronouns, demonstrative pronouns, quantifiers and *welch-*, 'which')
−F%:	Proportion of determiner omission in obligatory contexts
Adjective+N:	Noun phrases which contain a noun, an adjective and an obligatory context for an overt nominal functional element (e.g. *die kleine Katze*, 'the small cat', *großer Hund*, 'big dog')
Adjective:	Noun phrases without an overt nominal head which contain an adjective and an obligatory context for an overt nominal functional element (e.g. *die kleine*, 'the small (one)', *großer*, 'big (one)')
Total:	All noun phrases which contain an adjective and an obligatory context for an overt nominal functional element

TABLE 2.16   Nominal functional elements in noun phrases with adjectives –
Annelie

Nr	Adjective+N		Adjective		Total	
	n	−F%	n	−F%	n	−F%
I	2	100	0	–	2	100
2	0	–	0	–	0	–
3	4	100	0	–	4	100
4	I	100	3	100	4	100
5	0	–	0	–	0	–
6	I	0	2	0	3	0

TABLE 2.17   Nominal functional elements in noun phrases with adjectives –
Carsten

Nr	Adjective+N		Adjective		Total	
	n	−F%	n	−F%	n	−F%
I	65	5	27	0	92	3

TABLE 2.18 Nominal functional elements in noun phrases with adjectives –
Hannah

Nr	Adjective+N		Adjective		Total	
	n	–F%	n	–F%	n	–F%
1	0	–	2	100	2	100
2	0	–	10	100	10	100
3	0	–	6	100	6	100
4	2	100	1	100	3	100
5	1	0	4	100	5	80
6	3	0	0	–	3	0
7	7	14	0	–	7	14
8	1	0	1	0	2	0

TABLE 2.19 Nominal functional elements in noun phrases with adjectives –
Leonie

Nr	Adjective+N		Adjective		Total	
	n	–F%	n	–F%	n	–F%
1	4	100	1	100	5	100
2	15	100	4	100	19	100
3	18	94	1	100	19	95
4	4	100	14	100	18	100
5	19	100	8	88	27	96
6	17	100	6	83	23	96
7	11	55	3	67	14	57
8	11	64	5	60	16	63
9	5	80	12	58	17	65
10	9	44	22	41	31	42
11	9	22	30	30	39	28
12	12	8	13	8	25	8
13	23	13	47	6	70	9
14	12	0	27	7	39	5
15	12	8	20	5	32	6

TABLE 2.20   Nominal functional elements in noun phrases with adjectives – Mathias

Nr	Adjective+N		Adjective		Total	
	n	−F%	n	−F%	n	−F%
9	0	–	0	–	0	–
10	I	100	0	–	I	100
11	0	–	0	–	0	–
12	0	–	I	100	I	100
13	I	100	0	–	I	100
14	0	–	0	–	0	–
15	I	100	I	100	2	100
16	3	100	0	–	3	100
17	0	–	0	–	0	–
18	3	100	0	–	3	100
19	I	0	2	0	3	0
21	I	0	I	100	2	50
22	5	40	2	0	7	29
23	0	–	0	–	0	–
24	2	50	2	0	4	25
25	2	50	3	0	5	20
26	7	29	6	17	13	23
27	4	25	3	0	7	14

TABLE 2.21   Nominal functional elements in noun phrases with adjectives – Svenja

Nr	Adjective+N		Adjective		Total	
	n	−F%	n	−F%	n	−F%
2	0	–	4	0	4	0
3	2	0	8	0	10	0
4	0	–	3	0	3	0
5	3	33	7	0	10	10
6	2	0	I	0	3	0
7	0	–	0	–	0	–
8	4	0	5	0	9	0
9	3	0	I	0	4	0
10	I	0	0	–	I	0
11	4	0	4	0	8	0
12	0	–	5	0	5	0
13	11	18	12	0	23	9
14	3	0	I	0	4	0
15	9	11	16	0	25	4
16	10	0	10	0	20	0

TABLE 2.22   Types of nominal functional elements – Andreas

Nr	Common nouns and proper names					Proper names	
	n	def.art. %	indef.art. %	others %	−F%	n	+F%
I	389	21	43	23	13	126	20

Nr:	Number of file
Common nouns and proper names:	All noun phrases in which a determiner was required (common nouns) or appeared though it was optional (proper names). Thus, in addition to noun phrases with an obligatory context for overt nominal functional elements (Tables 2.8–2.14), noun phrases with a proper name and an overt determiner were taken into account.
n:	Total number of noun phrases with a common noun or a proper name
def.art. %:	Proportion of definite articles
indef.art. %:	Proportion of indefinite articles
others %:	Proportion of other overt nominal functional elements (possessive pronouns, demonstrative pronouns, inflected and uninflected quantifiers and numerals, the negator *kein-*, 'no', the prenominal *wh*-word *welch-*, 'which')
−F%:	Proportion of determiner omission in obligatory contexts
Proper names:	All noun phrases with a proper name in which a determiner may appear; vocatives and possessive nouns were not taken into account
n:	Total number of noun phrases with a proper name
+F%:	Proportion of noun phrases with a proper name and an overt determiner

TABLE 2.23   Types of nominal functional elements – Annelie

Nr	Common nouns and proper names					Proper names	
	n	def.art. %	indef.art. %	others %	−F%	n	+F%
I	46	4	33	0	63	2	0
2	27	19	26	22	33	14	14
3	84	18	20	5	57	19	5
4	100	21	35	21	23	18	39
5	63	32	46	17	5	15	47
6	79	61	10	23	6	3	100

TABLE 2.24 Types of nominal functional elements – Carsten

Nr	Common nouns and proper names					Proper names	
	n	def.art. %	indef.art. %	others %	−F%	n	+F%
1	690	41	21	29	9	38	76

TABLE 2.25 Types of nominal functional elements – Hannah

Nr	Common nouns and proper names					Proper names	
	n	def.art. %	indef.art. %	others %	−F%	n	+F%
1	16	0	56	0	44	−	−
2	17	6	47	6	41	1	0
3	24	0	0	4	96	1	0
4	26	8	27	0	65	−	−
5	10	20	50	0	30	−	−
6	39	62	28	2	8	7	71
7	73	70	26	3	1	8	75
8	40	60	28	9	3	5	100

TABLE 2.26 Types of nominal functional elements – Leonie

Nr	Common nouns and proper names					Proper names	
	n	def.art. %	indef.art. %	others %	−F%	n	+F%
1	17	0	35	0	65	1	0
2	10	20	40	0	40	2	0
3	19	0	32	5	63	4	0
4	13	0	31	0	69	28	0
5	32	3	47	9	41	9	11
6	67	4	54	14	28	14	14
7	56	5	54	14	27	5	0
8	31	3	65	16	16	7	0
9	64	13	66	10	11	26	8
10	78	29	56	2	13	12	50
11	104	42	41	7	10	9	78
12	89	62	25	11	2	20	80
13	77	32	53	10	5	4	25
14	75	28	53	14	5	1	0
15	102	48	34	9	9	14	86

TABLE 2.27   Types of nominal functional elements – Mathias

Nr	Common nouns and proper names					Proper names	
	n	def.art. %	indef.art. %	others %	$-F\%$	n	$+F\%$
9	11	0	0	0	100	–	–
10	29	3	0	4	93	5	0
11	17	0	0	0	100	3	0
12	23	0	0	0	100	10	0
13	29	0	0	7	93	10	0
14	3	0	0	0	100	–	–
15	31	0	3	7	90	7	0
16	14	0	7	7	86	9	0
17	21	10	19	33	38	6	0
18	18	6	0	16	78	4	0
19	30	33	40	14	13	1	0
21	41	27	39	22	12	9	44
22	52	35	42	15	8	6	0
23	10	40	20	0	40	6	0
24	33	52	15	12	21	2	0
25	38	53	11	36	0	2	100
26	43	44	33	14	9	6	17
27	32	53	28	13	6	12	0

TABLE 2.28   Types of nominal functional elements – Svenja

Nr	Common nouns and proper names					Proper names	
	n	def.art. %	indef.art. %	others %	$-F\%$	n	$+F\%$
2	9	78	11	0	11	3	100
3	41	49	29	5	17	–	–
4	59	80	14	3	3	5	100
5	70	74	9	11	6	4	100
6	27	56	44	0	0	3	33
7	22	64	32	0	5	4	100
8	132	55	24	16	5	3	67
9	29	41	28	28	3	2	50
10	34	53	24	20	3	3	33
11	70	67	19	13	1	6	33
12	31	77	3	20	0	5	80
13	116	73	9	12	6	14	79
14	54	59	20	19	2	7	86
15	132	75	11	7	7	11	91
16	120	55	17	25	3	5	40

Acknowledgements

The research in this chapter was supported by a grant of the German Science Foundation (DFG; grants Cl97/1–1–3) to Harald Clahsen. I am grateful for comments from Joana Cholin, Harald Clahsen, Manfred Consten, Marc-Ariel Friedemann, Meike Hadler, Bettina Landgraf, Sebastian Löbner, Martina Penke, Thomas Roeper, Luigi Rizzi, Ingrid Sonnenstuhl-Henning and Dieter Wunderlich.

Notes

1 Cf. note 8.
2 A similar prediction might be derived from the truncation approach developed by Rizzi and his collaborators for the development of clause structure (see e.g. Rizzi 1994, this volume, Haegemann 1996, Friedemann 1993–1994). In this approach it is assumed that children have the adult-like capacity of projecting full phrase-structure trees, but may leave part of the structure unprojected. So far, the development of DP has not been described in the truncation approach; but see Friedemann (1993–1994) for some suggestions how the optionality of early determiners could be treated as an instance of the co-occurence of utterances with full-fledged and truncated phrase-structure representations.
3 See Pinker 1984 for the mechanisms which create morphological paradigms.
4 Therefore, this view of underspecification is also compatible with Merger Theory, an approach developed by Roeper (1996; see also Pérez-Leroux and Roeper 1996, 1997) on the basis of the Minimalist Program. Just as the proposed version of the Lexical Learning approach, this approach is based on the assumption of lexeme-specific maximal projections and lexical entries which are underspecified with respect to certain grammatical features.
5 The MLU values were computed on the basis of words.
6 See Clahsen, Vainikka and Young-Scholten (1990) for a description of the project.
7 See Wagner (1985).
8 It is not quite clear to me whether the trigger data for possessor raising involve a vocative/non-vocative contrast. In vocative noun phrases, we do not find any possessive constructions – neither with a raised possessor nor with a possessor in situ. Thus, there is an asymmetry between structures with and without possessor, but no asymmetry between possessive constructions with possessor raising and constructions without possessor raising.
9 The data of Carsten do not contain any possessive constructions with obligatory contexts for -s.
10 In German, only proper names can be used with -s in possessive constructions.
11 The data of Simone (cf. Miller 1976) have been made available by Jürgen Weissenborn. Cf. Clahsen, Eisenbeiss and Vainikka (1994) and Penner and Weissenborn (1996) for Simone's acquisition of DP.
12 Recall, however, that structures with the order 'possessor < possessum' are marked in adult language (see section 2). Thus, their late occurrence might be due to input frequency or the lack of relevant contexts for such structures.

In order to rule out this possibility, elicitation experiments which create contexts for 'possessor < possessum' would be required.

13 In contrast to Mathias, all other children in this study show relatively high proportions of overt determiners at the beginning of the recording period. Note, however, that Mathias has comparatively low MLU values at this stage (see Table 2.1). This suggests that the early data of the other children represent more advanced stages in which either impostors or adult-like determiners are used more frequently.

14 In recording 23 and in recording 24 of the Mathias-corpus, the proportion of overt nominal functional elements drops again. However, the relatively high omission rate in these recordings seems to be a sampling artefact. Taken together, the recordings 23 and 24 contain only 10 omissions of nominal functional elements, 5 of them in prepositional phrases, i.e. in contexts which show relatively high omission rates even in later stages of development.

15 See Eisenbeiss and Penke (1996) for a possible explanation of this fact.

References

BHATT, C. 1990. *Die syntaktische Struktur der Nominalphrase im Deutschen.* Tübingen: Narr.

BROWN, R. 1973. *A First Language: The Early Stages.* Cambridge, MA: Harvard University Press.

CHOMSKY, N. 1995. *The Minimalist Program.* Cambridge, MA: MIT Press.

CLAHSEN, H. 1990. 'Constraints on Parameter Setting: A Grammatical Analysis of some Acquisition Stages in German Child Language'. *Language Acquisition* 1 361–91.

CLAHSEN, H. (ed.) 1996. *Generative Perspectives on Language Acquisition.* Amsterdam: Benjamins.

CLAHSEN, H., S. EISENBEISS and M. PENKE. 1996. Lexical Learning in Early Syntactic Development. In: H. Clahsen (ed.), *Generative Perspectives on Language Acquisition.* Amsterdam: Benjamins, 129–60.

CLAHSEN, H., S. EISENBEISS and A. VAINIKKA. 1994. 'The Seeds of Structure. A Syntactic Analysis of the Acquisition of Case Marking'. In: T. Hoekstra and B. Schwartz (eds), *Language Acquisition Studies in Generative Grammar.* Amsterdam: Benjamins, 85–118.

CLAHSEN, H., C. KURSAWE and M. PENKE. 1996. 'Introducing CP. The Development of wh-Questions and Embedded Clauses in German Child Language'. In: C. Koster and F. Wijnen (eds), *Proceedings of the Groningen Assembly on Language Acquisition,* 5–22.

CLAHSEN, H. and M. PENKE. 1992. 'The Acquisition of Agreement Morphology and its Syntactic Consequences: New Evidence on German Child Language from the Simone-Corpus'. In: J. Meisel (ed.), *The Acquisition of Verb Placement: Functional Categories and V2 Phenomena in Language Acquisition.* Dordrecht: Kluwer, 181–224.

CLAHSEN, H., M. PENKE and T. PARODI. 1993. 'Functional Categories in Early Child German'. *Language Acquisition* 3, 395–429.

CLAHSEN, H., A. VAINIKKA and M. YOUNG-SCHOLTEN. 1990. 'Lernbarkeitstheorie und Lexikalisches Lernen. Eine kurze Darstellung des LEXLERN-Projekts'. *Linguistische Berichte* **130**, 466–78.

CRAIN, S. 1991. 'Language Acquisition in the Absence of Experience'. *Behavioral and Brain Sciences* **14**, 597–650.

EISENBEISS, S. 1994a. 'Raising to Spec and Adjunction Scrambling in German Child Language'. Paper presented at the Workshop on the Acquisition of Clause-Internal Rules: Scrambling and Cliticization, University of Berne.

EISENBEISS, S. 1994b. 'Kasus und Wortstellungsvariation im deutschen Mittelfeld. Theoretische Überlegungen und Untersuchungen zum Erstspracherwerb'. In: B. Haftka (ed.), *Was determiniert Wortstellungsvariation? Studien zu einem Interaktionsfeld von Grammatik, Pragmatik und Sprachtypologie.* Westdeutscher Verlag: Opladen, 277–98.

EISENBEISS, S. and M. PENKE. 1996. 'Children Checking Checking Theory'. Paper presented at the WCHTSALT-workshop, University of Utrecht.

FRIEDEMANN, M.-A. 1993–1994. 'The Underlying Position of External Arguments in French: A Study in Adult and Child Grammar'. *Language Acquisition* **3**, 209–55.

HAEGEMANN, L. 1996. 'Root Infinitives, Clitics and Truncated Structures'. In: H. Clahsen (ed.), *Generative Perspectives on Language Acquisition.* Amsterdam: Benjamins, 271–308.

HAIDER, H. 1988. 'Die Struktur der deutschen Nominalphrase'. *Zeitschrift für Sprachwissenschaft* **7**, 32–59.

HAIDER, H. 1993. *Deutsche Syntax – generativ. Vorstudien zur Theorie einer projektiven Grammatik.* Tübingen: Narr.

HOEKSTRA, T., N. HYAMS and M. BECKER. 1996. 'The Role of the Specifier and Finiteness in Early Grammar'. Ms. Leiden University / University of California, Los Angeles.

HOEKSTRA, T. and S. SCHWARTZ (eds). 1994. *Language Acquisition Studies in Generative Grammar.* Amsterdam: Benjamins.

JOHNSON, K., S. BATEMAN, D. MOORE, T. ROEPER and J. DEVILLIERS. 1996. 'On the Acquisition of Word Order in Nominals'. Ms. University of Massachusetts, Amherst/Smith College.

KAYNE, R. 1994. *The Antisymmetry of Syntax.* Cambridge, MA: MIT Press.

LEOPOLD, W. F. 1949. *Speech Development of a Bilingual Child. A Linguist's Record.* Volume III: Grammar and General Problems in the First Two Years. New York: AMS Press.

LINDAUER, T. 1995. *Genitivattribute. Eine morphosyntaktische Untersuchung zum deutschen DP/NP-System.* Tübingen: Niemeyer.

LÖBEL, E. 1990. 'D und Q als funktionale Kategorien in der Nominalphrase'. *Linguistische Berichte* **127**, 232–64.

MARCUS, G., S. PINKER, M. ULLMAN, M. HOLLANDER, T. J. ROSEN and F. XU. 1992. 'Overregularizations in Language Acquisition'. *Monographs of the Society for Research in Child Development* **57.4**.

MEISEL, J. (ed.). 1992. *The Acquisition of Verb Placement.* Dordrecht: Kluwer.

MILLER, M. 1976. *Zur Logik der frühkindlichen Sprachentwicklung.* Stuttgart: Klett.

MILLS, A. 1985. 'The Acquisition of German'. In: D. Slobin (ed.), *The Cross Linguistic Study of Language Acquisition.* Hillsdale, NJ: Erlbaum, 141–254.

62 THE ACQUISITION OF SYNTAX

MÜLLER, N. 1994. 'Gender and Number Agreement within DP'. In: J. Meisel (ed.), *Bilingual First Language Acquisition. French and German Grammatical Development*. Amsterdam: Benjamins, 53–88.

OLSEN, S. 1991. 'Die deutsche Nominalphrase als Determinansphrase'. In: S. Olsen and G. Fanselow (eds), *DET, COMP und INFL: Zur Syntax funktionaler Kategorien und grammatischer Funktionen*. Tübingen: Niemeyer, 35–56.

PENNER, Z. 1993. 'The Earliest Stage in the Acquisition of the Nominal Phrase in Bernese Swiss German: Syntactic Bootstrapping and the Architecture of Language Learning'. Ms. University of Berne.

PENNER, Z. and J. WEISSENBORN. 1996. 'Strong Continuity, Parameter Setting and the Trigger Hierarchy: On the Acquisition of the DP in Bernese Swiss German and High German'. In: H. Clahsen (ed.), *Generative Perspectives on Language Acquisition*. Amsterdam: Benjamins, 161–200.

PÉREZ-LEROUX, A. and T. ROEPER. 1996. *Learning 'Home': The Acquisition of Inherent Binding and Economy of Representation*. BUCLD 20, 552–63.

PÉREZ-LEROUX, A. and T. ROEPER. 1997. 'Scope and the Structure of Bare Nominals: Evidence from Child Language'. Ms. Pennsylvania State University / University of Massachusetts, Amherst.

PINKER, STEVEN 1984. *Language Learnability and Language Development*. Cambridge, MA: Havard University Press.

RADFORD, A. 1990. *Syntactic Theory and the Acquisition of English Syntax*. Oxford: Basil Blackwell.

RITTER, E. 1991. 'Two Functional Categories in Noun Phrases: Evidence from Modern Hebrew'. In: S. Rothstein (ed.), *Perspectives on Phrase Structure: Heads and Licensing*. New York: Academic Press, 37–62.

RIZZI, L. 1994. 'Early Null Subjects and Root Null Subjects'. In: T. Hoekstra and B. Schwartz (eds), *Language Acquisition Studies in Generative Grammar*. Amsterdam: Benjamins, 151–77.

ROEPER, T. 1996. 'The Role of Merger Theory and Formal Features in Acquisition'. In: H. Clahsen (ed.), *Generative Perspectives on Language Acquisition*. Amsterdam: Benjamins, 415–50.

SCUPIN, E. and G. SCUPIN. 1910. *Bubi im vierten bis sechsten Lebensjahre*. Leipzig: Th. Grieben's Verlag.

SILONI, T. 1997. *Noun Phrases and Nominalizations. The Syntax of DP*. Dordrecht: Kluwer.

SZABOLCSI, A. 1987. 'Functional Categories in the Noun Phrase'. In: F. Kiefer and K. Kiss (eds), *Syntax and Semantics* 27, 197–274.

VALOIS, D. 1991. *The Internal Syntax of DP*. PhD dissertation, UCLA.

WAGNER, K. 1985. 'How Much Do Children Say in a Day?' *Journal of Child Language* 12, 475–87.

Chapter 3

Early French postverbal subjects
Marc-Ariel Friedemann

1 Introduction

Around the age of two years, children acquiring French produce a considerable number of target inconsistent utterances containing a postverbal subject:

(1) a. A   chanté Victor. (Grégoire, 2;1: Champaud)
     has sung Victor
  b. Fait   du bruit la voiture. (Philippe, 2;2: Suppes, Smith and
     makes noise the car   Léveillé 1973)
  c. Veux une montre moi. (Philippe, 2;3)
     want a   watch me

The phenomenon illustrated in (1) has received a good deal of attention in the last few years, and two distinct grammatical hypotheses have emerged. Some linguists (e.g. Pierce 1989, 1992, Friedemann 1993–94) have seen in utterances such as (1) manifestations of VP-internal subjects. Others (e.g. Ferdinand 1993, Labelle and Valois 1996) have argued that these postverbal subjects constitute instances of right-dislocation.

In this chapter, I would like to review the arguments presented for each approach. As will become clear, at the present stage of research it is hardly possible to decide between the two proposals by looking at specific utterances. However, on the basis of quantitative and cross-linguistic considerations, it seems necessary to maintain a version of the VP-internal subject approach. This does not necessarily exclude a right-dislocation analysis for some instances. Further, I will suggest that under either approach, the truncation hypothesis, discussed throughout this volume, best captures the child specificity of sentence-final subjects. More generally, the issue at stake illustrates the fruitful interaction between theoretical linguistics and acquisition studies developed in recent years, as it crucially utilizes acquisition data to shed light on adult structures.

Sections 2 and 3 present a critical review of the arguments in favor of the VP-internal subject approach and the right-dislocation approach, respectively. Section 4 argues that subject-final constructions are truncated structures (whether the subject is VP-internal or right-dislocated). This explains why the canonical subject position, SpecIP, can be left unpronounced in child French, and derives the distribution of the construction and its child specificity. Section 5 is devoted to a tentative evaluation of the two approaches, examining aspects of a more general character. The last section deals with some important remaining issues such as Case and parameter setting, including a brief discussion of the resulting situation if one is to adopt an articulated theory of phrase structure, in particular Kayne's (1994) antisymmetric approach and multiple functional projections.

2 The VP-internal hypothesis

Postverbal subjects are massively attested in early French. Based on files from Grégoire (Champaud) and Philippe (Suppes, Smith and Léveillé 1973), Friedemann (1993–94) found 161 postverbal subjects, that is 73 percent of all lexical non-dislocated subjects (220) (for more details, see Table 3.2 in the appendix). Similar figures are found in corpora of other children, such as Lightbown's (1977) corpus studied by Pierce (1989, 1992), or Cynthia, studied by Labelle and Valois (1996). Some examples are given in (2).[1]

(2) a. Est là   voisine. (Grégoire, 1;11)
       is here neighbor
    b. Est belle la   poussette. (Grégoire, 2;0)
       is nice the baby carriage
    c. Ranger   tout seul Grégoire. (Grégoire, 2;1)
       to+put in order all   alone Grégoire
    d. Va   dedans Christian. (Grégoire, 2;3)
       goes inside Christian
    e. Faire   boum sur camion maman. (Philippe, 2;1)
       to+make boom on   truck   Mummy
    f. Fait   du bruit la voiture. (Philippe, 2;2)
       makes noise   the car
    g. Font du feu les dames. (Philippe, 2;3)
       make fire   the women

Noticeably, early postverbal subjects systematically follow VP complements, as can be seen in the preceding examples. Further, the phenomenon extends to infinitival structures, as illustrated in (2c,e) (see Tables 3.2 and 3.3 in the appendix for figures). The latter fact raises the question as to why, contrary to adult French, lexical subjects are allowed with infinitivals; I briefly address this question in sections 5 and 6.

Pierce (1989, 1992) and Déprez and Pierce (1993) convincingly show that at the stage under consideration, learners of French master V-to-I movement, raising only finite verbs to I^0 (see also Weissenborn 1988, Weissenborn, Verrips and Berman 1989, and the introduction to this volume for discussion). Elaborating on that, Pierce and Déprez and Pierce suggest that structures like (2) result from raising of the verb over the subject in its VP-internal position, to a higher inflectional head. The subject, according to them, receives nominative Case under government from I^0. The VP-internal subject position is considered left-branching or not fixed. To account for the VOS surface order, the suggestion is made that accusative Case assignment by the verb in I^0 to its object requires strict adjacency, therefore forcing the subject to be extraposed in the relevant cases. This is schematized in (3).

(3) veux$_i$ [$_{VP}$ t$_j$ t$_i$ une montre] moi$_j$
    want   a watch   me

Importantly, Déprez and Pierce (1993) furnish crosslinguistic evidence (from English, German and Swedish) for the existence of early VP-internal subjects.

However, the above proposal encounters some difficulties. First, adult French does not normally allow overt VP-internal subjects (I return below to stylistic inversion, an adult construction that is often argued to show overt VP-internal subjects). If so, all other things being equal, it is unclear how children acquiring French can unlearn the option of leaving the subject in its VP-internal position, given the lack of negative evidence (the input does not contain any information about impossible sentences).

Second, a strict adjacency requirement on accusative Case assignment cannot explain why postverbal subjects systematically follow the complements of the verb. It does not account for the fact that PP complements or other non-accusative complements do not appear to the right of the subject. The italicized complements in (4) do not have to satisfy the putative Case adjacency condition.

(4) a. Faire   boum *sur camion* maman. (Philippe, 2;1)
      to+make boom on truck   Mummy
  b. Tourner *dans l'autre sens*   maman. (Philippe, 2;2)
      to+turn in the other direction Mummy
  c. Va   *dedans* Christian. (Grégoire, 2;3)
      goes inside Christian

Finally, in adult French the verb and its direct object do not have to be adjacent. (5a) shows that adverbials can intervene between the verb and its direct object; (5b) instantiates a (derived) VSO word order. Their acceptability indicates that no Case problem arises in that environment.

(5) a. Jean voit$_i$ probablement trop souvent t$_i$ des films.
       Jean sees probably   too often   movies
    b. Où$_j$ achètent$_i$-t-ils tous t$_i$ le pain t$_j$?
       where buy-they   all   the bread

These examples suggest that if there is an adjacency requirement on accusative Case assignment at all, it involves the verbal trace rather than I^0 or the verb itself.

Friedemann (1993–94) proposes that the external argument is generated in a right-branching specifier of VP in French (see also Levow 1995).[2] Obviously, this straightforwardly accounts for the fact that early postverbal subjects systematically appear to the right of any complement of the verb, under a VP-internal approach. Further, Friedemann claims that a right-branching SpecVP in French allows accounting for otherwise obscure restrictions imposed on stylistic inversion (6). Stylistic inversion is one of the few adult constructions that may present the external argument in its basic, VP-internal position:[3]

(6) a. Où   a   mangé Jean?
       where has eaten Jean
    b. Le livre qu' achètera Marie
       the book that will+buy Marie

In other words, early French data are not only argued to receive an explanation under the right-branching hypothesis, but also to be of direct relevance in determining the exact VP-internal position of the subject in a language that only rarely displays this position overtly. Developmental data such as (2) then supply a type of evidence that is not available in the adult language.

Next, Friedemann (1993–94) argues that early main-clause infinitives provide further support to the right-branching hypothesis (I henceforth refer to them as root infinitives, following Rizzi's (1993–94) terminology). It is well known that lexical subjects appear with infinitives in early child grammar (see section 5 for some discussion). Now, since infinitives do not move to I^0 in French, nor in early French as mentioned above, their co-occurrence with postverbal subjects suggests again that SpecVP, containing the lexical subject, is right-branching.[4] Moreover, as shown by Table 3.2 in the appendix, preverbal lexical subjects are rare in untensed contexts: they amount to 5 infinitival plus 5 bare participle structures (the latter could involve a null auxiliary) out of 220 lexical subjects, that is 4.5 percent (2.3 percent if one excludes bare participles) of all utterances with lexical subjects. They are roughly 5 times less frequent than postverbal subject in the same context. This small percentage indicates that SpecIP is not likely to be the host for lexical subjects of root infinitives – a question to which we shall return. Importantly, it also casts doubts upon the plausibility that SpecVP is left-branching in French; if it were, we would expect the percentage of preverbal subjects of infinitives to be much higher.

So far, the VP-internal subject approach in its right-branching version seems simple and rather straightforward. It immediately accounts for the V(XP)S order found in early child language. It is claimed to have advantageous consequences with regard to stylistic inversion (Friedemann 1997a). It correctly expects a very low rate of preverbal subjects within root infinitivals. Of course, it remains to be understood why postverbal subjects, and especially simple declarative VOS structures, are by and large child-specific. I return to this question in sections 4 and 6. Let me first examine the alternative approach to early French postverbal subjects proposed in the recent literature.

3 The right-dislocation hypothesis

Ferdinand (1993) and Labelle and Valois (1996) argue that early postverbal subjects constitute instances of right-dislocation. They thus assimilate a child utterance such as (2g), repeated in (7a), to the adult construction (7b):

(7) a. Font du feu les dames. (Philippe, 2;3)
        make fire   the women
    b. Elles₍ᵢ₎ font du feu, les dames₍ᵢ₎.
       they make fire   the women

Under this view, the child structure differs from the adult one only in that the subject pronoun, which is obligatory in the adult grammar, is dropped or left unpronounced in the early grammar. This difference will be discussed in section 4, which is devoted to the question of why SpecIP can apparently be empty in child language.

The authors provide three main arguments in favor of the right-dislocation analysis (and against the VP-internal approach). The first argument concerns the nature of the lexical subject. It is well known that by and large, dislocations cannot involve quantified DPs, nor (non-generic) indefinites, which has been related to their incompatibility with new information (for a detailed discussion of dislocations in colloquial French, see in particular Ashby 1988, Lambrecht 1981, 1984). Indeed, Ferdinand and Labelle and Valois found no indefinite nor quantified postverbal subject in their corpora. This is also true for the corpus under consideration here.[5]

However, indefinite or quantified subjects appear to be rare altogether in our corpus: they amount to 9 instances (listed below) in the 1084 utterances under consideration, less than 1 percent. Moreover, most of them are target inconsistent, including three cases of left-dislocated, quantified (8i) or indefinite (8b,f) subjects. This considerably weakens the argument. Not only are quantified and indefinite subjects extremely rare in the corpus, but additionally children do use them in dislocations. Their rarity and misapplication may suggest that children at this stage do not yet master indefinite subjects, independently.

(8) a. Des motos fait   du bruit.
       motorcycles makes noise (Grégoire, 2;1)
   b. Une voiture elle roule.
      a   car   she runs (Philippe, 2;2)
   c. Un vert écrit   bien.
      a   green writes well
   d. Une pelle ramasser   les feuilles.
      a   shovel to+pick+up the leaves
   e. Un petit bout de croissant tombé.
      a   small piece of croissant fallen
   f. Un cheveau elle court.
      a   horse   she runs
   g. Un camion perdu   sa roue. (Philippe, 2;3)
      a   truck   lost (part.) its wheel
   h. Un trou arrivé.
      a   hole arrived (part.)
   i. Tout le monde il veut   une cigarette.
      everybody   he wants a   cigarette

Second, Labelle and Valois (1996) observe that the expression *tout seul* ('all alone') systematically precedes postverbal subjects in child language (9a,b), although it has to follow the noun it modifies in adult French (9c,d).

(9) a. Marcher tout seul la voiture. (Philippe, 2;2)
      to+work all alone the car
   b. Me suis mouché   tout seul moi. (Philippe, 2;3)
      blow (part.) my nose all alone me
   c. Qui a fait   cela? Lui tout seul / *Tout seul lui.
      who has done that   he all alone / all alone he
   d. Philippe tout seul / *tout seul Philippe
      Philippe all alone / all alone Philippe

Whether *tout seul* ('all alone') in (9a,b) is generated within the DP or as an adjoined adverbial, the subject must be right-adjoined and hence dislocated, Labelle and Valois argue. If *tout seul* is a DP modifier, the

subject should have preceded it (given the adult order in (9c,d)), but it
does not; hence it was moved rightwards. If *tout seul* is an adverbial, it
is right-adjoined to VP or IP; hence the subject is also right-adjoined.
First, a few words on *tout seul* are in order here. The expression *tout
seul* consists of an adjective modified by the quantifier *tout* ('all'). In
adult French, it can appear either DP-internally as a restrictive modifier
(essentially limited to generic environments) (10a), or as a predicative
expression predicated of an argument taking part in the event/state
denoted by the verb. In the latter case, it can occur in various positions
(10b):

(10) a. [Un homme tout seul] ne peut pas donner un cadeau a
          a man   all alone cannot   give   a gift   to
          une femme.
          a woman
      b. Un homme ne peut pas (tout seul) donner (tout seul)
          a man   cannot   all alone give   all alone
          un cadeau (tout seul) a   une femme (tout seul).
          a gift   all alone   to a woman   all alone

In all the child utterances I examined so far, *tout seul* is a predicative
expression (hence, not originating DP-internally). Further, it never agrees
in contexts where agreement is mandatory in the target grammar ((9a),
for example). Finally, *tout seul* can also precede an accusative argument, as in (11a) and possibly in (11b). One would not like to claim on
this basis that all objects are right-dislocated.[6]

(11) a. Faire rouler tout seul la voiture. (Philippe, 2;2)
          make roll   all alone the car
      b. Va casser tout seul les petites boules. (Philippe, 2;2)
          go break   all alone the small balls

Given its relatively free distribution in the target language, the apparent inability of *tout seul* to be right-adjacent to the noun it refers to in
the early grammar is indeed intriguing (and should further be verified
in additional corpora). More generally, one would like to understand in
what way child *tout seul* differs from its adult counterpart. Presently,
there is not sufficient evidence to answer these questions, neither to
deduce from the distribution of *tout seul* that postverbal subjects must
be dislocated in the relevant cases. And even if they (or some of them)
turn out to be dislocated, the few examples involving *tout seul* would of
course not lead us to a generalized right-dislocation approach.
    The third argument for right-dislocation concerns prosody. Labelle
and Valois (1996) assume that phonetically, right-dislocated elements
are somewhat separated from the rest of the sentence in French. They
therefore conducted a phonetic analysis on a small sample of utterances

(four VS sentences) in order to find out whether a significant intonational break could be revealed before the postverbal subject, with positive results. As the authors emphasize, a more thorough analysis would be needed to certify a dislocation-specific intonation, but at this stage the tests seem to point towards an analysis of early VS sequences in terms of right-dislocated constructions.

How strong is the prosodic argument? On the one hand, genuine right-dislocations (with an overt pronominal subject) are known to be present in both the child's output (Table 3.1 in the appendix) and input. If one observes that some postverbal subjects are phonetically detached and that pronominal subjects can independently be dropped in early grammars (see next section), then there is a good argument in favor of right-dislocations without a subject clitic in child French. Still, quantitative considerations are important here; the existence of four potential right-dislocations without subject clitics does not allow the conclusion that all postverbal subjects are right-dislocated.

On the other hand, it has been argued that (right-)dislocated elements need not be clearly detached from the rest of the sentence in colloquial French (Lambrecht 1981, Ashby 1988). It could then be that the conclusive argument for dislocated structures should not rely on such phonetic evidence. Now, notice that a single tested VS sequence is reported in Labelle and Valois' paper, which unfortunately may involve an intonational break in between the verb and the subject independently of any dislocation. The sentence is *Tombe Benoît* ('falls Benoît'): given that the phonetic string [tɔ̃mb # bənwa] manifests a sequence of two occlusives precisely at the word boundaries, it would hardly be possible to pronounce the utterance without a significant break between the verb and the subject. In short, the prosodic argument, though potentially interesting, is not significant at the present stage.

To summarize, the proponents of the dislocation approach draw a parallelism between adult right-dislocated subjects and early postverbal subjects. The main arguments they supply rely on the lack of indefinites, the behavior of *tout seul* ('all alone') and prosody considerations. It is possible that some instances of sentence-final subjects are cases of right-dislocations, but the evidence at this stage is not conclusive. At any rate, the question arises as to whether the dislocation approach can be generalized to all cases of postverbal subjects. Before trying to evaluate the dislocation approach alongside the VP-internal approach, I would like to examine why SpecIP can apparently be left empty in early French.

4 The higher subject position

Both approaches to early postverbal subjects presented above need to explain why children can leave SpecIP, the higher subject position, unpronounced. Recall that genuine postverbal subjects are rare in adult French. Under the VP-internal hypothesis, the question is why in child French the subject can stay in SpecVP, in apparent violation of whatever version of the Extended Projection Principle (Chomsky 1982, 1995). Under the dislocation hypothesis, one needs to understand why an overt pronominal subject is not mandatory, contrary to the situation in the adult grammar.

It has been noticed that postverbal subjects are mostly limited to main declaratives. Crisma (1992) and Levow (1995) found a very small amount of V(X)S structures in *wh*-contexts, most of them of the form *Où est X* ('Where is X'), a structure that is target consistent and very common in colloquial French.[7] This is reminiscent of the distributional constraint characterizing early null subjects (12), which also appear to be restricted to contexts in which the CP layer is not activated. Moreover, a random search in later files indicates that both phenomena, null and postverbal subjects, disappear around the same age (Table 3.4). As discussed in the introduction to this volume (and see Rizzi 1992), there is mounting evidence that early null subjects in non pro-drop languages are limited to truncated (reduced) structures and are hence incompatible with CP material. Structures truncated at the level of IP can license a null subject in the highest position of the structure, that is in the specifier of the root (SpecIP). In this position, the null subject can escape the formal licensing requirement imposed on empty categories, because the structure does not provide room to host a candidate to formally license it (I put aside the question of which type of empty category is at stake here: see Rizzi this volume for a reformulation of the 'null constant' approach of Rizzi (1992) in terms of unpronounced lexical material at the root):

(12) [$_{IP}$ <ec> a chanté]
     has sung

Early subject-final structures, then, can resort to the same kind of empty category in SpecIP as early null subject structures do. Their limited distribution immediately follows from the assumption that they, too, are truncated structures:

(13) [$_{IP}$ <ec> a chanté Victor]
     has sung Victor

Note that this proposal is compatible with the VP-internal as well as with the right-dislocation approach to postverbal subjects. Under the VP-internal approach, the empty category in SpecIP qualifies as an expletive (similar to the expletive *pro* occupying SpecIP in say Italian free inversion, under standard assumptions). Under the right-dislocation approach, the argumental status of the empty category depends on the

precise analysis of dislocations. If the dislocated element originates
in its A′-position, the empty category is argumental. If it is rightward
moved from the argument position, the empty category would arguably
be an expletive.[8]

Alternatively, instead of inserting an expletive in SpecIP, one could
suggest that truncation applies to I′. In the absence of SpecIP, subject-
final constructions would not require an empty category to fill the
canonical subject position (whether I′ is a possible truncation site depends on the exact formulation of the EPP). Such a solution is not
immediately available to the base-generation approach to dislocations,
which takes the empty category to be the argument.

5 Evaluating the hypotheses

Section 3 discussed the possibility that certain early postverbal subjects
are right-dislocated. Is it possible to generalize the approach to all postverbal subjects? I will try to provide a partial answer to this question by
addressing the following issues:

(i)   On a quantitative basis, is it reasonable that all early postverbal
      subjects constitute instances of right-dislocation?
(ii) Is a generalized right-dislocation approach to early French com-
      patible with crosslinguistic findings?

In order to deal with the first issue, one needs to rely on some
statistical observations with regard to subject right-dislocations in adult
colloquial French. It has long been observed that dislocations are extremely frequent in spoken French: over 60 percent of the cases where
a dislocation would a priori be possible, according to Barnes (1986).
Usually, however, right-dislocations are considered much less frequent
than left-dislocations. In Ashby's (1988) corpus, right-dislocated subjects represent only around 20 percent of all dislocated subjects; Pierce
(1989) estimates right-dislocations to account for only 6 percent of the
input in Lightbown's child corpus. More exceptional are the results of
Labelle and Valois (1996), who counted twice as many right-dislocated
subjects than left-dislocated ones in the children's input.

As to child production, Table 3.1 in the appendix indicates a low
amount of 7 percent of genuine dislocated subjects (with an overt pronominal subject). But if one is to count all postverbal subjects as dislocated subjects, the situation changes drastically: we would arrive at 209
right-dislocated subjects (48 genuine right-dislocations plus 161 simple
postverbal subjects) in comparison with 32 left-dislocated ones, that is
around 6.5 times as many right-dislocations as left-dislocations.[9] This is
well over any estimation of the frequency of right-dislocations in adult
French. Also, under such a count dislocations would represent around

80 percent of all lexical subjects (240 out of 299). Since dislocations are standardly viewed as syntactically marked, one would not expect children to produce more such constructions than adults. Hence, on a quantitative basis, and especially in view of the distribution of left- and right-dislocations, it does not seem likely that all early postverbal subjects are right-dislocated.

With respect to the second issue, Déprez and Pierce (1993) have convincingly shown that early VP-internal subjects are attested cross-linguistically: in English, German and Swedish. Now, as in early French, potential instances of VP-internal subjects happen to appear in a sentence-final position, a generalized right-dislocation approach is the equivalent of denying the existence of overt VP-internal subjects in this early grammar. Why, in contrast to other languages, should that be so?

I would like to illustrate the crosslinguistic issue in some more detail, taking as an example the root infinitive phenomenon. It has already been mentioned that sentence-final subjects are found in early French root infinitivals. As can be seen in Table 3.2 (and see (2c,e) for example), more than a quarter of all lexical subjects appear with infinitivals in the child corpus under consideration.[10] We have seen in section 2 that their large majority is postverbal, which we took as support for ordering SpecVP to the right of V' in French. But recall that the very existence of lexical subjects with infinitives is target inconsistent, presumably because only a tensed verb / inflection can check nominative Case.

Now, no genuine subject dislocations are found within infinitivals in early French. This is not surprising, as pronominal subjects appear only with finite verbs in child French, too (Pierce 1989, 1992). Lack of nominative Case is arguably responsible for this state of affairs. Nonetheless, child grammars avail themselves of an empty category in the specifier of the root (see section 4). It could then very well be that this empty category is available also with root infinitives. If so, their lexical subjects could be in a dislocated position, thereby avoiding the Case problem. This seems to be a clear advantage of the right-dislocation approach:[11]

(14) <ec>$_i$ faire   boum sur camion, maman$_i$.
      to+make boom on truck   mummy

However, two problems immediately come to mind. The first is again the quantitative one: why would the overwhelming majority of root infinitives involve right-dislocations and only few left-dislocations? The second concerns the crosslinguistic aspect. Lexical subjects with root infinitives are attested in many other early grammars, and apparently very clearly so in all early Germanic languages (see Wexler 1992, 1995 for an overview). Their adult counterparts do not exhibit a rate of dislocations comparable with French, but still the rate of overt subjects in child infinitivals is considerable (ranging from 11 to 32 percent, with an exceptionally high proportion of 80 percent of lexical subjects with bare forms in English, according to a summary provided in Hoekstra and Hyams 1998). Why then would children acquiring a Germanic language produce massive dislocations? Generalizing the dislocation approach to these languages does not seem promising.

Further, Germanic languages seem to exhibit (almost) only preverbal subjects in this context. Under a generalized dislocation approach to lexical subjects of infinitives, it would remain mysterious why French children quite systematically opt for right-dislocations, whereas children acquiring a Germanic language choose left-dislocations. Under a VP-internal approach, in contrast, there is an obvious solution to this puzzle. Root infinitives have been argued to be structures truncated lower than tense (I^0) (Friedemann 1993–94, Rizzi 1993–94; see also the introduction to this volume). As SpecIP is not available to host the lexical subject under this view, the asymmetry between Germanic languages and French ought to be traced back to the base position of the subject. It follows straightforwardly if SpecVP is right-branching in French, and left-branching in Germanic languages.

In sum, even if some early French postverbal subjects may (and possibly should) be accounted for in terms of right-dislocation, it is very unlikely that all the occurrences of sentence-final subjects could be treated along these lines. First, the total of subject right-dislocations would be much higher than what is observed in the input. Second, a completely different analysis would be required to derive similar phenomena in other early grammars. The right-branching SpecVP hypothesis, which of course is not incompatible with right-dislocations, appears to be independently required to account for the whole array of data.

6 Remaining issues

If right-branching VP-internal subjects indeed exist in early (and adult) French, some important questions related to Case and to parameter setting arise. I will not develop them here (see Friedemann 1993–94 for more elaboration, though in an older framework), but just briefly sketch some possible solutions to the Case problem, consider the incompatibility of right-branching specifiers with an LCA-based approach (Kayne 1994), and suggest a few possible triggers for parameter setting.

An approach claiming that postverbal subjects are not (always) dislocated, but rather occupy an argumental position, must deal with the question of how these subjects can check their Case. A possible solution to this problem could be looked for in Chomsky's (1995) approach to expletive replacement, if SpecIP is filled with an expletive, as suggested above: in the covert syntax, the lexical postverbal subject adjoins to the expletive, thereby checking nominative Case and avoiding a violation of Full Interpretation caused by an isolated expletive. (Alternatively, if no expletive is involved, covert subject raising could create SpecIP, along the lines suggested by Chomsky 1994.) But this cannot be the whole story. Although this kind of solution might be plausible for finite utterances, we have seen that lexical subjects are found with root infinitives, which cannot check nominative under standard assumptions, even less so if they do not contain a tense projection at all, as claimed by the truncation approach (see above). Also, it has been noted throughout the acquisition literature that early pronominal subjects can appear as inherently non-nominative subjects, like *moi* ('me'), *toi* ('you') (see for example (1c)).

Various (possibly complementary) hypotheses have been entertained in the literature. For instance, one may imagine that children have access to default Case more freely than adults (Vainikka 1993–94, Rizzi 1993–94, Wexler 1995). Yet, the reason for that has to be rendered precise, especially since it is unclear how the mechanism could be delearned.

Another possibility would be to extend the truncation approach to DPs. Suppose D is responsible for Case transmission to NPs, as has commonly been suggested. It can be further proposed that on a par with the CP level, the DP level is not obligatory in early grammars, and can be truncated. And as long as the DP level is not systematically projected, Case requirements may be vacuously satisfied. It is fairly clear that determiner-like elements are indeed optional in early stages: not only are articles often missing, but in addition object clitics are rare (Friedemann 1993–94, Hamann, Rizzi and Frauenfelder 1996), and postnominal possessors can surface instead of possessive pronouns (Friedemann 1993–94). If this solution is on the right track, the Case puzzle and the optionality of determiners in child language could be related (as originally proposed by Radford 1990) and reduced to the optional projection of the DP-level in early grammars. This hypothesis awaits a careful examination. Note, however, that a solution along these lines would allow deducing three important child-specific peculiarities – early null and postverbal subjects, root infinitives, and optional determiners – from a single cause, truncation (Friedemann 1993–94 and, in a different framework, Hoekstra and Hyams 1995, Eisenbeiss this volume).

Next, the proposal advanced in the chapter is at odds with Kayne's (1994) antisymmetric view of syntax. Postulating a right-branching SpecVP appears to be fully incompatible with Kayne's Linear Correspondence Axiom (LCA), which allows only left-branching specifiers. Notice, though, that the standard analysis of right-dislocations involves a right-adjoined A'-position, and is as incompatible with the antisymmetric approach as right-branching specifiers are. Indeed, according to the LCA, there is no difference between specifiers and adjuncts. How, then, could the data be reconciled with the antisymmetric theory? According to Kayne (1994) himself, French right-dislocations are to be analyzed basically as clitic-doubling structures, with the dislocated element in its canonical position. In the covert syntax, the lexical element moves to a position on the extreme left of the clause, resulting in a left-dislocation at LF.

With respect to our postverbal subjects, then, the LCA essentially reduces right-dislocated subjects to subjects in their argumental position in the overt syntax. Presumably, sentence-final subjects would be located in a left-branching SpecVP, and the rest of the VP content would move to functional projections located higher than the VP itself, thereby deriving the overt word order. Structurally, right-dislocated subjects and VP-internal subjects therefore occupy the same position at spell-out. The difference between the two constructions has to be looked for at the interface: topic interpretation at LF, and (possibly) intonation at PF.

In short, we are back to our original conclusions: in the absence of reliable empirical tests, deciding between the VP-internal hypothesis and the right-dislocation approach rests mainly on statistical and cross-linguistic considerations. On these grounds, the previous section concluded that early right-dislocations without an overt pronominal subject should not be excluded, but cannot be generalized to all early postverbal subjects. Thus, independently of the chosen framework, we have to deal with overt VP-internal subjects.

Still, the LCA technically excludes right-branching specifiers and hence right-branching subjects. In order to account for the observed VOS surface order, it appeals to multiple functional projections. Estimating the theoretical and empirical impact of such a move is a subtle question. For the purposes of this chapter, it suffices to consider it as a technical alternative. For reasons of simplicity and mnemonics, I hence continue designating VP-internal subjects following the complement(s) of the verb right-branching subjects. Independently of the chosen label and technique, however, the appearance of massive surface VOS structures is clearly not a universal phenomenon, and raises the important question of parameter setting. I would like to close this chapter by briefly mentioning a few possible triggers that could allow children acquiring French to set the value of the relevant parameter.

As already mentioned (note 7), stylistic inversion is rare in colloquial French; it would hence not be reasonable to argue that in itself it forces the right setting of the ordering parameter. Two other and more common constructions, though, manifest sentence-final subjects and may help the child set the ordering parameter to right-branching subjects: causative constructions (15a) (see Guasti 1993 for extensive discussion), and constructions involving distinctive pronouns (15b) (Ronat 1979).

(15) a. Grégoire fait   travailler les linguistes.
     Grégoire makes to+work the linguists
   b. Il l' a fait   LUI.
     he it$_{cl}$ has done HE

Moreover, genuine right-dislocations, which are very common in the input and present clear VOS order, could also serve as a trigger. And they could do so, I believe, even if one takes right-dislocations to be right-adjoined structures and not VP-internal ones à la Kayne. It would not be implausible that children make a good choice for parameter setting on the basis of a wrong analysis of dislocations, and use right-dislocation structures to determine the base position of the subject in French. Nothing should force them to initially reject the simpler assumption generating the lexical subject in its base position (see Clark 1991 for an acquisition model favoring simpler and non-movement analyses), and later, once equipped with the right evidence, to correct their original, wrong evaluation.

7 Conclusion

This chapter has proposed an overview of the hypotheses made in recent years to account for early French postverbal subjects. It has reached the conclusion that sentence-final subjects may include both right-dislocations and right-branching VP-internal subjects, and that there is presently no sufficient empirical evidence to decide case by case which construction is involved. Nonetheless, crosslinguistic and statistical considerations strongly suggest that the VP-internal analysis is required to account for the high frequency and distribution of sentence-final subjects. Finally, it has been argued that early postverbal subject constructions are truncated structures. This explains their configurational sensitivity and their child specificity.

Appendix

These tables are from Friedemann (1993–94). The data are from 'Child Language Data Exchange System' (MacWhinney and Snow (1985)). The corpus contained records of two children, Grégoire (collected by Christian Champaud) and Philippe (cf. Suppes, Smith and Léveillé (1973)). I had access to files corresponding to one tape each month between the age of 1;11 and 2;3 for Grégoire (2;2 was not available). Philippe was recorded one hour each week, and I analyzed files between 2;1 and 2;3, and additionally some files from 2;6 and on for comparison (Philippe was not recorded at 2;4 and 2;5).

TABLE 3.1 Distribution of subjects in all utterances examined

		Weak pron.	Dislocations	Null subj.	Lexical subj.	Total
Grégoire	1;11	4	2	27	11	**44**
	2;0	7	6	28	17	**58**
	2;1	2	2	13	7	**24**
	2;3	20	4	22	19	**65**
	Total	33 *17%*	14 *7%*	90 *47%*	54 *28%*	**191**
Philippe	2;1	35	14	91	40	**180**
	2;2	44	26	231	86	**387**
	2;3	80	26	180	40	**326**
	Total	159 *18%*	66 *7%*	502 *56%*	166 *19%*	**893**
TOTAL		192 *18%*	80 *7%*	592 *55%*	220 *20%*	**1084**

TABLE 3.2 Distribution of lexical subjects (without unstressed pronouns and dislocations)

		$S{-}V_{+\text{finite}}$	$S{-}V_{-\text{finite}}$	$V_{+\text{finite}}{-}S$	$V_{-\text{finite}}{-}S$	S_{lexical}
Grégoire	1;11	2	1	7	1	**11**
	2;0	5	0	5	7	**17**
	2;1	4	0	2	1	**7**
	2;3	3	1	12	3	**19**
	Total	14 *26%*	2 *4%*	26 *48%*	12 *22%*	**54**
Philippe	2;1	8	2	16	14	**40**
	2;2	16	3	50	17	**86**
	2;3	11	3	21	5	**40**
	Total	35 *21%*	8 *5%*	87 *52%*	36 *22%*	**166**
TOTAL		49 *22%*	10 *5%*	113 *51%*	48 *22%*	**220**

TABLE 3.3 VP-internal position of postverbal subjects

		$V_{+\text{fin}}{-}S$	$V_{-\text{fin}}{-}S$	$V_{+\text{fin}}{-}XP{-}S$	$V_{-\text{fin}}{-}XP{-}S$	$V{-}S{-}XP$	VS
Grégoire	1;11	6	1	1			**8**
	2;0	3	3	2	3	1	**12**
	2;1	1		1	1		**3**
	2;3			12	3		**15**
	Total	10 *26%*	4 *11%*	16 *42%*	7 *18%*	1[12] *3%*	**38**
Philippe	2;1	5	4	11	10		**30**
	2;2	15	8	35	9		**67**
	2;3	10	2	11	3		**26**
	Total	30 *24%*	14 *11%*	57 *46%*	22 *18%*	0 *0%*	**123**
TOTAL		40[13] *25%*	18 *11%*	73 *45%*	29 *18%*	1 *<1%*	**161**

TABLE 3.4   Later stages[14]

		Subjectless sentences	Root infinitives	Postverbal subjects	**Total utterances**
Philippe	2;6;13	20 9%	11 5%	3 1,3%	**219**
	2;8;29	10 6,3%	2 1,3%	0 0%	**160**
	3;3;12	10 6,2%	2 1,2%	0 0%	**161**

Acknowledgements

This work has been supported by grant N° 8210-042998 of the *Fonds national suisse de la recherche scientifique* and the *Programme plurifacultaire 'Langage et communication'* (University of Geneva). I would like to thank Luigi Rizzi and Tali Siloni for helpful comments.

Notes

1 Grégoire and Philippe's files were taken from CHILDES (MacWhinney and Snow 1985). Unless mentioned differently, I will henceforth use the figures from Friedemann (1993–94) when I refer to early French data; I am not aware of any seriously conflicting results based on other corpora. The Geneva Corpora, though, discussed elsewhere in this volume (Augustin and Marie; see the contributions by Hamann, Rasetti, Rizzi) seem to show fewer overt subjects – and hence fewer postverbal subjects – in infinitival contexts (2c,e). There has not yet been any work done on postverbal subjects which took these corpora into consideration.

2 And possibly more generally in Romance; see also Giorgi and Longobardi (1991), Roberts (1993).

3 For reasons of space, I will not discuss the construction here, nor the complex restrictions it exhibits. Various restrictions were already noted in Kayne (1973, 1986), Kayne and Pollock (1978). Accounts in terms of (left-branching) VP-internal subjects include Déprez (1988), Valois and Dupuis (1992), Watanabe (1994) among others, and Pollock (1986) for certain contexts. For a detailed analysis that shows why a right-branching SpecVP allows a more fine-tuned account of the facts, see Friedemann (1997a, 1997b).

4 Based on the relative order of verbs and adverbs, Pollock (1989) observes that infinitives can move to an intermediate head position between VP and IP (say, InfP), as in (i). This observation does not refute the claim in the text. Short movement of infinitival forms is at best optional in French, as shown by the (more natural) option (ii). For obvious reasons of delearning, one would not like to claim that children obligatorily move the verb in a context where adults do it optionally:

(i) Perdre$_i$ [$_{VP}$ complètement [$_{VP}$ t$_i$ la tête]] . . .
     to+loose completely   the head . . .

(ii) [$_{VP}$ Complètement [$_{VP}$ perdre   la tête] . . .
        completely   to+loose the head . . .

(Pollock 1989)

5 Subjects without determiners are not counted as indefinites. Determiners are
   known to be independently optional in early child language; I return to this
   briefly in section 6.
6 I take *la voiture* ('the car') to be in complement position in (11a). (11b)
   may have several interpretations. It is not certain that *casser* ('break') is a
   transitive verb, with *tout seul* referring to the unexpressed agent. If the
   intransitive variant is involved (with *tout seul* referring to the subject *les
   petites boules* ('the small balls'), the utterance would not be relevant for our
   purposes.
      Additionally, *tout seul* may refer to the accusative argument; under this
   interpretation, it precedes the argument that it would follow in the adult
   grammar, as in the postverbal subject cases. This would then be the child-
   particular behavior awaiting an explanation, and no conclusion could be
   drawn with respect to the base position of the subject.
      Finally, if one argues that *tout seul* may be left-adjoined in (11), the same
   reasoning could carry over to (9a,b) (and all other instances of *tout seul*
   with a postverbal subject I encountered).
7 Genuine cases of stylistic inversion are typical of a more literary French, as
   the name of the construction indicates. Thus, we do not expect them to
   occur in child French.
8 Labelle and Valois (1996) are not explicit as to which theory of dislocation
   they adopt. If one judges according to the structure they attribute to infinitivals
   (see note 11), they seem to consider postverbal subjects as base-generated
   dislocated elements, because they posit PRO, which cannot be an expletive,
   in SpecIP.
9 In this count, I do not take simple preverbal subjects (59 cases) to be
   possible instances of left-dislocations without subject clitics. This would
   amount to saying that all lexical subjects are dislocated in early French.
10 This might appear to be an unusually high number in comparison with
   certain figures presented in the literature. The difference may result from
   the fact that often only preverbal subjects are counted as non-null subjects.
11 Labelle and Valois (1996) suggest, relying on a proposal by Hoekstra and
   Hyams (1995), that in infinitival structures a dislocated DP can function as
   discourse antecedent to a PRO subject in SpecIP:

   (i) [$_{IP}$ PRO$_i$ faire   boum sur camion] maman$_i$
           to+make boom on   truck   mummy

   As I take (i) to rely on assumptions not needed in the text proposal, I will
   not consider it here. At any rate, it is irrelevant for the ensuing discussion.
12 (i) (faut) fermer   Pinpin (les) lunettes. (Grégoire, 2;0)
       (has) to+close Pinpin (the) glasses

   I found another (unclear) instance of 'Subject–Complement' word order in
   a structure involving two subjects (which therefore does not appear in this
   table):

(ii) Il tourne le (?) monsieur la (?) titite. (Grégoire, 2;0)
     he turns the (?) man the (?) titite

It is not clear to me how to interpret this example, since right-dislocations always manifest sentence-final subjects. One possibility may be that the object has undergone a topic-like movement over the dislocated subject. But then, this example is not relevant for the relative basic order of subjects and complements.

13 23 utterances out of the 40 represent complex tenses.
14 As in Table 3.1, subjectless sentences here include both finite and non-finite contexts. Note that some subjectless sentences are expected to occur in finite contexts, too, as imperative or root expletive subject constructions (see Rizzi 1992), for instance, can appear without a lexical subject, even in adult grammars. The subjectless sentences found here are mainly of this sort:

(i) Regarde, il passe par   la fenêtre (Philippe, 2;8;29)
     look,   he passes through the window
(ii) Faut pas les balancer exprès   comme ça. (Philippe, 3;3;12)
     should not them to+swing voluntarily so

Furthermore, the few root infinitives also seem to correspond to grammatical adult forms; for example, the following answer Philippe (P) gives to his mother (M):

(iii) M: Qu' est-ce que tu   veux qu' il fasse avec (Philippe, 2;8;29)
         what is it   that you want that he do   with
         ton cartable?
         your bag
      P: Manger.
         to+eat

References

ASHBY, W. J. (1988) 'The Syntax, Pragmatics, and Sociolinguistics of Left- and Right-Dislocations in French', *Lingua* **75**, 203–29.

BARNES, B. (1986) 'An Empirical Study of the Syntax and Pragmatics of Left Dislocations in Spoken French', in O. Jaeggli and C. Silva-Corvalan (eds), *Studies in Romance Linguistics*, Foris, Dordrecht, 207–23.

CHOMSKY, N. (1982) *Some Concepts and Consequences of the Theory of Government and Binding*, MIT Press, Cambridge, MA.

CHOMSKY, N. (1994) 'Bare Phrase Structure', *MIT Occasional Papers in Linguistics* 5, MIT, Cambridge, MA, reprinted in G. Webelhuth (ed.) (1995), *Government and Binding Theory and the Minimalist Program*, Blackwell, Oxford.

CHOMSKY, N. (1995) *The Minimalist Program*, MIT Press, Cambridge, MA.

CLARK, R. (1991) 'The Selection of Syntactic Knowledge', ms., Université de Genève.

CRISMA, P. (1992) 'On the Acquisition of *wh*-questions in French', *GenGenP* **0.1–2**, 115–22.

DÉPREZ, V. (1988) 'Stylistic Inversion and Verb Movement', ms., MIT.

DÉPREZ, V. and A. PIERCE (1993) 'Negation and Functional Projections in Early Grammar', *Linguistic Inquiry* **24**, 25–67.

FERDINAND, A. (1993) 'Subject Dislocations in Child Language', *HIL Manuscripts*, 54–64.

FRIEDEMANN, M.-A. (1993–94) 'The Underlying Position of External Arguments in French: A Study in Adult and Child Grammar', *Language Acquisition* **3.3**, 209–55.

FRIEDEMANN, M.-A. (1997a) 'Inversion stylistique et position de base du sujet', *Revue canadienne de linguistique* **42**, 379–413.

FRIEDEMANN, M.-A. (1997b) *Sujets syntaxiques: positions, inversions et pro*, Peter Lang, Bern.

GIORGI, A. and G. LONGOBARDI (1991) *The Syntax of Noun Phrases: Configuration, Parameters and Empty Categories*, Cambridge University Press, Cambridge.

GUASTI, M. T. (1993) *Causatives and Perception Verbs*, Rosenberg & Sellier, Torino.

HAMANN, C., L. RIZZI and U. FRAUENFELDER (1996) 'On the Acquisition of Object Clitics in French', in H. Clahsen (ed.), *Generative Perspective on Language Acquisition*, Benjamins, Amsterdam and Philadelphia.

HOEKSTRA, T. and N. HYAMS (1995) 'The Syntax and Interpretation of Dropped Categories in Child Language: A Unified Account', *Proceedings of the XIVth West Coast Conference on Formal Linguistics* **14**, 123–36.

HOEKSTRA, T. and N. HYAMS (1998) 'Aspects of Root Infinitives', ms., University of Leiden and UCLA.

KAYNE, R. (1973) 'L'inversion du sujet en français dans les propositions interrogatives', *Le français moderne* **41**, 10–42, 131–51.

KAYNE, R. (1986) 'Connexité et inversion du sujet', in M. Ronat and D. Couquaux (eds), *La grammaire modulaire*, Les Editions de Minuit, Paris, 127–47.

KAYNE, R. (1994) *The Antisymmetry of Syntax*, MIT Press, Cambridge, MA.

KAYNE, R. and POLLOCK, J. Y. (1978) 'Stylistic Inversion, Successive Cyclicity, and Move NP in French', *Linguistic Inquiry* **9**, 595–621.

LABELLE, M. and D. VALOIS (1996) 'The Status of Post-verbal Subjects in French Child Language', *Probus* **8**, 53–80.

LAMBRECHT, K. (1981) *Topic, Antitopic and Verb Agreement in Non-Standard French. Pragmatics and Beyond*, Benjamins, Amsterdam.

LAMBRECHT, K. (1984) 'A Pragmatic Constraint on Lexical Subjects in Spoken French', *Chicago Linguistic Society* **20**.

LEVOW, G. (1995) 'Tense and Subject Positions in Interrogatives and Negatives in Child French: Evidence for and against Truncated Structures', *MIT Working Papers in Linguistics* **26**, 281–304.

LIGHTBOWN, P. (1977) *Consistency and Variation in the Acquisition of French*, Doctoral dissertation, Columbia University.

MACWHINNEY, B. and C. SNOW (1985) 'The Child Language Data Exchange System', *Journal of Child Language* **12**, 271–96.

PIERCE, A. (1989) *On the Emergence of Syntax: A Crosslinguistic Study*, Doctoral dissertation, MIT.

PIERCE, A. (1992) *Language Acquisition and Syntactic Theory: A Comparative Analysis of French and English Child Grammars*, Kluwer, Dordrecht.

POLLOCK, J. Y. (1986) 'Sur la syntaxe de *en* et le paramètre du sujet nul', in M. Ronat and D. Couquaux (eds), *La grammaire modulaire*, Les Editions de Minuit, Paris, 211–46.

POLLOCK, J. Y. (1989) 'Verb Movement, UG and the Structure of IP', *Linguistic Inquiry* 20, 365–424.

RADFORD, A. (1990) *Syntactic Theory and the Acquisition of English Syntax: The Nature of Early Child Grammars of English*, Oxford University Press, Oxford.

RIZZI, L. (1992) 'Early Null Subjects and Root Null Subjects', *GenGenP* 0.1–2, Université de Genève, 102–14. Published in T. Hoekstra and B. Schwartz (eds) (1994), *Language Acquisition: Studies in Generative Grammar*, John Benjamins, Amsterdam and Philadelphia.

RIZZI, L. (1993–94) 'Some Notes on Linguistic Theory and Language Development: The Case of Root Infinitives' *Language Acquisition* 3.4, 371–93.

ROBERTS, I. (1993) *Verbs and Diachronic Syntax*, Kluwer, Dordrecht.

RONAT, M. (1979) 'Pronoms topiques et pronoms distinctifs', in M. Ronat (ed.), *Grammaire de phrase et grammaire de discours. Langue française* 44, 106–28.

SUPPES, P., R. SMITH and M. LÉVEILLÉ (1973) 'The French Syntax of a Child's Noun Phrase', *Archives de Psychologie* 42.

VAINIKKA, A. (1993–94) 'Case in the Development of English Syntax', *Language Acquisition* 3.3, 257–325.

VALOIS, D. and F. DUPUIS (1992) 'On the Status of (Verbal) Traces in French: The Case of Stylistic Inversion', in P. Hirschbühler and K. Koerner (eds), *Romance Languages and Modern Linguistics*, John Benjamins, Amsterdam, 325–38.

WATANABE, A. (1994) 'A Crosslinguistic Perspective on Japanese Nominative–Genitive Conversion and its Implication for Japanese Syntax', ms., Kanda University of International Studies, Tokyo.

WEISSENBORN, J. (1988) 'The Acquisition of Clitic Object Pronouns and Word Order in French: Syntax or Morphology?', ms., Max-Planck Institute, Nijmegen.

WEISSENBORN, J., M. VERRIPS and R. BERMAN (1989) 'Negation as a Window to the Syntax of Early Child Language', ms., Max-Planck Institute, Nijmegen, and Tel Aviv University.

WEXLER, K. (1992) 'Optional Infinitives, Head Movement and the Economy of Derivations in Child Grammar', *MIT Occasional Paper* 45. Published in D. Lightfoot and N. Hornstein (eds) (1994), *Verb Movement*, Cambridge University Press, Cambridge.

WEXLER, K. (1995) 'The New Look in Inflectional Development', ms., MIT.

Chapter 4

Split inflection in neurolinguistics
Na'ama Friedmann and Yosef Grodzinsky

Since Pollock's 1989 paper, much linguistic argumentation has been mounted in favor of the split inflection hypothesis. This chapter presents evidence from a neuropsychological angle in support of this hypothesis. Given that agrammatic aphasic patients demonstrate a selective deficit in the syntactic domain, it is tempting to look for impairment patterns that pertain to issues debated in current syntactic theory. Some arguments from agrammatism to linguistics have already been put forth in the past (Grodzinsky, 1990; Grodzinsky et al., 1993). We will focus on the inflectional domain, and show that the agrammatic selective breakdown pattern follows the exact same line that the theory sketches between subparts of inflection: tense and agreement. Thus, we will present corroborating evidence to the theory, by showing how natural classes within it behave differentially in aphasia. In addition, we will show that the impairment in tense node has implications upon higher nodes in the syntactic tree.

We believe that these claims are relevant to anyone interested in psycholinguistic and neurolinguistic aspects of the theory of syntax. Moreover, they are of special interest to students of language acquisition, where somewhat parallel (yet very different) developments have taken place, and, in fact, inspired us in our investigation (see Rizzi, 1994).

This study is a detailed examination of the speech production abilities in agrammatic aphasic patients. Agrammatism is a language deficit following damage to Broca's area in the left cerebral hemisphere (Damasio, 1992; Zurif, 1995). It is usually viewed as an impairment to functional elements (or 'grammatical morphemes' in common use). However, this description is far too crude, and, as will become apparent below, a precise description of the fine patterns of impairment and sparing in this syndrome requires a lot of syntactic machinery. The standard view is that all functional elements are impaired in the production of such brain-damaged patients (see, for instance, Goodglass, 1976; Grodzinsky, 1984; Kean, 1977; Ouhalla, 1993). We show, however, that the pattern of selectivity is more refined than previously thought, and that distinctions provided by the split inflection hypothesis must be part of the proper description of the impairment pattern. We have, in short, documented a dissociation between tense and agreement: while tense is impaired, agreement is intact. Beyond the clinical implications that this finding has, it supports the split inflection hypothesis. This dissociation, we claim, is derived from an impaired phrase marker. Furthermore, the impairment is not restricted to tense inflection. There is a cluster of syntactic disruptions related to the T(ense) node: subject omissions, copula difficulties and word order problems. By contrast, properties related to Agr(eement) (and to the VP in general) are intact. Thus, a distinction between tense and agreement is neurologically demonstrated. This pattern of impairment is associated, furthermore, with problems in higher nodes of the tree, namely in the CP layer: Wh-questions and embedded clauses are either nonexistent or ill-formed in the speech production of patients suffering from this syndrome.

The major part of our data is based upon an extensive experimental study on the speech production abilities of a Hebrew-speaking agrammatic aphasic. Special tests were devised to examine the split inflection hypothesis, and at the same time investigate the exact nature of the agrammatic impairment. We then sought, and found, additional empirical evidence supporting our claims in previously published cross-linguistic neuropsychological data, and in 12 more agrammatic patients: 10 Hebrew speakers, and 2 speakers of Palestinian Arabic.

1 First step: deficit to tense but not agreement

In order to assess our patient's abilities, we began with a comparison between tense and agreement in her production of verbal inflection. Since data from spontaneous speech (which are commonly used in aphasia research) are not enough to pursue errors in detail, we used structured tasks.[1]

Two tasks were employed: a sentence repetition task, in which the patient was asked to repeat the sentences she had heard (after counting to 3), and a sentence completion task, in which the patient was required to inflect a verb for either tense or one of the agreement features. The patient first heard a sentence containing an inflected verb, and then a second sentence without the verb, with a change in either the subject or the time adverb. The subject had to produce the missing verb with the proper inflection (1).

(1)   etmol   ha-yeled katav,
                                           yesterday *the-boy* *write-3ʳᵈ-masc-sg-past,*

              Tense condition

              maxar   ha-yeled ____. (yixtov)   Agreement
              tomorrow *the-boy* ____.   condition
              (write-3ʳᵈ-masc-sg-future)

                                           etmol   ha-yeladim ____. (katvu)
                                           yesterday the-boys ____.
                                           (write-3ʳᵈ-masc-pl-past)

Each test consisted of a large number of token sentences, to allow
for quantitative analysis. The tests consisted of simple sentences (3–5
words), which included verbs inflected for one of the 3 tenses and one
of 10 agreement forms. In the completion test, sentences were devised
to elicit each of the 30 forms. (See Table 4.1 for an example of Hebrew
inflectional paradigm.) (For more details on the experiments, see
Friedmann and Grodzinsky, 1997.)

The results were remarkable. While agreement was normal, tense
was severely impaired, even though the patient's perception of time,
as well as comprehension of temporal adverbs, proved to be intact
through tests.[2] There were mainly tense substitutions (with no preferred
'unmarked' form), and some 'don't know' responses in tense completion tasks, but almost no agreement errors. Table 4.2 summarizes the
results, followed by typical substitution errors – in repetition (2), and in
completion (3).

TABLE 4.1   Hebrew inflectional paradigm

		Past	*Present*	*Future*
1st	singular	KaTaVti	KoTeV	EXToV
	plural	KaTaVnu	KoTVim	NiXToV
2nd masc	singular	KaTaVta	KoTeV	TiXToV
	plural	KaTaVtem	KoTVim	TiXTeVu
fem	singular	KaTaVt	KoTeVet	TiXTeVi
	plural	KaTaVten	KoTVot	TiXToVna
3rd masc	singular	KaTaV	KoTeV	YiXToV
	plural	KaTVu	KoTVim	YiXTeVu
fem	singular	KaTVa	KoTeVet	TiXToV
	plural	KaTVu	KoTVot	TiXToVna

(in caps – the root KTV (= *write*))

SPLIT INFLECTION IN NEUROLINGUISTICS

TABLE 4.2   Tense vs. agreement production: patient RS

	Tense		Agreement	
	% correct	(correct/total)	% correct	(correct/total)
Repetition	77	(43/56)	100	(56/56)
Completion	46	(41/90)	93	(66/71)
Total	58	(84/146)	96	(122/127)

TABLE 4.3   Tense vs. agreement production in Hebrew and Arabic
(Friedmann, 1998)

		Tense		Agreement	
		% correct	(correct/total)	% correct	(correct/total)
Hebrew	Repetition	84	(769/912)	100	(908/912)
	Completion	58	(438/760)	96	(572/596)
Arabic	Completion	31	(14/45)	91	(42/46)
Total		71	(1221/1717)	98	(1522/1554)

(2) Target: ha-anašim **yixtevu**   mixtav
                        *the-people write-**future**-3-m-pl letter*
                        la-bank.
                        to-the-bank
    Actual repetition: ha-anašim **katvu**   mixtav
                        *the-people write-**past**-3-m-pl letter*
                        la-bank.
                        to-the-bank

(3) Target: axšav ata holex,   etmol   ata
                        now   you go-pres-2-m-sg yesterday you
                        ____. (expected: **halaxta**)
                        ____ *(go-**past**-2-m-sg)*
    Actual completion: axšav ata holex,   etmol   ata
                        now   you go-pres-2-m-sg yesterday you
                        telex.
                        *go-**future**–2-m-sg*

   A later study of 11 Hebrew-speaking agrammatics and 2 Palestinian Arabic-speaking agrammatics yielded the same results: impaired
tense inflection (29% errors) with intact agreement (only 2% errors)
(Table 4.3) (Friedmann, 1998).

A retrospective literature review indicates that cross-linguistic evidence goes in the same direction: although very few studies have examined verbal inflection through structured tests, it seems that there is a group of patients (mostly Italian and French aphasics) impaired in tense but not agreement, yet the opposite (i.e. agreement impairment with intact tense) is never found.

For example, the French-speaking agrammatic Mr. Clermont, reported in Nespoulous *et al.* (1988, 1990), had only tense errors but no verb agreement errors, avoided the use of complex tenses, omitted 50% of the copulas (7/14) and 50% of the auxiliaries (10/20). An example of his tense errors in reading aloud from Little Red Riding Hood is given in (4).

(4) Target: Bonjour,   grand-mère, je vous   **ai**
             *Good morning, grandma,   I to-you **have**
             apporté   un panier de gâteaux.
             ***bring-pres-perf** a bowl   of cake*
    Read: Bonjour, grand-mère, je **porterai** euh je /pu/ /zɛda/ . . .
                                       carry-future
             a-apporté un-un panier de gâteaux.

In Romance, the picture is more complicated, first of all, because structured tests of tense and agreement are not available and the only existing data is spontaneous speech,[3] and secondly, because tense substitutions in Romance are mainly to the nonfinite forms: participles and infinitives.

In Germanic languages such as Dutch, German and Icelandic, patients frequently use the infinitive instead of the inflected verb. Crucially, a nonfinite form always appears in a sentence-final position, indicating that the verb has not moved up the tree to C, where tensed verbs in matrix clauses of V2 languages should move (Bastiaanse and van Zonneveld, 1998; Kolk and Heeschen, 1992).

These findings immediately suggest a deficit that implicates tense but not agreement features. This, in itself, is new, for agrammatic aphasia has always been thought to implicate all functional elements equally, and the striking difference we observe appears to have been overlooked.

Before making a syntactic claim that T node is impaired and Agr node (or the node where agreement is checked) is intact, other imaginable accounts, such as a lexical account, should be considered. The syntactic and lexical approaches are contrasted clearly. A split inflection based approach would claim that the phrase marker is impaired in the T node. A lexical (or morphological) approach, on the other hand, would somehow attribute the problem to the lexical representation of tense features.

Even without fully elaborating upon these alternatives, we can easily see that each has different empirical consequences. What data can be used to decide between the accounts?

A deficit in the T node predicts that all of its other functions will be implicated as well, and does not predict any problem at the single-word level. A lexical account contains the opposite predictions: no impairment in other functions of T node, and a problem with inflections of verbs, whether isolated or embedded in sentences. Furthermore, the observed deficit to higher nodes of the syntactic tree (specifically to CP) can be explained only in a syntactic framework.

Thus, in order to decide between lexical and syntactic accounts, we had to test three levels: single-word production, other functions of T, and the CP.

First, we tested production in single-word level. The subject repeated verbs and copulas presented outside sentence context: as single items and as quadruplets of items. The results (40/43 correct) indicated the preserved ability at the single-word level.

We were thus led to the next experimental step in which we looked for deficits in other syntactic functions of the T node.

2 Second step: deficits related to the T node

Three functions of T were examined:

(i) Copula production
(ii) The relative ordering of negation and copula
(iii) Subject pronoun production

2.1 Copular errors

If the Hebrew copula is at T prior to Spell-Out (whether moved, or base-generated there) then impairment to the T node will affect it as well.[4] We thus used the same experimental paradigm, asking our patient to repeat or complete sentences that required her to inflect copulas (for tense and agreement). (5)

(5) *Copula completion tasks*
    a. *Tense completion*
        ha-šana galia hi   xavert-i   ha-tova be-yoter.
        the-year Galia cop-pres friend-my the-best
        gam ba-šana   ha-ba'aa galia ____ xavert-i
        also in-the-year the-next Galia ____ friend-my
        ha-tova be-yoter.
        the-best
        '**This year** Galia *is* my best friend. Also **Next year** Galia ____ my best friend.'

TABLE 4.4   Copula inflection production in Hebrew

	Tense		Agreement	
	% correct	(correct/total)	% correct	(correct/total)
Repetition	50	(30/60)	100	(60/60)
Completion	20	(9/46)	100	(36/36)
Total	37	(39/106)	100	(96/96)

    b. *Agreement completion*
      etmol   hu haya   acuv. etmol   gam
      yesterday he cop-past–3rd-sg-mas sad   yesterday also
      hi _____ acuva.
      she _____ *sad-fem*
      'Yesterday **he** was sad. Yesterday **she** _____ sad too.'[5]

In Hebrew, copula inflects like the main verb, for 3 tenses, 10 agreement forms in the past and future, and 4 forms in the present (the participle).

The results show that the ability to inflect copulas for tense was seriously impaired, as predicted by the syntactic account. The patient made many tense substitutions and copula omission errors in repetition and completion tasks, but no agreement error.[6] The results are shown in Table 4.4, and a typical error in (6).

    (6) maxar   dani   haya ba-yam
        tomorrow Danny was in-the-sea

Again, a review of the literature shows a consistent impairment in copula production in many other languages (Dutch, Swedish, French, Finnish and Japanese, among others – in the spontaneous speech corpora in Menn and Obler, 1990). In all of these languages, agrammatics omit the copula in 36%–60% of the obligatory contexts, and substitute the copula's tense.

2.2 Copula–negation order
Aspects of word order in which T plays a role should also be informative for the functioning of T. We therefore looked at the relative placement of negation and copula.

In Hebrew, the relative order of copula and negation depends on tense: past and future tense copulas follow negation (7a), while present tense copulas precede their negation (7b) (unlike in regular verbs, where negation always precedes the verb, regardless of tense).

(7) a. David <u>lo</u>   haya/yihye melex anglia.
    David NEG was/will-be king-of England
  b. David <u>hu</u> <u>lo</u>   melex anglia.
    David is NEG king-of England

The content of T thus plays a critical role in the determination of the relative ordering of negation and copula. If T is impaired in agrammatic aphasia, negation and copula will not be ordered properly. We devised two varieties of sentence anagram ordering tasks: the first required the patient to create a sentence from 4 cards: a negation card, a copula card, and two with other sentence parts (8a); in the second task, the patient was asked to insert a card with a copula into a given sentence containing negation (8b), or to insert negation into a sentence containing a copula (8c) (for instance: insert *not* into *Dan is happy*).

(8) a. | David || hu || lo || melex anglia |

  b. David lo melex anglia | hu |

  c. David hu melex anglia | lo |

The patient failed to come up with the correct relative ordering of copula and negation. Instead, she came up with an almost random order of negation and copulas: she performed correctly only on 24% of the sentences (18 out of 76 sentences). Her errors were of three main types: placing negation in front of the whole sentence, using constituent negation instead of sentential negation such as (9), and sometimes just giving up, holding the negation card helplessly in her hand.

(9) *David <u>haya</u>   <u>lo</u>   melex anglia
   David copula-past NEG king-of England

A parallel test of verb–negation ordering was carried out, yielding a 4% error rate. Again, this contrast does not mean that NegP is intact: recall that Hebrew systematically shows Neg–Vmain order, irrespective of tense. Negation of main verbs in Hebrew appears in the same position whether or not the verb rises to T. The patients can thus negate the whole VP correctly even without knowing its precise position, and without being aware of the verbal tense.

2.3 Subject omissions
Next, we looked at the subject position, which depends on T for several functions. For instance, if T checks (or assigns) Nominative case (Chomsky, 1993), then an impaired T node would have implications upon the subject position: Nominative case cannot be checked (or assigned), and hence the subject cannot be realized, even in mandatory contexts (Hebrew is only partially null-subject).

TABLE 4.5   Pronoun production in repetition

	% correct	(produced/total)
Subject – transitive sentence	36	(5/14)
Subject – intransitive sentence	94	(14/15)
Object	100	(6/6)

In spontaneous speech, subjects were frequently omitted. We therefore conducted a sentence repetition test, and found that subject pronouns were missing in contexts where pro-drop is illicit,[7] whereas object pronouns were never omitted[8] (Table 4.5).

This evidence is indirect, but it is hard to find direct evidence for lack of Nominative case, since Hebrew does not show Nominative case overtly. The fact that subjects, whenever they appear, do not carry a wrong case, might stem from a similar reason to the one suggested by Friedemann (1993–94) for language acquisition: the agrammatics may use subjects as topicalized elements, and assign them a default case (which in Hebrew is Nominative case).

A relation between verb inflection errors and subject pronoun omission has also been observed for children acquiring language (Pierce, 1989), but the case of agrammatism differs in an important respect: in agrammatism subject omissions co-occur with tense *substitutions*, not only with the use of nonfinite forms in matrix clauses.

Summarizing our findings so far, several seemingly separate impairments all follow from a single assumption – a Tense node deficit.

(10) a. Tense, but not agreement, errors in main verbs
     b. Tense, but not agreement, errors in copular constructions
     c. Copula omissions
     d. Errors in negation of copular constructions
     e. Subject pronoun omissions (in mandatory contexts)

This cluster of phenomena indicates that not only tense inflection, but also other functions of T are impaired. They support a syntactic theory of impaired T node. No other hypothesis we are aware of can account for these findings. Crucially, the theory of split inflection – the distinction between T and Agr, and the assignment of other functions to T (Nominative case, and a landing site for copulas), receives powerful neurological support.

(11) Generalization: T is impaired in agrammatic production.

The structural generalization in (11) has the desired consequences: errors in tense follow immediately, for both main verbs and copulas; subject omissions follow from lack of case features, necessary for Nominative case assignment to the subject, or from lack of landing site for the subject in spec TP; finally, problems of negation placement would result from the fact that the tense features of copulas cannot reside in T, and since the relative position of negation and copula crucially depends on these features (cf. (7) above). As for the omission of copulas, we adopted an idea of Guasti (1993). She claims that causatives in Romance do not allow for auxiliaries because they do not contain TP. Since AUX must move to T or otherwise violate Full Interpretation (FI), they are prohibited in structures that do not contain T (see also Rizzi (1994) for a similar point concerning auxiliaries in root infinitives). This account explains why auxiliaries and copulas are omitted or poorly used in the agrammatic sentence: since agrammatic trees contain a defective TP, or do not contain TP at all, auxiliaries and copulas are impossible to check. This results in either violating FI or avoiding the auxiliary/copula in the first place. In terms of sentence production, the first might look like tense substitution, and the second like auxiliary or copula omission.

Thus, the functional impairment subsequent to anterior lesions in the left cerebral hemisphere, or, more precisely, damage to Broca's area and its vicinity, is an impaired T node.[9]

3 Climbing higher in the tree: deficits in the CP

So far, we have been looking at a cluster of syntactic properties that are directly related to the T node, and saw that they are all impaired in agrammatism. We have proposed that T is impaired, and that this deficit is at the heart of the agrammatic impairment in speech production. What would happen to higher parts of the tree, given the crucial role of heads in projecting phrasal nodes? If a fully specified head is critical for phrasal projection, then the construction of nodes higher than T may be hampered, with the result of pruned trees (Rizzi, 1994 and this volume; Friedemann and Rizzi, this volume). This would have rather radical empirical consequences: it would mean that nodes above TP do not exist in agrammatic representation. Note that we assume here Pollock's original order TP–Agr$_S$P, which was also advocated for Arabic by Ouhalla (1994).

To test this possibility, we looked both at the corpus of spontaneous speech we had collected from the patient and assessed tests in search of evidence of higher projections – elements of CP. The results were clear-cut: both complementizers and Wh-questions were severely impaired.

3.1 Question production
Out of 440 sentences in the corpus of spontaneous speech of our patient (obtained in the large part from free conversation between the experimenter and the patient), only 3 were Wh-questions, of the type: Wh NP (*where the-pin*[10]) (which are grammatical in Hebrew).

In contrast to Wh-questions, the patient produced 11 (matrix) well-formed yes/no questions, some of them instead of properly formed Wh-questions. Since word order in yes/no questions in Hebrew is identical to that in declarative sentences, and does not require movement of a constituent to CP, this type of question is available to the patient.[11] Moreover, this finding proves that the agrammatic problem in question production is not a general problem with questions, but rather a problem that stems directly from the CP impairment.

An attempt to elicit Wh- and yes/no questions led to similar results: out of 20 Wh-questions *no* trial was successful. In repetition tasks, the patient repeated only 2/23 Wh-questions correctly.

Friedmann (1998) conducted a more extensive study with 8 additional patients: 7 Hebrew-speaking and 1 Palestinian Arabic-speaking agrammatics. This study also presented a marked dissociation between production of Wh-questions and production of yes/no questions. (Arabic yes/no questions do not require the CP as well.)

While the patients succeeded in 90% of the yes/no questions, they produced only 24% of the Wh-questions correctly (Table 4.6).

TABLE 4.6   Question elicitation: Wh- and yes/no questions in Hebrew and Arabic

	Wh-		Yes/No	
	% correct	*(correct/total)*	*% correct*	*(correct/total)*
Hebrew	25	(45/182)	95	(100/105)
Arabic	21	(5/24)	65	(15/23)
Total	24	(50/206)	90	(115/128)

The main error types in Wh-question production according to frequency of occurrence were:

(i)   Producing a yes/no question instead of a Wh-question (12)
(ii) 'Don't know' responses
(iii) Wrong Wh-morpheme selection
(iv) Unmoved Wh-morpheme in the beginning of the sentence, with filled gap (13)
(v)   Wh- in situ

(12) Ex: The sun rose today at a certain hour. You want to know about the hour. So you ask . . .
     Pa: bešeš . . . ha-šemeš zarxa . . . ha-šemeš ha-yom . . .
          at-six . . . the-sun   rose . . .   the-sun   today . . .
          lo   yoda'at. ha-šemeš zarxa ha-yom?
          (I) NEG know.   the-sun   rose   today?

(13) a. Patient: *ma* Dani hidlik *et ha-or*
       what** Danny lit   ACC **the-light
     b. Patient: *eix* Dani noheg *bi-zhirut*
       how** Danny drives **carefully

This problem in question production has been found in English as well (treatment studies in Thompson and Shapiro, 1995; Thompson *et al.*, 1996). Here, again, language-specific properties correlate with performance. Thus, unlike in Hebrew, English-speaking patients require intact C node for the auxiliary 'do' in do-support constructions, and therefore need an intact CP for yes/no question production.

The literature on the subject indicates that English-speaking agrammatics are indeed unable to produce yes/no questions. The patient reported in Goodglass *et al.* (1972) produced 0/14 yes/no questions in elicitation tasks.

This corroborates the claim that agrammatics do not have a general question production deficit, but rather a syntactically well-defined deficit, stemming from inaccessibility of CP.

3.2 Embedded sentence production

We proceeded to test another function of the CP layer: embedding. Our first step was to look at spontaneous speech, which can give qualitative, though not quantitative, information about the ability to embed. We found no evidence of such ability. To avoid the need for embedded constructions, the patient either omitted most of the embedded sentence (14), or omitted complementizers (15), or avoided such structures altogether in spontaneous speech.

(14) dorit ba'aa . . . etmol . . .   tilpena la-rofe   **še** . . .
     *Dorit came . . . yesterday . . . called to-the-Doctor **that** . . .*
     tor.
     appointment

(15) siparti la . . . nir   xayal
     told-I her . . . Nir (is a) soldier

Since it is difficult to determine the target sentence in spontaneous speech, structured tasks were assessed. Repetition results have shown the same pattern: repetition of sentences with embedding was only 4/23 successful.

A study with 7 additional agrammatics (5 speakers of Hebrew and 2 speakers of Palestinian Arabic) compared elicited production of embedded sentences (subject relatives (16)) with similar nonembedded sentences (adjectival modification (17)). This study yielded the same results, summarized in Table 4.7: embedding production proved to be severely impaired (Friedmann, 1998).

TABLE 4.7   Elicitation of embedded and nonembedded sentences

	Relative clause		Adjectival modification	
	% correct	(correct/total)	% correct	(correct/total)
Hebrew	21	(44/207)	100	(76/76)
Arabic	28	(10/36)	92	(22/24)
Total	22	(54/243)	98	(98/100)

(16) zo   ha-iša   še-mesaxeket tenis
this the-woman that-plays   tennis
'This is the woman who plays tennis'

(17) ze   ha-dag ha-kaxol
this the-fish the-blue
'This is the blue fish'

The two most frequent error types in embedding repetition and elicitation were complementizer omission and getting 'stuck' after the complementizer without being able to complete the sentence.

Severe impairment in CP embedding production has been documented for other languages as well (see de Roo, 1995, for Dutch, and Hagiwara, 1995, for Japanese). The pattern of errors is very similar to the ones reported for Hebrew, mainly complementizer omission and omission of most of the embedded sentence.

The following examples demonstrate agrammatic embedding difficulties in repetition in Palestinian Arabic (18), and in spontaneous speech in Finnish (19) and Japanese (20).

(18) *Palestinian Arabic-repetition*
Target: rula šaafat il-film **illi** ṣubḥi xaḍḍaro
*Rula saw   the-film **that** Subhi made-ACC*
Repeated: rula šaafat il-film . . . xallas! . . . rula šaafat
Rula saw   the-film . . . enough! . . . Rula saw
il-film . . . ṣubḥi xaḍḍaro
the-film . . . Subhi made-ACC
(Friedmann, 1998)

(19) *Finnish*
Vahtimestari toteaa-kin   **että** . . . **että** . . . voi veljet
*Watchman   even-remarks **that** . . . **that** . . . oh, brother,*
kun . . . vahtimestary huomaa sitten **että** . . . toteaa
*how . . . watchman   notices   then **that** . . . remarks*
että . . . vahtimestari huomaa . . . voi . . . tapauksen
that . . . watchman   notices . . . oh . . . incident:GEN
(Niemi *et al.*, 1990)

(20) *Japanese*
    'Hippat-te kudasai'   **[to]**   atasi [ga] ii-mas-u
    'Please   pull (me)' [comp] I say
                           (Sasanuma, Kamio and Kubota, 1990)

The results show a severe embedding deficit. Can it be only a general deficit in the construction of complex sentences, as some aphasiologists have claimed, and not a selective deficit to parts of the tree, as claimed here? A type of complex sentence that is preserved and does not involve C may help to decide between these approaches.

When testing different types of embeddings, Friedmann (1998) found that only CP embedding is problematic for the Hebrew-speaking agrammatics: untensed clausal complements (infinitival and participial complements) exist in agrammatic spontaneous speech, and were elicited and repeated normally.

Other languages behave in a similar manner with respect to embeddings. The French-speaking Mr. Clermont, for example (Nespoulous *et al.*, 1990), produced only 2 relative clauses and *no* other CP embeddings compared with 33 and 49 respectively produced by his control subject. On the other hand, his untensed clause embedding proved to be completely normal.

In the untensed embedded constructions, patients probably produce a partial tree that does not contain CP (which is required in these constructions according to standard analysis).

These findings indicate that the embedding impairment is not a general deficit in complex sentence production, but rather a problem with accessing CP, that leaves other embedding constructions intact.

To conclude, data from spontaneous speech and structured tasks in Hebrew and Arabic, as well as a retrospective review of spontaneous speech data from other languages, show a clear deficit in embedding of clauses headed by C in agrammatic aphasia. This, we suggest, follows from the inaccessibility of the C node in agrammatic production.

4 Discussion

4.1 Summary of the findings

  a. **AgrP level**: Intact agreement inflection

    ∿∿∿∿∿∿∿∿∿∿∿∿∿∿∿∿∿∿∿∿∿∿∿∿∿∿∿

  b. **TP level**:   Impaired tense inflection
                  Copula omissions
                  Subject pronoun omissions
                  Ordering errors of copulas and negation
  c. **CP level**:   No Wh-question production
                  No CP embedding

In sum, we have found that nodes higher than TP (namely CP) are also severely impaired in agrammatism. This impairment follows from the principle of an impaired head blocking further construction of higher phrasal nodes. This principle, together with the T node impairment, constitutes the grammatical deficit in agrammatic Broca's aphasia.

(21) The Tree Pruning Hypothesis
      a. T is impaired in agrammatic production.
      b. An impaired node cannot project any higher.

Having seen that the data fall under a structural generalization, it is now time to examine the generalization in greater detail. In what sense are the T node and its functions impaired? Whatever representational deficit we assume, it must have the consequences summarized above. This can be achieved in two possible ways: through a deficit in T node, or through a deficit to checking mechanisms. According to the former, the content of T, namely, the φ-features of the lexical head it dominates, is eliminated; moreover, the T node may not be projected at all. A deficit in checking mechanisms derives the data similarly, yet a question immediately arises: given that mechanisms of checking operate in an identical fashion everywhere, why is the failure in checking restricted to T? The answer, then, must lie in T itself, leading us to conclude that this node is impaired, and that this is the deficit in the syntactic representation of agrammatic speech production.[12]

Another possibility that should be considered is that it is not the T node which is defective, causing deficit in C also, but rather only the C node. The work by Stowell (1982), Enç (1987) and Guéron and Hoekstra (1989) suggests that tense is anchored in C. Is it possible to assume a C impairment only, that hampers tense anchoring and thus tense inflection, and dispense with an impairment in T? The answer is probably *no*, since pruning at C will not be able to explain subject omissions, and T deficit will have to be assumed anyway.[13]

4.2 Implications for the relative order of functional categories

The intactness of subject–verb agreement in the presence of poor tense bears on one of the central issues in clausal architecture: the relative order of functional categories, and, in particular, the relative order of Agr_s and T.

If we adopt the truncation constraint, then no node above the impaired TP can project (see Grimshaw (1991) for a similar account at least in the IP, and Rizzi (1994), for the root infinitive stage). Based on this theoretical stand, a poor T node and a well-projected Agr above it are out of the question. Taking these together, our claim has the consequence that subject–verb agreement is checked below T, hence it remains intact

in agrammatism. For Hebrew and Arabic, at least, this is not an unreasonable assumption.
An account of these finding is consistent with two approaches:

(i) Agreement and tense are both checked in spec–head relation in designated nodes – tense is checked in T node, and subject–verb agreement in Agr node. Under this assumption, in the normal Hebrew and Arabic phrase markers, the relative order of functional categories is CP>TP>Agr$_s$P. This is actually the order proposed by Pollock (1989, 1993) for English and French, and by Demirdache (1988) and Ouhalla (1994) for Arabic. It is, nevertheless, the opposite of the relative order suggested by Chomsky (1991, 1993) and Belletti (1990) for Romance.

(ii) Agreement is checked in a mechanism different from that for tense. It may not have a node of itself, but it checks in one of the other checking points below T, and is thus preserved. So, if the phrase marker is pruned above VP, and agreement is checked in VP spec–head, this is the expected result: VP and subject–verb agreement are intact, but tense inflection is impaired (and so are Wh-structures and subordinations).[14]

Our findings also refute an accepted view in neurolinguistics: some researchers explain inflectional marker omissions and substitutions by way of a general tendency of ignoring items of low semantic value. This study shows that this cannot be the reason for inflectional impairment: it is widely agreed that while agreement does not have semantic content, tense does. If only low-semantic-value items are neglected, we would expect agreement to be impaired, and tense to be preserved. Yet the empirical data point in the opposite direction.

To conclude, in aphasia research, very much like in language acquisition (Radford, 1990), researchers have claimed that agrammatics lack all functional categories (Ouhalla, 1993; Caplan, 1985). Like current studies in language acquisition (Hyams, 1992, and Poeppel and Wexler, 1993, for full phrase marker; Clahsen, 1990, for partial phrase marker), we show that agrammatics do have at least some of the functional categories. We claim that the agrammatic phrase marker is pruned in T and above: it contains an Agr node, but does not include the higher nodes: TP and CP.

In verb inflection production, the resemblance between children and agrammatics is only apparent: indeed both children and agrammatics produce main verbs which are not correctly inflected. But while agrammatics substitute tense inflection, children never substitute inflection, they only use the nonfinite forms (Wexler, 1994; Borer and Rohrbacher, to appear).

When children use nonfinite verbs in matrix clauses, these clauses usually do *not* contain negation (Friedemann, 1993–94), Wh-questions and complementizers (Clahsen, Penke and Parody, 1994; Weissenborn, 1992) subject pronouns (Pierce, 1989; Friedemann, 1993–94) or auxiliaries (Guasti, 1993–94; Poeppel and Wexler, 1993). But the crucial difference between children and agrammatics lies exactly here: children are able to build these constructions and use these elements (Rizzi, 1994), and agrammatics cannot project any higher than T.

When children do have an additional motivation to build the whole tree up to CP, they do it, and use a finite verb (Crisma, 1992). These constructions that children consistently use with finite verbs are exactly the ones which are impaired in agrammatic production: Wh-questions, auxiliaries and copulas, and pronoun subjects.

While speech production in language acquisition and agrammatism is similar in many respects, the underlying cause is very different: while agrammatics cannot construct the tree up to T and higher, children do not always find it necessary.

Notes

Address correspondence to: Na'ama Friedmann, department of psychology, Tel-Aviv University, Tel Aviv 69978, Israel. naamal@freud.tau.ac.il.

1 Tense errors which are easily detected in structured tense tasks may not be evident even in the spontaneous speech of the same patient, since patients can avoid using specific tenses or even avoid verb use. Furthermore, when patients do use tense, it is usually impossible to determine what the target tense was, hence it is impossible to detect tense substitutions.

2 An additional type of completion task was used, which did not include time adverbs ('The girls wanted to swim, so they jumped into the pool and _____.' See Friedmann (1998) for further details about the procedure). The results in this task were identical to the results in the described completion method which included time adverbs.

3 One structured test of participial agreement is available in Italian. De Bleser and Luzzatti (1994) examined two agrammatics, and found intact participle agreement completion. Unfortunately, subject agreement was not tested in this study.

4 Under the previous theoretical framework, copula in Hebrew is held to be located under INFL (Rothstein, 1995; Rapoport, 1987; and Borer, 1995, for 'a functional node outside VP'). Based on its semantic function, we suggest that the exact node in INFL in which copula resides is the T node.

5 In present tense sentences, we used only sentences in which present tense copula is obligatory (identity and generic sentences).

6 Existing theories for the Hebrew present tense copula describe it as a different entity from the past and future copulas ('pron' in Doron, 1983, 1986; Shlonsky, 1995). The fact that RS made errors in repetition and completion which were substitution of past and future copula for the present copula and vice versa, might indicate that this claim needs reconsideration.

7 Subjects in the repetition sentences were in third person, where pro-drop is illicit in Hebrew.

8 An unresolved question remains as to why the asymmetry is apparent with pronouns, but not with lexical NPs. This problem is similar to that encountered in child language.

9 See Friedmann and Grodzinsky (1997) for further elaboration, and for the definition of degrees of severity within agrammatic Broca's aphasia.

10 Interestingly, these are questions without a finite T.

11 The fact that agrammatic patients succeed in producing yes/no questions might indicate that 'force' (Rizzi, 1997) does not necessarily reside in C, since although they lack the C node, sentence force is still available to them.

12 We remain agnostic as to whether the deficit is in representation or in processing. We are not aware of a way to decide empirically between the two (especially in the absence of a well-articulated syntactic theory of on-line sentence production). But one point is crucial: if it is a processing deficit, this deficit *must* follow very strict syntactic constraints.

13 Another fact which rules out an account of C pruning for tense errors is the existence of a group of less severe agrammatics who show intact tense and copula inflections with impaired embedding and Wh-question formation. This can only be accounted for by describing the tree of this group of mild agrammatics as pruned at C, and the tree of the more severe patients as pruned at T (Friedmann, 1998).

14 This possibility is reminiscent of Chomsky's (1995) proposal, where he dispenses with Agr nodes, but there he suggests that subject agreement is checked in TP, which does not conform with the data presented here.

References

BASTIAANSE, R. and VAN ZONNEVELD, R. 1998. 'On the Relation between Verb Inflection and Verb Position in Dutch Agrammatic Aphasics'. *Brain and Language* **64**, 165–81.

BELLETTI, A. 1990. *Generalized Verb Movement: Aspects of Verb Syntax*. Turin, Rosenberg & Sellier.

BORER, H. 1995. 'The Ups and Downs of Hebrew Verb Movement'. *Natural Language and Linguistic Theory* **13**, 527–606.

BORER, H. and ROHRBACHER, B. To appear. 'Features and Projections: Arguments for the Full Competence Hypothesis'. *Proceedings of the 21st Annual Boston University Conference on Language Development*.

CAPLAN, D. 1985. 'Syntactic and Semantic Structures in Agrammatism'. In M.-L. Kean (ed.), *Agrammatism*, New York, Academic Press.

CHOMSKY, N. 1991. 'Some Notes on Economy of Derivation and Representation'. In R. Freidin (ed.), *Principles and Parameters in Comparative Grammar*. Current Studies in Linguistics Series, **20**, Cambridge MA, MIT Press, 417–54.

CHOMSKY, N. 1993. 'A Minimalist Program for Linguistic Theory'. In K. Hale and J. Keyser (eds), *The View from Building 20*, Cambridge, MA, MIT Press, 1–52.

CHOMSKY, N. 1995. *The Minimalist Program*. Cambridge, MA, MIT Press.
CLAHSEN, H. 1990. 'Constraints on Parameter Setting: A Grammatical Analysis of Some Acquisition Stages in German Child Language'. *Language Acquisition* 1, 361–91.
CLAHSEN, H., PENKE, M. and PARODY, P. 1994. 'Functional Categories in Early Child German'. *Language Acquisition* 3, 395–429.
CRISMA, P. 1992. 'On the Acquisition of Wh-questions in French'. *Geneva Generative Papers* 1–2, 115–22.
DAMASIO, A. R. 1992. Aphasia. *New England Journal Of Medicine* 326, 531–39.
DE BLESER, R. and LUZZATTI, C. 1994. 'Morphological processing in Italian agrammatic speakers syntactic implementation of inflectional morphology'. *Brain and Language* 46, 21–40.
DE ROO, E. 1995. 'Articles and Finite Verb Inflections in Dutch Agrammatism'. Poster presented at RuG-SAN-VKL conference on aphasiology, Groningen.
DEMIRDACHE, H. 1988. 'Nominative NPs in Modern Standard Arabic'. Unpublished ms.
DORON, I. 1983. 'Verbless Predicates in Hebrew'. PhD dissertation, University of Texas at Austin.
DORON, I. 1986. 'The Pronominal Copula as Agreement Clitic'. In *The Syntax of Pronominal Clitics*, H. Borer (ed.), Syntax and Semantics 19, New York, Academic Press, 313–32.
ENÇ, M. 1987. 'Anchoring Conditions for Tense'. *Linguistic Inquiry* 18, 633–57.
FRIEDEMANN, M.-A. 1993–94. 'The Underlying Position of External Arguments in French'. *Language Acquisition* 3, 209–55.
FRIEDMANN, N. 1998. 'Functional Categories in Agrammatic Production: a cross linguistic study'. PhD thesis, Tel-Aviv University.
FRIEDMANN, N. and GRODZINSKY, Y. 1997. 'Tense and Agreement in Agrammatic Production: Pruning the Syntactic Tree'. *Brain and Language* 56, 397–425.
GOODGLASS, H. 1976. 'Agrammatism'. In H. Whitaker and H. A. Whitaker (eds), *Studies in Neurolinguistics (1)*. New York, Academic Press.
GOODGLASS, H., GLEASON, J. B., BERNHOLTZ, N. A. and HYDE, M. R. 1972. 'Some Linguistic Structures in the Speech of Broca's Aphasic'. *Cortex* 8, 191–212.
GRIMSHAW, J. 1991. 'Extended Projection'. Ms, Brandeis.
GRODZINSKY, Y. 1984. 'The Syntactic Characterization of Agrammatism'. *Cognition* 16, 99–120.
GRODZINSKY, Y. 1990. *Theoretical Perspectives on Language Deficits*. Cambridge, MA, MIT Press.
GRODZINSKY, Y., WEXLER, K., CHIEN, Y. C., MARAKOVITZ, S. and SOLOMON, J. 1993. 'The Breakdown of Binding Relations'. *Brain and Language* 45, 396–422.
GUASTI, M. T. 1993. *Causatives and perception verbs*. Turin, Rosenberg & Sellier.
GUASTI, M. T. 1993–94. 'Verb Syntax in Italian Child Grammar: Finite and Nonfinite Verbs'. *Language Acquisition* 3, 1–40.
GUÉRON, J. and HOEKSTRA, T. 1989. 'T-Chains and the Constituent Structure of Auxiliaries'. In A. Cardinaletti, G. Cinque and G. Giusti (eds), *Constituent Structure*, Dordrecht, Foris.
HAGIWARA, H. 1995. 'The Breakdown of Functional Categories and the Economy of Derivation'. *Brain and Language* 50, 92–116.

HYAMS, N. 1992. 'The Genesis of Clausal Structure'. In J. M. Meisel (ed.), *The Acquisition of Verb Placement*, The Netherlands, Kluwer, 371–400.
KEAN, M. L. 1977. 'The Linguistic Interpretation of Aphasic Syndromes'. *Cognition* 5, 9–46.
KOLK, H. and HEESCHEN, C. 1992. 'Agrammatism, Paragrammatism and the Management of Language'. *Language and Cognitive Processes* 7, 89–129.
MENN, L. and OBLER, L. (eds). 1990. *Agrammatic Aphasia: A Cross-language Narrative Sourcebook*. Philadelphia, John Benjamin's Publishing Company.
NESPOULOUS, J.-L., DORDAIN, M., PERRON, C., JAREMA, G. and CHAZAL, M. 1990. 'Agrammatism in French: Two Case Studies'. In L. Menn and L. Obler (eds), *Agrammatic Aphasia: A Cross-language Narrative Sourcebook*. Philadelphia, John Benjamin's Publishing Company.
NESPOULOUS, J.-L., DORDAIN, M., PERRON, C., SKA, B., BUB, D., CAPLAN, D., MEHLER, J. and LECOURS, A. R. 1988. 'Agrammatism in Sentence Production without Comprehension Deficits: Reduced Availability of Syntactic Structures and/or of Grammatical Morphemes? A Case Study'. *Brain and Language* 33, 273–95.
NIEMI, J., LAINE, M., HÄNNINEN, R. and KOIVUSELKÄ-SALLINEN, P. 1990. 'Agrammatism in Finnish: Two Case Studies'. In L. Menn and L. Obler (eds), *Agrammatic Aphasia: A Cross-language Narrative Sourcebook*. Philadelphia, John Benjamin's Publishing Company.
OUHALLA, J. 1993. 'Functional Categories, Agrammatism and Language Acquisition'. *Linguistische Berichte* 143, 3–36.
OUHALLA, J. 1994. 'Verb Movement and Word Order in Arabic'. In N. Hornstein and D. Lightfoot (eds), *Verb Movement*, Cambridge University Press.
PIERCE, A. 1989. 'On the Emergence of Syntax: A Cross-linguistic Study'. Doctoral dissertation, Cambridge, MA, MIT.
POEPPEL, D. and WEXLER, K. 1993. 'The Full Competence Hypothesis'. *Language* 69, 1–33.
POLLOCK, J. Y. 1989. 'Verb Movement, Universal Grammar and the Structure of IP'. *Linguistic Inquiry* 20, 365–424.
POLLOCK, J. Y. 1993. 'Notes on Clause Structure'. Ms., Amiens, Université de Picardie.
RADFORD, A. 1990. *Syntactic Theory and the Acquisition of English Syntax: The Nature of Early Child Grammars of English*. Oxford, Basil Blackwell.
RAPOPORT, T. R. 1987. 'Copular, Nominal and Small Clauses: A Study of Israeli Hebrew'. PhD dissertation, Cambridge, MA, MIT.
RIZZI, L. 1994. 'Some Notes on Linguistic Theory and Language Development: The Case of Root Infinitives'. *Language Acquisition* 3, 371–93.
RIZZI, L. 1997. 'The Fine Structure of the Left Periphery'. In L. Haegeman (ed.), *Elements of Grammar: Handbook in Generative Syntax* (Kluwer International Handbooks of Linguistics, Vol. 1), Dordrecht, Kluwer.
ROTHSTEIN, S. 1995. 'Small Clauses and Copular Constructions'. In A. Cardinaletti and M. T. Guasti (eds), *Syntax and Semantics: Small Clauses*, 28.
SASANUMA, S., KAMIO, A. and KUBOTA, M. 1990. 'Agrammatism in Japanese: Two Case Studies'. In L. Menn and L. Obler (eds), *Agrammatic Aphasia: A Cross-language Narrative Sourcebook*, Philadelphia, John Benjamin's Publishing Company.

SHLONSKY, U. 1995. 'Clause Structure and Word Order in Hebrew'. Ms., Université de Genève.
STOWELL, T. 1982. 'The Tense of Infinitives'. *Linguistic Inquiry* **19**, 561–70.
THOMPSON, C. K. and SHAPIRO, L. P. 1995. 'Training Sentence Production in Agrammatism: Implications for Normal and Disordered Language'. *Brain and Language* **50**, 201–24.
THOMPSON, C. K., SHAPIRO, L. P., TAIT, M. E., JACOBS, B. J. and SCHNEIDER, S. L. 1996. 'Training Wh-question Production in Agrammatic Aphasia: Analysis of Argument and Adjunct Movement'. *Brain and Language* **52**, 175–228.
WEISSENBORN, J. 1992. 'Null Subjects in Early Grammars: Implications for Parameter Setting Theory'. In J. Weissenborn, H. Goodluck and T. Roeper (eds), *Theoretical Issues in Language Acquisition*, Hillsdale, NJ, Lawrence Erlbaum.
WEXLER, K. 1994. 'Optional Infinitives, Head Movement and the Economy of Derivations'. In D. Lightfoot and N. Hornstein (eds), *Verb Movement*, Cambridge University Press.
ZURIF, E. B. 1995. 'Language and the Brain'. In D. Osherson (ed.), *Invitation to Cognitive Science*, 2nd Edition, Cambridge, MA, MIT Press.

Chapter 5

An excursion into interrogatives in Early English and Italian
Maria Teresa Guasti

1 Introduction

The formation of non-subject constituent questions in English requires inversion of the subject and the auxiliary (SAI) and fronting of
a wh-operator, thus creating an adjacency configuration between the
wh-operator and the verb, as illustrated in (1):

(1) a. What does he want?
    b. What has he done?

The requirement of adjacency between the wh-operator and the verb
in (1) has been interpreted by Rizzi (1990) in terms of a well-formedness
constraint on question formation: the wh-criterion which is given in (2)
(see also May, 1985):

(2) *Wh-criterion*
    a. A wh-operator must be in a Spec–head relation with a head
       carrying the wh-feature.
    b. A head carrying the wh-feature must be in a Spec–head rela-
       tion with a wh-operator.

Suppose that the wh-feature is generated as a specification of T. In its
base-generated position, the wh-feature does not satisfy the wh-criterion.
Similarly, the wh-operator being base-generated in the complement
position is not in a Spec–head relation with the wh-feature. Therefore,
in order to enter into the Spec–head configuration required by the wh-
criterion, the wh-operator moves to SpecCP; the wh-feature also needs
to move and be carried to C. Lexical verbs do not move in English and
thus cannot carry the wh-feature to C, but auxiliaries and modal do, as
in (1a). These will move and take the wh-feature to C. If auxiliaries or
modal are not present, the carrier will be the pleonastic verb *do*, as in
(1b). The results of these two movements, that of the wh-operator and

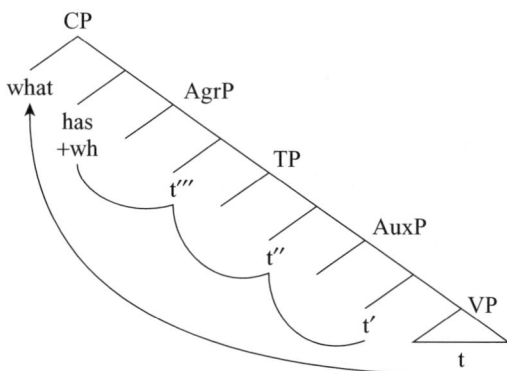

FIGURE 5.1

that of the wh-feature specified on a head, give us the surface structure given Figure 5.1.

Unlike its target language, Early English (EE) seems to deviate from the pattern in (1) in several ways. One way concerns the raising of the wh-feature to C, which results in the inversion of the auxiliary and the subject. Perhaps one of the most influential study of EE interrogatives is Bellugi's (1971). She argued, based on the natural production of Adam, Eve and Sarah (Brown, 1973), that children pass through three stages before they achieve the adult grammar for question formation. These stages are schematized in (3).

> (3) *Stages of the acquisition of SAI*
>   a. Failure to perform SAI
>   b. SAI is performed in yes/no-questions, but not in wh-questions
>   c. SAI is performed both in positive yes/no- and wh-questions, but not in the negative ones

In the last twenty-five years, many scholars have examined EE interrogatives and found evidence in favor of or against Bellugi's alleged stages. A wide discussion of these studies, along with several new results and conclusions, is found in Stromswold (1990). For a discussion related to the third stage, the reader can refer to Guasti, Thornton and Wexler (1995).

Bellugi's stages are concerned with questions including an auxiliary or a modal or *do*. Another way in which children's questions deviate from the adult pattern is represented by questions lacking an auxiliary, as in *What you cleaning?* These display the order Wh-S-V (Bellugi, 1971; Brown, 1968; Guasti and Rizzi, 1996; Stromswold, 1990).

In this chapter, we will focus on two issues of children's deviant questions. First, based on an investigation of wh-questions, we will establish whether the wh-criterion is part and parcel of the EE grammar from the initial production. In this context, beside data from EE, we will consider data from Early Italian and point out the relevance of the cross-linguistic perspective in studies of language development. This dimension will shed new light on the nature of properties or mechanisms that may be problematic for children. Next, we will carry out an examination of children's aux-less questions. This chapter does not examine Bellugi's stages, except for issues concerned with the first one.

2 Method

2.1 Subjects

The data examined come from the transcripts of 4 English-speaking children – Adam, Eve and Sarah (Brown, 1973) and Nina (Suppes, 1973) – and of 5 Italian-speaking children – Martina, Diana, Guglielmo, Viola and Raffaello (Cipriani *et al.*, 1989, from the Istituto Stella Maris of Calambrone, Pisa) – included in the CHILDES database (version 1994; MacWhinney and Snow, 1985). The age of the children studied, their MLU and the files examined are reported in Table 5.1.

2.2 Corpora

The Combo utility (MacWhinney, 1990) was used to search the transcripts and cull all the lines containing a wh-word or an interrogation mark. The search using an interrogation mark was carried out as a control, because children may have modified the wh-word. For example, Italian *dove* (where) sometimes is spelled out as *ove*. When searching for specific words, it is important to search for all their variants. Irrelevant

TABLE 5.1   Data examined

Child	Age	MLU	Files
Adam	2;3–4;3;2	2;1–4;9	45
Eve	1;6–2;3	1;9–2;7	20
Sarah	2;3–5;1	1;7–3;2	139
Nina	1;11–3;3	1;8–3;2	56
Diana	1;8–2;6	2;6–4;7	10
Martina*	1;8–2;7	1;3–2;5	14
Guglielmo	2;2–2;11	2;6–5;0	9
Raffaello	1;7–2;11	1;2–2;9	17
Viola	1;11–2;10	1;6–1;8	10

* Martina produced her first scorable question at MIR04.
MLU is calculated based on words.

sequences were discarded by hand. These include: embedded questions, matrix questions with a contracted auxiliary, which, at least initially, could involve unanalyzed units as pointed out in Brown (1973), routines, unclear and repetitive questions. Possible (partial) imitations of adult sentences were not discarded.

3 The wh-criterion in English child grammar

3.1 The specifier component: wh-movement or wh-in-situ?

As seen in (2), the wh-criterion includes two clauses, which are two sides of the same coin. However, one is concerned with the wh-operator, the specifier component, and the other with the head carrying the wh-feature. The operativity of this criterion predicts that children produce adult questions of the type in (1). Its non-operativity predicts that children produce questions with wh-in-situ and/or a non-inverted aux. Three possible non-adult structures could be expected:

(4) a. John has washed what? (wh-in-situ and non-inverted aux)
    b. Has John washed what? (wh-in-situ and inverted aux)
    c. What John has washed? (wh movement and non-inverted aux)

In this section, we focus on the status of the specifier component of the wh-criterion in EE. The question we will address is: do children produce questions like (4a) and (4b) at any stage of linguistic development? We will postpone the discussion of (4c) to 3.2.3.

An examination of the transcripts of Adam, Eve, Nina and Sarah was carried out. Overall these four children asked 2809 questions, 41 of which had a wh-in-situ, i.e. 1%. From context, most or perhaps all of the in-situ questions are echo questions. In addition, with the exception of 5 examples, all the in-situ questions do not contain an auxiliary. Finally, the 41 examples of wh-in-situ are not concentrated in the earliest files, but scattered throughout the period investigated. Some examples of wh-in-situ questions are given below:

(5) eating what (Eve 1;8)
    gone where (Adam 2;8)
    they are for who? (Adam 3;2,21)
    can I try # (# = pause) which way? (Sarah 4;1,4)

From these data, it clearly emerges that wh-in-situ is not an option entertained by English-speaking children, i.e. neither (4a) nor (4b) are productively used by children. Wh-in-situ is not problematic per se, since French children do produce questions featuring wh-in-situ, an option that is available in the adult grammar (see Hamann, this volume). Then, we can safely conclude that syntactic wh-movement is operative as soon as the children produce their first questions.

TABLE 5.2   Frequency of questions by type of structure

Children	+SAI	−SAI	Wh S V	Wh S V-ing	Wh S Vfin
Adam	816	64	469	268	207
Eve	58	2	42	44	3
Sarah	250	15	127	23	26
Nina	316	4	14	19	1

3.2 Non-adult questions
In this section, we investigate the head component of the wh-criterion in child grammar.

3.2.1 The data
Table 5.2 summarizes the frequency of the various types of questions produced by the four children.[1] It contains only positive non-subject wh-questions with an overt subject (for an investigation of subject questions see Guasti and Rizzi (1996)).

The first two columns include questions containing an auxiliary: in the first the auxiliary is inverted (+SAI) and in the second it is non-inverted (−SAI). The last three columns include wh-questions lacking an auxiliary (aux-less questions) and having the main verb in the bare form (Wh S V), e.g., *What he/you like?*, in a form inflected for -ing (Wh S V-ing), e.g., *What he/you doing?* and in a form inflected for tense or agreement (Wh S Vfin), e.g., *What he likes/liked?* or *What you liked?* (see section 6).

These data show that children make extensive use of non-adult structures represented by the last four columns of Table 5.2. Overall, we have 48% of non-adult questions. At first glance it could appear that the head component of the wh-criterion is not operative: SAI is not performed (second column) or is not visible (last three columns).

3.2.2 Commission and omission errors
It is worth noticing that Table 5.2 reports two different types of errors. Failure of SAI, in the second column, represents an error of commission: the child fails to place the auxiliary in the appropriate position, before the subject. Questions with a main inflected verb represent an error of commission too: the child inflects the lexical verb, while inflection should have been carried by an auxiliary; the third and fourth columns represent errors of omission: the auxiliary is omitted.[2] As noted by Stromswold (1996), these two types of errors need to be evaluated differently. A significant number of errors of commission may be evidence that the child and the adult grammar are different in some respects.

TABLE 5.3   Children's inversion rate in non-subject positive
wh-questions (%)

	Adam	Eve	Sarah	Nina
+SAI	93	96.6	94.3	98.7
	(88.3)	(96.5)	92.9	(98.5)
−SAI	7	3.3	5.6	1.2

Errors of omission are potentially compatible with the view that the child and the adult grammar are the same. The omission may be due to performance limitations or to the unavailability in the child lexicon of a particular lexical item.

3.2.3   The head component: when is SAI performed?
A superficial impression that one gets from an examination of Table 5.2 is that children experience, in one way or another, some difficulties with the head component of the wh-criterion. Recall that the head component of the wh-criterion requires overt movement of the wh-feature to C, resulting in the inversion of the subject and the auxiliary (SAI). Since lexical verbs do not move in English, raising of the wh-feature is ensured by auxiliaries or *do*. Our concern is whether children abide by the requirement of the head component of the wh-criterion: do they invert auxiliaries? To investigate this issue, we need to rely only on informative questions: these include only those questions containing an auxiliary. Aux-less questions are not relevant, because no auxiliary is present. Later, we will see how the wh-criterion is satisfied in these questions. Table 5.3 reports the individual rate of inversion for the four children examined (these are calculated on the basis of the first two columns of Table 5.2). The results presented here comport with those found by Stromswold, which are put in parentheses in Table 5.3. This author investigated the spontaneous production of 12 children (CHILDES, MacWhinney and Snow, 1985), among which are the four children examined in this study. She found that the overall inversion rate in positive questions (containing an auxiliary) is 93.4%, with individual rates ranging from 54% (Nathan) to 98%, with a median inversion rate of 95% (see Stromswold's Table 5.5).[3,4]

In the vast majority of the cases, above 90%, the auxiliary is correctly placed before the subject (see also Pinker, 1984). Sequences in which the auxiliary is not moved are (relatively) rare. Moreover, they are not concentrated in the earliest files, as we will see later (Figures 5.5 and 5.6). These findings suggest that also the head component of the wh-criterion is part and parcel of the EE grammar: children know that the wh-feature generated in T must be raised to C by an auxiliary. In section 3.1, we conjectured that children might be expected to produce questions like (4c), if they do not know the wh-criterion. Our investigation shows that (4c) is not a common structure in children's production. We should keep in mind that children's performance of SAI is not perfect, however. Later, we will examine the errors and provide an interpretation for them.

3.3 Summary

The wh-criterion is responsible for movement of the wh-operator to SpecCP and of I to C. These two movements ensure the establishment of a Spec–head configuration between the wh-operator and the head endowed with the wh-feature. If the wh-criterion were not operative in the EE grammar, we should have found questions with wh-in-situ and/or non-inverted auxiliaries. Wh-in-situ is never an option in the EE grammar. Despite the presence of many non-adult structures in the speech of children, an examination of questions including an auxiliary, which are the only ones relevant for our point, has revealed that children do not initially fail to perform SAI. In this respect, as pointed out by Stromswold (1990), we can conclude that there is no evidence for the first of Bellugi's stages, namely one in which SAI or the head component of the wh-criterion is missing from children's grammar.

4 The wh-criterion in Italian child grammar

The conclusion that children respect the requirements imposed by the wh-criterion or by its equivalent counterpart in other frameworks is further supported by an investigation of Early Italian (EI) interrogatives.

4.1 The structure of Italian interrogatives

In Italian interrogatives, the wh-operator is fronted to an initial position. Moreover, adjacency between wh-operator and the verb is required, as in the English examples in (1). Thus, questions like those in (6a) are not grammatical. Inversion of the subject and the auxiliary does not produce a well-formed question either, as seen in (6b). Adjacency is obtained by placing the lexical subject in a sentence-initial or sentence-final position, as in (6c) (see Guasti, 1996) or by not expressing the subject, as in (6d):

(6) a. *Cosa Gianni ha fatto?
        What Gianni has done?
    b. *Cosa ha Gianni fatto?
        What has Gianni done?

c. (Gianni) Cosa ha fatto (Gianni)?
    (Gianni) What has done (Gianni)?
    'What has Gianni done?'
d. Cosa ha fatto?
    'What has (he) done?'

Rizzi (1990) interprets the requirement of adjacency between the wh-operator and the verb as a manifestation of the wh-criterion as it is for English: the verb carrying the wh-feature and the wh-operator move to the CP to enter in a Spec–head configuration. Thus, (6a) violates the wh-criterion because the wh-feature has not been raised to C. To explain the unavailability in Italian, but not in English, of the order Wh Aux Subject ((1 vs. (6b)), Rizzi assumes that the Italian verb in C does not have the option of assigning case under government to the subject in SpecIP, whereas it can do so in English. Since the subject cannot stay in SpecIP, the adjacency between the wh-operator and the verb carrying the wh-feature must be obtained by exploiting other grammatical options offered by the Italian grammar. Italian is a pro-drop language; this opens the possibility of forming questions with a null subject (see (6d)), which unlike an overt subject can stay in SpecIP.[5] Another related possibility consists in placing the overt subject in a sentence-final or sentence-initial position (see (6c)) and leaving in SpecIP a null subject (possibly an expletive), connected to the overt one.

4.2 Early Italian questions

4.2.1 The specifier component
In this section, we are going to investigate EI questions. The investigation is based on the transcripts of 5 Italian-speaking children. As a group, the 5 children produced 296 spontaneous positive questions, all having a fronted wh-operator. As in EE, wh-in-situ is not an option in EI.[6] So, the specifier component of the wh-criterion is part of the EI grammar.

4.2.2 The head component
We shall now deal with the head component. Among the 296 questions, 166 have a null subject, an option admitted in the adult grammar, and 130, i.e. 43.9%, have an overt subject. Only the latter group of sentences is relevant to establish whether the child respects the adjacency between the wh-operator and the verb expressed by the wh-criterion. Null-subject questions are not informative because one cannot see where the null subject is placed. The analysis of the 130 informative questions reveals that in all but 5 questions, the subject is placed in peripheral positions. Just 5 examples had the order Wh S V and all these were

examples headed by the wh-operator *perchè* (why), which admits this order even in the adult grammar. Thus, even these questions are not ungrammatical. Natural production data show that Italian-speaking children never place the subject between the wh-element and the verb, producing ungrammatical structures such as those in (6a). This conclusion is further reinforced by the results of an elicited production experiment carried out by Guasti (1996). In this experiment, positive and negative questions were evoked from Italian-speaking children aged between 3;1 and 4;8. Overall, children produced 86 positive and 113 negative questions for a total of 199 questions. Thirthy-eight of these questions had an overt subject, which was always placed in a sentence-final or sentence-initial position. The order Wh S V was displayed only by 6 questions introduced by the question word *perchè*, as was the case for the spontaneous production. On the basis of these data, we can confidently conclude that the Italian-speaking children also conform to the requirement of the head component of the wh-criterion from their earliest questions.

5 The relevance of cross-linguistic language acquisition studies

The investigation of EI and EE questions has revealed that the wh-operator is invariably fronted in both languages and the verb is adjacent to the wh-operator. Thus, the basic ingredients of question formation are in the grammar of children from the first multi-word utterances. This may not be an accident, but is likely to be the result of an early sensitivity to a language-specific choice. Whether a language requires overt wh-movement or admits wh-in-situ (as in Chinese or Japanese) is subject to parametric variation. The data examined show that our children have operated the correct parametric choice from the onset of syntactic production. Nevertheless, we should not forget that English-speaking children experience some difficulties in forming questions, as proven by the high number of non-adult questions in Table 5.2. Given the results obtained so far, both for EE and for EI, the difficulties cannot hinge on the wh-criterion per se. If this were the case, we should have found non-adult questions in EI, as well. In this respect, the comparative dimension is crucial, because it restricts the space of hypotheses to be evaluated: if some piece of universal knowledge is defective, it should affect all early languages, but this does not appear to be the case here. Since the wh-criterion is operative in EE, we must find the source of aux-less questions and of questions violating SAI in EE in some specific property of the English grammar. This will be the topic of the following sections. We will start with the investigation of aux-less questions and later examine the violations of SAI.

6 Aux-less questions

In EE questions, the auxiliary is frequently omitted, as shown by the
last three columns of Table 5.2. Aux-less questions take three forms in
children speech, as illustrated in (7):

(7) a. What John cleaning?
    b. What John clean?
    c. What John cleans/cleaned?

In (7a) the verb is inflected for -ing, in (7b) it is a bare verbal root and
in (7c) the verb is inflected for agreement or tense. Notice that aux-less
questions are attested along with adult-like questions in which SAI has
applied. As we noticed in section 3.2.2, aux-less questions of the type
in (7a) and (7b) are the expression of an omission error (see note 2 for
some details). The child is not providing an overt expression of inflection, as would be required in the adult grammar. Instead, the aux-less
question in (7c), with a main inflected verb, represents an error of
commission. This time the child is expressing inflection, but not in the
way an adult would express the inflection in questions: in the adult
grammar *do* would have been used and it would carry the inflection.
The evaluation of these two types of errors may be different. Earlier we
established that the child grammar includes the ingredients for question
formation: wh-movement is acquired and so is SAI. In the face of this,
the following questions arise: How is the wh-criterion satisfied in aux-less
questions? What is the source of these questions? In keeping with our
conclusions so far, in the next section, we will examine a hypothesis
according to which aux-less questions conform to the requirements
of the wh-criterion: the wh-feature is carried from Agr/T to C by an
auxiliary, but, unlike in the adult grammar, this auxiliary is null.

6.1 The null auxiliary hypothesis

Let us first consider aux-less questions with a verb inflected for -ing.
We have been assuming that the landing site for wh-movement is
SpecCP. We know that the wh-criterion requires that the wh-feature be
in C. How is this criterion satisfied in aux-less questions? In line with
the conclusion that the wh-criterion is respected in the English child
grammar, a rather natural proposal is that in the structure in (7a) there is
a null auxiliary *be*, the counterpart of lexical *be*. This null element, like
its overt counterpart, is generated under an Aux projection and moves
in the overt syntax through T (and Agr), thus carrying the wh-feature
from Agr/T to C (see Guasti and Rizzi, 1996; Stromswold, 1990). The
structure with a null and an overt aux is reported in (8):[7]

(8) [$_{CP}$ What [$_C$ o/is] [John ... [$_{AgrP}$ t [$_{TP}$ t [$_{AuxP}$ t [cleaning]]]]]]?

According to this proposal, the adult and the EE grammar for questions differ minimally: whereas in the adult grammar (of standard English) aux is always overt, in the child grammar it may optionally be null. This hypothesis can be extended very naturally to questions containing a bare verbal form, as in (7b), repeated below:

(7b) What John clean?

As in the case of questions with a verb inflected for -ing, in these questions a null auxiliary is likely to be present. This auxiliary is a null *do*, which, like the null *be*, carries the wh-feature from T to C.[8]

This proposal treats in a uniform way all children's questions, except for the aux-less questions with an inflected verb, for which a separate treatment will be justified later; despite surface differences, questions with an overt auxiliary and aux-less questions are the product of the same underlying mechanism: the wh-criterion. It minimizes the divergence between the child and the adult grammars, since this is reduced to the fact that the former includes a null aux while the latter does not. These two aspects make the present analysis preferable to any other analysis that may have to appeal to different mechanisms for question formation. As usual, in the scientific enterprise, *entia non sunt multiplicanda praeter necessitatem*.

6.2 A root null auxiliary

In aux-less questions including a non-finite verb (V-ing and bare verbal forms), a null aux is present to satisfy the wh-criterion. Since the null aux does not exist in the standard grammar of adult English, we need to explain why. Guasti and Rizzi (1996), exploiting the root character of the null *be*, draw a parallel between the null aux and the early null subject.[9] Rizzi (1994) argues that early null subjects as well as null subjects belonging to the diary style (see Haegeman, 1990, this volume) are possible in the specifier of the root. This position is the highest position of the clause, and elements hosted there are not subject to the principle of identification. This principle requires that empty categories be identified through chain-connection to an antecedent. But this principle is not enforced for the specifier of the root due to the lack of a potential identifier for this position. Extending this approach to questions amounts to saying that a null aux is possible in a structure, provided that it is located in the head of the root. In main sentences, the head of the root is C; so a null aux is allowed provided that it raises to C, as is the case in questions. As it stands, this proposal is too permissive. It predicts that the null aux may occur in all varieties and registers of adult English, since it would always be in the head of the root. While some varieties and registers (see Akmajian *et al.*, 1984; Labov, 1995) allow this option, others do not.

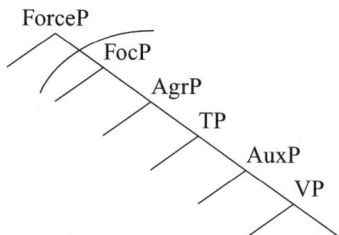

FIGURE 5.2

To fully develop the hypothesis of the null aux, we need to examine the internal structure of the CP system. Rizzi (1997) has proposed that the CP system is layered: ForceP is the highest projection, which determines the clausal type; it dominates a FocP (focus phrase) whose specifier is the landing site for wh-movement and whose head hosts inverted auxiliaries (FocP corresponds to what we have been calling CP until now). Thus, adult questions require the projection of ForceP beyond that of FocP, the latter to host wh-movement and the former to determine the type of the clause, question in the present case. We can now return to children's aux-less questions and see how they arise in this framework. Some telegraphic aspects of early production, such as the omission of subjects and root infinitives (see Rizzi, this volume), have been attributed to the availability in child grammar of the truncation process (Rizzi, 1994). Child grammar allows the production of reduced clausal structures; rather than projecting the full CP, the child can truncate at different levels below the ForceP, e.g. at the IP or at the VP level. Truncating at a certain level, for example at the VP level, implies that no phrase dominating the VP in the clausal architecture will be projected and the truncated phrase becomes the root of the clause. Clausal truncation accounts for the root character of early subject omission and of root infinitives: they are only allowed in the Spec and in the head of the root, respectively. In the spirit of the truncation hypothesis, one may suppose that children can truncate the CP system under ForceP and take just the portion under FocP, as shown in Figure 5.2.

In this way, children would have enough of the C system to accommodate the wh-operator and invert the null aux, which could then be the head of the root. In the head of the root, auxiliaries could be null, since the principle of clause-internal identification is not enforced, because there is no other head higher than Foc. In the adult system, ForceP is the necessary end point of syntactic representations and thus must always be projected: the null aux in Foc will never be the head of the root, since ForceP dominates it.[10] Thus, a null aux in Foc will be submitted to the usual requirement of clause-internal identification and turn out to be illegitimate, since it cannot be connected to an antecedent.

6.3 Predictions of the null aux hypothesis

The null aux is legitimate only in the head of the root. This view leads us to expect that a null aux will not be allowed in contexts in which I to C does not apply; this is because in this case the null aux would not stay in the head of the root and hence would not be able to escape the principle of identification holding for empty categories. One such context is subject questions. According to Rizzi (1990), in subject questions, there is no movement of the auxiliary to C, probably because of the ECP. Evidence for this claim is the fact that in subject questions, unlike in non-subject questions, *do* support is not possible, except when it is emphatic:

(9)   Who speaks Greek?

(10) *Who does speak Greek?

Under the proposal advanced here, we do not expect to find a null aux in subject questions. Guasti and Rizzi investigate this issue with respect to the null *be*. Let us discuss their proposal. We have seen that non-subject aux-less questions with a V inflected for -*ing* include a null aux *be*, which raises to C. Since the auxiliary does not raise to C in subject questions, we do not expect to find subject questions including a verb inflected for -*ing*, e.g. *who speaking?* In fact, the V-*ing* form was rarely used in subject questions. Overall, Guasti and Rizzi report that it represents the 2% of Adam, Sarah and Eve's subject questions, in striking contrast with what they found in non-subject questions: the 3 children mentioned produced 16% non-subject questions with a V-*ing* form.[11] This sharp asymmetry is expected if I raises to C and carries the null aux in the head of the root only in non-subject questions. Hence, the limited distribution of V-*ing* form supports the analysis of aux-less questions as involving a null auxiliary.[12]

We have seen that the null auxiliary may occur with V-*ing* forms or with bare forms (7b). In subject questions, V-*ing* forms are rare; this is expected under the view that in these questions the null auxiliary is not legitimate, since it cannot rise in the head of the root. By parity of reasoning, we expect subject questions with bare verbal forms not to be attested: the null auxiliary is not legitimate there. In other words, while (7b) is legitimate, the subject question *Who clean that?* should not be allowed even in child grammar, under the approach elaborated up to now. However, Guasti and Rizzi found that overall 41% of the 3 children's subject questions were with bare verbal forms. The remaining 56% is represented by subject questions with inflected verbs. (2% were questions with verbs ending in -ing, e.g., 'who singing') How can we explain the high rate of bare forms in subject questions? One possibility is to say that in these questions the bare form is not bare, despite appearances, but is a finite form with a morphological error. Evidence

that English-speaking children make morphological errors comes from
Guasti and Rizzi's study (1998) on *do* support. These authors found
that for a certain period (up to 3/3;6 years), English-speaking children
provide *do* in negative sentences with third person subjects, but do not
correctly inflect it, i.e. they produce sentences such as (11):

(11) he don't have a bug (Adam28)
      he don't talk (Sarah58)
      he don't use (Nina12)

In these sentences, *does* should have been employed, instead of a bare
do. We can analyze the form in (11) as a finite form (the auxiliary *do*
can never be non-finite) with a morphological error; rather than the
morpheme -*s*, it is inflected with a null morpheme (see Halle and Marantz
(1994) for a discussion of null morphemes). We may extend this analysis
to subject questions and say that even there the bare verb is not bare, but
is a finite form, as *do* in (11), with a zero suffix.[13]

7 A third structure: aux-less questions with an inflected verb

In section 6, we noticed that aux-less questions with inflected verbs
are instances of commission errors: the child is placing inflection on
the wrong verbal item. Commission errors need to be evaluated differently from omission errors. For this reason, and other reasons that will
become clear in the course of the exposition, we will discuss aux-less
questions with an inflected main verb separately from the other two
types of aux-less questions.

7.1 Some considerations
A third variety of aux-less questions has the lexical verb inflected for
tense or agreement:

(12) What John cleaned/cleans?

While the verbal form with the -*s* morpheme is unambiguous, the one
with the -*ed* morpheme is potentially ambiguous: it can be a simple past
or a past particle, as pointed out in Stromswold (1990). For this reason,
we will base our analysis only on questions with verbs inflected with
the -*s* morpheme.

Aux-less questions of the type in (12) are peculiar in several ways.
First, they do not seem to be used by all children: Eve and Nina almost
never employ them. Second, they display a developmental trend different from the one of aux-less questions including non-finite forms.
To better understand aux-less questions with inflected verbs, we can

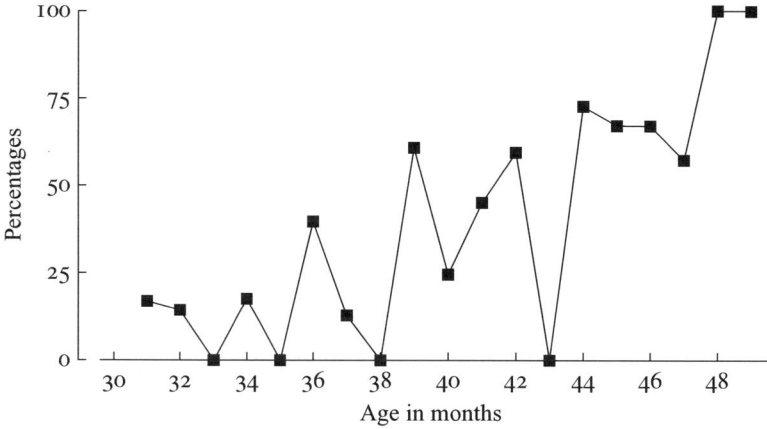

FIGURE 5.3   Adam's verb + -s in questions

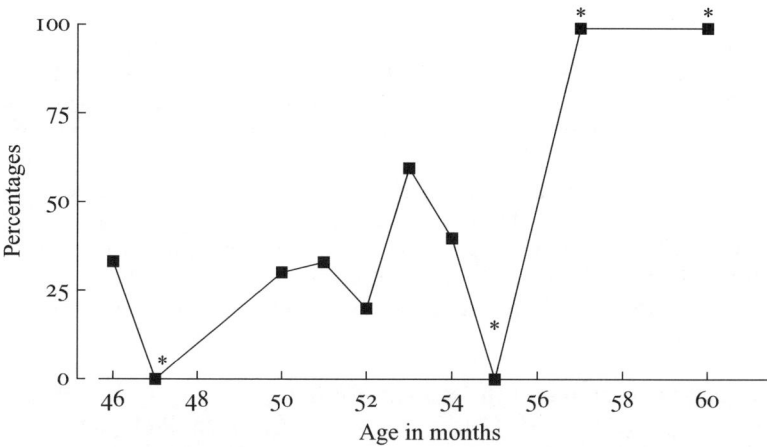

* 1 example

FIGURE 5.4   Sarah's verb + -s in questions

compare them with aux-less questions with bare verbs. Figures 5.3 and
5.4 depict the developmental curve of aux-less questions with a verb
inflected with the -s morpheme. To calculate these percentages, we
have used as the denominator the number of verbs inflected with -s plus
the number of bare forms occurring with third person subjects. The
reason for this choice is that bare verbs occurring with non-third person
subjects may be either bare forms or forms with a zero morpheme, as is
presumably the case in adult grammar (see note 2). The Y-axis reports

the percentage of questions with a verb inflected with the -*s* morpheme and the X-axis reports the age.

From these graphs, it appears that aux-less questions with inflected verbs tend to increase with age and consequently aux-less questions with bare forms tend to decrease (see also Stromswold, 1990). In addition, while aux-less questions with non-finite verbs are present from the first transcripts, aux-less questions with a verb inflected with the -*s* morpheme start to appear at 3;10 for Sarah and 2;7 for Adam. Thus, aux-less questions do not all observe the same trend: those with inflected verbs are set apart from the other two types of aux-less questions including non-finite verbs and need to be treated separately. For this reason and for theoretical reasons, a direct extension of the null *do* hypothesis to this case is not desirable. Let us spell out the reasoning. If we inserted a null aux under the AuxP, this would have to rise in the overt component through T/Agr to C. In this way, it would check its tense and agreement features. But the main verb is inflected and it will also need to check its tense/agreement features in the covert component of the grammar, as is generally the case in English. This entails that the lexical verb will have to move covertly to the TP/AgrP projection. But T/Agr has already checked the features of the auxiliary and would be unable to check the features of the lexical verb, which would remain unchecked. Then, an ill-formed structure would ensue. If we want to accommodate the morphosyntactic properties of the inflected verb, we cannot include a null auxiliary in the same structure: a lexical inflected verb and a null aux both need to check their features against the same Agr/T.

The hypothesis of a null aux is not viable for aux-less questions with inflected verbs. Then, we must explore some other hypothesis. From our perspective, the question is how the wh-criterion is satisfied in this type of structure.

7.2 Base generation of the wh-feature in C
In some languages, such as Hebrew and Brazilian Portuguese, the wh-feature is generated directly in C (see Rizzi, 1990). To satisfy the wh-criterion, only the wh-operator must move to SpecCP; there is no need for the verb to raise to C, since the wh-feature is already in the relevant position. Thus, in these languages, adjacency between the wh-operator and the verb is not required and the order Wh S V is grammatical, as shown by the example in (13) from Hebrew:

(13) Ma Jean 'axal?
     What Jean ate?

It could be that English speaking children entertain, for a while, the hypothesis that in their grammar, base generation of the wh-feature in C is permitted, along with the possibility of generating the same feature in the IP and carrying it to C through movement. This option would allow them to produce aux-less questions with an inflected verb: the verb checks its features in T/Agr. The wh-criterion is satisfied in the CP between the wh- operator and the base-generated wh-feature.[14] This hypothesis predicts that, along with aux-less questions with an inflected verb, children should produce questions including an auxiliary in a non-inverted position, at least occasionally, as exemplified in (14):

(14) What John has read?

In these questions, the wh-feature is generated in C and the auxiliary does not need to rise to C. Another prediction concerns *do*. Since this auxiliary is inserted just to raise the wh-feature to C, we expect that whenever *do* is lexically spelled out, it will be in the inverted position, i.e. questions like (15) are not expected to be found in children's speech:

(15) What John does read?

In the next section, we are going to investigate these predictions.

7.3 Testing the predictions: failure of SAI
Figures 5.5 and 5.6 depict the developmental curve of inversion for Adam and Sarah. The analysis is limited to these two children because they were the ones who produced a relatively high number of inflected main verbs in questions. The graphs show that these children experience a dip in the inversion rate after a period of near-perfect performance. Stromswold reports that other children manifest the same behavior. Thus, the dip seems a characteristic of English acquisition of

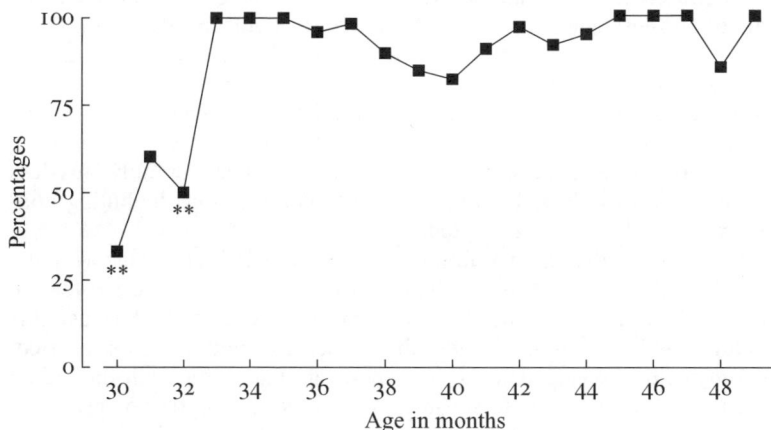

** 2 examples

FIGURE 5.5   Adam's development of SAI

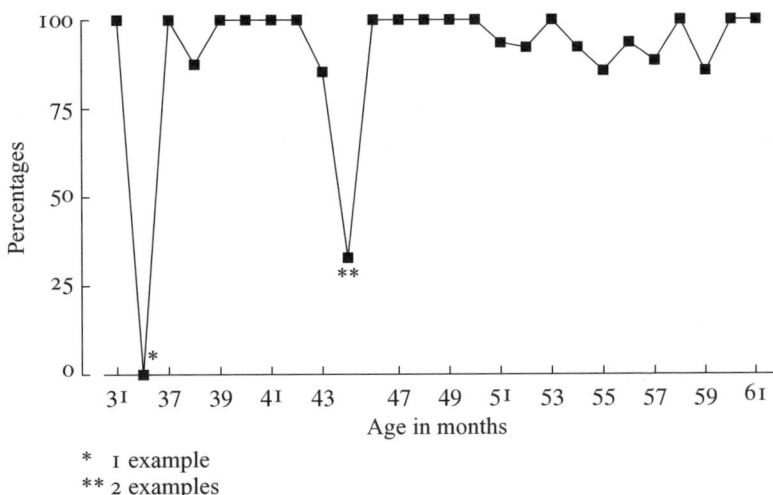

* 1 example
** 2 examples

FIGURE 5.6   Sarah's development of SAI

SAI. Notice also that, especially after the dip, the trend of the curve is irregular: inversion is not performed in 100% of the cases and its rate varies depending on the file.

Aux-less questions with an inflected verb and questions with a non-inverted auxiliary are phenomena that show up in advanced stages of development, although their trend is completely similar.[15] We interpret failure of SAI as another manifestation of the fact that English-speaking children form questions with the wh-feature generated in C. The rate of aux-less questions with inflected verbs tends to steadily increase, while the rate of questions violating SAI is rather irregular. This difference between the two phenomena may depend on the fact that their ultimate source is not the same, although the escape hatch to satisfy the wh-criterion is the same (i.e. base generation of the wh-feature in C). All in all, these data show that children produce not only aux-less questions with inflected main verbs, but also questions including non-inverted auxiliaries, as expected.

We also predicted that failure of SAI should not occur with the auxiliary *do*, because this verb is employed just to raise the wh-feature to C. When there is no need to raise the wh-feature to C, because this feature has been base-generated there, then *do* should not be inserted. Stromswold observes that the inversion rate varies for each individual auxiliary (see Stromswold's Tables 5.7 and 5.8). The rate of inversion for *do* is the highest, among the auxiliaries. Taking the different forms of the auxiliary together, she found that the 14 children she examined invert *be* 87.9% of the time, *do* 98.7% of the time, *have* 90.9% and modals 91.8% of the time. These data confirm our prediction that whenever *do* is used, it is raised to C. They also reveal that with auxiliaries other than *do*, inversion errors are found, in agreement with our previous expectation. To recap: in our view, these errors stem from the fact that the child conjectures, for some reason or another yet to be identified, that the wh-feature can be generated in C in EE.

At this point one may wonder whether the hypothesis of base generation of the wh-feature in C is manifested in other early languages whose adult target does not have this option. Let us see what we should expect to find in EI, if this hypothesis were to hold. Under our approach, a manifestation of the wh-feature in C in EI would be represented by questions with the order Wh S V. Under this view, we should expect to find questions such as (16):

(16) *Cosa Gianni vuole?
       What Gianni wants?

As in Hebrew (see example (13)), this order should surface if the wh-feature was generated in C, as we have seen in section 7.2. However, questions of this kind are not found in EI, as discussed in section 4.2.2. Why do English-speaking children entertain the hypothesis of base generation of the wh-feature in C, while their Italian peers do not? If base generation of the wh-feature in C was enforced by the logic of acquisition of the wh-criterion or by some inherent difficulty of this criterion, such an asymmetry between early languages should have no reason to exist. The discrepancy between EI and EE leads us to conjecture that base generation of the wh-feature in C is a by-product of some properties of the English grammar that interact with the wh-criterion. A formal account of these facts will take us too far away. Nevertheless, we will indicate some lines of investigation for future research. A likely candidate responsible for English non-adult questions are the morphosyntactic properties of verb movement and, related to these, the syntax of *do* support (Stromswold, 1990). Under this view, when children have no means of raising the wh-feature to C, they are forced to search in UG for a mechanism to satisfy the wh-criterion: base generation of the wh-feature in C is such a mechanism. This view may explain why in EI non-adult questions of the type in (16) are not found. Given the comparative approach developed so far, the contrast must depend on the different morphosyntactic properties of verbs, as originally proposed by Guasti (1996). Italian verbs all raise and there is neither a special class of auxiliary nor a dummy verb such as *do*. From very early, verb raising is performed by Italian-speaking children (Guasti, 1993/4) and no difference is found in the treatment of verbs. Hence, children perform verb raising to check the features inherent to the verb, tense and agreement, but also to carry features in appropriate configurations, as is the case for the wh-feature in questions, and no adult questions are expected.

8 Conclusion

In this chapter, we have seen that children satisfy the well-formedness requirements on question formation from their first productions. EI displays this very clearly. The data are more complex in the case of EE, however. A careful investigation, combined with an evaluation of the data from a cross-linguistic perspective, has revealed first that English-speaking children comply with the requirement on question formation from very early, as their Italian peers. English-speaking children produce some non-adult questions, however. One type of questions, which shows up from the earliest productions, is aux-less questions with bare verbal forms. These involve a null auxiliary in the Spec of the root and arise from the option of truncating structures. Another type is aux-less questions with inflected verbs and questions with non-inverted auxiliaries. Both types show up in later stages of development and are likely the product of the intricate morphosyntactic properties of English verbs. These properties interact with the wh-criterion and give us the impression that it is the criterion that creates problems for children, whereas it is some other factors on which the criterion is parasitic.

Notes

1 Adam (up to file 34), Eve and Sarah's data are taken from Guasti and Rizzi (1996).
2 This description may not be totally accurate. While in questions of the type in (i) the verb is a bare form and in (ii) it is a finite form, in questions of the type in (iii), which are included in the fourth column, together with the question in (i), the verb is ambiguous: it can be either a bare form on a par with (i) or a finite form with a null agreement marker on a par with (ii). Unfortunately, it is impossible to distinguish the two forms. Thus, the figures in the fourth column are somewhat inflated. This point will be taken into account in 7.1.

   (i)   What he like?
   (ii) What he likes?
   (iii) What you like?

3 Sometimes the results of an investigation vary from study to study, although the same transcripts have been examined. This may be attributed to different criteria used, to a subjective evaluation of some data, a source of difference which is not easy to avoid, or to the use of different version of the CHILDES database. For this reason, it is important to state the criteria of classification clearly.
4 In the present study, we will not examine yes/no-questions. However, it suffices to know that the overall rate of inversion for these questions is 93.7%, according to Stromswold.
5 We must assume that a null subject in SpecIP, unlike an overt one, may receive case, perhaps by incorporation.

6 There were a few negative questions that I did not include in the count to be coherent with the choice I made for English. In any case, even these questions were adult in form. In addition, questions like (i) and (ii) were not counted, because the wh-operator is ambiguous: it can be the subject or the predicate (see Moro, 1996).

(i) Chi è?
     Who is (it)?
(ii) Cos'è?
     What is (this)?

7 It has been proposed that questions displaying the order Wh S V, as is the case for our aux-less questions, or for questions displaying failure of SAI, result from movement of the wh-operator, not to SpecCP, as in the adult grammar, but to a position adjoined to IP (see Roeper and de Villiers, 1990; Radford, 1995). Under this view, questions have the same structure as sentences involving topicalization, as in (i). Topic movement does not require SAI. Likewise, IP-adjoined interrogatives do not require SAI.

(i) John, I did not see

This proposal holds that children assign to questions two different structural analyses, depending on the surface form of a question. When the auxiliary is present and is correctly inverted, the question is a CP; in the other cases, it is an IP. It is clear that such a view is highly uneconomical because it forces us to say that wh-movement is due to different requirements: the wh-criterion for CP interrogatives and some other triggering factor for the IP-adjoined interrogatives (see Thornton and Crain, 1993, for a criticism of this view).

8 We have not been specific about the features of the null auxiliary. It can either be finite or non-finite.

9 Guasti and Rizzi adopt the null auxiliary hypothesis only for questions. In this respect, their proposal is different from that of Boser et al. (1992), Pesetsky (1993) and Withman (1994), who have generalized the null auxiliary hypothesis to all cases of non-finite verbal forms.

10 Root null subjects disappear at around the age of 3; null auxiliaries, however, seem to last longer, even up to $4\frac{1}{2}$ years. If the two phenomena ensue from the truncation mechanism such developmental discrepancy is not expected. Guasti and Rizzi suggest that the discrepancy may follow from the different nature of the IP and the CP system (see Rizzi, 1997). Principles governing the IP architecture preclude the truncation at this level earlier than principles governing the CP architecture. Haegeman (1995) has found a somewhat analogous discrepancy: in Early Dutch, root infinitives disappear earlier than root null subjects. She proposes that this asymmetry may depend on the fact that root infinitives require truncation at a lower point of the clausal structure than root null subjects. The proposal that truncation is sensitive to the categorial status of the truncated category (IP or CP) needs to be further elaborated. Haegeman (this volume) accounts for instances of non-initial null subjects in early languages (e.g. *after dinner – go to bed*) by appealing to the option of truncating structure at the level of the TOPP, a

layer belonging to the CP system. Hence, the availability of null auxiliaries and of non-initial null subjects depends on the truncation of some categories at the level of CP. The two phenomena do not display the same trend, however. Null auxiliaries may last up to 4 years, while non-initial null subjects end at the age of 3. Further research may shed light on whether and how this range of facts can be accommodated in the framework adopted here.

11 While in this study we have used Adam's transcripts from 1 to 45, Guasti and Rizzi (1996) based their analysis on Adam's transcripts from 1 to 34.

12 If our reasoning is correct, the asymmetry between subject and non-subject questions lends support to an analysis of subject questions according to which the wh-operator moves to SpecCP, rather than stays in SpecIP. Let us see why. If wh-movement is vacuous in subjet questions, then the wh-operator would stay in SpecIP. Children may apply the truncation mechanism and just project up to IP. This would be enough to accommodate subject questions. But a null auxiliary in I would be legitimate, since it would occur in the head of the root. Consequently, we should find subject questions of the form *Who speaking?*, contrary to the facts.

13 This implies that superficially bare verbal forms in English child language can be three ways ambiguous: they can be bare forms, forms selected by *do* or forms affixed with a zero morpheme (see also Hoekstra and Hyams (1999) for evidence in this direction). The first corresponds to infinitives in other early languages, the second and the third are probably found only in EE, since they are a product of the English verbal system.

14 Aux-less questions including bare verbal forms or verbs inflected with the *-ing* morpheme continue to involve a null aux raising from I to C. In the latter case, this analysis conforms to the observation that the verb inflected with *-ing* does not need to and cannot check agreement and tense features, unlike what happens in the case of inflected verbs. The same remark carries over to questions involving bare verbs, modulo the consequences of the observation in note 2.

15 One may wonder why there is a dip after some time. A plausible conjecture is that some confounding data start to be considered by the children at the point when they dip. Indirect questions can be a likely candidate: children hear that SAI does not apply in embedded contexts. Correctly, they assume that this is because the wh-feature is generated in C in these contexts. Then, they try to extend this option to matrix questions with the entitlement of UG, which makes this option available in some adult languages.

References

AKMAJIAN, A., R. A. DEMERS and R. M. HARNISH (1984) *Linguistics*. Cambridge, MA: MIT Press.

BELLUGI, U. (1968) 'Simplification in Children's Language'. In *Methods and Models in Language Acquisition* edited by R. Huxley and E. Ingram, New York: Academic Press.

BOSER, K., B. LUST, L. SANTELMANN and J. WHITMAN (1992) 'The Syntax of

CP and V-2 in Early Child German: The Strong Continuity Hypothesis'. In *Proceedings of NELS 23*, edited by K. Broderick, Amherst, MA: GLSA.
BROWN, R. (1968) 'The Development of Wh-questions in Child Speech'. *Journal of Verbal Learning and Verbal Behavior* **7**: 279–90.
BROWN, R. (1973) *A First Language*. Cambridge, MA: Harvard University Press.
CHOMSKY, N. (1993) 'A minimalist program for linguistic theory'. In *The View from Building 20: Essays in Linguistics in Honour of Sylavain Bromberger*, edited by K. Hale and S. J. Keyser, Cambridge: MIT Press.
CIPRIANI, P., P. PFANNER, L. CITTADONI, A. CIUTI, A. MACCARI, N. PANTANO, L. PFANNER, P. POLI, S. SARNO, P. BOTTARI, G. CAPPELLI, C. COLOMBO and E. VENEZIANO (1989) *Protocolli diagnostici e terapeutici nello sviluppo e nella patologia del linguaggio* (1/84 Italian Ministry of Health). Stella Maris Foundation.
GUASTI, M. T. (1993/4) Verb Syntax in Italian Child Grammar. *Language Acquisition* **3**: 1–40.
GUASTI, M. T. (1996) 'The Acquisition of Italian Interrogatives'. In *The Acquisition of Inflection*, edited by Harald Clahsen, Amsterdam: Benjamin.
GUASTI, M. T. and L. RIZZI (1996) 'Null Aux and the Acquisition of Residual V2'. In *Proceedings of the Boston Conference on Language Development*, edited by A. Stringfellow, D. Cahana-Amytay, E. Hughes and A. Zukowski, Sommerville: Cascadilla Press.
GUASTI, M. T. and L. RIZZI (1998) 'Non-agreeing Do in Child English and the Expression of Agr'. *Glow Newsletter*.
GUASTI, M. T., R. THORNTON and K. WEXLER (1995) 'Negation in Children's Questions: The Case of English'. In *Proceeding of the Boston Conference on Language Development*, edited by D. MacLaughlin and S. McEwen, Sommerville: Cascadilla Press.
HAEGEMAN, L. (1990) 'Understood Subjects in English Diaries'. *Multilingua* **9**: 157–99.
HAEGEMAN, L. (1995) 'Root Infinitives and the Initial Root Null Subject'. Ms. University of Geneva.
HALLE, M. and A. MARANTZ (1994) 'Distributed Morphology and the Pieces of Inflection'. In *The View from Building 20*, edited by K. Hale and S. J. Keyser. Cambridge, MA: MIT Press.
HOEKSTRA, T. and N. HYAMS (1999) 'Aspects of Root Infinitives'. To appear in *Proceedings of the Edinburgh Assembly on Child Language*.
MACWHINNEY, B. (1991) *The CHILDES Project: Tools for Analyzing Talk*, Hillsdale, NJ: LEA.
MACWHINNEY, B. and C. SNOW (1985) 'The Child Language Data Exchange System'. *Journal of Child Language* **12**: 271–96.
MANZINI, M. R. and K. WEXLER (1987) 'Parameters, Binding and Learnability'. *Linguistic Inquiry* **18**: 413–44.
MAY, R. (1985) *Logical Form: Its Structure and Derivation*, Cambridge, MA: MIT Press.
MORO, A. (1996) *The Raising of Predicates*. Cambridge: Cambridge University Press.
PESETSKY, D. (1993) *Some Possible Alternative Explanations for Early Language Phenomena*. Paper presented at the Workshop on language acquisition. SISSA, Trieste.

PINKER, S. (1984) *Language Learnability and Language Development*. Cambridge, MA: Harvard University Press.

PINKER, S. and A. PRINCE (1988) 'On Language and Connectionism: Analysis of a Parallel Distributed Processing Model of Language Acquisition'. *Cognition* **28**: 73–193.

PLUNKETT, B. (1991) 'Inversion and Early WH-questions'. In *Papers on the Acquisition of WH*, edited by T. L. Maxfield and B. Plunkett, Amherst, MA: GLSA Publications.

RADFORD, A. (1995) 'Children – Architects or Brickies?' In *Proceeding of the Boston Conference on Language Development*, edited by D. MacLaughlin and S. McEwen, Sommerville: Cascadilla Press.

RIZZI, L. (1990) 'The Wh-Criterion'. *Technical Report, Département de linguistique générale et française* I.

RIZZI, L. (1994) 'Early Null Subjects and Root Null Subjects'. In *Language Acquisition Studies in Generative Grammar*, edited by T. Hoekstra and B. Schwartz, Amsterdam: Benjamins.

RIZZI, L. (1996) 'A Note on Do Support'. Ms. University of Geneva.

RIZZI, L. (1997) 'The Fine Structure of the Left Periphery'. In *Elements of Grammar*, edited by L. Haegeman, Dordrecht: Kluwer.

ROEPER, T. and J. DE VILLIERS (1990) 'Ordered Decision in Wh-questions'. In *Theoretical Issues in Language Acquisition*, edited by J. Weissenborn, H. Goodluck and T. Roeper, Hillsdale, NJ: LEA.

STROMSWOLD, K. (1989) 'How Conservative are Children? Evidence from Auxiliary Errors'. In *Papers and Reports on Child Language*, Stanford, CA: Stanford University.

STROMSWOLD, K. (1990) 'Learnability and the Acquisition of Auxiliaries'. Ph.D. dissertation, Cambridge, MA.

STROMSWOLD, K. (1996) 'Analyzing Children's Spontaneous Speech'. In *Methods for Assessing Children's Grammar*, edited by McDaniel *et al.*, Cambridge, MA: MIT Press.

SUPPES, P. (1973) 'The Semantics of Children's Language'. *American Psychologist* **88**: 103–14.

THORNTON, R. and S. CRAIN (1993) 'Successive Cyclic Movement'. In *Language Acquisition Studies in Generative Grammar*, edited by T. Hoekstra and B. Schwartz, Amsterdam: Benjamins.

VILLIERS, J. DE (1991) 'Why questions?' In *Papers on the Acquisition of WH*, edited by T. L. Maxfield and B. Plunkett, Amherst MA: GLSA Publications.

WITHMAN, J. (1994) 'In Defense of the Strong Continuity Account of the Acquisition of Verb-second. In *Syntactic theory and first language acquisition* edited by B. Lust *et al.*, Hillsdale, NJ: Erlbaum.

Chapter 6

Adult null subjects in non pro-drop languages
Liliane Haegeman

1 Introduction: early null subjects and diary drop

A well-known parameter of cross-linguistic variation is the pro-drop parameter, which accounts for the contrast between Italian (1a), on the one hand, and English (1b) and French (1c), on the other hand (for an introduction, see Haegeman 1994, Chapter 8). In all registers of Italian, from the informal to the formal, the subject of a finite clause may remain non-overt; this is not the case in most types of usage of English and French. Italian is a pro-drop language, English and French are not.

(1) a. (Io) Parlo italiano.
        (I) speak-1sg Italian.
    b. *(I) speak English.
    c. *(Je) parle français.[1]
        (I) speak French.

It has been observed, though, that in the early production of non pro-drop languages such as French and English, null subjects are attested with a relatively high frequency in finite clauses. This is illustrated in (2a) for English and in (2b) for French (see Hyams 1986, Rizzi 1994a, Rasetti 1995).

(2) a. Want more. (Rizzi 1994a: 1, from Hyams 1986)
    b. Oh! Est pour maman – A tout mangé. (Augustin 2.0.2)
        oh, is for mummy – has all eaten.
                                    (see Hamann *et al.* 1996)

An important question for acquisition studies is to determine whether the data in (2) reflect a property exclusive to the early production or whether they find an analogue in the adult production. In the literature, the data in (2) have often been related to the observation that English and French adult grammars allow non-overt subjects in specific registers, the writing of diaries, illustrated in (3), being perhaps the best-known example (Haegeman 1990a, 1990b).

(3) a. Cried yesterday morning: as if it were an hour for keening: why is crying so pleasurable. (Sylvia Plath, 10.1.1959, p. 288)
   b. Reread all before to Jan 1,[2] and. . . . Has structure. . . . Can't see whole thing yet. (Allen Ginsberg, 10.1.1955, p. 97)
   c. Have always wanted to 'make something' by hand. (Sylvia Plath, 28.1.1959, p. 293)
   d. Elle est alsacienne. Paraît intelligente, (Paul Léautaud, 9.2.1933, p. 48)
   she is Alsatian. seems intelligent.

The early null subject in (2) is often assimilated to the adult null subject in (3) with which, as we will see presently, it shares the distributional properties. Bromberg and Wexler (1995: 243), for instance, signal the parallelism:

it is well known that even English can drop its subjects when they are topics, as in rejoinders [4a], or in diary contexts [4b–c]:

[4] a. What happened to Mary?
   – went away for a while.
   b. – pulled a piece of skin off my lip last night.
   c. – felt a joy yesterday. – soon clouded.
                                (S. Plath, *Journals*, McCollough 1982)

Bromberg and Wexler (1995: 243) propose a null topic analysis for the data in (4) and extend the analysis to the null subject in finite clauses of the early English production (2a) (see also de Haan and Tuijnman 1988, Hyams and Wexler 1993):

It may be the case that children in English are performing Topic-Drop with finite sentences in a way which the adult language allows, except that the children may be performing it in a wider range of contexts, including these infelicitous for adults. . . . Young children are less discriminating than adults as to the variety of pragmatic contexts in which they will allow null topics. (Bromberg and Wexler 1995: 243–244)

In this chapter, I study the adult null subject (henceforth ANS) in (3) and (4) in detail.[3] I will evaluate three analyses for the ANS: (i) the pro-drop analysis, (ii) the topic drop analysis (Haegeman 1990a, 1990b, Weissenborn 1992, Bromberg and Wexler 1995), and (iii) the ante-cedentless empty category analysis (Rizzi 1994a). Neither a pro-drop analysis nor a topic drop analysis accounts for the properties of the ANS.

I will conclude that the ANS in the special registers in English and in French can best be analysed as an antecedentless empty category.[4]
The chapter is organized as follows. Section 2 is an overview of the main properties of the ANS in French and English. Section 3 examines and discards the *pro*-drop analysis. Section 4 examines and discards the topic drop analysis. Section 5 shows that Rizzi's (1994a) analysis of the early null subject in terms of an antecedentless empty category in the specifier of the root is best able to capture the ANS phenomenon. Section 6 is the conclusion to the chapter.

2 The null subject in adult English and French finite clauses

2.1 Distribution of the ANS
The illustrations of subject omission in (3) are quotations from English and French diary-writing, a register in which the phenomenon is quite regularly attested. Table 6.1 provides a survey of the frequency of subject omission in finite clauses in two short diary extracts: Sylvia Plath's entry for 10 January 1959 and Paul Léautaud's entry for 9 February 1933.[5]
In the extracts examined, the ANS is attested only in root clauses, with a frequency of between around 10% in Léautaud's diary and 25% in Plath's diary.[6] Table 6.2 is based on Ihsane's (1998) study of null subjects in the diary register. In this work Ihsane studies thirty pages of Virginia Woolf's diary for 1940.

TABLE 6.1   Distribution of non-overt subject in diary samples

Writer	Clause type	Finite sentences	Null subjects	% null subject
PLATH	Root clauses	54	14	25.92
	Embedded clauses	30	0	0.00
LÉAUTAUD	Root clauses	52	6	11.54
	Embedded clauses	42	0	0.00

TABLE 6.2   Distribution of non-overt subjects in Virginia Woolf

Writer	Clause type	Finite sentences	Null subjects	% null subject
WOOLF	Root clauses	989	111	11.22
	Embedded clauses	287	0	0.00

The restriction to root clauses found in the diaries examined here (but see note 6) also applies to the early null subject (cf. Rizzi 1994a).

The ANS is not limited to the diary register. In English and in French, the ANS phenomenon is attested in other written registers in which pressures of economy seem to over-rule the 'core' grammar. For instance, the ANS is attested in short notes:

(5) a. Wish you were here.
    b. Brilliant could have stayed all day.
       Could see everything from wheelchair.
                    (*Visitors Book '91*, The Green, Beaumaris,
                                          Anglesey, North Wales)
    c. Could do better. (school report)

There is also evidence for subject omission in casual spoken English. This kind of usage is reflected in the following dialogue extracts from British (6a–b) and American (6c) fiction:[7]

(6) a. he said, 'Does the name Farriner mean anything to you?'
       'Can't say it does.' . . .
       Her habit of omitting pronouns from her otherwise not particularly economical speech irritated him.[8]
       '. . . Couldn't get herself a man, so she was always showing what she could get. Wonder who'll get her money? Won't be me, though, not so likely.'
                                          (Rendell 1994: 87–88)
    b. Came to England a couple of days ago, thought I've only got one brother, blood's thicker than water, I'll pay a visit. Called at Malbite Street, got address from Mrs Whatever-her-name-is, said it was care of Rider. Rider, I thought, I know that name, it's Geoff's friend and employer Billy. Doesn't call himself Billy any more, though. (Symons 1973: 67)
    c. 'No. Oh, I know why. 'Cause Norman was home that whole weekend. . . . Didn't want to have any fun. Kept sleeping and drinking and sleeping.' (Isaacs 1997: 465)

Subject omission in informal spoken English is signalled in the linguistics literature. Quirk *et al.* (1985: 896–897) provide the following examples of first person subject omission (7a), of third person referential subject omission (7b) and of third person non-referential subject omission (7c):

(7) a. Beg your pardon.
       Wonder what they're doing.
       Don't know what to say.
       Told you so.
       Hope he's there.
       Think I'll go now.

b. Doesn't look too well.
   Can't play at all.
   Serves you right.
   Doesn't matter.
c. Looks like rain.
   Must be hot in Panama.
   Ought to be some coffee in the pot.
   Must be somebody waiting for you.
   May be some children outside.
   Appears to be a big crowd in the hall.

Observe that all examples given concern root clauses. In the generative literature, we find discussion of the subject omission phenomenon in spoken American English in Thrasher (1977) and in Schmerling (1973):

(8) a. Thought I heard something. (Thrasher 1977: 12)
    b. Will be there as soon as I finish this report. (Thrasher 1977: 13)
    c. Sounds even better than I expected. (Thrasher 1977: 15)
    d. Guess I should have been more careful. (Schmerling 1973: 579)

The discussion in the present chapter mainly concentrates on the English ANS in written abbreviated registers, and is based on attested data from written sources supplemented with native speakers' intuitions. I will also extend the discussion to the ANS phenomenon in informal spoken English and to French, where the ANS seems to be restricted to the written register.[9]

2.2. The interpretation of the ANS

2.2.1 Referential ANS

So far we have illustrated the referential ANS with first and third person singular interpretations. In (9a) the implied subject is the first person plural[10]:

(9) a. Climbed Rue Vieuville & series of angled steps to Place du Tertre . . . ; Tony and I walked about and looked about and looked at paintings. (Sylvia Plath, 26.5.1956, p. 136)

Second person null subjects are not attested in diary extracts, but this is due to the non-interactive nature of diary-writing. In the following citations from fiction, the second person subject is non-overt:

(9) b. 'Can't understand you newspaper chaps.' . . . 'Fill up the papers with all kinds of stuff nobody wants to read, and often miss what's right under your noses. *The Gazette,* now, that's a local paper –.' (Symons 1967: 12)

    c. 'Chap as always wears an old duffle coat, . . . he lives up the
       road a couple of mile, Pebwater Farm, can't mistake it . . .'
       (Symons 1967a: 130)
    d. 'No, it wouldn't do for me. Sharing everything with your
       neighbours, haven't even got a bit of garden to call your
       own except for that pocket handkerchief out there. . . .'
       (Symons 1967b: 30)

2.2.2 Non-referential ANS

Omission of non-referential subjects has already been illustrated in (7c)
from the linguistics literature. Thrasher (1977: 44) gives the following:

    (10) a. Won't be too difficult to reconstruct his argument.
        b. Isn't much we can do about it.
        c. Aren't enough left to worry about.

(10d–e) are from Schmerling (1973):

    (10) d. Seems like the class always wakes up five minutes before
         the bell rings. (1973: 597)
        e. Must be an accident up ahead. (1973: 582)

(10f–j) are attested examples, the first represents written ANS, the last
four, spoken ANS.

    (10) f. Rained in the night, wind, rain and hail. (Elizabeth Smart,
         On the side of the Angels, 19.1.1945, p. 27)
        g. It was after they got back from their nature walk. Must have
         been after six. (Isaacs 1997: 168)
        h. Looks like he's letting the fields go wild. (Shields 1996: 159)
        i. Won't be long till the snow flies. (Shields 1996: 152)
        j. 'We've got her scared all right,' thought Sergeant Martin.
         'Might be something here after all.' (James 1989: 92)

So far I have not come across any examples of omission of non-
referential subjects in French diaries, but native speakers confirm that
they accept the following examples in the relevant written register (see
also note 1):

    (11) a. A plu toute la journée.
         has rained all the day.
        b. M'est arrivé quelque chose de bizarre.
         me is arrived something of strange.
         'Something strange has happened to me.'

I conclude that ANS may be both referential and non-referential.

2.3 The non-overt subject

The subjectless sentences are interpreted as if they have a subject. The understood subject can be shown to be syntactically active, in that it interacts with other constituents of the sentence. In English (12a) (from (6a)), the non-overt subject of *couldn't* binds the reflexive pronoun *herself*. We represent the non-overt subject as *ec*; the binding relation is expressed by coindexation. French (12b) illustrates the same phenomenon:

(12) a. $[ec]_i$ Couldn't get herself$_i$ a man, so she was always showing what she could get.
      b. $[ec]_i$ s$_i$'est donné souvent l'illusion de l'amour à P.
          refl. is given often the illusion of the love to P.
          (Paul Léautaud, 20.3.1920, pp. 69–70)

Similarly, an ANS can control the PRO subject of a non-finite clause. In English (13a), the non-overt subject of *walked* controls the subject of the non-finite verb *feeling*. In French (13b) the non-overt subject of *est donné* controls the subject of *pensant*.

(13) a. $[ec]_i$ Walked there – [PRO$_i$ feeling] light and airy. (Elizabeth Smart, *Necessary Secrets*, 7.3.1933, p. 15)
      b. $[ec]_i$ s$_i$'est donné souvent l'illusion de l'amour à P. en [PRO$_i$ pensant] à moi . . .
          refl. is given often the illusion of the love to P. while thinking of me . . .
          (Paul Léautaud, 20.3.1920, pp. 69–70)

Since the understood subject in apparently subjectless sentences can be shown to be syntactically active, we postulate an empty category in the subject position. Let us try to determine the nature of this empty category. In generative approaches, different types of non-overt categories are distinguished:[11]

(14) a. Trace of A-movement (A-trace).
          John$_i$ seems [$_{IP}$ t$_i$ to have arrived].
      b. Trace of A'-movement (A'-trace).
          Who$_i$ do you think [$_{CP}$ t$_i$ [$_{IP}$ t$_i$ will get here first]]?
          John$_i$, I don't think [$_{CP}$ t$_i$ [$_{IP}$ t$_i$ will get here first]].
      c. *pro*
          pro parlo italiano.
          speak-1sg Italian. (cf. 1a)
      d. PRO
          [PRO to go there] is important.
      e. Null A'-operator
          The woman [$_{CP}$ OP$_i$ that [$_{IP}$ you see t$_i$ over there]] is his wife.

The question arises whether the ANS corresponds to any one of these empty categories. Both the A-trace (14a) and PRO in (14d) can be excluded from consideration: they do not alternate with overt DPs (Determiner Phrases) (15), while the ANS does alternate with overt DPs (16):

(15) a. John seems (*he) to have arrived.
     b. (*You) to go there is important.

(16) a. (I) Reread all before to Jan 1, and. . . .
     b. (It) Has structure. . . .

                                    (Allen Ginsberg, 10.1.1955, p. 97)

This leaves us with three potential candidates: the non-overt pronoun *pro* postulated for Italian finite clauses such as (1a) above, the A'-trace and the non-overt A'-operator which is used, among others, to introduce relative clauses (cf. Lasnik and Stowell 1991 for other uses of the null operator). The *pro* analysis is examined in section 3, the null operator analysis is evaluated in section 4, and the A'-trace analysis is explored in section 5. We will conclude that the ANS is an antecedentless empty category with the properties of A'-traces, i.e. an empty category with the features [−anaphoric, −pronominal] and we will refer to this empty category by the shorthand term 'antecedentless A'-trace'.[12]

3 The ANS as pro

It is not plausible that the English and French ANS corresponds to the non-overt pronominal subject of finite clauses in Italian, represented as *pro* in (17).

(17) *pro* parlo italiano.
     pro speak-1sg Italian.

First, as shown in section 3.1, the English and French registers allowing ANS do not have any of the properties standardly associated with pro-drop languages. Second, as discussed in section 3.2, the distribution of the ANS is subject to a number of constraints not associated with pro.

3.1 The syntactic properties of pro-drop languages
The positive setting of the pro-drop parameter is associated with a cluster of syntactic properties (cf. Rizzi 1982, 1986, 1993, Jaeggli and Safir 1989, Haegeman 1994, Chapter 8, for an introduction).

(i) Empty categories are licit in a grammar as long as (i) they are formally licensed in the structure and (ii) their content can be recovered. These two conditions are captured in two clauses of the Empty Category Principle (ECP) (see Rizzi 1986, 1990).

(18) *ECP (i): formal licensing*
An empty category must be governed by an appropriate head.

(19) *ECP (ii): identification*
An empty category must be chain-connected to an antecedent.

For the unmarked adult grammar, the difference between the verbal inflection in Italian, on the one hand, and that in English and French, on the other, accounts for the contrast in the licensing of the null subject. The inflectional paradigm of Italian is 'rich' (20a): each person–number combination is associated with a distinct form, while the inflectional paradigms of English (20b) or French (20c) are 'poor':

(20)	a. Italian	b. English	c. French
1sg	parlo	speak	parle
2sg	parli	speak	parles
3sg	parla	speaks	parle
1pl	parliamo	speak	parlons
2pl	parlate	speak	parlez
3pl	parlent	speak	parlent

In Italian, the rich finite inflection licenses and identifies the non-overt subject in finite clauses. In English, the poor finite inflection cannot license a null subject (cf. Rizzi 1986; see Jaeggli and Safir 1989 and especially Huang 1986 for a more subtle discussion of the relation inflection–pro drop). Similarly, French has only four verb-forms which are phonetically distinct, the contrast between *parle*, *parles* and *parlent* becomes clear only in contexts of *liaison*. French cannot have non-overt subjects. Clearly, in the registers of English and French allowing ANS, the inflectional paradigms of the verb are no different from those in the registers which do not allow the ANS.

(ii) In pro-drop languages such as Italian, the definite subject can occupy a post-verbal position, an option not generally available in English or in French (but see Friedemann 1992, 1997, for stylistic inversion in French):

(21) a.   Ha telefonato il decano.
has telephoned the dean.
'The dean has phoned.'
b. *Has telephoned the dean.
c. *A téléphoné le doyen.

Again, the post-verbal subject of the pro-drop language (21a) finds no parallel in the English and French registers allowing the ANS, and native speakers agree that such registers do not allow post-verbal subjects of this type. (21b) and (21c) remain ungrammatical.

(iii) In Italian, a subject can be extracted from an embedded clause across the overt complementizer *che* ('that'), without giving rise to a *that*-trace violation. In English and French, this is not possible (Perlmutter 1971).

> (22) a. Chi$_i$ credi che abbia telefonato t$_i$?[13]
>   who believe you that have (subj) telephoned.
>   'Who do you think has called?'
>   b. *Who$_i$ do you think that t$_i$ has telephoned?
>   c. *Qui$_i$ crois-tu que t$_i$ a téléphoné?

English (22b) and French (22c) violate the ECP (i): the embedded subject trace, t$_i$, is not head-governed because, by hypothesis, the complementizers *that* and *que* are inert for government. Sentences such as (22b) and (22c) are also not attested in the registers allowing ANS, and native speakers agree that they remain ungrammatical in such registers.

If we were to equate the ANS in special registers with pro, this would be tantamount to saying that English and French have a positive setting for the pro-drop parameter. We would then expect the other properties of pro-drop grammars to also be attested, contrary to fact.

The pro-drop analysis also raises a theoretical issue. If register variation could trigger parameter-resetting, one might expect to find other instances of register-related parameter-resetting. One case that might be advocated is the long extraction data discussed in Haegeman (1987), another concerns the null topic phenomena in recipe texts and other kinds of instructions (Haegeman 1988). For reasons of space, I cannot develop these points here and refer the reader to the earlier papers.

3.2 The distributional constraints on ANS

3.2.1 ANS as a root phenomenon
The ANS is subject to distributional constraints not applicable to pro. As suggested by Tables 6.1 and 6.2, the ANS is restricted to root clauses (but see note 6): in the extracts examined there are no instances of subject omission in embedded clauses. Consider, for instance, the English extract (23a) and the French extract (23b). Root subjects are non-overt, but embedded subjects consistently remain overt. Native speakers agree that the omission of the italicised subjects in embedded clauses would lead to ungrammaticality.

> (23) a. Cried yesterday morning: as if *it* were an hour for keening:
>   why is *crying* so pleasurable? I feel clean, absolutely purged
>   after it. As if *I* had a grief to get over with, some deep
>   sorrow. I cried about other mothers coming to take care of
>   their daughters for a while, with babies. Talked of how *I*

could let Mother have her limited pleasure if *I* were 'grown
up' enough not to feel jeopardized by her manipulating me.
(Sylvia Plath, 10.1.1959, p. 288)

b. A tenu à m'assurer en m'en donnant sa parole qu'*elle* ignorait
. . .

has held to me ensure by me giving her word that she
ignored . . .

le soir de notre rencontre, que *je* suis au Mercure,
the evening of our meeting, that I am at the Mercure.

qu'*elle* tenait à m'assurer de cela pour le cas où . . .
that she held to me ensure of that in case if . . .

. . . A tout de suite protesté qu'*elle* s'en doutait bien.
. . . has immediately protested that she it doubted well.
(Paul Léautaud, 9.2.1993, p. 47)

The Italian non-overt subject pro is licit in embedded clauses:

(23) c. Gianni canta quando *pro* è felice.
Gianni sings when pro be-3sg happy.
'Gianni sings when he is happy.'

3.2.2 ANS and the left periphery of the clause
The ANS is not freely available in root sentences. As a first approximation (but see section 5.3), let us say that the ANS must be the initial, i.e.
leftmost, constituent in the sentence. Whenever the pre-subject left
periphery of the clause is activated as a result of *wh*-preposing, or of
subject–auxiliary inversion, the ANS is not attested. Table 6.3 provides
a survey of the distribution of the ANS in the English extracts. In non-
subject *wh*-questions, in exclamative sentences with *wh*-preposing, and
in inverted *yes/no* questions,[14] the subject is always overt. As there are
no sentences with *wh*-preposing in the Léautaud extract, there is no
quantitative information for French.

TABLE 6.3   ANS and the left periphery

	Clause type	Total	Null subjects	Percentage
PLATH		54	14	25.92
	wh	15	0	0.00
	decl	39	14	35.90
WOOLF		989	111	11.22
(Ihsane 1998)	*wh*	51	0	0.00
	decl	938	111	11.83

Sentences classified as *wh* in Table 6.3 amalgamate *wh*-preposing in interrogatives (24a), in exclamatives (24b) and in *yes/no* questions with inversion (24c).

> (24) a. Whence does *it* come, how can *I* triumph over it? (Sylvia Plath, 10.1.1959, p. 288)
> b. What a mess *I* am. (Sylvia Plath, 10.1.1959, p. 290)
> c. Am *I* crude to say 'The New Yorker sort'. (Sylvia Plath, 28.1.1959, p. 293)

Native speakers agree that in (24), the italicized subject remains obligatory in the register allowing the ANS:

> (25) a. *Whence does come,
> *how can triumph over it? (Sylvia Plath, 10.1.1959, p. 288)
> b. *What a mess am. (Sylvia Plath, 10.1.1959, p. 290)
> c. *Am crude to say 'The New Yorker sort'. (Sylvia Plath, 28.1.1959, p. 293)

Native speakers also confirm these judgements for the French ANS:

> (26) a. Quand reviendra-t-*(elle) à Paris?
> when return-future-*(she) to Paris.
> b. Quelle belle surprise *(elle) avait pour nous.
> what nice surprise *(she) had for us.
> c. Reviendra-t-*(elle) à Paris?[15]
> return-future-*(she) to Paris.

Unlike the English and French ANS, the Italian non-overt pronominal subject pro is compatible with interrogative *wh*-preposing (27a), with exclamative *wh*-preposing (27b), and with inversion in *yes/no* questions (27c):

> (27) a. Quando [pro] tornerà?
> when return-future-3sg.
> 'When will he/she return?'
> b. Che bel regalo [pro] mi hanno dato!
> what nice present me have given.
> 'What a nice present they gave me!'
> c. Tornerà [pro] presto?
> return-future-3sg soon?
> 'Will he/she return soon?'

3.3 The ANS is not *pro*

Based on the data discussed above, we conclude that the English and French ANS is not an instantiation of the non-overt pronominal *pro*.

The special registers do not provide any evidence for a resetting of the parameter (3.1) and the ANS is subject to specific distributional constraints (3.2): the ANS is not available in embedded sentences, which typically implicate the CP-level (28a), nor in *wh*-questions, *wh*-exclamatives and *yes/no* questions, three construction which also involve the CP-domain (28b).

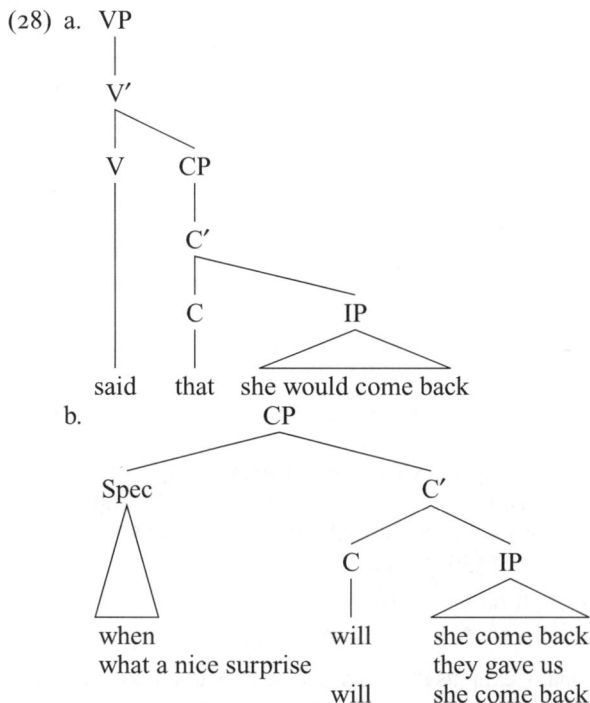

(28) a. VP

b.

4 ANS as topic drop

Haegeman (1990a, 1990b), Weissenborn (1992), and Bromberg and Wexler (1995) propose that the ANS is a null topic operator (cf. (14e)). I first show that the original argumentation on which their analysis is based, which crucially exploits the observed complementarity of ANS and *wh*-preposing (see section 3.2.2), is faulted and must be revised. I then re-examine the evidence and show that while the complementarity of ANS and *wh*-preposing might still be advanced in support of a null topic analysis of the ANS, further evidence shows that this analysis is not tenable.

4.1 Topic drop: introduction

In English (29a), the preposed constituent, *that film*, functions as the discourse topic.

(29) a. [$_{CP}$ That film$_i$, [$_{IP}$ I saw t$_i$ last night (and not last week).]]

In some languages the discourse topic may be non-overt. This is referred to as topic drop (cf. Ross 1982, Huang 1984, Raposo 1986). Topic drop is illustrated in Portuguese (29b), in which the verb *viu* ('saw') lacks an overt direct object. The interpretation of this sentence is that 'Joana saw "it"/"him"/"her"/"them"', i.e. she saw some entity which is salient in the discourse.

(29) b. A Joana viu na televisao ontem é noite.
Joana saw on television last night.

By analogy with the overt topic preposing in English (29a), and using the null operator analysis postulated for relative clause formation (14e), we assign to Portuguese (29b) the representation (29c). The object of *viu* is a null operator which, like the overt topic, is moved to a left-peripheral position, leaving a coindexed A'-trace in the base position (cf. Raposo 1986).

(29) c. [$_{CP}$ OP$_i$ [$_{IP}$ A Joana viu t$_i$ na televisao ontem é noite]].

4.2 The incompatibility of ANS and *wh*-preposing

Haegeman (1990a, 1990b) and Bromberg and Wexler (1995) propose that the ANS be analysed as a null topic operator. In this view, (30a) is assigned representation (30b).

(30) a. Reread all before to Jan 1.
b. [$_{CP}$ OP$_i$ [$_{IP}$ t$_i$ reread all before to Jan 1]].

The analysis crucially exploits the observed incompatibility of the ANS and *wh*-movement (cf. section 3.2.2). It rests on two related assumptions:

(i) The left periphery of the clause consists of a unique projection CP.
(ii) *Wh*-preposing and topicalization target the same position, [Spec,CP]:

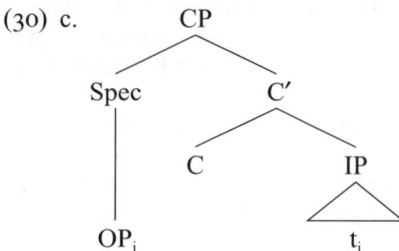

(30) c.

CP
Spec   C'
| C   IP
OP$_i$ t$_i$

Based on assumptions (i)–(ii), preposed topics and *wh*-preposing must be in complementary distribution. Bromberg and Wexler (1995: 227, note 15) say explicitly, 'the existence of the *wh*-phrase in Spec,C prevents there being a topic in the sentence'. However, the analysis is subject to a number of criticisms.

First, the idea that topics are in complementary distribution with *wh*-preposing is problematic on interpretative grounds, as pointed out by Bromberg and Wexler themselves (1995: 227, note 15).

> . . . a *wh*-phrase is usually considered to be a focus, not a topic, since a topic is old information and a *wh*-phrase is usually not old information. Thus we would not expect the *wh*-phrase itself to delete by Topic Drop.

Second, there are problems with the assumption that ANS are incompatible with *wh*-preposing because they compete for the single XP-position in the CP-domain. The two assumptions cited above on which the argumentation is based are incorrect. (i) It is not the case that the CP-domain consists of a unique projection; (30c) must be abandoned for an articulated CP. (ii) Preposed topics and preposed *wh*-constituents can be shown to have distinct landing sites and they are in general not in complementary distribution. I will discuss both these points.

Various authors (Bresnan 1977, Reinhart 1981a, Culicover 1991, Müller and Sternefeld 1992, Aboh 1995, Nakajima 1996, Puskas 1997, Rizzi 1997) provide evidence against the unitary CP (30c) and in favour of an articulated CP-domain composed of discrete functional projections each with a specialized function. CP contains, among others, the unique Focus Phrase (FocP), whose specifier is the landing site for *wh*-movement,[16] and the recursive Topic Phrase (TopP), whose specifier is the landing site for topicalization. The projections have the hierarchical organization in (31) (adapted from Rizzi 1997):

(31) CP> (TopP)*> (FocP)> (TopP)*> IP

Topicalization targets [Spec,TopP]; focalization and *wh*-movement target [Spec,FocP]; I-to-C movement (giving rise to Subject Auxiliary Inversion (SAI)) targets Foc. In other words, a preposed *wh*-phrase and a topicalized constituent are not in complementary distribution. In (32a) the object DP *Tom* has moved to the specifier of TopP and it co-occurs with the preposed *wh*-phrase *why* in [Spec,FocP]; in (32b) the topicalized PP *to Tom* cooccurs with preposed *what*:

(32) a. $[_{CP}[_{TopP}$ Tom$_i$ $[_{FocP}$ why $[_{Foc}$ would$_v]$ $[_{IP}$ anyone t$_v$ want to invite t$_i$?]]]]
      b. $[_{CP}[_{TopP}$ To Tom$_i$ $[_{FocP}$ what$_j$ $[_{Foc}$ can$_v]$ $[_{IP}$ I t$_v$ say t$_j$ t$_i$?]]]]

The same point is also made by Italian (32c), in which the preposed *wh*-phrase *che cosa* ('what') in [Spec,FocP] cooccurs with a topicalized subject, *Gianni*, in [Spec,TopP].

(32) c. $[_{CP} [_{TopP}$ Gianni$_j$ $[_{FocP}$ **che cosa**$_i$ $[_{Foc}$ ha$_v$] $[_{IP}$ t$_j$ t$_v$ fatto t$_i$]]]]?
    Gianni what has (he) done.

The argumentation used for equating the ANS with a null topic is inadequate since it incorrectly relies on an assumed incompatibility between topicalization and *wh*-preposing.[17] The explanation for the alleged incompatibility of *wh*-preposing and topicalization rests in turn on the incorrect assumption that there is a unique projection in the CP-domain and that preposed topics and preposed *wh*-phrases target the same position.

To uphold the null topic analysis for the English and French ANS (Haegeman 1990a, 1990b, and Bromberg and Wexler 1995, etc.), one has to admit the general compatibility of topicalization and *wh*-preposing, while specifically excluding the cooccurrence of the (null) subject topic (i.e. the ANS) and *wh*-movement. Such a position can be motivated: in English we observe a subject/object asymmetry with respect to the compatibility of topicalization and *wh*-preposing. While object topicalization and *wh*-preposing are compatible (32a), subject topicalization and *wh*-preposing are incompatible:

(33) *$[_{CP} [_{TopP}$ Tom$_i$ $[_{FocP}$ why $[_{Foc}$ should] $[_{IP}$ t$_i$ be invited?]]]]

In this respect, English contrasts with Italian, in which subject topicalization is compatible with *wh*-preposing (32c).

The subject/object asymmetry shown by the contrast between English (33) and (32a) is reminiscent of the subject/object asymmetry in (34):

(34) a. *This is a man $[_{CP}$ who$_i$ $[_{IP}$ I think $[_{CP}$ t$_i$ that $[_{IP}$ t$_i$ will invite Mary]]]].
     b. This is a man $[_{CP}$ who$_i$ $[_{IP}$ I think $[_{CP}$ t$_i$ that $[_{IP}$ Mary will invite t$_i$]]]].

The contrast between (34a) and (34b) is accounted for in terms of the formal licensing condition on traces (18). Traces must be head-governed. In (34a), the trace in [Spec,IP] is not head-governed: the complementizer *that* is, by hypothesis, inert for government. In (34b), the object trace is head-governed by the verb *invite*. In the grammatical (34c), the appropriate head-governor for the subject trace is the non-overt complementizer (o). As the subject transits via the specifier of the non-overt complementizer, the agreement features of the complementizer are activated, and the agreeing complementizer head-governs the subject trace.

(34) c. This is a man [$_{CP}$ who$_i$ [$_{IP}$ I think [$_{CP}$ t$_i$ o$_{AGR}$ [$_{IP}$ t$_i$ will invite Mary]]]].

Let us now return to the illicit cooccurrence of subject topicalization and *wh*-movement in (33). The subject is extracted across the preposed *wh*-phrase in [Spec,FocP] and the auxiliary in Foc. The trace in [Spec,IP] is not head-governed. An inverted auxiliary cannot head-govern a trace in [Spec,IP], as shown by the ungrammaticality of (35). I refer the reader to Rizzi and Roberts (1991) for discussion.

(35) *Who$_i$ did t$_i$ go there?

In Italian, subject topicalization is compatible with *wh*-preposing, as shown by (32c) above. The contrast between English and Italian follows from the different settings of the pro-drop parameter. Recall that in Italian, the subject can occupy a post-verbal position (21a). The subject can be extracted from that post-verbal position, since the trace will be head-governed (22a), satisfying the licensing condition (18).

The null topic analysis for the English and French ANS could thus account for the incompatibility of ANS and *wh*-preposing not by appealing to there being a unique landing site in CP but rather by appealing to the ECP. However, in the next section I show that there are additional conclusive arguments for discarding the null topic analysis.

4.3 Two objections to the null topic analysis

4.3.1 No object omission

The null topic hypothesis for ANS runs into a problem (see also Rizzi 1994a, Wilder 1994) when we take into account the observation that while null subjects are instantiated in the relevant register, null objects are not. In the passage from Plath's diary which yields 25.92% instances of subject omission, there are 58 transitive verbs, none of which has comparable object omission. In the light of the null topic analysis, the lack of null objects is unexpected: as illustrated above, the Portuguese null topic is typically an object (29b).

4.3.2 Non-referential null subjects

Another objection to the null topic analysis concerns the interpretation of the ANS. If the ANS is a null topic, it should not be able to function as a non-referential subject (quasi-argument, expletive): non-referential subjects cannot topicalize, as shown by the ungrammaticality of (36):

(36) a. *It tomorrow will rain.[18]
     b. *There tomorrow will be more snow.

This expectation is not borne out: the ANS can have a non-referential reading (cf. section 2.2.2).

5 The ANS as an antecedentless empty category

5.1 Early null subjects

The distribution of the early null subject in finite clauses (cf. (2)) is the same as that of the ANS: it is restricted to the leftmost position of root clauses, and it is incompatible with *wh*-preposing[19] and with SAI. Rizzi (1994a, 1998) analyses the early null subject as an antecedentless empty category.[20] In order to make this analysis work, two auxiliary hypotheses are needed. First, Rizzi reformulates the identification clause of the ECP, (19), as in (37):

(37) *ECP: identification*
A non-pronominal empty category must be chain-connected to an antecedent if it can be.

Condition (19) rigorously applies to **all** empty categories. (37) allows for one exception. If an empty category is the highest specifier in the structure, hence is not c-commanded by any maximal projection, then there exists no potential antecedent position. In this case, the empty category cannot be chain-connected to an antecedent and, by (37), it can legitimately remain antecedentless.

A second hypothesis concerns the projection of structure. Rizzi (1997) proposes (38), a principle which derives from economy considerations (cf. Chomsky 1991, Cardinaletti and Starke 1994):

(38) Avoid Structure.

According to (38), structure is only projected when required by selection and other fundamental structure-building principles. Syntactic structure cannot be added, for instance, to salvage a potential ECP violation. Thus, one cannot simply insert an abstract projection to ensure head-government of the subject trace in (34a) above (see Rizzi's paper for exemplification).

Principle (38) cannot cancel out the fundamental structure-building principles. For the standard adult grammar, Rizzi assumes that every root clause must be assigned an illocutionary force. Since CP encodes the illocutionary force, a root clause must be dominated by CP.

(39) Root → CP

Because of (39), a fundamental structure-building principle, CP must be projected.

In order to account for the English and French early null subject, Rizzi (1994a) postulates that early grammars differ from adult grammars in that they offer the possibility of structural truncation (see also the introduction to this volume for a general discussion of truncation). Root clauses in the adult grammar must be projected up to CP (39). Root clauses in the child grammar may be truncated, i.e. the projection may stop at some level lower than CP. Finite clauses may, for instance, be truncated at IP, which then becomes the root. Rizzi interprets the early null subject as an antecedentless empty category in the specifier of such a (truncated) root-IP.

(40) a. [$_{IP}$ ec [$_{VP}$ want more]].

The antecedentless empty category in [Spec,IP] of (40a) will not violate the identification clause of the ECP (37). Occurring in the highest specifier position of the clause, the empty category in (40a) can remain antecedentless: not being c-commanded by a potential antecedent it cannot (and, by (37), need not) be chain-connected to an antecedent.

In the standard adult grammar, representation (40a) is illicit; by (39), root clauses must be CP. If CP is projected, giving (40b), an antecedent-less empty category in [Spec,IP] will violate the identification condition of ECP (37): [Spec,CP] can host an antecedent.

(40) b. *[$_{CP}$ [$_{Spec}$] [$_{IP}$ ec want some milk]].

5.2 Adult null subjects (ANS)

Early null subjects are incompatible with *wh*-movement and only occur in root clauses. The same distributional constraints apply to ANS. Given the similarities in distribution between the early null subject and the adult ANS, I will examine the hypothesis that the ANS is an antecedentless empty category in [Spec,IP], with CP being truncated. Truncation then becomes a device characteristic of the 'informal' or 'abbreviated' styles.

In terms of Rizzi's analysis, the observed incompatibility of ANS with *wh*-preposing is expected. In sentences with *wh*-preposing, the CP-level must be projected. If CP is projected, [Spec,CP] may host an antecedent and by the identification clause of the ECP (37), an empty category in [Spec,IP] will not be allowed to remain antecedentless (cf. (40b)).

According to this analysis, only subjects will be non-overt. Consider (41) with a null object:

(41)

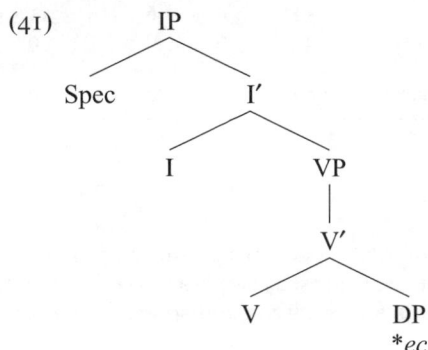

In (41) [Spec,IP] c-commands the object position, hence [Spec,IP] could host an antecedent of the empty category. (41) violates (37): the object empty category can, hence must, be identified, i.e. chain-connected to an antecedent. By (37) the empty category cannot remain antecedentless.

An empirical prediction of the analysis is that the null subject in the special register will be the leftmost constituent of the root clause. The availability of any constituent XP to the left of the antecedentless empty category ought to trigger the projection of a higher projection, 'FP', to host XP. If FP is projected above IP, [Spec,FP] will be an antecedent position for an empty category in [Spec,IP] and the empty category in [Spec,IP] cannot remain antecedentless by (37). This prediction is initially borne out by (42):

(42) a. *That book, don't like. (Wilder 1994: 36–37)
     b. *More problems don't need. (Thrasher 1977: 83)

But, although the examples in (42) are ungrammatical, the ANS may cooccur with preposed adjuncts. I turn to this point in the next section.

ANS also will be excluded from embedded clauses. A non-overt subject in an embedded clause will always be c-commanded by potential antecedents, i.e. the specifier of the embedded CP itself and the specifiers in the root clause. Hence an embedded null subject will always have a potential antecedent. As shown by the results displayed in Tables 6.1 and 6.2, which are grouped below for the readers' convenience in Table 6.4, embedded clauses lack null subjects. See also the discussion of (23) and note 6 above.

TABLE 6.4   Distribution of non-overt subject in diary samples

Writer	Clause type	Finite sentences	Null subjects	% null subject
PLATH	Root clauses	54	14	25.92
	Embedded clauses	30	0	0.00
LÉAUTAUD	Root clauses	52	6	11.54
	Embedded clauses	42	0	0.00
WOOLF	Root clauses	989	111	11.22
(Ihsane 1998)	Embedded clauses	287	0	0.00

5.3 Non-initial ANS?

5.3.1 The data
While there are no instances of ANS cooccurring with preposed arguments (42) in the extracts examined here (see also Ihsane 1998), the ANS does cooccur with preposed adjuncts, both in English and in French.[21]

(43) a. After Dr. Krook, had good lunch at Eagle with Gary [Hamp].
     (Sylvia Plath, 6.3.1956, p. 126)
     b. Here, studies under [David] Daiches... (Sylvia Plath,
     6.3.1956, p. 126)

(44) a. *Tout de suite* m'a parlé de ma visite chez elle (Paul Léautaud,
     immediately me has talked about my visit 9.2.1933, p. 45)
     to her
     b. *Après chaque oblitération* donne droit (Geneva public
     à la libre circulation pendant 60 min.   transport card 'Carte
     after each checking gives right to   multiparcours')[22]
     free circulation during 60 min.

For spoken American English, Thrasher (1977) signals the contrast
in (45):

(45) a. Next time you get to Kobe, want you to buy me an umbrella.
     (1977: 80)
     b. *More problems don't need. (1977: 83)

5.3.2 The syntax of adjunct preposing
Based on the observed absence of ANS with object preposing, and
based on Thrasher's judgements (45), let us adopt the hypothesis that
the ANS is incompatible with a preposed argument (46a) and it may
cooccur with a preposed adjunct (46b).

(46) a. *Dr. Krook, met for lunch at Eagle.
     b. After Dr. Krook, *ec* had good lunch at Eagle with Gary
     [Hamp].
                              (Sylvia Plath, 10.1.1959, p. 126)

If the null subject of *had* in (46b) is an antecedentless empty category
in [Spec,IP], it should violate the ECP (37) since the preposed PP *after
Dr. Krook* is a c-commanding maximal projection and hence could be
an antecedent.
    A first option, which we will discard, would be to relate the compat-
ibility of the preposed adjunct with the ANS in (46b) to the intrinsic
properties of the preposed constituents. It could be argued that adjuncts,
i.e. non-arguments, simply do not qualify as antecedents for argumental
empty categories. This explanation is inadequate, though, as it would
no longer allow us to exclude the examples in (47), in which *wh*-
adjuncts are shown to be incompatible with the ANS. As discussed in
section 3.2.2, there are no examples of preposed *wh*-phrases and ANS
in the material examined (see Table 6.3).

(47) a. *After which date will come back?
     b. *When will come back?

An alternative would be to attempt a purely configurational explanation. One might propose that a preposed adjunct fails to qualify as an antecedent for the ANS because it occupies an (IP)-**adjoined** position (Lasnik and Saito 1984). We might stipulate that only constituents in specifier positions can function as antecedents.

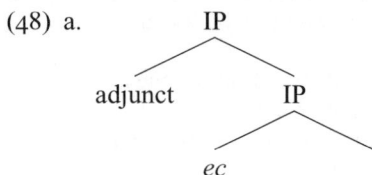

(48) a.

```
              IP
            /    \
      adjunct      IP
                 /    \
              ec
```

Preposed arguments in [Spec,TopP] would qualify as antecedents:

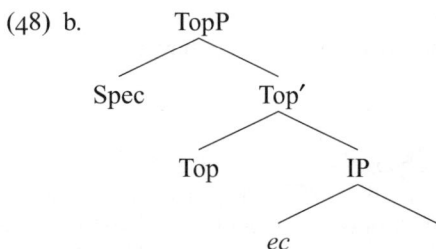

(48) b.

```
               TopP
             /      \
        Spec          Top'
                    /      \
                 Top          IP
                            /    \
                          ec
```

The question would arise, though, why the adjoined constituent in (48a) disqualifies as a binder for an *ec* in [Spec,IP]. Furthermore, empirical evidence suggests that preposed adjuncts are not merely IP-adjoined but that, like preposed arguments, they are licensed by a specialized functional head. Thus the alleged contrast between the two structures in (48) evaporates.[23] Support for the idea that preposed adjuncts are associated with a specialized functional head is obtained from the interaction of SAI and adjunct preposing in (49):

(49) a.   After lunch, what are you going to do?
     b.   *What are after lunch you going to do?

Recall that [Spec,FocP] hosts, among others, the preposed *wh*-constituent, and that Foc hosts the inverted auxiliary. As shown by (49), subject–auxiliary inversion and adjunct preposing are compatible as long as the preposed adjunct precedes the inversion structure.

Let us postulate that the preposed adjunct *after lunch* in (49) is associated with a specific projection in the CP-domain. Adjunct preposing does not give rise to SAI (cf. Rizzi 1997: note 22). We conclude that the head of the adjunct-related projection cannot host the auxiliary. Based on these assumptions, the contrast in (49) follows from the Head Movement Constraint (HMC) (Travis 1984), which says that in the course of movement a head *x* cannot skip an intervening head *y* (Haegeman 1994, Chapter 12, for discussion). For the sake of the argument, let us assume that the preposed adjunct *after lunch* occupies [Spec,TopP]. (50a) and (50b) represent the grammatical (49a) and the ungrammatical (49b) respectively:

(50) a.

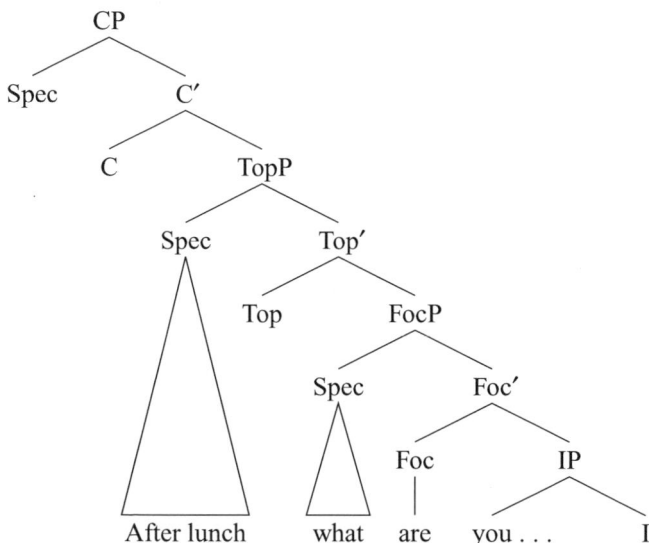

b.*

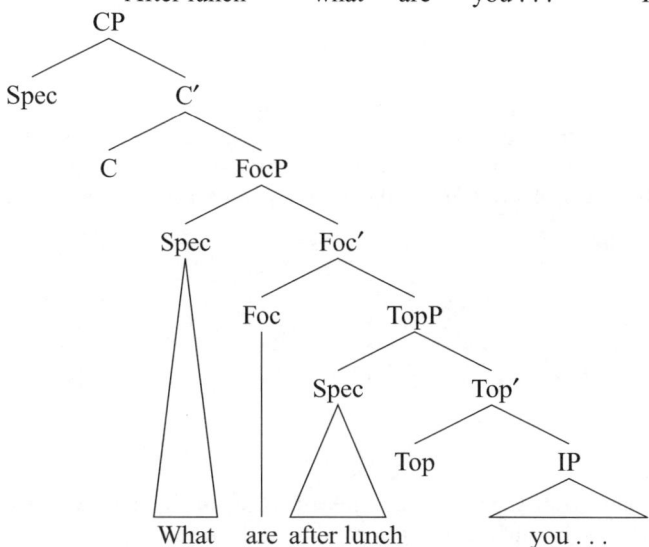

In (50a) the auxiliary *are* inverts with the subject: it occupies Foc. The head Top, which is associated with the preposed adjunct,[24] *after lunch,* does not intervene in the movement of the auxiliary. (50b) is ungrammatical. To reach Foc, *are* would have to skip the intervening head, Top. If *are* cannot move to Top, (50b) violates the HMC: the head Top blocks head-movement to the c-commanding head Foc.

It is clear that the adjunction analysis represented by (48a) cannot account for the ungrammaticality of (49b) (see Rizzi 1997).

We now return to the interaction of the ANS with preposing. Recall the adjunct/argument asymmetry in (46) repeated here for convenience in (51):

(51) a.   *Dr. Krook, met for lunch at Eagle.
     b.   After Dr. Krook, had good lunch at Eagle with Gary [Hamp].
                               (Sylvia Plath, 10.1.1959, p. 126)

In (51a) the preposed object, *Dr. Krook*, occupies [Spec,TopP], hence the *ec* in [Spec,IP] violates the identification condition of the ECP (37).

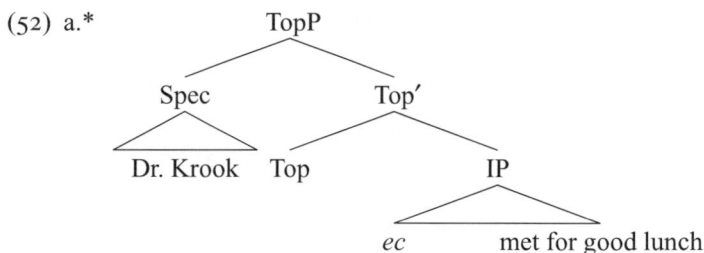

(52) a.*

```
                    TopP
                   /    \
              Spec        Top'
             /    \       /    \
       Dr. Krook  Top         IP
                            /    \
                          ec    met for good lunch
```

(52a) is the only representation for (51a), hence the sentence is ungrammatical.

In (51b), the preposed adjunct, *after Dr. Krook*, is, by hypothesis, also associated with a specialized projection. As in (52a), an antecedentless empty category cannot survive in [Spec,IP]. The specifier of the higher projection is available as a position for a potential antecedent.

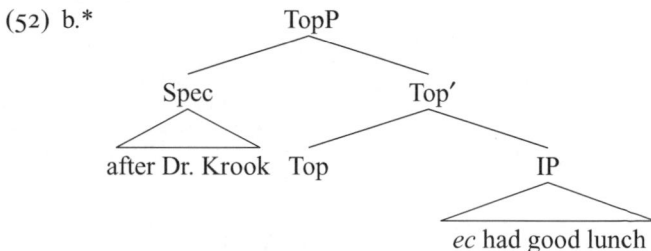

(52) b.*

```
                    TopP
                   /    \
              Spec        Top'
             /    \       /    \
    after Dr. Krook Top        IP
                            /    \
                         ec had good lunch
```

[Spec,TopP] can host an antecedent for the subject *ec*, thus the subject *ec* is submitted to the reformulated identification condition of the ECP

(37). Coindexation of the *ec* with the PP *after Dr. Krook* obviously leads to ungrammaticality. If the ec and *after Dr. Krook* are not coindexed, the representation violates the identification condition (37) of the ECP. In the next section, I show that while there is no alternative representation to (52a) for (51a), which therefore is ungrammatical, there is an alternative to (52b) for (51b), which therefore is licit.

5.3.3 By-passing the adjunct in the CP-domain

5.3.3.1 A first sketch Our analysis should continue to exclude an ANS with a preposed argument (51a), while allowing an ANS with a preposed adjunct (51b).

In this section, I elaborate a representation for (51b) in which the non-overt subject does not occupy [Spec,IP], a position to the right of the preposed adjunct. Rather, the null subject by-passes the preposed adjunct, leaving a coindexed trace in [Spec,IP]:

(53) a. *ec*$_i$ After Dr. Krook, t$_i$ had good lunch at Eagle with Gary
       <----------------------
       [Hamp]. [Sylvia Plath, 10.1.1959, p. 126)

While admitting representation (53a) with adjunct preposing, our analysis must exclude by-passing of an argument (53b). If only the illicit representation (52a) is available with argument preposing, (51a) remains ungrammatical.

(53) b. *ec*$_i$ Dr Krook t$_i$ met for lunch at Eagle.
       <--------*-----

5.3.3.2 Subject extraction and argument/adjunct asymmetries The adjunct/argument asymmetry for subject-extraction postulated in (53) is not an idiosyncratic property of ANS. In French (54a) the interrogative pronoun *qui* has been extracted from the embedded clause across a preposed adjunct. In (54b) the subject of the embedded clause cannot be extracted: crossing the preposed argument is not possible.

(54) a. Qui$_i$ crois-tu qui *l'année prochaine* t$_i$ pourra nous aider?
      <-----------------------------------
     who think you that next year will-be-able us help.
     'Who do you think that next year will be able to help us?'
   b. *Qui$_i$ crois-tu qui *ton livre*, t$_i$ pourra l'acheter?
      <--------------------*------
     who think-you that your book will-be-able to buy.
     'Who do you think will be able to buy your book'?'

For our analysis of the adjunct/argument asymmetry with the ANS, we will capitalize on the contrast in (54).[25]

Before examining the interaction between long *wh*-extraction of the subject and preposing in French in (54), we briefly discuss the French *que/qui* alternation in relation to *wh*-extraction of the subject. The contrast in (55) is well known from the literature (Rizzi 1997: 33, his (111)):

(55) a. *[$_{CP}$ Qui$_i$ crois-[$_{IP}$tu [$_{CP}$ t$_i$ que [$_{IP}$ t$_i$ pourra nous aider l'année prochaine]]]]?
        who think you that can-fut us help the next year
     b. [$_{CP}$ Qui$_i$ crois-[$_{IP}$ tu [$_{CP}$ t$_i$ qui [$_{IP}$ t$_i$ pourra nous aider l'année prochaine]]]]?

The standard analysis of the contrast in (55) is that in (55a) the complementizer *que*, like English *that*, is inert for head-government; the trace of the moved subject *qui* violates the formal licensing condition (18) of the ECP. In (55b) the lower complementizer *qui* is the spell out of the agreement features on the complementizer. These features are triggered by the transition of the subject via the specifier of the complementizer and they enable the complementizer to head-govern the subject trace:

(55) c. [$_{CP}$ Qui$_i$ crois-[$_{IP}$ tu [$_{CP}$ t$_i$ qui [$_{IP}$ t$_i$ pourra nous aider l'année prochaine]]]]
                            → [+ AGR].

We restrict our attention to sentences with the agreeing complementizer *qui*, and consider the interaction of subject extraction with preposing. (54) above shows that *wh*-extraction of the subject *qui* can by-pass a preposed adjunct without creating an ECP violation, while it cannot by-pass a preposed argument. Following Rizzi (1997) postulate that the preposed adjunct allows an agreement projection to be created whose specifier serves as an escape hatch for the moved subject.

(56) a. [$_{CP}$ Qui$_i$ crois-[$_{IP}$ tu [$_{CP}$ t$_i$ qui [$_{AgrP}$ t$_i$ [$_{TopP}$ *l'année prochaine* [$_{IP}$ t$_i$ pourra nous aider?]]]]].

Based on Rizzi (1997), I assume that this particular kind of agreement projection in the CP-domain is not available when an argument is preposed;[26] one-step movement from the [Spec,IP] position to [Spec,CP] leads to ungrammaticality.

(56) b. *[$_{CP}$ Qui crois-[$_{IP}$ tu [$_{CP}$ t$_i$ qui [$_{TopP}$ *ton livre*, [$_{IP}$ t$_i$ pourra l'acheter?]]]]].

5.3.3.3 ANS and argument/adjunct asymmetries   If the adjunct-related [Spec,AgrP] in the CP-domain is postulated as an escape hatch for subject movement (56a), it is natural to assume that the position is also available in the case of adjunct preposing with ANS, i.e. the antecedentless empty category. The ANS may move to the specifier of the adjunct-related AgrP in the CP-domain, in order to by-pass the preposed adjunct.

Starting from (56a) let us terminate the projection with the adjunct-related AgrP in the embedded CP.

(57) a. [$_{\text{AgrP}}$ t$_i$ [$_{\text{TopP}}$ *l'année prochaine* [$_{\text{IP}}$ t$_i$ pourra nous aider?]]].

In (57a) there is a trace in the specifier of the adjunct-related AgrP. This trace is antecedentless, i.e. it is an antecedentless empty category. Representation (57a) equals representation (57b):

(57) b. [$_{\text{AgrP}}$ ec$_i$ [$_{\text{TopP}}$ *l'année prochaine* [$_{\text{IP}}$ t$_i$ pourra nous aider?]]].

Following the identification condition (37) of the ECP, (57b) is grammatical: the antecedentless empty category is the highest specifier position in the structure. (57b) is a grammatical sentence in the diary register:

(57) c. L'année prochaine, pourra nous aider.
next year, will-be-able us help.
'Next year, (he) will be able to help us'

Recall that the AgrP in the CP-domain is adjunct-dependent. Such an AgrP is unavailable in the case of argument preposing (56b): the escape hatch [Spec,AgrP] is unavailable for subject extraction when an argument is preposed.

Suppose now that we also terminate (56b) at the level of the lower clause. The AgrP in the CP-domain being unavailable, by hypothesis, we end up with the structure in (58a), in which an antecedentless trace occupies [Spec,IP]. This trace is an illicit antecedentless empty category: there is a position ([Spec,TopP]) available which could host the antecedent and (58b) violates the identification clause of the ECP (37).

(58) a. *[$_{\text{TopP}}$ *ton livre*, [$_{\text{IP}}$ t$_i$ pourra l'acheter?]].
b. *[$_{\text{TopP}}$ *ton livre*, [$_{\text{IP}}$ ec$_i$ pourra l'acheter?]].
c. *Ton livre, pourra l'acheter.
your book, will-be-able it buy.

Truncated structures with preposed adjuncts and ANS such as (57c) are attested in specialized registers; truncated structures with preposed arguments and ANS such as (58c) are not found in those registers.

Capitalizing on the adjunct/argument asymmetry in French subject extraction, we postulate that the ANS can by-pass a preposed adjunct via the specifier of an adjunct-related AgrP. The ANS moves to the initial position and escapes the identification clause of the ECP (37). This escape hatch is, by hypothesis, not available with preposed arguments, the ANS cannot by-pass the topicalized object and remains stuck in [Spec,IP], where it violates the identification clause (37) of the ECP.[27, 28]

As shown by (59), subject *wh*-movement cannot by-pass the preposed adjunct *wh*-phrase.[29] We deduce that in such examples the escape hatch, [Spec,AgrP], is also unavailable.

(59) a. *Qui te demandes-tu quand reviendra?
  who yourself ask-you when will return.

We predict that an antecedentless category will not be able to by-pass preposed *wh*-phrases, hence that null subjects do not occur in *wh*-questions (cf. Table 6.3).

(59) b. *When will come back?

5.4 By-passing and principle C
The analysis outlined leads to certain predictions with respect to the interpretation of the ANS. I have formulated an account in which the ANS by-passes a preposed adjunct, and moves to a specifier of an adjunct-related AgrP. A specifier position of AgrP is, by definition (Rizzi 1991), an A-position. The prediction is that from this higher A-position, an ANS will count as a binder for any lower A-position. Notably, the ANS in the specifier of the higher adjunct-related AgrP is a potential binder for a DP within the adjunct itself. The data in (60)–(61) confirm this expectation, both for English and for French.

(60) a. [On John's$_i$ birthday], he$_i$ bought a car.
  b. [ec_i [On John's$_i$ birthday],[$t_{j/*i}$ bought a car.]]].

(61) a. [Sur cette photo de Marie$_i$], elle$_i$ sourit.
  on this picture of Marie she smiles.
  b. [ec_i [Sur cette photo de Marie$_i$],[$t_{j/*i}$ sourit.]]].

(60a) and (61a) are grammatical with coreference between the matrix subject pronoun, and the DP contained in the adjunct. (60b) and (61b) are ungrammatical if the null subject is coreferential with the adjunct-contained DP.

The Principle C effects observed in these examples confirm the analysis developed here. They also bring out quite clearly that the null subject is not strictly equivalent to the pronominal counterpart.[30, 31]

6 Conclusion

In the acquisition literature, the parallelism between the early null subject in non pro-drop languages and the adult null subject in specialized registers of the same languages has often been pointed out. This chapter discusses the adult null subject in specialized registers of French and English. I have argued that the adult null subject in the specialized registers (ANS) cannot be an instantiation of the pronominal null subject pro attested in pro-drop languages: the distribution of the ANS differs markedly from that of pro. We have also discarded the topic drop analysis for the null subject. The basic arguments against the null topic analysis concern the observation that while null subjects are available, null objects are not, and the fact that null subjects may have a non-referential interpretation.

Based on Rizzi's (1994a) analysis for early null subjects, I elaborate an analysis of the ANS as an antecedentless empty category in the specifier of the root. This analysis presupposes a reformulation of the ECP in terms of potential antecedent.

In the final part of the chapter, I extend the analysis to cases in which the null subject is preceded by a preposed adjunct. In restricted environments, the ANS can by-pass a constituent in CP. This escape hatch is not available with argument preposing.

Acknowledgements

Versions of this chapter were presented at a number of conferences: the Going Romance Conference (Amsterdam, 1995), the Graduate Students Conference (Manchester, 1994), the Workshop on Theory and Data (Salford, 1996) and the Conference on Grammar and Knowledge (Keio University, 1996). It was also presented at DIPSCO, San Raffaelle, Milan. I thank the audiences for their comments and discussion. Thanks are due to Siobhan Cottell, Paul Rowlett and Neil Smith for help with the English data. Thanks to Marc-Ariel Friedemann and to Luigi Rizzi for their comments on an earlier version of the chapter. Thanks to Tabea Ihsane for making her material available. Needless to say, none of those mentioned above can be held responsible for the remaining errors. For a version of the chapter which is more focused on English, see Haegeman (1997c).

At the moment of finalizing this chapter I have come across data which are problematic for the analysis. I have not been able to incorporate them into the chapter. For some discussion, see note 6 and also Haegeman and Ihsane (1999).

Notes

1 Expletive null subjects seem to be allowed in colloquial French. Typically, the verb *falloir* ('must') allows such an expletive null subject:

(i) a. Faut que je parte
   must that I leave-subjunctive
   'I must go'

It is not entirely clear what the constraints on the distribution of this null subject are. Observe that it may, for instance, appear in embedded clauses, though not as productively as it appears in main clauses:

(i) b. Quand faut partir, faut partir (Example due to Corinne Grange, p.c.)
　　　　when must leave, must leave

More generally, French native speakers seem to agree that expletive null subjects are possible in colloquial French:

(i) c. Semble que Marie est malade

Again, the distribution and properties of these null subjects are not clear to me at this point. I will not go into this issue here.

2 Jan 1 is 'January first'.

3 For a discussion of null subjects in 'What About Answers' (WAA) as in (i) below, see Laporte-Grimes (1996).

(i) Leigh:　Sandra walks
　　Masao:　What about Kazuko?
　　Leigh:　Runs/Can Run/*Has run

(Laporte-Grimes 1996: 13)

The non-overt subject in WAAs is argued by Laporte-Grimes to be different from the null subject discussed in this chapter. Notably, WAAs do not contain aspectual auxiliaries. This contrasts with the adult null subject in the diary style, as shown by text-example (3c). Ihsane (1998) shows that in the thirty-page extract from Virginia Woolf's diary which she has examined, 13 out of the 111 ANSs occur with an aspectual auxiliary.

4 Wilder (1994), followed by Laporte-Grimes (1996), proposes that the ANS is the result of left-peripheral deletion. See note 31 for the problems raised for such a view.

5 Coordinated clauses were not included in the survey, as these allow non-overt subject in all registers of English and French. See note 31.

(i) a. John arrived and started talking about the problem
　　b. Jean est arrivé et a commencé à parler du problème

6 My informants, and the many native-speaking audiences confronted with the data at issue here, agreed that embedded null subjects are illicit in the relevant registers. The diaries which I examined confirm this generalization. See also Ihsane (1998). At the time of finishing this chapter, though, I have come to the conclusion that the data are not that clear-cut, and that certain types of abbreviated writing do allow embedded ANS.

　Ginsberg's diary (published in 1995) contains some embedded null subjects, as illustrated by (i):

(i) a. When saw him at noon, he'd been in North Beah all last night (Allen Ginsberg, 9.1.1955, p. xxx 92)
　　b. Then I resolved to stay night here, though with money might have gone to 755 pine. (Allen Ginsberg, 3.1.1955, p. 78)
　　c. next time see him must be alive (Allen Ginsberg, 4.1.1995, p. 77)

Embedded null subjects are significantly more frequent in Helen Fielding's *Bridget Jones's Diary*, a work of fiction written in diary style. This book was first published as a diary style column in *The Independent*.

(i) d. Think might wear short black skirt tomorrow (p. 19)
   e. Delighted by, well, anything – as always am if is not work – I quickly pressed RMS Execute and nearly jumped out of my skin when I saw Cleave at the bottom of the passage (p. 22)
   f. This is what sent (p. 23)
   g. Think will cross last bit out as contains mild accusation of sexual harassment . . . (p. 25)
   h. Just managed to press Alt Screen in nick of time but big mistake as merely put CV back up on screen. (p. 25)

In Table 6.5 I provide a survey of the frequencies of null subjects according to clause types. By and large, root null subjects are more frequent than embedded null subjects.

So far, I have not come across any comparable data for the French diary register.

In future research I will return to what Ihsane calls Unexplored Null Subjects (UNS). At this point no syntactic constraints on embedded null subjects have been identified (Ihsane 1998, Haegeman and Ihsane 1999). The text-analysis is restricted to those types of diaries in which embedded null subjects are not attested and the account is not obviously applicable to the data discussed in the present note.

TABLE 6.5   Null subjects according to clause types

Extract	Clause type	Overt SU	Null SU	Total finite S	% null SU
Ginsberg:	*wh*+*y/n* root	34	0	34	0
73–92	decl root	301	150	451	33.26
	embedded	162	7	169	4.14
Ginsberg:	*wh*+*y/n* root	21	0	21	0
85–119	decl root	258	126	384	32.81
	embedded	101	3	104	2.88
Fielding:	*wh*+*y/n*-root	5	0	5	0
7–27	decl root	146	29	175	16.75
	embedded	107	15	122	12.29
Fielding:	*wh*+*y/n*-root	8	0	8	0
139–159	decl root	137	55	192	28.6
	embedded	133	17	150	11.3
Fielding:	*wh*+*y/n*-root	3	0	3	0.00
204–224	decl root	154	19	173	10.98
	embedded	77	9	86	10.47

7 The contexts in which subjects are omitted are not restricted to the rejoinders discussed in Laporte-Grimes (1996) (see note 3 above).
8 Observe the author's reference to 'economy' as the force behind pronoun omission.
9 As the early production data concern spoken English and French, it might at first sight seem preferable to compare the early null subject only with the null subject in the informal spoken register. There are differences, however, between the early production and the spoken register.

In his discussion of the casual speech which allows null subjects, Thrasher (1977: 34) discusses a range of omission phenomena, including article omission, as illustrated in (i):

(i)   a. Damn dogs are taking over the city
        b. Man your age shouldn't be working that hard

Thrasher (1977: 35) shows that article omission is restricted to the initial position in the clause – sentence-internal omissions leading to ungrammaticality:

(ii)   a. *The truth of matter is, I don't have the money
        b. *That is really busy intersection.

In the written registers which we are concerned with here, on the other hand, article omission is also found clause-internally:

(iii)   Finished, almost, story of Shadow (Sylvia Plath, 7.1.1959, p. 287)

In the early production data too, article omission is not restricted to initial position, as illustrated by the examples in (iv) from Radford (1996: 44):

(iv)   Wayne taken bubble (Daniel 1.9)
        Paula play with ball (Paula 1.6)
        Machine make noise (Kathryn 1.9) (from Bloom (1970))

So as far as article omission is concerned, a comparison with data from the written register might be more relevant.

Similarly, in spoken English, auxiliary and copula deletion is by and large confined to initial position. (See the discussion in Thrasher 1977: 22, and Akmajian *et al.* 1980, Haegeman 1997c: 32–34, for apparent counterevidence.) Typically, *be* deletes in *yes/no* questions such as (v):

(v)   (Is) Bill busy (Thrasher 1977: 41)

Concerning (vi), Thrasher (1977: 41) says: 'Auxiliary verbs also delete in statements but, *of course, only after the subject has been lost*' (my italics):

(vi)   (I'm) Afraid there's not much we can do.

Again, in the written registers, auxiliaries delete sentence-internally (see also Ihsane 1998):

(vii)   All most reassuring (Sylvia Plath, 26.3.1957, p. 135)

And again, the acquisition data are similar to the data from the written register:

(viii) Daddy gone (Hayley 1.8) (from Radford 1996: 44)

In the present chapter, I will group subject omission in casual spoken English together with that in written English and in written French, because in fact the subject omission data do not seem at first sight to differentiate between the two kinds of registers (see note 6, though). However, it may well be that for further comparisons between adult registers and early production, the written register paradoxically turns out to be more relevant. I leave this issue for future study.

10 Example (i) is a French e-mail message:

   (i) Préparons les copies (1993)
      prepare (1pl) the copies

11 (14a–d) are based on the features [±anaphoric], [±pronominal] (see Haegeman 1994: Chapter 8)

12 As pointed out by Marc-Ariel Friedemann, the term 'antecedentless trace' seems to contain a contradiction since traces are by definition created by the movement of an antecedent. The reader should bear in mind, however, that I use the term 'trace' as a shorthand for a [–anaphoric, –pronominal] empty category.

13 Following by now standard analyses, I assume that in Italian the subject is extracted from the post-verbal position. For the possibility of post-verbal subjects, see the discussion of text-example (21).

14 Non-inverted yes/no questions are not attested in the extracts I have examined. It seems to me, though, that subject omission would be grammatical. The question in (i) could be used in informal English.

   (i) Went away, did he?

The non-inverted structure went away allows a null subject. This pattern is as expected, since the non-inverted question does not implicate the left periphery. For inverted yes/no questions, I assume that the auxiliary moves to a head position in the CP-domain whose specifier position hosts a null operator.

15 There are no instances of non-inverted questions of the type illustrated in (i). Example (ia) is an instance with wh-in-situ, (ib) a yes/no question:

   (i) a. Elle reviendra à Paris quand?
           she returns to Paris when
      b. Elle reviendra encore à Paris avant de partir?
           she returns again to Paris before to leave

My conjecture is that in the relevant register they would allow a null subject:

   (ii) a. Reviendra à Paris quand?
       b. Reviendra encore à Paris avant de partir?

There are also no instances of non-inverted *wh*-questions with *wh*-preposing:

(iii) a. Quand elle reviendra à Paris?

My conjecture is that these would not allow null subjects:

(iii) b. *Quand reviendra à Paris?

16 In English and French embedded questions and relatives, *wh*-movement targets [Spec,CP]. See Rizzi (1997).

17 To maintain the null topic analysis for ANS whilst accounting for the incompatibility of ANS and *wh*-preposing, one might propose (Michal Starke p.c.) that the null topic differs from the overt topic in that it has to move to the landing site normally reserved for *wh*-preposing, [Spec,FocP]. This is not a natural move: Portuguese topic drop is compatible with *wh*-preposing (data from Lucienne Rasetti, p.c.):

(i) Quando você viu
     when you see

18 I assume that *tomorrow* is in the CP-domain. (36) contrasts with (i):

(i) a. It probably will rain tomorrow.
     b. There probably will be more snow tomorrow.

In (i) I assume that *it* and *there* are in the canonical subject position, hence not topicalized, and that *probably* is IP-internal.

The ban on topicalization of the [−human] pronoun *it* extends beyond expletives: as a weak pronoun, *it* never topicalizes (see Cardinaletti and Starke 1994):

(iii) a. Don't try this cake now. *It tomorrow will taste better.

Again (iiib) is grammatical, suggesting that *probably* is not in the CP-domain and that *it* occupies the canonical subject position:

(iii) b. Don't try this cake now. It probably will taste better tomorrow.

A full discussion of the syntax of pronouns is beyond the scope of this chapter.

19 Cf. Valian (1991) and Crisma (1992). See Roeper and Rohrbacher (1994), Bromberg and Wexler (1995), for English.

20 In line with Chomsky (1993), Rizzi (1998, this volume) interprets the antecedentless empty category in terms of an independent grammatical option of leaving a position unpronounced. This particular implementation does not entail any particular modification of the analysis.

21 Haegeman (1990b) signals (i) without discussion:

(i) ?After I had left the party, saw no one

22 Thanks to Eric Haeberli for pointing out this example to me.

23 For a generalized approach to the syntax of adverbials along these lines, I refer the reader to Cinque (1995). For a discussion of intervention effects of adjuncts in CP, see also Haegeman (1997d).

24 The label of the functional projection as such is not crucial. What is import-ant is that there **is** a specific adjunct-related projection.
25 The data are simplified. Notably, indirect objects pose intricate problems which I cannot go into here. For discussion of the French data, I refer to Rizzi (1997).
26 The reader should note that argument topicalization involves a doubling clitic in most cases in French:

(i) Ton livre, je pourrai *(l)'acheter la semaine prochaine
your book, I will be able to *(it) buy next week
'Your book, I will be able to buy next week'

For reasons of space I cannot provide a full explanation for the ungrammaticality of (56b) here. Let me sketch a much simplified summary of Rizzi's account. If the TopP-related AgrP were to be projected in the CP-domain with a topicalized DP-argument, its features would be exhausted by the preposed DP-argument itself. Rizzi suggests that an adjunct does not exhaust the TopP-related agreement features. For discussion of preposed PPs, see Rizzi (1997).
27 In order to check whether the parallelism with the adult null subject holds, it would be interesting to examine the cooccurrence of the early null subject with topicalized material.
A first survey of the French data of Augustin (Hamann *et al.* 1996) reveals that early null subjects are compatible with preposed material. There are 18 instances of topicalization in the material examined, 6 of which with a null subject:

(i) a. encore veux jouer (Augustin 2.9.2)
      still want play
    b. tout là haut essuie, tout là-haut, essuie (Augustin 2.4.22)
      high up wipes
    c. pis a payé (Augustin 2.9.2)
      then has paid
    d. et pis a yamenees (Augustin 2.9.2)
      and then has taken back
    e. A la poste a aussi magasin (Augustin 2.9.2)
      at the post have also shop
    f. encore faut demonter le pont (Augustin 2.9.30)
      still must take apart the bridge

Example (if) concerns a null expletive with *falloir* ('must'), a possibility available in colloquial French (see note 1). None of the examples involves object topicalization.
Friedemann (1992) signals 14 instances of topicalization in Early French, 3 of which with a non-overt subject. Among the latter, there is one instance of a null subject with object preposing, again an instance of the expletive null subject with *falloir* ('must') (cf. note 1).

(ii) Celui-la, faut couper (Friedemann 1992, from Philippe 2.2)
that one there must cut

Rasetti (1995) cites (iii), signalling that it is not clear wether the DP *le chien* ('the dog') is a separate unit or integrated in the structure.

(iii) Le chien dessine (Jean 1.7)
      the dog (object) draws

28 As pointed out by Friedemann (p.c.), the by-passing mechanism is potentially in conflict with the Avoid Structure principle. The exact scope of the Avoid Structure principle and its interaction with other principles of the grammar requires further study.

29 For a discussion of the landing sites of *wh*-movement, I refer the reader to Rizzi (1997). Suffice it to say here that in French and in English, root *wh*-movement targets [Spec,FocP] and embedded *wh*-movement targets [Spec,CP].

30 The data are slightly more complex when we turn to clausal adjuncts. Some speakers accept (i) with coreference between *John* and the non-overt subject:

(i) Although John smokes, never touches alcohol

While it remains to be seen how to account for the acceptability of this example for some speakers, it seems to me that a number of considerations come into play. First, it is known that Principle C effects are weakened with the intervention of clausal projections (cf. Reinhart 1981b and much work (also by others) written later). Moreover, it is conceivable that for speakers who accept (i) the adjunct clause is less directly integrated in the structure (cf. Haegeman 1984).

31 Wilder's (1994: 35ff) analysis of ANS is an extension of his analysis of forward deletion in coordination. He proposes that like the null subject in the second conjunct of (ia), ANS in (ib) is the result of a left-peripheral deletion process:

(i) a. He left the office and went to the cinema.
    b. Went to the cinema.

Wilder 's analysis correctly excludes object deletion:

(i) c. *I saw Bill and invited for lunch.

In order to rule out (ii), where a post-auxiliary subject is deleted, Wilder appeals to the Head condition (iii) which also governs forward deletion in coordination. Both a diary sentence such as (iia) and a coordinated sentence such as (iib) are ungrammatical because the null subject in the canonical subject position is governed by the auxiliary to its left.

(ii) a. *% Did see anyone?
     b. *Did he go there and did see anyone?
(iii) Head condition
      Root is ellipsis not possible in the c-command domain of an overt head. (1995: 36)

Wilder does not account for the ungrammaticality of (iva) – unexpected in his account – in which the subject is not governed by an overt head. He simply signals the parallelism with (ivb):

(iv) a. *This book, do not approve of.
      b. *This book, I like and that record, did not approve of.

Wilder does not discuss the adjunct/argument asymmetry discussed in 5.3; the question of what excludes the null subject with preposed complements (iv) and what allows it with adjunct preposing remains unanswered. It is not clear how Wilder's deletion analysis would account for the Principle C effects in section 5.4.

The question arises whether null subjects in coordination might be given the same analysis as that developed for the ANS in this chapter.

References

ABNEY, STEVE (1987) *The English Noun Phrase in its Sentential Aspect.* Dissertation, MIT.

ABOH, ENOCH (1995) 'Notes on Focalization in Gungbe'. Ms, University of Geneva.

AKMAJIAN, ADRIAN, RICHARD A. DEMERS and ROBERT M. HARNISH (1980) *Linguistics.* Cambridge, MA: MIT Press.

BLOOM, LOIS (1970) *Language Development.* Cambridge MA: MIT Press.

BRESNAN, JOAN (1977) 'Variables in the Theory of Transformations', in P. Culicover *et al.* (eds), *Formal Syntax,* New York: Academic Press.

BROMBERG, HILARY and KEN WEXLER (1995) 'Null subjects in wh-questions', in C. T. Schütze *et al.* (eds), *Papers on Language Processing and Acquisition,* 221–48.

CARDINALETTI, ANNA and MICHAL STARKE (1994) 'The Typology of Structural Deficiency'. Ms, University of Geneva, University of Venice.

CHOMSKY, NOAM (1991) 'Some Notes on the Economy of Derivation', in R. Freidin (ed.), *Principles and Parameters in Comparative Grammar* Cambridge MA: MIT Press, pp. 417–54.

CHOMSKY, NOAM (1993) 'A Minimalist Program for Linguistic Theory', in Ken Hale and Jay Keyser (eds), *A View from Building 20.* Cambridge, MA: MIT Press, 1–52.

CINQUE, GUGLIELMO (1995) *Adverbs and the Universal Hierarchy of Functional Projections.* Glow paper, Tromsö.

CLAHSEN, HARALD (ed.) (1996) *Generative Perspectives on Language Acquisition,* Amsterdam: John Benjamins, pp. 309–34.

CRISMA, PAOLA (1992) 'On the Acquisition of Wh-questions in French', *GenGenP* 0, 1–2 115–22.

CULICOVER, PETER (1991) 'Topicalization, Inversion and Complementizers in English', in D. Delfitto *et al.* (eds), *OTS Working Papers. Going Romance and Beyond,* Department of Linguistics, University of Utrecht, 1–45.

FRIEDEMANN, MARC-ARIEL (1992) 'The Underlying Position of External Arguments in French: A Study in Adult and Child Grammar', *GenGenP* 0, 1–2: 123–44.

FRIEDEMANN, MARC-ARIEL (1997) *Sujets syntaxiques. Positions, inversions et pro.* Bern, etc.: Peter Lang.

GRIMSHAW, JANE (1993) 'Minimal Projection and Clause Structure'. Ms, Rutgers University.

HAAN, GER DE and K. TUIJNMAN (1988) 'Missing Subjects and Objects in Child Grammar', in Peter Jordens and Josien Lalleman (eds), *Language Development*, Dordrecht: Foris, 101–22.

HAEGEMAN, LILIANE (1984) 'Remarks on Adverbial Clauses and Definite Anaphora', *Linguistic Inquiry* (USA) **15**: 4.

HAEGEMAN, LILIANE (1987) 'Complexity and Literary Prose: Some Suggestions for Formalization', *Language and Style* **20**/3: 214–22.

HAEGEMAN, LILIANE (1988) 'Register Variation in English: Some Theoretical Observations', *Journal of English Linguistics* **20**/2: 230–48.

HAEGEMAN, LILIANE (1990a) 'Non-overt Subjects in Diary Contexts', in Juan Mascaro and Marina Nespor (eds), *Grammar in Progress*, Foris: Dordrecht.

HAEGEMAN, LILIANE (1990b) 'Understood Subjects in English Diaries', *Multilingua* **9**: 157–99.

HAEGEMAN, LILIANE (1992) *Generative Syntax: Theory and Description. A Case Study of West Flemish*. CUP: Cambridge.

HAEGEMAN, LILIANE (1994) 'The Typology of Syntactic Positions: L-relatedness and the A/A'-distinction', *GAGL*, Thematic issue on Minimalism.

HAEGEMAN, LILIANE (ed.) (1997a) *The New Comparative Syntax*. Longman: London.

HAEGEMAN, LILIANE (ed.) (1997b) *Elements of Grammar*. Kluwer Academic Publishers: Dordrecht.

HAEGEMAN, LILIANE (1997c) 'Register Variation, Truncation and Subject Omission in English and in French', *English Language and Linguistics* **1**: 233–70.

HAEGEMAN, LILIANE (1997d) 'Negative Inversion and the Structure of CP. Paper presented at the Linguistic Colloquium, University of Wuppertal.

HAEGEMAN, LILIANE TABEA, IHSANE (1999) 'Subject Ellipsis in Embedded Clauses in English', *English Language and Linguistics* **3**, 117–45.

HAMANN, CORNELIA, LUIGI RIZZI and ULI FRAUENFELDER (1996) *On the Acquisiton of the Pronominal System in French*, in Harald Clahsen (ed.)

HUANG, JAMES (1984) 'On the Distribution and Reference of Empty Pronouns', *Linguistic Inquiry* **15**: 531–574.

HUANG, JAMES (1986) 'Pro Drop in Chinese: A Generalized Control Theory', in Oswaldo Jacggli and Ken Safir (eds), *The Null Subject Parameter*, Dordrecht: Kluwer, 185–214.

HYAMS, NINA (1986) *Language Acquisition and the Theory of Parameters*. Reidel: Dordrecht.

HYAMS, NINA and KEN WEXLER (1993) 'On the Grammatical Basis of Null Subjects in Child Language', *Linguistic Inquiry* **24**: 412–59.

IHSANE, TABEA (1998) 'The Syntax of Diaries: Grammar and Register Variation'. Mémoire de licence. Department of Linguistics, University of Geneva.

JAEGGLI, OSWALDO and KEN SAFIR (1989) *The Null Subject Parameter*, Dordrecht: Kluwer.

LAPORTE-GRIMES, LAUREL (1996) 'Pf Merger and LF Verb Raising'. General Examination Paper, University of Connecticut.

LASNIK, HOWARD and MAMORO SAITO (1984) 'On the Nature of Proper Government', *Linguistic Inquiry* **14**: 235–98.

LASNIK, HOWARD and TIM STOWELL (1991) 'Weakest Crossover', *Linguistic Inquiry* **22**: 687–720.

MÜLLER, GEREON and WOLFGANG STERNEFELD (1992) 'Improper Movement and Unambiguous Binding', *Linguistic Inquiry* **24**: 461–507.

NAKAJIMA, HEIZO (1996) 'Complementizer Selection', *The Linguistic Review* **13**: 143–64.

PERLMUTTER, DAVID (1971) *Deep and Surface Structure Constraints in Syntax.* New York: Holt, Rinehart and Winston.

PIERCE, AMY (1989) *On the Emergence of Syntax: A Cross linguistic Study.* Ph.D. dissertation, MIT.

PUSKAS, GENOVEVA (1997) 'Focus and the CP domain', in Liliane Haegeman (ed.), *The New Comparative Syntax*, London: Longman, 145–64.

QUIRK, RANDOLPH, GEOFFREY LEECH, SIDNEY GREENBAUM and JAN SVARTVIK (1985) *A Comprehensive Grammar of English.* London: Longman.

RADFORD, ANDREW (1990) *Syntactic Theory and the Acquisition of English Syntax.* Oxford: Blackwell.

RADFORD, ANDREW (1994) *The Nature of Children's Initial Clauses.* Ms, Essex University.

RADFORD, ANDREW (1996) 'Towards a Structure-building Model of Acquisition', in H. Clahsen (ed.), *Generative Perspectives on Language Acquisition*, Amsterdam: John Benjamins, 43–90.

RAPOSO, EDUARDO (1986) 'The Null Object in European Portuguese', in Oswaldo Jaeggli and Carmen Silva-Corvalan (eds), *Studies in Romance Linguistics*, Dordrecht: Foris 373–90.

RASETTI, LUCIENNE (1995) 'La distribution du sujet nul dans la grammaire enfantine du français'. Licence paper, University of Geneva.

REINHART, TANYA (1981a) 'Two COMP positions', in A. Belletti, L. Brandi, and L. Rizzi (eds), *Theory of Markedness in Generative Grammar*, Pisa: Sucola Normale Superiore.

REINHART, TANYA (1981b) 'Definite NP-anaphora and C-command Domains', *Linguistic Inquiry* **12**: 605–35.

RIZZI, LUIGI (1982) *Issues in Italian Syntax.* Dordrecht: Foris.

RIZZI, LUIGI (1986) 'Null Objects in Italian and the Theory of Pro' *Linguistic Inquiry* **17**: 501–58.

RIZZI, LUIGI (1990) *Relativized Minimality.* Cambridge: MIT Press.

RIZZI, LUIGI (1991) 'Proper Head Government and the Definition of A Positions'. Glow paper, Leiden.

RIZZI, LUIGI (1993) 'A Parametric Approach to Comparative Syntax: Properties of the Pronominal System', *English Linguistics* **10**: 1–27. Also in Liliane Haegeman (ed.), (1997a),

RIZZI, LUIGI (1994a) 'Early Null Subjects and Root Null subjects', in Teun Hoekstra and Bonny Schwartz (eds), *Language Acquisition Studies in Generative Grammar*, Amsterdam: John Benjamins, 151–77.

RIZZI, LUIGI (1994b) 'Some Notes on Linguistic Theory and Language Development: The Case of Root Infinitives', *Language Acquisition* **3**/4: 371–93.

RIZZI, LUIGI (1997) 'The Fine Structure of the Left Periphery', in Liliane Haegeman (ed.), 1997b, *Elements of Grammar*, Dordrecht: Kluwer Academic Publishers.

RIZZI, LUIGI (1998) *Remarks on Early Null Subjects.* Ms, University of Siena, University of Geneva.

RIZZI, LUIGI and IAN ROBERTS (1991) 'Complex Inversion in French', *Probus* 1: 1–30.

ROEPER, TOM and BERNHARD ROHRBACHER (1994) 'Null Subjects in Early Child English and the Theory of Economy of Projection'. Ms, University of Massachusetts at Amherst and University of Pennsylvania.

ROSS, JOHN ROBERT (1982) 'Pronoun Deleting Processes in German'. Paper presented at the Annual Meeting of the Linguistics Society of America, San Diego, California.

SCHMERLING, SUSAN (1973) 'Subjectless Sentences and the Notion of Surface Structure', in Claudia Corum, T. Cedric Smith and Ann Weiser (eds), *Papers from the Ninth Regional Meeting of the Chicago Linguistics Society* 577–86.

SCHÜTZE, CARSON T., JENNIFER B. GANDER and KEVIN BROIHIER (1995) *Papers on Language Processing and Acquisition*, MIT Working papers in Linguistics **26**.

THRASHER, RANDOLPH (1977) *One Way to Say More by Saying Less. A Study of So-called Subjectless Sentences.* Kwansei Gakuin University Monograph Series Vol. 11. Tokyo: The Eihosha Ltd.

TRAVIS, LISA (1984) 'Parameters and Effects of Word Order Variation'. MIT dissertation.

VALIAN, VIRGINIA (1991) 'Syntactic Subjects in the Early Speech of American and Italian Children', *Cognition* **40**: 21–81.

WEISSENBORN, JURGEN (1992) 'Null Subjects in Early Grammars: Implications for Parameter Setting Theory', in Jurgen Weissenborn, Helen Goodluck and Tom Roeper (eds), *Theoretical Issues in Language Acquisition*, Hillsdale, NJ: Lawrence Erlbaum.

WILDER, CHRIS (1994) 'Some Properties of Ellipsis in Coordination', *GenGenP* **2**/2: 23–61.

Corpus material

GINSBERG, ALLEN (1995) *Journals 1954–1958*, edited by Gordon Ball. London: Penguin Books.

HELEN FIELDING (1997) *Bridget Jones's Diary*. Picador.

ISAACS, SUSAN (1997) *Lily White*. London: Penguin Books.

JAMES, P.D. (1989) (1962) *Cover her Face*. Faber and Faber; London: Penguin Books.

LÉAUTAUD, PAUL (1989) *Le Fléau. Journal Particulier. 1917–1939*. Paris: Mercure de France.

PLATH, SYLVIA (1983) *The Journals of Sylvia Plath*, edited by Ted Hughes and Frances McCollough. New York: Ballantine Books.

RENDELL, RUTH (1994) *A Sleeping Life. An Inspector Wexford Mystery.* London: Arrow Books.

SHIELDS, CAROL (1996) *Swann*. London: Flamingo.

SMART, ELIZABETH (1992) *Necessary Secrets*, edited by Alice Van Wart. London: Paladin/Harper Collins.

SMART, ELIZABETH (1995), *On the Side of the Angels*, edited by Alice Van Wart. London: Flamingo/Harper Collins.

SYMONS, JULIAN (1967) *The End of Solomon Grundy*. London: The Crime Club.

SYMONS, JULIAN (1973) *The Plot against Roger Rider*. London: Penguin Books.

SYMONS, JULIAN (1967) *The Progress of a Crime*. London: The Crime Club.
VISITORS BOOK '91, The Green, Beamaris, Anglesey, North Wales.
WOOLF, VIRGINIA (1985) *The Diary of Virginia Woolf, Volume 5: 1936–1941*, edited by Anne Olivier Bell, assisted by Andrew McNeillie. London: Penguin Books. First published 1984 by Chatto and Windus.

Chapter 7

The acquisition of constituent questions and the requirements of interpretation
Cornelia Hamann

1 Introduction

From the age of 2 years, children never seem to make mistakes with respect to the order of the verbal element and its complement. In accordance with their target language, German children place the complement before the uninflected verb, whereas Danish, English and French children place it after the verb, see (1a–d).

(1) a. hubsauber putzn (Andreas, 2.1, German)
   helicopter clean(v/inf)
 b. gribe bold (Anne, 1.7.18, Danish)
   catch ball
 c. man drive truck (Allison, 1.10, English)
 d. oter la coquille (Augustin, 2.0.23, French)
   take off the shell

In contrast to this early development, fully adult-like constituent questions (Wh-questions) appear 'late': around 2.6, and often as late as 3.6. Early questions are mostly formulaic or are systematically deviant from adult usage. Klima and Bellugi (1966) found that English children either do not invert the subject and the auxiliary in their first Wh-questions or do not insert the auxiliary at all, (2). Guasti (this volume) finds about 40% non-adult questions in Child English. Likewise, French children prefer questions without inversion of the verbal element and the subject, as shown in (3). This form, though not allowed in Standard French, also occurs in adult Colloquial French. So early questions such as (3) are not target deviant. It has been observed for German, Swiss German and Dutch (Penner 1994, Tracy 1994, Clahsen *et al.* 1995, van Kampen 1997) that children often use forerunners of constituent questions where the Wh-element is missing, as in (4) and (5). In Child English the use of finite non-inverted main verbs in Wh-questions can occur quite late, as Guasti shows for Adam's and Sarah's use of finite non-inverted main verbs (Guasti, this volume). The developmental curve for Laura's acquisition of constituent questions in Dutch (van Kampen 1997:81) shows questions with a missing Wh-element till the age of 3.7.

(2) where dis goes (Adam, 2.8, Brown)

(3) a. où il est? (Philippe, 2.1.19, Childes, Leveillé)
       where he is
    b. où il est canard? (Marie, 2.1.28, Geneva Corpus)
       where he is duck

(4) a. isch das? (S., 2.0) (Penner 1994)
       is that
       'what is that'

(5) a. ga jij nou heen? (Sarah, 2.3.26) (van Kampen 1997)
       go you then to
       'where are you going'
    b. is deze vor nou? (Laura, 3.2.9) (van Kampen 1997)
       is this for then
       'whom is this for then'

What is so difficult or special about questions? To investigate this problem, we have to look more closely at the syntax and semantics of constituent questions: the projections which are involved and the fact that a question necessarily contains a scope-marking element which indicates which part of the utterance falls under the question force.

2 Theoretical background

2.1 The interpretation of questions
In generative theories of grammar, it is assumed that 'there is a level of linguistic interpretation at which all grammatical structure relevant to semantic interpretation is provided', (Hornstein 1995: 3). This level is called Logical Form (LF). Semantic interpretation operates off this level providing the truth conditions for the sentence. Quite often, interpretation is possible directly from the overt form of the utterance. There are sentences, however, which look structurally alike on the surface, but have a completely different LF-structure. This can happen if a surface subject is not a simple name (*John*), but involves a quantifier (*everybody*). In such a case, scope relations have to be made explicit at LF.

Exactly the same holds for questions: like utterances containing negation or tense, they require operators for their interpretation. This is so because one can think of the interpretation of a question as the set of propositions, here written as {P}, which are appropriate answers to it. Question (6a) has the possible answers: Jane has bought shoes, Jane has bought a dress, Jane has bought a dog, etc. Such a list of alternatives is captured semantically by the use of a variable as in (6b) and the actual interpretation, the set of true answers, is (6c).

    (6) a. What has Jane bought?
          b. Jane has bought x
          c. $\{P|\ \exists\ x\ ((x$ is an entity) $\&\ P=$ Jane has bought x $\&$ true $(P))\}$

In the English question (6a), the Wh-element occupies sentence-initial position and serves to mark question scope over the propositional frame. This helps to determine the appropriate answers. At the same time, it indicates which particular argument of the predicate the question is about. This also narrows down the possible answers, compare (6a,b) and (7a,b).

    (7) a. Who bought a book?
          b. x bought a book

The standard syntactic treatment of (6a) assumes that the Wh-element is generated in object position, but moves to sentence-initial position and leaves behind a trace, which serves as the variable. This gives (8a). Here, *what* functions as an operator which marks the structure in its scope, i.e. the rest of the sentence, as a question. The inner bracket provides a propositional frame closely resembling (6b). In a more articulated system which assumes at least three shells of sentence structure (VP, IP and CP),[1] such an analysis has the form shown in (8b), where the specifier–head relation of Wh-word and auxiliary is a necessary consequence of either a feature-checking mechanism as assumed in Chomsky (1995) or of the Wh-criterion as introduced by Rizzi (1991) and discussed by Guasti (this volume). The interpretation remains as in (6c).

    (8) a. [$what_i$ has [Jane bought t_i]]
          b. [$_{CP}$ $what_i$ [$_{C'}$ has_j [$_{IP}$ $Jane_k$ [$_{I'}$ t_j [$_{VP}$ t_k [$_{V'}$ bought t_i]]]]]]

So the overt syntax of the Standard English question (6a) makes the interpretation explicit. But not all languages do this. In Asian languages, the Wh-element remains in-situ and the same possibility exists in Colloquial French, see (9).

    (9) Jeanne a acheté quoi?
          Jane has bought what

If the semantic frame is not given overtly, the question interpretation, especially question scope, must be read off some other level. The usual assumption is that the Wh-element of an in-situ question moves covertly at LF. Leaving aside the problem of auxiliary movement to

Comp here, the French question (9) has roughly the same LF as shown in (8) with the French words substituted for the English ones. This sameness is the result of design, of course, making a natural assumption about human languages. Interpretations are constant across languages, only the overt syntax may vary. In other words, Logical Form, the level which provides the input for semantic interpretation, is universal.

2.2 Assumptions about acquisition

These standard assumptions about the interpretation and syntax of questions help to make the child's difficulties more precise, especially in the light of certain approaches to the acquisition of language. Let us adopt a view of Full Continuity modified in the sense of Borer and Wexler (1987) or Rizzi (1994). This implies that Universal Grammar (UG) is available from the beginning and that principles are never violated. But it also implies that not only parameters, but also principles of UG, can be underspecified and mature. Wexler (1994), Hyams (1996) and Schütze and Wexler (1996) assume that the tense projection is underspecified, Rizzi assumes that it is the CP which is not obligatorily projected in the first phases of syntactic development. Subsequently, maturation of some principle of discourse grounding or selection will oblige the child to use these projections. Both approaches presuppose that projections are universal. Radford (1990) also adheres to the view of Full Continuity, but assumes that projections are not universal and have to be acquired, one after and on top of the other, triggered by the acquisition of lexico-morphological material.

The Full Continuity Hypothesis, even with a maturational modification, makes it likely that the difficulties in the acquisition of questions and the differences found cross-linguistically in their development are due to syntax, not interpretation. Most researchers agree that children have 'CP-trouble' of some kind. So the problems almost certainly involve the CP-level.

If CP is missing in the early phases of language development (cf. Radford 1990, Clahsen 1991, Clahsen et al. 1995), then operator movement to SpecCP cannot take place and the correct scope relations cannot be established unless the Wh-word is simply adjoined or merged to IP. Radford (1990) and also Roeper (1996) take the non-inversion of subject and auxiliary in the Wh-questions of young English children as evidence for the adjunction/merger analysis. Moreover, the occurrence of finite fronted Wh-questions with a sentence-final main verb in Child German as reported by Penner (1994) and Tracy (1994), but not found by Clahsen et al. (1995), is most easily explained by a merger analysis. A closer look at the Early English data as provided by Guasti (this volume) gives a different interpretation of this sort of evidence, however, which could be transferred to the German data.

Another approach which presumes 'CP-trouble' is Rizzi (1994)'s truncation hypothesis. Rizzi observes that every root clause must be connected to discourse and be marked for illocutionary force. Because it is the CP-projection which is selected by discourse and where illocutionary force can be marked, he assumes that (10) is an axiom of adult grammar. He further assumes that this axiom is suspended in child grammar. If (10) is not yet in force, any projection can be the root, so that higher projections can be truncated. However, projections can never be truncated if there is material to be accommodated.

(10) Root = CP

The approach implies that every higher projection must be truncated once a projection has been truncated. Conversely, if a projection is activated by material, then all lower projections are selected and thus activated. It follows that a fronted Wh-word activates the CP-projection, so that the IP must be projected and root infinitives cannot occur. Moreover, subjects cannot be omitted from a fronted Wh-question because subject omission must be licensed and the Wh-element, which is in the right c-commanding position, does not qualify as a licenser.

2.3 The problem
With regard to interpretation, the following predictions are obtained. If the CP is not obligatory, but is always projected in the presence of morphological material, then Wh-questions with a fronted Wh-element activate the CP and the correct interpretation can be established. This seems to be borne out in a general fashion because root infinitives have not been found in French or German fronted Wh-questions, see section 3.2.3.[2] However, early questions without Wh-elements as occurring in Dutch and German or early Wh-in-situ questions as occurring in French could be syntactically different if the CP can be truncated. This follows, if we assume that only morphological material can activate a projection.

In section 3.2.3 I show that root infinitives (RIs) do not occur in fronted Wh in Early French, but neither do they occur in Wh-in-situ. Syntactic differences have been found, however, with respect to null subjects. Crisma (1992) reports no missing subjects in the fronted Wh-questions of the French corpus of Philippe, but predicts French Wh-in-situ questions without subjects. This prediction is borne out: my data on Augustin and Marie (see Tables 7.3 and 7.5 and the appendix) show that subjects are frequently missing from Wh-in-situ questions. A similar phenomenon has been observed by Clahsen *et al.* (1995) for German. Covering an age span of 1.7 to 3.8 over 9 children, there are very few (4%) missing subjects in fronted Wh-questions, but about 18% missing subjects in questions without the Wh-element.

Clahsen *et al.* (1995) use these data as an argument for the Lexical Learning Hypothesis. In the absence of the Wh-element or the complementizer there are syntactic differences, they reason, which show that only the full acquisition of the paradigm of lexical Wh-pronouns and complementizers can create the full CP-projection. They use the idea of economy of projection to argue for the view that 'silent' elements do not create a projection and they provide the evidence of syntactic differences as a proof. With respect to complementizers they conclude their argument: 'Hence if the child does not produce any complementizers, we cannot treat these sentences [complementizerless subordinate clauses] as full CPs even though they might have similar meanings as subordinate clauses in the adult language' (Clahsen *et al.* 1995:14, my addition in square brackets).

There is a problem here, however. Having 'similar meanings' implies that the LFs of the clauses with or without complementizers have the same structure and thus necessarily both have a CP at LF. The same applies to constituent questions without Wh-elements and to French Wh-in-situ. Clahsen *et al.* (1995) are aware of this problem and argue that though both types of clauses have the same LF, they still may have different phrase structures (Clahsen *et al.* 1995:19, footnote 4). If this were intended to mean that there must be certain structural differences at Spell-out, I would totally agree. But I do not think that the differences could be as radical as missing out a projection or a position important for the interpretation.

Crisma (1992) speculates about the same problem in the framework of the Truncation Hypothesis. She observes that Philippe only uses fronted Wh in a first phase, though Wh-in-situ occurs frequently in colloquial French. She proposes that Philippe avoids this construction because it obligatorily requires CP at LF, which clashes with the option to truncate this projection in the absence of morphological material. The data I present in section 3.2.2 show that this explanation does not hold across children. Some French children use Wh-in-situ quite frequently so that there cannot be any clash which has to be avoided.

The problem which emerges from this brief discussion is whether interpretational material can force syntactic projection just as morphological material can. Let us return to the interpretation of Wh-questions. If the German child marks question force not by the Wh-element, which is left out, but by the intonational pattern, one can still assume that the child knows that s/he is asking a question. So there must be something which marks this utterance with question force at LF. This could be an abstract, non-overt question morpheme Q, structurally encoding what is given by the intonation. Such an abstract Q-morpheme is no ad-hoc invention. It is standardly assumed for adult Yes–No questions, which in many languages exist in two forms, one (see 11a,b) syntactically distinct from a declarative (though without a Wh-element), but the other (see 12a,b) exactly like a declarative, marked as a question only by intonation.[3]

(11) a. Est-ce que il a achéte le livre?
     b. Has he bought the book?

(12) a. Il a acheté le livre?
     b. He has bought the book?

So at LF at the latest, this abstract Q-morpheme will have to be placed in its usual scope position, i.e. in SpecCP. If the child is communicating and so pairing utterances with meanings, the derivation cannot stop at Spell-out but must provide the LF. It follows that for questions, especially for their interpretative content, there must be CP and SpecCP.

This argument is problematic for the Lexical Learning Hypothesis. For the Truncation Hypothesis it poses a problem only as long as it is assumed that a projection is activated if and only if there is morphological material to be accommodated. I therefore propose that interpretative material which is not available through a default (situational) interpretation also activates projections. If this is the case, however, the obvious explanation for the syntactic differences of fronted-Wh on the one hand, and questions without Wh-elements or Wh-in-situ on the other hand, is not available any longer.

The solution proposed in section 4.5 is straightforward. Just as subordinate clauses introduced by *that* have different syntactic properties from clauses introduced by the null complementizer in English (see 4.3), the syntactic differences observed may be due to different properties of the overt or non-overt question morphemes. Capturing the fact that French child Wh-in-situ and German child questions without a Wh-element both allow null subjects ultimately requires that the movement analysis discussed for Wh-in-situ be abandoned.

Before I investigate French child data with respect to the syntax of different question forms, I will discuss the analysis of Wh-in-situ. The presentation of the data will be followed by a discussion and the outline of a solution.

3 French fronted Wh and Wh-in-situ

3.1 Two approaches to adult in-situ questions
Following 2.1, a French question with a fronted Wh-pronoun (13a) has the representation (14a). For the question (13b), the Wh-word, though in situ on the surface, also needs to have wide scope in order to achieve the correct reading.

(13) a. qui as-tu vu?
     who have-you seen
   b. tu as vu qui?
     you have seen who

(14) a. $[_{CP}$ qui$_i$ $[_{C'}$ as$_j$ $[_{IP}$ tu$_k$ $[_{I'}$ t$_j$ $[_{VP}$ t$_k$ $[_{V'}$ vu t$_i$]]]]]]

The standard solution (see 2.1) is to assign representation (14a) not only to (13a) but also to (13b). The difference is explained by assuming covert LF-movement for (13b), whereas in (13a) the question word has moved overtly before Spell-out. This – apart from differences in Aux-movement – outlines the movement approach to scope marking, originating from Chomsky (1976) and developed notably by Huang (1982).

Certain syntactic differences in the two question forms in adult language were explained by the assumption of different constraints for overt and covert movement. Such differences cannot be stated in the minimalist framework (Chomsky 1995) because there is only one type of movement before and after Spell-out. Moreover, even in older models of grammar, it can be shown that the two types of movement are in fact constrained in the same manner (Reinhart 1995). So the movement analysis of Wh-in-situ was always controversial.

A competing analysis goes back to Baker (1970), who suggested that every question contains an abstract Q-morpheme. This captures the intuition that an interrogative pronoun contains an abstract question morpheme and the basic existential pronoun 'someone' or 'something'. In Baker's approach, in-situ Wh-constituents are bound directly by Q, as shown in (14b), where Q is in a scope position (adjoined or as a specifier).

(14) b. [Q$_i$ [$_{IP}$ tu [as [$_{VP}$ vu qui$_i$]]]]

The idea that scope assignment does not necessarily involve movement has since been elaborated by Williams (1986), Pesetsky (1987) and Reinhart (1995).[4] The last argues that a movement analysis is inappropriate for all types of in-situ questions, and suggests that the question operator binds a choice function.

Let us sketch the basic concepts of Reinhart (1995)'s analysis. Wh-NPs are analysed as indefinites. *Which lady* thus could be analysed as (15a). However, structure (15a) coupled with an in-situ analysis leads to scope problems whenever the Wh-NP is embedded under other operators such as the universal quantifier, negation or *if*. These problems can be avoided if a choice function is employed instead of the existential operator. This analysis is shown in (15b), which denotes the value of the function f applied to the set of ladies.

(15) a. $[_{Det}$ ∃ x $[_{N}$ lady (x)]]
   b. $[_{Det}$ f $[_{N}$ {x| lady(x)}]]

A choice function f selects one element out of the set of entities which appears as its argument. So the choice function f in (15b) selects one element x out of the set of entities which are ladies, and the value of f is a specific lady. This treatment guarantees that it is a semantic argument which stays in situ. Moreover, an operator acting on the choice function can be arbitrarily far away from this argument, which solves the above-mentioned scope problems.

This analysis is then extended to Wh-pronouns such that the N-restriction is more general, just giving the selectional restrictions. Roughly speaking, one can analyse *who*, *what* and *where* and their French equivalents as (16a,b,c).[5]

> (16) a. who   qui [$_{Det}$ f [$_N$ {x| person(x)}]
>   b. what   quoi [$_{Det}$ f [$_N$ {x| thing(x)}]
>   c. where où   [$_{Det}$ f [$_N$ {x| place(x)}]

Using the choice function analysis of indefinites, a Baker-type in-situ analysis and the notations 'Q f' for the locution 'for which f' and 'f(person)' for (16a), gives (17a,b) as the LF and interpretation of (13b). For the interpretation (17b), 'Q' is replaced by the existential operator.

> (17) a. [Q f [tu [as [vu f(person)]]]]
>   b. {P| ∃ f (P= you have seen f(person) & true(P))}

Two alternative approaches have emerged. For fronted Wh, scope marking takes place overtly by the Wh-operator. For Wh-in-situ there are two possibilities: covert Wh-movement or binding by a base-inserted operator.

3.2 The data from Child French

3.2.1 The method and the subjects
In the light of the theoretical discussion and the questions raised in section 2.3, I investigate data from Child French which provides the test case for the use of both fronted-Wh and Wh-in-situ questions. I investigate the spontaneous production of three monolingual French children, Philippe (2.1.19–2.7.18) from Leveillé (Childes, MacWhinney 1991) analysed by Crisma (1992), Augustin (2.0.1–2.9.30) from (Hamann *et al.* 1996), and Marie (1.8.26–2.3.3), who, like Augustin, was recorded in the Interfaculty Project in Geneva and whose data have recently become available. See Rasetti (this volume) for details on Marie, and the Childes Corpus for details on Philippe. Augustin was studied longitudinally over a period of 10 months. He was recorded 10 times at his home in 45-minute sessions in the intervals shown in Table 7.7 in the appendix. For this analysis, the transcriptions of the first 30 minutes of each recording were used. Direct repetitions were not included;

TABLE 7.1   Development of Wh-questions for Philippe, Augustin and Marie

			% RIs	% NS	Fronted Wh	Wh-in-situ
Philippe	T1	2.1.19–2.2.17	21.8	38.6	35	0
	T2	2.2.26–2.3.21	8.6	33.2	78	1
	T3	2.6.13–2.7.18	1.6	9.8	118	81
Augustin	T1	2.0.2–2.4.22	17.5	49.1	1	27
	T2	2.6.16–2.9.30	6.1	26.6	7	59
Marie	T1	1.8.26–2.3.3	17.9	40.2	3	27

neither were question types without a verbal element. Utterances such as (18a,b), which, following Friedemann (1992), I analyse as having a postverbal lexical subject, were not counted as null-subject utterances, but as utterances with an overt subject. The same criteria were applied to the count on Marie.[6]

(18) a. mas su quoi Cedric (Augustin, 2.6.16)
         marche sur quoi Cedric
         walks on what Cedric
         'on what does Cedric walk'
     b. Est où maman (Augustin, 2.6.16)
         is where mummy
         'where is mummy'

3.2.2 Individual variation

Table 7.1 compares the development of question formation for Philippe, Augustin and Marie in relation to these children's overall use of RIs and their overall null subject use (finite and non-finite declaratives, Yes–No questions and Wh-questions). For Philippe the percentages of overall null subjects and of RIs are calculated from Crisma (1992)'s data, but see Rasetti (this volume) for slightly different numbers. The percentages of Augustin's overall null subject use and RI-use are fully compatible with Rasetti (1996 and this volume). The recordings analysed for Marie span five months of early speech and do not show a notable development in the use of null subjects or RIs. Therefore I have summed up this period as Marie's T1. The percentages given for Marie's use of null subjects and RIs are based on counts made available to me by L. Rasetti. For more detailed analyses, see Tables 7.6, 7.7 and 7.8 in the appendix.

First, Table 7.1 shows that there is variation in the development of Wh-questions. Philippe has fronted Wh before he has Wh-in-situ. In this period his use of RIs is as high as 36.8% and his overall use of null

TABLE 7.2   Finite and non-finite questions, Philippe, Augustin and Marie

	Phililppe		Augustin		Marie	
	Fronted Wh	Wh-in-situ	Fronted Wh	Wh-in-situ	Fronted Wh	Wh-in-situ
FIN	231	82	8	86	3	27
INF	0	0	0	0	0	0

subjects is 38.6% (Crisma 1992) or even 43.5% (Rasetti 1996). He acquires Wh-in-situ in T3 at the age of 2.6 when his use of root infinitives has dropped to 1.6% and his overall null subject use has dropped to 9.8% (Crisma 1992). In contrast, Augustin has Wh-in-situ before he has fronted Wh, at a time when he still uses about 17% root infinitives and has about 50% overall null subjects. In T2 he uses some rare fronted Wh. Marie's data corroborate the findings for Augustin. She has Wh-in-situ first (14 Wh-in-situ in the time from 1.8.26 to 2.1.7) and then acquires the routine inversion *qu'est-ce que c'est* (2 times at age 2.1.28). At the same time, she uses the first fronted Wh-question without inversion as sometimes admitted in Colloquial French, see (19). In the observed period, she has about 17% RIs and 40% overall null subjects.

(19) où il est canard? (Marie, 2.1.28)
      where he is duck

The existence of these markedly different acquisition routes is a strong indication for the involvement of two different processes. Note that the asymmetry in question production is most marked at a time when Philippe, Augustin and Marie are undoubtedly in the root infinitive phase. If the use of child Wh-in-situ, parallel to the use of RIs, were crucially dependent on the truncation option, one would expect Philippe to make use of this option in his question production as well as in his production of declaratives. Therefore, this marked asymmetry in the 'RI-phase' argues for a more sophisticated analysis of child Wh-in-situ than assuming a simple truncation of CP.

3.2.3 Root infinitives in Wh-questions
Next, I investigate the occurrence of root infinitives in Wh-questions. Under the Truncation Hypothesis, RIs in fronted Wh-questions are not expected. Their occurrence in Wh-in-situ, however, would be an indication that projections can be truncated in this structure. No such evidence is found, however.

Table 7.2 shows that RIs occur in neither question type. So the expectations are borne out for fronted Wh. Moreover, the absence of root infinitives in Wh-in-situ indicates that this question type projects high enough to be interpretable, certainly as far as tense and possibly higher.

It has been suggested (Phillips 1995) that this clear result may be an artifact of the data, especially in the case of Philippe. Philippe's Wh-questions contain almost exclusively auxiliaries, and so root infinitives seem to be a priori excluded. Child data show cross-linguistically that auxiliaries do not occur in the infinitive, see Sano and Hyams (1994). The numbers presented in Phillips (1995) corroborate this. Of 166 auxiliaries used by Philippe in declaratives (T1+T2), all are finite and none is in the infinitive. This is predicted by the fact that auxiliaries involve tense, whereas root infinitives do not activate this projection.

The question therefore is how many main verbs occur in Philippe's Wh-questions. Using the criteria (20) for exclusion of an utterance, Phillips (1995) finds 444 finite main verbs compared with 182 main-verb RIs in Philippe's declaratives in T1 and T2, but only one main-verb Wh-question (which is finite) in the same period.

(20) a. multiple repetition of the same utterance
     b. repetitions of all or a large part of the preceding adult utterance
     c. common routines such as *c'est* and *il y a*

These criteria are too strict because they obscure some important developmental steps in Philippe's acquisition of the target forms *qu'est ce que c'est* and *est-ce que . . .* as shown in Hamann (1997). Moreover, they cut out a very revealing main-verb example. Philippe has 10 main-verb questions in his first 10 recordings, i.e. in the period where he uses RIs. Eight of these are verbatim repetitions of adult questions and so have to be excluded by any standard. The remaining two relevant questions are given in (21) and (22).[7]

(21) Mad: qu'est-ce que tu fais?
           what are you doing?
     Phil: je coupe le bois
           I cut the wood
     Mad: tu coupe le bois
           you cut the wood
     Mad: et alors qu'est-ce qui se passe?
           and what is happening then
     Fat: c'est vraiment un gros foutoir
           it's really a pigsty
     Phil: pourquoi coupe le bois
           why cut (fin) the wood

                                        (Philippe, 2.2.17)

(22) Phil: va monter au pied
           go go-up on foot
     Phil: enlever son pneu
           take off its wheel
     Phil: enlever son pneu
           take off its wheel
     Mad: pourquoi?
          why
     Phil: oh. a plus pneu la voiture
           oh, has no more wheel the car
     Phil: pourquoi j'enleve le pneu?
           why I take off the wheel

                                          (Philippe, 2.3.17)

Example (21) passes the criteria of (20) and is probably the one
main-verb Wh-question mentioned by Phillips (1995). Example (22) is
excluded, however, by criterion (20b). This is not a correct decision,
I believe. In an investigation of question formation, the creative act
of transforming an adult or child foregoing declarative into a question
should be one of the most interesting sources for our observations.
Consider (22) in this light: The child has taken up the question word
from the adult as an important cue. But then he changes his own
declarative infinitive into a finite utterance to form the question. This is
extremely important because in the absence of any significant statistics
it indicates that infinitives are not allowed in questions in the child
grammar. Excluding such examples from the count just misses the point.

For Augustin, the picture is clearer. Twenty-three of his 94 Wh-
questions have a main verb, 20 of these meet the strict criteria of (20),
and none of these occurs in the infinitive. The data from Marie support
this. Of her 30 identifiable, non-repetitive Wh-questions, 6 contain a
main verb (*faire, aller, avoir*) and 4 of these occur at 2.1.28 where she
has about 20% root infinitives, one of these 4 is a fronted Wh-question.
None of her questions contains a root infinitive.

Moreover, it emerges from other children's data that so far not one
infinitive has been documented in French Wh-questions (cf. Levow
1995). The main-verb data from Augustin and Marie, though not abso-
lutely conclusive because of few examples in the case of Marie and
because of Augustin's overall low use of infinitives, still support Crisma
(1992)'s result.

We can thus state that RIs are not found in French Wh-questions.
This holds for fronted-Wh, as predicted by the Truncation Hypothesis
and first corroborated by Crisma (1992). But it also holds for Wh-
in-situ. This shows that the child is aware of the requirements of interpretation of questions and so cannot produce *manger quoi* along with

manger pomme. It shows that the interpretation of in-situ questions involves at least tense and probably part of the CP-layer, as argued later. This is not surprising in view of the fact that the question operator modifies a proposition and an untensed clause with the event not properly placed on the time line does not provide a proposition.

3.2.4 Null subjects and French Wh-questions

As to the occurrence of null subjects, Table 7.3 gives an overview for all three children. The data from Augustin and Marie show that Wh-in-situ allows null subjects. For Philippe not much can be said because by the time he uses Wh-in-situ (T3), he has passed out of the root infinitive phase and uses null subjects only infrequently (13%). Moreover, his use of Wh-in-situ seems to be rather limited in productivity. There are 40.7% Wh-in-situ in T3, about 90% of these are of the form *c'est quoi* which has routine characteristics. During T1 and T2, (23) is the typical question for Philippe, whereas it is (24a) for Augustin through the whole period of observation. For Augustin, however, in-situ questions with clitic subjects like (24b,c) occur side by side with the more frequent (24a). Lexical fronted subjects in Wh-in-situ questions occur three times for Augustin, see (25a,b,c). The other overt lexical subjects are postverbal subjects of the kind quoted in (18a,b).

(23) où il est? (Philippe, 2.1.19)
      where he is

(24) a. est où? (Augustin, 2.6.16)
         is where
      b. c'est où? (Augustin, 2.6.16)
         it is where
      c. elle est où? (Augustin, 2.9.30)
         she is where

(25) a. Madam Veco habite où (Augustin, 2.4.1)
         madam Veco lives where
      b. tous les moutons là-bas est où (Augustin, 2.6.16)
         all the sheep down there are where
      c. le mouton i(l) fait comment:bee (Augustin, 2.6.16)
         the sheep he makes how:beh
         'what does the sheep do: beh'

Table 7.3 shows that in 242 fronted Wh-questions, there are only four cases of (finite) null subjects, which amounts to 1.6%, whereas the overall use of finite null subjects averages about 25% (see Tables 7.6 and 7.7 in the appendix and Rasetti (this volume) for more details). I propose that French fronted Wh-questions do not allow null subjects.

TABLE 7.3   Null subject use in fronted Wh and Wh-in-situ, Philippe,
Augustin and Marie

	Philippe		Augustin		Marie	
	Fronted Wh	Wh-in-situ	Fronted Wh	Wh-in-situ	Fronted Wh	Wh-in-situ
0-subject	1	1	3	23	0	2
Overt subject	230	81	5	63	3	25

The 1.6% of null subjects could well be just the natural percentage of errors. However, the striking fact is that all four cases involve *pourquoi*, 1 case is found in Philippe's corpus and 3 cases in Augustin's recordings, whereas Marie does not yet use *pourquoi*. A natural explanation of this fact is found in the special status of *pourquoi*, as discussed in Rizzi (1990). There it is maintained that *pourquoi* does not undergo movement but is base-generated in the Comp system. The reasons for this assumption are that *pourquoi* does not occur in French in-situ questions and does not license stylistic inversion, see (26b,c). So it is clear that *pourqoui* does not have the same properties as a true Wh-operator; see section 3.3.

(26) a.   Pourquoi tu verse de l'eau?
          why you pour of the water
      b. *Tu verse de l'eau pourquoi?
          you pour of the water why
      c. *Pourquoi part Jean?
          why leaves John

The data from Levow (1995) confirm the finding that null subjects do not occur in French fronted Wh-questions, as can be seen in Table 7.4. The three children produce 39 Wh-questions in total and only two of these occur with a null subject (5%), whereas the occurrence of null subjects in declaratives is as high as 55%. The two null subject questions involve *où* and *quoi*, but are produced by the same child.

Summing up these findings on null subjects in child Wh-questions, I propose that fronted Wh does not allow null subjects, whereas Wh-in-situ admits null subjects (22% total in the corpora of the two children, Marie and Augustin, who use Wh-in-situ in their null subject phase). So there is a syntactic difference which needs explaining.

Note that null subjects also occur in French Yes–No questions, as shown by Crisma (1992) and corroborated by Lewov (1995), see Table 7.4 also Table 7.6 in the appendix. They also occur in the Wh-less forerunners of German questions as reported by Penner (1994) and

TABLE 7.4 The occurrence of null subjects in Wh-questions, Yes–No questions and declaratives (adapted from Levow 1995:293)

Child	Type	NS	Total	% NS
Gregoire	declarative	156	396	39.4
	Wh-qu	2	14	14.2
	Yes–No qu	16	30	53.3
Daniel	declarative	457	664	68.8
	Wh-qu	0	23	0
	Yes–No qu	0	1	0
Nathalie	declarative	166	352	47.2
	Wh-qu	0	2	0
	Yes–No qu	2	3	66.6
Total	declarative	779	1412	55.2
	Wh-qu	2	39	5.1
	Yes–No qu	18	34	52.9

TABLE 7.5 Occurrence of null subjects in specific question types

French			German		
Fronted Wh	Wh-in-situ	Yes–No	Fronted Wh	No Wh	Yes–No
–	+ 22%	+ 32%	–	+ 18%	+ 20%

Clahsen *et al.* (1995). Table 7.5 gives a summary of null subject occurrence in specific question types in French and German, putting together our findings with those of Crisma (1992), Levow (1995), Clahsen *et al.* (1995) and Hamann (1994, 1996a).[8]

3.3 Discussion

Since none of the questions is non-finite, an analysis of null subjects depending on underspecified tense can be excluded under standard assumptions about French inflection.[9] Note that the majority of questions for all three children are copula/auxiliary constructions, so that tense cannot be underspecified in the null subject cases. This is interesting, since 'Null Subject AUX' structures have not been observed in English and are rare in other languages (cf. Sano and Hyams 1994, Schütze and Wexler 1996, Hamann and Plunkett, 1998). In French child language, they occur to about 26%; see Rasetti (1995) and Hamann and Plunkett (1998).

Let us therefore test the hypothesis that the child null subject in French is licensed by agreement, whereas in English it is licensed by missing or underspecified tense. This implies that omitting the subject should be possible in (23). Because such clitic–auxiliary configurations are quite frequent for Philippe, null subjects in his questions are expected. These do not occur, however. It is thus extremely unlikely that the null subject in the in-situ case is licensed by agreement. Agreement does not license a null clitic in constructions such as (23) and both constructions have exactly the same local licensing and identification configuration.

However, if uninverted French child questions were clefts, a hypothesis which has been used to assign analysis (27b) to the English example (27a),[10] then Philippe's (23) is in fact (23a) and the non-occurrence of null subjects in this type of question would follow because null subjects are not found in subordinate clauses in child language.

(27) a. Where dis goes? (Adam, 2.8)
      b. Where (is it that) this goes

(23) a. Où (est-ce qu') il est? (Philippe, 2.1.19)
          where (is it that) he is

The last claim is true for English, but not for Italian, and just begs the question: if it is agreement which licenses the French child null subject then such null subjects are expected in subordinate clauses. It still remains to be explained why null subjects do not occur in subordinates in English. It is also not quite clear whether the French *est-ce que* can be analysed as a cleft at all. First, the French cleft which comes to mind for (23) is (23b) not (23a).

(23) b. Où   c'est qu' il est?
          where it is that he is

Second, in a Yes–No question *est-ce que* cannot be analysed as a cleft because it cannot be focalized (Rizzi, p.c.). Moreover, non-inverted adult questions have been analysed as involving dynamic agreement in French (Rizzi 1991), so that it is more likely that the French child uses this option instead of resorting to a cleft. I will come back to this question later. Once it is clear that a cleft analysis for French uninverted child questions is unlikely, the non-occurrence of null subjects in this question type argues against licensing of null subjects by agreement in Child French.

Licensing of null subjects by missing tense and licensing by agreement have thus been excluded. Hence, it seems to be the privileged initial position which makes omission possible in (24a), but not in (23). Therefore, an analysis which goes together with the possibility of truncation seems best.

This brings us back to the original problem. As mentioned in 2.3, Crisma (1992) argues that null subjects are expected in Wh-in-situ because the CP-level is not activated. Therefore, it can be truncated and the empty category is in topmost position and can survive. But if truncation were possible in this case, then the child could decide to truncate even lower than IP-level so that we expect infinitives such as *aller où* ('go where'), which are so far unattested.

The other problem for Crisma's idea was the assumption that the child is uttering meaningful sentences. This means that the derivation must converge at an LF-representation. If the derivation involves silent movement of the Wh-constituent, then CP must be activated at LF for Wh-in-situ, and a difference with fronted Wh is not expected. Augustin's and Marie's use of Wh-in-situ shows that there is no Spell-out/LF clash, and the 'delay of Wh-in-situ' does not exist. So there is a genuine problem for the truncation analysis. The CP must be projected at LF in both cases, and there is evidence at Spell-out (missing RIs) that the child indeed projects higher than tense in both cases. We are faced with the dilemma that null subjects are possible in one case, but not the other.

One possible solution is the following: if Wh-in-situ does not involve a silent Wh-operator, but another kind of operator, then the difference can be explained by the difference of the operators, especially their specific features. In a split CP analysis, as suggested by Rizzi (1997), the empty category could raise higher than the binder, thus exempting the ECP. Such a mechanism could by-pass an operator of the existential type in the manner suggested by Haegeman (1997a and this volume), but could never by-pass a Wh-operator.

The fact that Wh-in-situ and *pourquoi* both allow null subjects is another argument for a non-movement analysis. As *pourquoi* is base-inserted and has not moved, it is natural to assume the same for the scope assigning operator in Wh-in-situ. From Table 7.5 another asymmetry emerges. Null-subjects do not occur in fronted Wh-questions but occur quite freely in Yes–No questions (to about 32%, which is roughly comparable with the percentage of null subjects in Wh-in-situ). A similar observation holds for German. Hamann (1994, 1996a) found 20% null subjects in Yes–No questions of German 3-year-olds, Clahsen *et al.* (1995) found 18% null subjects in Wh-less questions in Early German. In the current line of argumentation, I suggest that the operator marking scope and question force in Yes–No questions is different in feature content from the genuine Wh-operator and can be assimilated to the Wh-in-situ operator. Moreover, the operator marking question force in the absence of the Wh-pronoun in German child questions seems to be not just a silent Wh-operator, but must share properties of the Yes–No operator, and, by inference, of the Wh-in-situ operator.

4 Towards a solution

4.1 The by-passing mechanism

Assuming different operators as the source of the observed difference
is only a first step. Haegeman (1997a and this volume) proposes a by-
passing mechanism for both (28a) and (28b).

(28) a. avant nc veux chocolat (Nathalie, 2.2)
        before want chocolate
     b. puis nc se colle à moi (adult diary)
        then herself presses to me

Her analysis of the child null subject is the same as for the diary null
subject. Following Rizzi (1994), she proposes that both are null constants (nc). The crucial ingredient for the licensing of this null constant
is either the existence of an anaphoric operator which can be identified
by context or its location in the topmost sentence position. An empty
category escapes the ECP only if there is no position from which it can
be licensed. As soon as there is a c-commanding position which is
not occupied by a licensing operator but by something else, the ECP is
violated, and the empty category cannot survive.

Therefore, the examples (28a,b) should be ruled out by the ECP.
This holds for an analysis in which the adjunct occupies the specifier
position of a dominating projection as well as for an analysis in which
the adjunct is adjoined to IP. In both cases the nc is c-commanded by
the higher position. There are reasons to assume that preposed adjuncts
are specifiers of dominating projections, however. This assumption, a
split CP, and the possibility of generating agreement projections above
projections with contentful functional heads all put together provide an
analysis.

4.2 A split CP analysis

The very task of the complementizer system as the interface between
the propositional content (expressed by the IP) and the superordinate
structure (a higher clause or the discourse) makes it necessary that it
codes information oriented at the higher structure and also information
oriented downwards, towards the IP. This results in a split into a ForceP
and a FinP, the first coding the specification of illocutionary force, i.e.
the declarative, interrogative, exclamative, relative or adverbial nature
of the clause, the latter the specification of finiteness, related to tense.
Additionally, the C-system codes functions which have traditionally
been called topic–comment relations. These must be sandwiched between
the Force and the Finiteness projection. This, together with the cross-
linguistic facts about the order of topic and focus (cf. Rizzi 1997), leads
to an articulated CP structure as in (29).

(29) ForceP > TopicP > FocusP > TopicP > FiniteP > IP

4.3 Topic projections

The fact that topics can be stacked, while focus is unique, seems to suggest an adjunction analysis for topics. Following Culicover (1991), Rizzi (1997) argues for independent projections. The observation is that sentences such as (30a), which are excluded because of the *that*-trace effect, become more acceptable if an adjunct is added, as in (30b):

(30) a.   *This is an amendment which I think that will be law next year.
      b.   (?) This is an amendment which I think that next year will be law.
      c.   This is an amendment which I think will be law next year.

The difference of (30a) and (30c) leads to the assumption that in English the two variants of the complementizer *that*, i.e. *that* and *null*, differ as to their feature specification. The null variant carries agreement features and can head-govern the trace. Therefore the amelioration in (30b) is explained by the involvement of agreement. The adjunct is not merely adjoined, but occupies the specifier of a topic phrase whose head hosts agreement features and so head-governs the trace. This presupposes that the adjunct does not enter into a spec–head relation with its head so that the agreement features remain available for other constituents. Haegeman (1997a and this volume) argues that every contentful functional head activates its own dominating agreement projection. Rizzi (1997) and Haegeman (1997a and this volume) exclude IP-adjunction for preposed adjuncts and postulate independent topic projections. To explain argument/non-argument asymmetries concerning subject extraction, a modification is necessary, however. Preposed adverbs are adjoined to the TopP, whereas arguments occupy the specifier position. Subjects cannot be extracted in the argument case because the agreement features are exhausted by the spec–head relation. The adjoined adverb leaves the agreement features unchecked and the subject can use the position in SpecAgrTopP as a landing site.

4.4 Child and diary null subjects

With these tools, I return to the analysis of (28a,b). Haegeman (1997a and this volume) assumes that the Force projection is truncated in both cases and makes use of the position in the agreement phrase dominating the topic phrase. The nc can move there, escaping the c-commanding adverb, using the agreement features of the topic head because these are not yet checked. As the topmost layer is missing, the nc is now in a licit position. The structure for (28a) then is (31).

(31)

```
              AgrPTop
             /      \
          Spec      Agr'Top
                    /      \
                 Agr⁰       TopP
                            /   \
                          TopP
                          /   \
                        Top'
                       /    \
                Top⁰Agrᵢ      FinP
                                /  \
                                    IP
                                   /  \
    ncᵢ    Agrᵢ      avant      t'ᵢ     veux chocolat
```

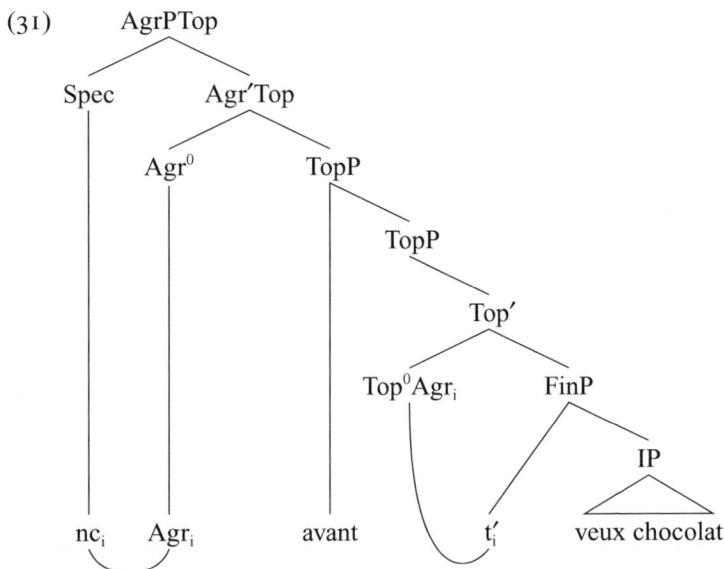

Preposed arguments with null subjects are very rare in the diary data and also in child speech. So one can assume that the same mechanism which excludes subject extraction across an argument also excludes the extraction of an nc: the agreement features are exhausted.

4.5 Null subjects and Wh

We now address the problem that null subjects occur freely in Wh-in-situ but not in fronted Wh-questions in Child French. Put differently: the nc can survive in Wh-in-situ but cannot survive in questions with a preposed Wh-constituent. Rizzi (1997) assumes that the question constituent occupies the specifier of the focus projection. This is motivated because the question word is also focal and because questions and focus are mutually exclusive. It follows that in a fronted Wh-question, the Wh-Criterion is satisfied in the FocP, which means that the Wh-constituent occupies the specifier of this projection and checks its Wh-features against the Wh-features present in the Foc head. This, especially if the Wh-pronoun as a pronoun contains phi-features and carries a minimal N-restriction (see (16)), which in the case of Wh-fronting is not separated from the operator part, exhausts the agreement option. So the antecedentless empty category cannot by-pass the Wh-constituent, just as it cannot by-pass a preposed object in Haegeman's account (see Haegeman 1997a: 257ff). Even if an agreement projection were projected on top of FocP, this would not provide an escape: the trace of the nc in SpecFinP would remain ungoverned by the head FocAgr, precisely because these features are already exhausted. For a full discussion I refer to Haegeman (1997a) and Rizzi (1997). Clearly, the nc does not have an escape hatch in Wh-questions, as shown in (32).

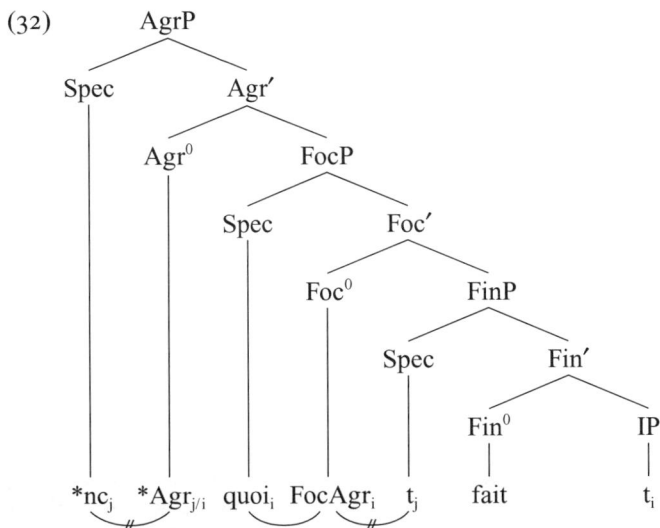

(32)

```
                    AgrP
                  /      \
              Spec        Agr'
                        /      \
                    Agr⁰        FocP
                              /      \
                          Spec        Foc'
                                    /      \
                                Foc⁰        FinP
                                          /      \
                                      Spec        Fin'
                                                /      \
                                            Fin⁰        IP
                                             |           |
    *ncⱼ    *Agrⱼ/ᵢ    quoiᵢ    FocAgrᵢ    tⱼ   fait     tᵢ
       \__#__/        \___/    \___#___/
```

It is crucially the Wh-Criterion (see Rizzi 1991) which ensures the matching of Wh-features in SpecFoc and Foc^0 and which exhausts the agreement features. I quote it as (33).

(33) *The Wh-Criterion*
  A: A Wh-operator must be in a spec–head configuration with an X^0 [+wh]
  B: An X^0 [+wh] must be in a spec–head configuration with a Wh-operator

The criterion is satisfied in English and in V2-languages because the auxiliary or verb carries the agreement features, among them the Wh-feature, up to a checking position. This way of looking at the Wh-phenomenon seems to imply that the typical question of Philippe, which does not involve subject–verb inversion, ignores the criterion. For Adult French it has been argued that non-inverted questions satisfy the criterion by dynamic agreement. This makes it possible that the Wh-operator endows the relevant head with the crucial feature. Dynamic agreement is the solution suggested by Rizzi (1991) for the obvious problem that in English the verb has to raise to a C-head in order to satisfy the criterion, while Adult French can raise the verb to a C-head in inversion structures but does not necessarily have to do so. In fact, many colloquial adult questions do not involve inversion and look exactly like the questions of Philippe. The point of the argument is that this peculiarity of French makes it inevitable that the Wh-Criterion is satisfied once the Wh-operator is fronted and no inversion has taken place. Dynamic agreement will always endow the features and establish the relevant agreement configuration. Therefore, in the question configuration typically produced by Philippe and other French children (if they are inspired by adult French, not Child English), the agreement options are necessarily exhausted and no by-passing can take place.

As to the nc in Wh-in-situ questions, I assume that the by-passing mechanism allows the nc to pass the in-situ-operator. This means in particular that there cannot be a silent Wh-operator in FocP at LF because its presence would block the passage of the nc, as in (32). If an analysis as suggested in (17a) is assumed, there are more options, however.

First, as the Wh-word remains an argument in argument position (cf. Rizzi 1991), the Wh-Criterion does not apply and therefore the operator does not have to enter into a spec–head relation with the Wh-features carried by the inflected verb. This means that the operator can well be adjoined to FocP, it does not have to occupy the specifier position. Moreover, the N-restriction of the Wh-word remains in situ and the Q-operator carries no relevant agreement features and has no features to check, neither the Wh-feature nor phi- or case features. Thus (34b) is obtained for (34a), where the nc can use the agreement features projected from the substantial Foc head because they are not already checked by the Q-operator. Here, I replace the analysis for 'quoi' in (16b) by the syntactically more suggestive 'quoi$_f$'.

(34a) fais quoi? (Marie, 2.3.3)
       does what

(34b)

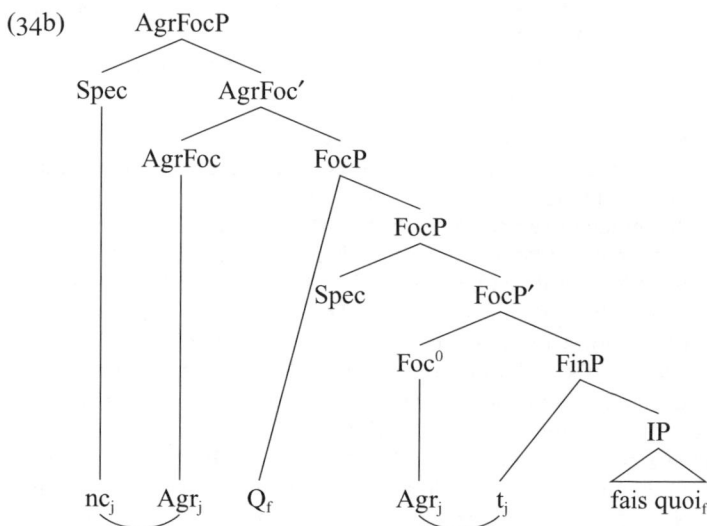

Even if the operator is not adjoined but appears in the specifier of FocP, the phi-features would still be available for the nc because the N-restriction part of the Wh-word has remained in situ. A similar mechanism could also explain the existence of null subjects in Yes–No questions – if it is assumed that the Wh-Criterion does not have to be satisfied there. Many languages mark this question type by inversion, which would suggest that the Wh-Criterion is operative, and so a problem ensues for the above explanation. On the other hand, Yes–No questions can often be expressed exactly like declaratives. So the Wh-Criterion is not necessarily involved. The alternative which comes to mind is binding by an unmarked Q-operator without N-restrictions. Then the mechanism will be exactly as suggested for Wh-in-situ, without the involvement of a choice function, of course. For *pourqoui*-questions the occurrence of null subjects would also follow from the fact that the operator is base-inserted and does not carry any N-restriction. Similarly, German (or Dutch) early Wh-less questions could involve a simple Q-operator. The analysis given in (34b) explains the occurrence of null subjects as well as the data presentend by Clahsen *et al.* (1995) with respect to verb placement and infinitives: infinitives do not occur in either question type (fronted Wh or Wh-less) and Verb Second is obeyed in both. The occurrence of finite verbs in clause-final position as observed by Penner (1994) or Tracy (1994) remains somewhat mysterious though and has to be investigated separately.

5 Conclusion

Detailed data on child question formation in French, and some less detailed data from German and Dutch were discussed. In German and Dutch, children often start with Wh-less constituent questions and this question type co-exists for a time with fronted Wh-questions. Developmental data on Child French were presented which correct the picture that French children start with fronted Wh. There is variation and some children start with Wh-in-situ and others with fronted Wh. The occurrence of null subjects in German Wh-less questions and in French Wh-in-situ led to an analysis involving question operators different from the Wh-operator. In this respect, I have presented acquisition evidence against a simple movement analysis of Wh-in-situ and in support of an alternative analysis going back to Baker (1970) and developed especially in Reinhart (1995).

Let me sum up what was used for allowing null subjects in Wh-in-situ but prohibiting them in fronted Wh. There are three essential assumptions. First, preposed topics and focus constituents are not simply IP-adjoined but create full projections with substantial heads. Second, substantial functional heads carry agreement and project a dominating agreement phrase. Third, adverbial topics and the Q-morpheme without the accompanying N-restriction do not exhaust the agreement features in the respective head so that the features are free to be checked in the AgrFP. This led to the idea that these constituents are not necessarily positioned in the specifier of the projection, but can be adjoined. This scenario made it possible for the nc to raise to the specifier of the AgrP concerned and thus avoid an ECP violation. This option is not open in the case of fronted Wh because there agreement is exhausted by the spec–head relation of Wh-head and operator. Last, ForceP must be truncated so that there is no higher position from which the nc could be c-commanded. As it is only the ForceP which is truncated, the utterance will be finite and root infinitives are not predicted.

Appendix

TABLE 7.6 The development of question formation concerning null subjects and root infinitives for Philippe (cf. Crisma 1992:117, 119)

		Total	% NS	% RI
T1	declarative	491	41.9	36.8
	Wh-question	35	2.8 (1)	0
	Yes–No question	28	25.0	14.3
T2	declarative	511	39.3	15.2
	Wh-question	79	0	0
	Yes–No question	29	13.8	3.4
T3	declarative	611	13.2	2.4
	Wh-question	199	0.5 (1)	0
	Yes–No question	100	7.0	0

Table 7.6 A new count of Philippe's Wh-questions which are not repetitions of a question involving the same question word, and counting only *comment, pourquoi*, spontaneous *que c'est ça, qui, quel(le), quoi, où* without considering the many occurrences of non-adult *qu'est ce* which might be attempted repetitions, gives 96 Wh-questions in T1+T2 compared with Crisma's 114. Because of the minimal difference, I do not set up my own table, but repeat Crisma's results. Null subjects here comprise all null subjects in finite and infinite structures. The analysis provided by Rasetti (1996 and this volume) differs in detail, but does not show new or different trends. For a file-by-file analysis of Philippe's overall and finite null subjects, I refer to Rasetti (this volume).

TABLE 7.7 Occurrence of Wh, root infinitives and null subjects in the Augustin corpus

Age	% all NS	% finite NS	% RI	Wh total	% RI	Fronted Wh	NS	Wh-in-situ	NS	% NS	inversion
2.0.2	46.0	34.1	14.0	0	0	0	0	0	0	0	0
2.0.23	57.7	31.3	34.6	0	0	0	0	0	0	0	0
2.1.15	63.2	36.4	36.8	0	0	0	0	0	0	0	0
2.2.13	36.6	28.6	12.2	3	0	1	0	2	0	0	0
2.3.10	35.3	32.1	11.8	0	0	0	0	0	0	0	0
2.4.1	54.8	49.1	11.3	12	0	0	0	12	6	50	0
2.4.22	54.4	45.8	10.5	16	0	0	0	13	8	61.5	0
2.6.16	37.7	29.7	7.5	46	0	4	3	42	9	21.4	1
2.9.2	28.6	19.8	6.1	8	0	1	0	7	0	0	1
2.9.30	16.2	10.7	6.3	12	0	2	0	10	0	0	1
Total	36.1	26.8	10.3	94	0	8	3	86	23	26.8	3

Table 7.7 This table is fully compatible with Rasetti's counts on Augustin (this volume) but may differ in detail from the numbers published in Hamann *et al.* (1996). As Rasetti's count is based on a newer machine coding, I adopt her figures.

TABLE 7.8   Occurrence of Wh, root infinitives and null subjects in the Marie corpus

Age	% all NS	% finite NS	% RI	Wh total	% RI	Fronted Wh	NS	Wh-in-situ	NS	% NS	inversion
1.8.26	51.4	26.3	23.6	4	0	0	0	4	0	0	0
1.9.3	32.0	10.9	24.0	8	0	0	0	8	0	0	0
1.9.10	46.6	31.7	19.0	(1)	0	0	0	(1)	0	0	0
1.10.1	27.8	16.1	11.1	0	0	0	0	0	0	0	0
1.11.5	35.4	29.3	6.2	1	0	0	0	1	0	0	0
2.0.9	45.6	34.5	13.2	0	0	0	0	0	0	0	0
2.1.7	44.2	32.5	15.4	1	0	0	0	1	0	0	0
2.1.28	32.0	17.8	16.4	11	0	3	0	8	1	12.5	2
2.3.3	51.9	33.3	23.1	5	0	0	0	5	1	20	0
Total	40.2	22.1	17.2	30	0	3	0	27	2	7.4	2

Table 7.8   See Rasetti (this volume) for an analysis of Marie's null subjects and RIs which takes into account 4 newly transcribed recordings. These were not available to me during the analysis of the Wh-data.

Acknowledgements

My thanks are due to my colleagues in Geneva, especially Liliane Haegeman and Lucienne Rasetti, to Ken Drozd, who pointed out some semantic and stylistic inadequacies, to Nina Hyams, who commented on an earlier version of this chapter given at WCHTSALT OTS 1996, to the participants in the discussion at that conference, and, of course, to the two editors whose comments helped shape the chapter.
This work was supported by Swiss National Fund Grant No. 1213–42219.94.

Notes

1 See Pollock (1989) for arguments for a tense phrase and an agreement phrase inside IP, and section 4.3 for one elaboration of the various hypotheses made about the composition of the CP.

2 Whereas in German and French child language no null subjects have been found in fronted Wh-questions (see Crisma 1992, Levow 1995 and this chapter for French, and Weissenborn 1990, Clahsen *et al.* 1995 for German), there is considerable controversy about Child English. Valian (1991) and Rizzi (1994) find practically no relevant examples, Radford (1996), quoting examples from Plunkett (1992), Vainikka (1994) and Hill (1983), is of a different opinion. Rohrbacher and Roeper (1994) and Bromberg and Wexler (1995) provide interesting statistics about the occurrence of null subjects in Adam's fronted Wh-questions.

3 Yes–No questions without inversion normally are restricted by special discourse conditions (cf. topic–focus relations).

4 Pesetsky (1987) originally suggested unselective binding as introduced by Heim (1982) as the mechanism which could correctly capture the properties of discourse-linked *which*-phrases. These, Pesetsky argued, cannot be analysed by movement in contrast to non discourse-linked Wh, which has to be so analysed.

5 This is an extension of Reinhart's analysis, valid, I believe, for the adverbial Wh-words *where* and *when* which I treat as spatial or temporal arguments because they are syntactically and semantically different from *how* and *why*. I also extend her analysis of English Wh-in-situ which occurs in multiple questions to the French case, where only one wh-word is present.

6 For a more detailed discussion and full question lists, see Hamann (1997).

7 The form *que il fait* which is quoted by Crisma (1992) as produced by Philippe at ages 2.2.3 and 2.3.21 could not be found by a UNIX 'egrep' search.

8 The percentage of null subjects in French Yes–No questions is calculated from Levow (1995) and from Crisma (1992)'s (T1 + T2); see Table 7.4 and Table 7.6 in the appendix. Unfortunately, no figures on RIs and overall null subject use could be found in Clahsen *et al.* (1995), so that a full comparison is hard to make. The children investigated by Clahsen are described as being in Stage I, however, so that about 40% RIs and null subjects can be inferred.

9 Wexler (1997) assumes that French finite verbs in the singular are specified for agreement but not for tense. Missing tense allows null subjects in his analysis.

198   THE ACQUISITION OF SYNTAX

10 The same approach to the acquisition of Bernese Swiss German and Standard German questions is proposed by Penner (1994), who points out that
children in the initial stages do not have the 'set' interpretation discussed
in 2.1., but prefer a 'singleton', a cleft reading for questions. Note, however,
that a singleton reading might also result if children have a choice function
in their question interpretation and analyse in-situ.

References

BAKER, C. L. (1970) 'Notes on the Description of English Questions. The Role of
an Abstract Question Morpheme', *Foundations of Language* **6**, pp. 107–219.
BORER, H. and K. WEXLER (1987) 'The Maturation of Syntax', in T. Roeper and
E. Williams (eds), pp. 123–72.
BROMBERG, H. S. and K. WEXLER (1995) 'Null, subjects in Wh-questions', in
C. Schütze, J. Ganger and K. Boihier (eds) pp. 221–48.
CHOMSKY, N. (1976) 'Conditions on Rules of Grammar', *Linguistic Analysis*,
vol **2**., no. 4. Reprinted in N. Chomsky, *Essays on Form and Interpretation*.
North Holland: Amsterdam, 1977.
CHOMSKY, N. (1995) *The Minimalist Program*. MIT Press: Cambridge, Mass.
CLAHSEN, H. (1991) 'Constraints on Parameter Setting', *Language Acqusition*
1, pp. 361–91.
CLAHSEN, H. (ed.) (1996) *Generative Perspectives on Language Acquisition*.
Benjamins: Amsterdam, Philadelphia.
CLAHSEN, H., C. KURSAWE and M. PENKE (1995) 'Introducing CP: Wh-questions
and Subordinate Clauses in German Child Language', *Essex Research
Reports in Linguistics* **7**, pp. 1–28.
CRISMA, P. (1992) 'On the Acquisition of Wh in French', *GenGenP* **0**(1–2),
pp. 115–12.
CULICOVER (1991) 'Topicalization, Inversion and Complementizers in English',
in D. Delfitto, M. Everaert, A. Evers and F. Stuurman (eds), pp. 1–45.
DELFITTO, D., M. EVERAERT, A. EVERS and F. STUURMAN (eds) (1991) *Going
Romance and Beyond*. OTS Working Papers, University of Utrecht.
FRIEDEMANN, M.-A. (1992) 'The Underlying Position of External Arguments in
French', *GenGenP* **0**(1–2), pp. 123–44.
GONZALEZ, M. (ed.) (1994) *NELS* **24** Proceedings of the North East Linguistic
Society. University of Mass. Amherst. Reproduced and distributed by GLSA
(Graduate Linguistic Student Association).
HAEGEMAN, L. (1997a) 'Register Variation, Truncation, and Subject Omission
in English and French', *Journal of English Language and Linguistics* **1**(2),
pp. 233–70.
HAEGEMAN, L. (ed.) (1997b) *Elements of Grammar. A Handbook of Generative
Syntax*. Kluwer: Dordrecht.
HALE, K. L. and S. J. KEYSER (eds) (1993) *The View from Building 20: Essays in
Linguistics in Honour of Sylvain Bromberger*. MIT Press: Cambridge, MA.
HAMANN, C. (1994) 'Null Arguments in German Child Language', *GenGenP*
2(2), pp. 62–90.
HAMANN, C. (1996a) 'Null Arguments in German Child Language', *Language
Acquisition* **5**, pp. 155–208.

HAMANN, C. (1996b) 'Wh-in situ, to Move or Not to Move', *GenGenP* 4(1), pp. 34–47.

HAMANN, C. (1997) 'From Syntax to Discourse: Children's Use of Pronominal Clitics, Null Arguments, Infinitives and Operators'. Habilitation thesis, University of Tübingen.

HAMANN, C. and K. PLUNKETT (1998) 'Subjectless Sentences in Child Danish', *Cognition* 69, pp. 35–72.

HAMANN, C. and S. POWERS (eds) (to appear) *The Acquisition of Scrambling and Cliticization*. Kluwer: Dordrecht.

HAMANN, C., L. RIZZI and U. FRAUENFELDER (1996) 'The Acquisition of Subject and Object Clitics in French', in H. Clahsen (ed.), pp. 309–34.

HEIM, I. (1982) 'The Semantics of Definite and Indefinite Noun Phrases'. Ph.D. dissertation, University of Massachusetts, Amherst. Published 1989 by Garland.

HILL, J. A. C. (1983) 'A Computational Model of Language Acquisition in the Two-Year-Old', *Indiana University Linguistics Club*, Bloomington.

HOEKSTRA, T. and B. SCHWARTZ (eds) (1994) *Language Acquisition Studies in Generative Grammar*. Benjamins: Amsterdam.

HORNSTEIN, N. (1995) *Logical Form*. Blackwells: Oxford.

HORNSTEIN, N. and D. LIGHTFOOT (eds) (1994) *Verb Movement*. CUP: Cambridge.

HUANG, J. (1982) 'Logical Relations in Chinese and the Theory of Grammar'. Ph.D dissertation, MIT.

HYAMS, N. (1996) 'The Underspecification of Functional Categories in Early Grammar', in H. Clahsen (ed.), pp. 91–128.

KLIMA, E. S. and U. BELLUGI (1966) 'Syntactic Regularities in the Speech of Children', in J. Lyons and R. Wales (eds), pp. 183–207.

LEVOW, G.-A. (1995) 'Tense and Subject Position in Interrogatives and Negatives in Child French: Evidence For and Against Truncated Structures', in C. Schütze, J. Ganger and K. Boihier (eds), *MITWPL 26*, pp. 281–304.

LYONS, J. and R. WALES (eds) (1966) *Psycholinguistic Papers*. Edinburgh University Press: Edinburgh.

MACWHINNEY, B. (1991) *The Childes Project: Tools for Analysing Talk*. Lawrence Erlbaum: Hillsdale, NJ.

PENNER, Z. (1994) 'Asking Questions without CPs', in T. Hoekstra and B. Schwartz (eds), pp. 177–214.

PESETSKY, D. (1987) 'Wh-in-situ: Movement and Unselective Binding', in E. Reuland and A. ter Meulen (eds), pp. 98–129.

PHILLIPS, C. (1995) 'Syntax at Age Two: Cross Linguistic Differences', in C. Schütze, J. Ganger and K. Boihier (eds), *MITWPL* 26, pp. 325–82.

PLUNKETT, B. (1992) 'Continuity and the Landing Site for Wh-movement', *Bangor Research Papers in Linguistics* 4, pp. 53–77.

POLLOCK, J. Y. (1989) 'Verb Movement, Universal Grammar and the Structure of IP', *Linguistic Inquiry* 20, pp. 365–424.

RADFORD, A. (1990) *Syntactic Theory and the Acquisition of English Syntax*. Blackwell: Oxford.

RADFORD, A. (1996) 'Towards a Structure Building Model of Acquisition', in H. Clahsen (ed.), pp. 43–90.

RASETTI, L. (1995) *La Distribution du Sujet Nul dans la Grammaire Enfantine du Francais*. Memoire de license, University of Geneva.

RASETTI, L. (1996) 'Null Subjects and Root Infinitives in the Child Grammar of French', *GenGenP* 4(2), pp. 120–32. TL-95-002.

REINHART, T. (1995) 'Interface Strategies', *OTS Working Papers*, University of Utrecht.

REULAND, E. and A. TER MEULEN (eds) (1987): *The Representation of (In)definites*. MIT Press, Cambridge, Mass.

RIZZI, L. (1990) *Relativized Minimality*. MIT Press: Cambridge, MA.

RIZZI, L. (1991) 'Residual Verb Second and the Wh-criterion', *Technical Reports on Formal and Computational Linguistics* no. 2, Geneva University.

RIZZI, L. (1994) 'Some Notes on Linguistic Theory and Language Development: the Case of Root Infinitives', *Language Acquisition* 3, pp. 371–93.

RIZZI, L. (1997) 'The Fine Structure of the Left Periphery', in L. Haegeman (1997b) (ed.), pp. 281–337.

ROEPER, T. (1996): 'The Role of Merger Theory and Formal Features in Acquisition', in H. Clahsen (ed.), pp. 415–50.

ROEPER, T. and E. WILLIAMS (eds) (1987) *Parameter Setting*. Reidel: Dordrecht.

ROHRBACHER, B. and T. ROEPER (1994) 'True Pro-drop in Child English and the Principle of Economy of Projection', paper presented at the Berne Conference on the Acqusition of Scrambling and Cliticization, to appear in C. Hamann and S. Powers (eds).

ROTHWEILER, M. (ed.) (1990) *Spracherwerb und Grammatik. Linguistische Untersuchungen zum Erwerb von Syntax und Morphologie*. Linguistische Berichte, Sonderheft 3, Westdeutscher Verlag: Opladen.

SANO, T. and N. HYAMS (1994) 'Agreement, Finiteness and the Development of Null Arguments', in M. Gonzàlez (ed.). *NELS* 24, pp. 543–58.

SCHÜTZE, C., J. GANGER and K. BOIHIER (eds) (1995) *Papers on Language Processing and Acquisition. MITWPL 26.*

SCHÜTZE, C. and K. WEXLER (1996) 'What Case Aquisition Data Have to Say about the Components of INFL', paper presented at *WCHTSALT*, OTS, Utrecht University, June 1996.

TRACY, R. (1994) 'Raising Questions: Formal and Functional Aspects of the Acquisition of Wh-questions in German', in R. Tracy and E. Lattney (eds), pp. 1–34.

TRACY, R. and E. LATTNEY (eds) (1994) *How Tolerant is Universal Grammar? Essays on Language Learnability and Language Variation*. Niemeyer: Tübingen.

VAINIKKA, A. (1994) 'Case in the Development of English Syntax', *Language Acquisition* 3, pp. 257–325.

VALIAN, V. (1991) 'Syntactic Subjects in the Early Speech of American and Italian Children', *Cognition* 40, pp. 21–81.

VAN KAMPEN, J. (1997) 'First Steps in Wh-Movement'. Doctoral dissertation, OTS, University of Utrecht.

WEISSENBORN, J. (1990) 'Functional Categories and Verb Movement: the Acquisition of German Syntax Reconsidered', in M. Rothweiler (ed.), pp. 166–89.

WEXLER, K. (1994) 'Optional Infinitives, Head Movement and the Economy of Derivations in Child Grammar', in N. Hornstein and D. Lightfoot (eds), pp. 305–50.

WEXLER, K. (1997) 'Explanatory Models of Language Acquisition', plenary
talk presented at *GALA*, Edinburgh, 1997.
WILLIAMS, E. (1986) 'A Reassignment of the Functions of LF', *Linguistic Inquiry*
17, pp. 265–99.

Chapter 8

Accounting for morphological variation in second language acquisition: truncation or missing inflection?

Philippe Prévost and Lydia White

1 Functional categories and variability

It is well known that first (L1) and second (L2) language learners show variability in their production of inflectional morphology and of lexical items associated with functional categories such as complementizers (Comp), inflection (Infl) and determiners (Det); failure to mark agreement and tense is common, and nonfinite morphology is found on verbs which would be finite in the language of adult native speakers. Such variability in L1 acquisition has been shown to be structurally determined; it is not the case that the children do not know the relevant morphology and that they use inflected and uninflected forms randomly and interchangeably. Rather, their use or nonuse of inflection co-occurs with other syntactic properties (types of subjects, verb raising, negative placement, etc.), suggesting that the variation reflects certain structural properties of the child grammar.

There is disagreement as to precisely what the relevant structural properties are. Wexler (1994) proposes that tense is underspecified, which explains the occurrence of optional (or 'root') infinitives in child language (i.e. nonfinite matrix verbs which vary systematically with finite forms); Hoekstra *et al.* (1997) and Hoekstra and Hyams (1995) argue that it is in fact number that is underspecified, with a somewhat broader range of consequences. Rizzi (1993/1994) proposes that it is the Root Principle that is underspecified or lacking. Each of these theories makes somewhat different predictions about the syntactic and morphological properties that should co-occur in the child's early grammar. However, they share the assumption that the child has 'full competence' with respect to functional categories. In other words, variable use or lack of inflection does not stem from the absence of some or all functional categories in the early stages, contrary to the claims of Clahsen, Eisenbeiss and Vainikka (1994), Guilfoyle and Noonan (1992) and Radford (1990), amongst others.

The question then arises as to whether L2 variability reveals similar properties and is due to similar causes. One possibility is that L1 and L2 differ in this respect. A number of researchers have argued that L2 learners have 'full competence' with respect to functional categories and that variability in use of L2 inflectional morphology (as well as other lexical items relating to functional categories) is due to relatively low level morphological problems (Epstein *et al.* 1996, 1998; Grondin and White 1996; Lardiere 1998; Lardiere and Schwartz 1997; Parodi *et al.* 1997; Schwartz 1998).[1] In other words, L2 learners 'know' the abstract properties of functional categories: the syntactic consequences of functional categories can be observed in their grammars. What is lacking is full knowledge of the specific realization of particular morphemes, such that errors in morphology may occur. Superficially nonfinite forms in L2 will often in fact be finite at an abstract level; superficially nonfinite clauses will share properties of finite ones. Haznedar and Schwartz (1997) refer to this as 'missing inflection', Epstein *et al.* (1996) term it 'ignorance of morphology'. We will refer to this position as the Missing Inflection Hypothesis.

An alternative possibility is that in L2 acquisition, as in L1, variation in incidence of inflection is structurally constrained, rather than being due to problems with realization of morphology. If so, the occurrence of nonfinite morphology on main verbs should be structurally determined and it should co-occur with other syntactic and morphological properties. The particular theory of structural determination that we adopt is the Truncation Hypothesis (Rizzi 1993/1994, this volume). We investigate the hypothesis that L2 grammars, both child and adult, allow truncation and that this accounts for variability in L2 production of lexical items and morphology associated with functional categories.

2 Truncation

For some researchers, full competence implies not only that all functional categories are present in the grammar but also that they must be represented in every sentence. Thus, every utterance is assumed to be a CP, even when certain features are apparently lacking. For example, Boser *et al.* (1992) account for the superficial absence of finite inflection on the assumption that L1 acquirers postulate null auxiliaries; this can be seen as a variant of the Missing Inflection Hypothesis – what is missing is a lexically realized auxiliary. For others, all functional categories are present in the representation underlying every utterance but some functional categories are underspecified (Hoekstra and Hyams 1995; Hoekstra *et al.* 1997; Wexler 1994).

There are other full competence theories, however, which make a somewhat different set of assumptions. While all functional categories are assumed to be present in the child's grammar from the beginning, this does not mean that all functional categories are projected in the representation underlying every utterance. Rizzi (1993/1994, this volume) and Haegeman (1995), for example, argue that early grammars possess the same set of functional categories as adult systems but that there is no restriction on what can be the root of a matrix declarative. As a result, learners project different types of roots. The child's structure may be truncated at any point below CP, such that root VPs, root TPs, root NegPs and root AgrPs are possible, in addition to CPs. Truncation at any particular point implies that all categories below that point are present, while none above it are, for that particular representation, as shown in (1).[2]

(1)

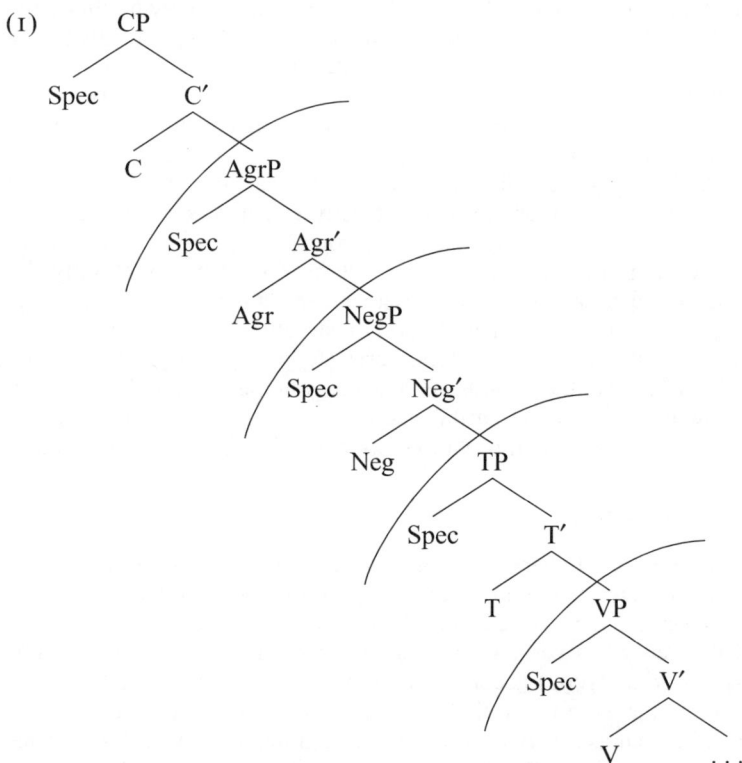

For Rizzi (1993/1994) and Haegeman (1995), truncation is a property of child grammars.[3] The child is assumed to lack the Root Principle, which dictates that a root clause must be a CP. Once the Root Principle matures, the possibility of truncation ceases. Others, however, have proposed that minimal projection is a property of grammars in general (Grimshaw 1994, 1997; Speas 1994). That is, loosely speaking, unnecessary structure should not be projected; every sentence does not necessarily have a CP root. Grimshaw (1994) suggests that what children do in L1 acquisition is simply a consequence of what grammars require in general (i.e. minimal projection) and that there is no qualitative difference between child and adult grammars in this respect.

3 Predictions for L2 acquisition

The Truncation Hypothesis and the Missing Inflection Hypothesis make different predictions for L2. If truncation obtains, variation in finiteness will be structurally determined and certain morphological and syntactic phenomena will be expected to co-occur, depending on the level of truncation (i.e. the nature of the root). On the Missing Inflection Hypothesis, on the other hand, such structural determination is not expected. Rather, finite and nonfinite forms should be found in similar contexts, since they are essentially alike at an abstract level, with nonfinite forms substituting for finite ones. We will look at three sets of predictions that distinguish the Truncation Hypothesis from the Missing Inflection Hypothesis, relating to finiteness, to the nature of subjects and to word order.

3.1 Finiteness
The Truncation Hypothesis assumes that truncation may, but need not, take place. Hence, VP, IP and CP roots are expected to be found at the same stages in the L2 learner's grammar. If a root VP is projected, there is no functional category under which the verb can appear and nonfinite matrix verbs should be observed. Verbs in IP and CP roots, on the other hand, will be finite, since these roots contain the necessary functional projections to host finiteness. In a number of cases, a particular sentence will be ambiguous as to the nature of the root (IP versus CP). Certain clause types are unambiguously CPs, however, and these must be finite. In other words, embedded clauses, wh-questions and yes/no questions should not contain nonfinite verbs, even when nonfinite verbs are otherwise being produced. The Missing Inflection Hypothesis also predicts variability between finite and nonfinite forms. In contrast to the Truncation Hypothesis, however, no difference is expected between CPs and other roots: nonfinite forms should show up in any syntactic context if the L2 learner's problem is due to inadequate knowledge of the specific realization of certain morphemes.

3.2 Subjects
The Truncation Hypothesis predicts differences in the distribution of subject types, depending on the nature of the root. We will consider

predictions for the distribution of null subjects, subject clitics and case-marking on DPs and pronouns.

3.2.1 Null subjects

For L1 acquisition of non pro-drop languages, Rizzi (1994) proposes that null subjects are null constants and that they have a limited distribution, only able to occur in the specifier of a root category, where they can be discourse identified. In the acquisition of a non pro-drop L2, null constants can be expected but only as subjects of VP and IP roots. As with finiteness, then, clauses that are clearly CPs are predicted to differ from VPs and IPs: null constants will be found as subjects of root VPs (nonfinite) and root IPs (finite) but not in CPs such as embedded clauses, wh-questions and yes/no questions. The Missing Inflection Hypothesis predicts no particular relationship between null subjects and root infinitives (Haznedar and Schwartz 1997); if L2 learners are omitting subjects (for whatever reason), the phenomenon should be independent of clause type. However, the Truncation Hypothesis and the Missing Inflection Hypothesis would be in agreement in the case of learners with pro-drop L1s. Assuming that the possibility of null subject *pro* is transferred from the L1 (e.g. White 1985), *pro* could occur in any context, including CPs.

A corollary prediction is that null constants and root infinitives will co-occur. If root infinitives decline or cease, null constants should disappear from finite roots. That is, as all root clauses become predominantly or exclusively CPs, the possibility of nonfinite main verbs and null subjects will disappear. As mentioned above, the Missing Inflection Hypothesis predicts no particular connection between null subjects and root infinitives.

3.2.2 Subject clitics

It is generally agreed that subject clitics attach to the finite verb in some functional projection (e.g. Auger 1994; Jaeggli 1982; Rizzi 1986; Roberge 1990). Since they require a functional category to host them, they minimally require an IP root. In other words, subject clitics should only be found in finite declaratives (CPs or IPs) and should not co-occur with root infinitives. Again, the Missing Inflection Hypothesis predicts no such contingency. If nonfinite forms are really finite, clitics should appear with nonfinite verbs.

3.2.3 Lexical subjects and case

Only elements that do not require structural case, such as bare NPs or pronouns bearing default case, should occur as overt subjects in root infinitives (Friedemann 1993/1994; see also Hoekstra *et al.* 1997). DPs should not be found as subjects of VP roots, as there is no mechanism for nominative case-assignment/checking. Finite declaratives (CPs or IPs) are expected to show the reverse properties, i.e. DP subjects should be found but not default case pronouns or bare NPs. The Missing Inflection Hypothesis, on the other hand, predicts that DP subjects should occur regardless of the form of the verb and that default pronoun subjects should not be possible with nonfinite verbs, since these are really finite.

3.3 Word order and negation

Word order may be affected by the type of root being projected, depending on properties of the L2s in question. The headedness characteristics of CP, IP and VP should determine the position of the verb in these roots. Thus, in the acquisition of German, root VPs and IPs should be verb-final, whereas CPs will be verb-second. In other words, if the verb is nonfinite, it should be found in final position. (This presupposes no effects of L1 headedness; we return to this point below.) The Missing Inflection Hypothesis predicts that nonfinite verbs should be found in second position, since they are in fact finite.

There are also predictions relating to negation which depend on the location of NegP, and which indirectly involve word order. If NegP is higher than TP (as in (1) above), a NegP root would entail the projection of T, hence the verb will move to T and the resulting sentences should be finite. The Truncation Hypothesis, then, predicts that if root NegPs are found, the word order will be Neg V and the verb will be finite. The Missing Inflection Hypothesis, on the other hand, assumes that most nonfinite forms are in fact finite; thus, they should show the same distribution as finite forms, yielding the order V Neg, since the verb will have moved past the negative to a higher functional projection in all cases.

4 L2 study

The data for this study are spontaneous production data drawn from four children and four adults learning French and German as L2s in naturalistic settings. Background information is summarized in Table 8.1. The two L2 French children, Greg and Kenny, were English native speakers learning French in Montreal (Lightbown 1977), who were enrolled in a French kindergarten. The children were 5 when recording started. They were recorded at regular intervals (roughly every month) from the kindergarten year until they were in Grade 2 (7–8 years).

The two child learners of German, Concetta and Luigina, were Italian speakers. They were 8 years old when they immigrated to Germany, with no prior exposure to German. They were first recorded one week after their arrival in the country (Pienemann 1981). Interviews took place on a monthly basis thereafter.

TABLE 8.1   Learner and interview details

	Greg	Kenny	Luigina	Concetta	Abdelmalek	Zahra	Zita	Ana
L1	English	English	Italian	Italian	Arabic	Arabic	Portuguese	Spanish
L2	French	French	German	German	French	French	German	German
Age at onset	5.8	5.4	8	8	adult	34	17	22
Files				*Months of exposure*				
1	—	0.3	0.7	0.2	14	12	3	3
2	—	0.5	1.4	1	15	14	3.5	4
3	—	1	2.3	1.8	16.7	15.5	3.7	4.5
4	—	2	3	2.5	17.7	17	4	4.7
5	—	3	3.7	3.2	18.7	18.5	5.6	5.2
6	—	4	4.4	4	20.5	20	6.5	7.2
7	5	5	5.4	5	21.5	21.7	6.7	7.4
8	—	7	6	5.6	24	23.2	7.5	8.2
9	—	8	7	6.8	25	23.7	8	11
10	9	9	7.9	8.4	25.7	24.5	9	11.7
11	—	9.5	8.6	9.1	27	25.5	9.5	13
12	10	10	8.8	11	27.7	26.7	10	13.5
13	11	11	9.5	12.4	30	27.7	11	14.2
14	14	14	11.4	13.5	30.7	28.2	11.7	23
15	15	15	12.8	14.5	31.7	29.2	13.7	23.5
16	18	18	14	—	32.5	33.7	15	24
17	20	20	14.9	—	33.5	34.4	16.5	24.7
18	25	25	19.8	—	34.5	36	19	—
19	27	27	—	—	35.7	36.5	22	—
20	29	29	—	—	36.7	38.5	22.7	—
21	—	—	—	—	38.7	39.5	23.4	—
22	—	—	—	—	43.5	40	24.4	—
23	—	—	—	—	51.5	41	25.4	—
24	—	—	—	—	52.5	42	25.6	—
25	—	—	—	—	54.5	43.5	25.8	—

The two adult learners of French, Abdelmalek and Zahra, were speakers of Moroccan Arabic, who immigrated as adults to France from Morocco and who were interviewed over a period of three years as part of the European Science Foundation (ESF) project on L2 Acquisition by Adult Immigrants (Perdue 1984, 1993).[4] They had had no exposure to French in their native country. At the time of their first interview, they had been living in France for one year but had had little contact with French and their proficiency was judged to be very limited. Each learner was interviewed roughly once every month.

The two adult German learners, Zita and Ana, were Portuguese and Spanish native speakers respectively who immigrated to Germany with no prior contact with the language. They were first interviewed by the ZISA project three months after their arrival (Clahsen, Meisel and Pienemann 1983). Each learner was then recorded every month for a little less than two years. (However, Ana went back to Spain for about 9 months, between month 14 and month 23.) Zita had little opportunity to interact with German speakers. In contrast, Ana had come to Germany to join her German boyfriend and hence was constantly exposed to the target language. She also had begun to attend German classes one month prior to the first interview.

Only verbal utterances consisting of at least two constituents were analysed. All instances of imitation and formulaic expressions were disregarded. Potential problems arise with homophony. Nonfinite markers in French and German sound like finite markers in some cases; we considered an ambiguous ending such as [e] and [i] in French, and -*en* in German as being nonfinite unless there was evidence to the contrary. Singular forms (1/2/3S) in French regular verbs are also homophonous. In addition, we encountered problems with words such as *je* (*I*) and *ne* (negative particle) in the transcription of the French ESF data, since these were not always phonetically transcribed and the status of *e* appears to be ambiguous between [e] and schwa, with very different consequences for the analysis. Therefore, we only analysed instances of *je* and *ne* that had been clearly transcribed with a schwa.

5 Results

5.1 Finiteness and clause type
Both hypotheses predict variable occurrence of finite and nonfinite morphology. According to the Truncation Hypothesis, finiteness will be structurally determined: if a VP is projected, the verb will be a root infinitive, if an IP or CP is projected, the verb will be finite. The Missing Inflection Hypothesis predicts no relationship between finiteness and clause type.

Co-occurrence of finite and nonfinite verbs was found for all the L2 learners, child and adult. It was not the case that the first occurrence of a verb systematically displayed the nonfinite form; most nonfinite verbs were also produced in the corresponding finite form, often during the course of the same interview, as in examples (2)–(9), suggesting it was not lack of knowledge of finiteness per se that caused learners to use nonfinite verbs.

(2) a. moi jouer   avec le train (Greg, month 5)
       me play-INF with the train
    b. moi je joue   avec une
       me I play-1/2/3S with one

(3) a. toi faire   ça (Kenny, month 8)
       you do-INF this
    b. Le papa   vache fait   ça
       the daddy cow   do-1/2/3S this

(4) a. mit Lehrer oder mit Mutter spielen? (Concetta, month 11)
       with teacher or   with mother play-INF
    b. spielt   Mutter
       play-3S mother

(5) a. ich schreiben (Luigina, month 14.9)
       I   write-INF
    b. schreibe ich?
       write-1S I

(6) a. pas demander les papiers (Abdelmalek, month 17.7)
       not ask-INF   the papers
    b. i demande
       he ask-1/2/3S

(7) a. tout le monde rester   à le salon (Zahra, month 23.7)
       everyone   stay-INF in the living-room
    b. deux restent le   bureau
       two   stay-3P (at) the office

(8) a. ich studieren in Porto (Zita, month 3.7)
       I   study-INF in Porto
    b. ich studiere nicht
       I   study-1S not

(9) a. das er kaufen   in en strant (=straße) (Ana, month 4)
       this he buy-INF in a   street
    b. er kaufe   ein Blume
       he buy-1S a   flower

TABLE 8.2 Distribution of finiteness and clause type

Age	L2	Learners	Finiteness	Declaratives	CPs
Children	French	Kenny	+ finite	428	138
			– finite	76 (15.1%)	9 (6.1%)
		Greg	+ finite	591	154
			– finite	58 (8.9%)	6 (3.8%)
	German	Concetta	+ finite	150	16
			– finite	23 (13.3%)	3 (15.8%)
		Luigina	+ finite	42	25
			– finite	8 (16%)	2 (7.4%)
Adults	French	Abdelmalek	+ finite	653	92
			– finite	272 (29.4%)	54 (37%)
		Zahra	+ finite	600	157
			– finite	236 (28.2%)	65 (29.3%)
	German	Zita	+ finite	587	64
			– finite	191 (24.6%)	18 (22%)
		Ana	+ finite	688	124
			– finite	74 (9.7%)	13 (9.5%)

In Table 8.2, we report the overall incidence of finite and nonfinite main verbs in root declaratives and CPs, for the total period during which root infinitives are found (i.e. up to month 18 for Kenny and Greg and the whole data collection period for everyone else). As far as child L2 French is concerned, the vast majority of root infinitives were found during the first 18 months of exposure (see Table 8.8 in the appendix for details).[5] During this period, 15% of Kenny's and 8.9% of Greg's declaratives contain root infinitives. After the 18th month, the proportion of root infinitives drops dramatically and becomes insignificant (0.56% for Kenny and 0.44% for Greg), suggesting that VPs are no longer possible roots from that point on. For the rest of this chapter, when analysing the child L2 French data, we concentrate on the first 18 months, i.e. the period during which finite and nonfinite forms coincide.

As for child L2 German, the proportion of root infinitives is around 15%, which is similar to Kenny (see Table 8.2 and Table 8.8 in the appendix). However, there is a considerable discrepancy in corpus size between the child German and child French. Concetta and Luigina produced many fewer declaratives than Greg and Kenny; their first utterances consisted mainly of nouns and noun phrases. A drop in production of root infinitives can be seen in Concetta's case at month 14.5; since this corresponds to the last interview, there is no way to tell whether or not this signals the end of the root infinitive period. As for Luigina, production was so low that it is impossible to establish any general developmental trend.

In contrast to the child data, the adult corpora were similar in size and hence more comparable. The adult French learners produced a higher proportion (about 29%) of root infinitives than the children (see Table 8.2 and Table 8.9 in the appendix); there was no evidence for a sudden drop in the incidence of root infinitives, nor did they disappear. The adult learners of German differ in their developmental patterns. Zita produced many more root infinitives than Ana. Overall, Zita's proportion of root infinitives was 24.6%, which is close to the adult L2 French learners' rate, compared with 9.7% for Ana. As was the case for the adult L2 French learners, there was no sharp decrease in Zita's production of root infinitives, except for the last interview. This is to be contrasted with Ana, whose root infinitives decreased at month 14.2, though without totally disappearing.

A crucial claim distinguishing the two hypotheses centres on finiteness in CPs. According to the Truncation Hypothesis, clauses that are clearly CPs (wh-questions, yes/no questions and embedded clauses, including relative clauses) should be finite, since the relevant functional categories are projected; the Missing Inflection Hypothesis, on the other hand, expects both finite and nonfinite verb forms to be found in CPs. The first appearance of CP was delayed for the children (see Grondin and White 1996) and the children learning German produced many fewer CPs than the children learning French. Nevertheless, CPs became productive during the period when root infinitives were still being used. CPs appeared early in the adult corpora.

As can be seen in Table 8.2, nonfinite CPs are rare in the child data. With the exception of Concetta, over 92% of child CPs are finite. In addition, the proportion of nonfinite verbs is lower in CPs than in root declaratives. The contingency between finiteness and clause type is significant for Kenny ($X^2 = 8.043$, p < .01) and for Greg ($X^2 = 4.74$, p < .05) but not for Concetta or Luiginia.

As for the adults, with the exception of Ana, the incidence of nonfinite CPs is much higher than for the children (see Table 8.2). Examples of nonfinite wh-questions, yes/no questions and embedded clauses produced by the adults are given in (10) and (11). For the four adults, there is no relationship between finiteness and clause type: a nonfinite verb was just as likely to be used in a CP as elsewhere.

(10) a. combien   tu   rester   ici? (Abdelmalek, month 24)
        how (long) you   stay-INF here
     b. et   Malika, pourquoi téléphoner (Zahra, month 38.5)
        and Malika why   call-INF
        à toi à la   maison?
        to you at the house

(11) a. möchten ma   du ein Kaffee? (Zita, month 10)
        want-INF then you a   coffee

    b. weil   ich hier nicht wohnen (Ana, month 11)
       because I   here not   live-INF

The results from the children, then, support the Truncation Hypothesis: very few of their CPs were nonfinite. In contrast, the adult learners used nonfinite forms in CPs, suggesting that the nature of the clause type does not determine the distribution of finite and nonfinite verbal forms in their case, consistent with the Missing Inflection Hypothesis.

5.2 Subjects

5.2.1 Null subjects

On the Truncation Hypothesis, null subjects are in fact null constants and can be expected in both finite (IP) and nonfinite (VP) declaratives but not in CPs. In addition, root infinitives and subjectless declaratives should disappear at the same time. The results concerning these predictions again show child/adult differences. While all learners produce null subjects in finite and nonfinite declaratives, the adults also produce them in CPs.

Examples of null subjects in finite and nonfinite contexts from the child L2 learners are given in (12) and (13). Kenny and Greg used null subjects in finite and non-finite declaratives (Kenny to a greater extent than Greg) until month 18 (20 in Kenny's case), after which they effectively disappeared (Table 8.10 in the appendix). As we have seen, this coincides with the disappearance of root infinitives for both children.

(12) a. va   là (Kenny, month 4)
       go-3S there
   b. jouer   de hockey (Kenny, month 9.5)
       play-INF of hockey
   c. et là   sont jaunes (Greg, month 9.5)
       and there are yellow
   d. manger les oreilles (Greg, month 10)
       eat-INF the ears

(13) a. macht de papier (Concetta, month 12.4)
       make-3S paper
   b. putzen   Haus (Concetta, month 12.4)
       clean-INF house
   c. ist kaputt (Luigina, month 3)
       is broken
   d. gehen   in die schule (Luigina, month 19.7)
       go-INF to the school

Table 8.3 summarizes the overall incidence of null subjects (looking only at the first 18 months for the child L2 French learners). Looking at

TABLE 8.3   Incidence of null subjects in different clause types

Age	L2	Learners	Subject types	Nonfinite declaratives	Finite declaratives	Finite CPs
Children	French	Kenny	overt	53	341	104
			null	23 (30.3%)	87 (20.3%)	6 (5.5%)
		Greg	overt	27	532	123
			null	31 (53.4%)	59 (10%)	5 (4%)
	German	Concetta	overt	12	127	12
			null	11 (47.8%)	23 (15.3%)	0 (0%)
		Luigina	overt	7	29	20
			null	1 (12.5%)	13 (30.9%)	4 (16.7%)
Adults	French	Abdelmalek	overt	205	601	79
			null	67 (24.6%)	52 (8%)	7 (8.1%)
		Zahra	overt	176	489	109
			null	60 (25.4%)	111 (18.5%)	39 (26.4%)
	German	Zita	overt	159	424	57
			null	32 (16.7%)	163 (27.8%)	7 (10.9%)
		Ana	overt	51	440	89
			null	23 (31.1%)	248 (36%)	26 (22.6%)

the children, with the exception of Luigina, who produced few root infinitives, a high proportion of root infinitives were subjectless. Roughly half of Greg's and Concetta's root infinitives and one third of Kenny's lacked a subject. The proportion of null subjects was lower in finite declaratives and they were rare in finite CPs, consistent with the hypothesis that null subjects in these grammars are null constants and hence unable to be licensed in a CP.

Turning to the adults, null subjects were produced in finite and non-finite declaratives, as well as in finite CPs, as shown in examples (14)–(17). (See Table 8.11 in the appendix for a detailed breakdown.) The proportion of adult CPs with null subjects is higher than was found for three of the four children (see Table 8.3).[6]

(14) a. jamais travaille   le   maroc (Abdelmalek, month 20.5)
        never work-1/2/3S the Marocco
     b. rester   à le bureau (Abdelmalek, month 20.5)
        stay-INF at the office
     c. parler   le   maroccain (Zahra, month 14)
        speak-INF the Maroccan
     d. gonfle   beaucoup (Zahra, month 28.2)
        swell-1/2/3S much

(15) a. koche   schnell (Zita, month 9)
        cook-1S quickly
     b. trinken   viele Kaffee (Zita, month 11.7)
        drink-INF much coffee
     c. und lerne   langsam (Ana, month 7.4)
        and learn-1S slowly
     d. fahren   in Autobahn (Ana, month 7.4)
        drive-INF in freeway

(16) a. il faut   marches (Abdelmalek, month 36.7)
        it has+to walk-1/2/3S (= it is required that you walk)
     b. quand toujours dort (Zahra, month 21.7)
        when always   sleep-1/2/3S

(17) a. wann kommt   in Deutschland (Zita, month 22)
        when come-3S in Germany
     b. weil   ist kleine (Ana, month 4.5)
        because is small

There appeared to be no relationship between incidence of null subjects and incidence of root infinitives in the adult data, in contrast to the children. Abdelmalek used null subjects until the last few interviews (see Table 8.11 in the appendix). Crucially, the point at which the proportion of null subjects dropped did not correspond to any decline in root infinitives. Ana, who did show a drop in root infinitives, did not show a corresponding drop in null subjects. This suggests that null subjects and root infinitives are not part of the same phenomenon in the adult grammar, as predicted by the Missing Inflection Hypothesis.

Finite declaratives are, in many cases, ambiguous between being root IPs or root CPs. If all declaratives are CPs, as the Missing Inflection Hypothesis implies (Epstein *et al.* 1996), then we predict no difference in the incidence of null subjects in finite declaratives compared with finite CPs. On the Truncation Hypothesis, there should be significantly more null subjects in finite declaratives, consistent with their being root IPs. The relationship of type of subject (overt vs. null) to clause type (finite declarative vs. finite CP) is significant for the French child L2ers (Kenny: $X^2 = 13.538$, p < .001; Greg: $X^2 = 4.791$, p < .05), while it is not significant for the German child L2ers, although their results are in the right direction. In the case of the adult French L2ers, incidence of null subjects is fairly low in both clause types for Abdelmalek and there is no relationship between the nature of the clause and the occurrence of null subjects. In Zahra's case, null subjects occur proportionally more in finite CPs than in other finite declaratives and the contingency is significant ($X^2 = 4.565$, p < .05), a finding that clearly goes against the Truncation Hypothesis. Significant differences conforming to the predictions of the Truncation Hypothesis are found in the adult L2 German data, in that null subjects occur to a greater extent in finite root declaratives than do CPs (Zita: $X^2 = 8.473$, p < .01; Ana: $X^2 = 7.915$, p < .01) but, in Ana's case at least, the incidence of null subjects in CPs is quite high (22.6% of her CPs have null subjects). While the data support the hypothesis that finite declaratives are truncated IPs as far as the children are concerned, the adult data are consistent with the hypothesis that all their clauses are CPs.

However, this then requires an explanation for why the adults were producing sentences with null subjects at all. The adult learners all had pro-drop L1s, as did two of the children. Thus, it is conceivable that the adult null subjects are in fact *pro*, rather than null constants, which would explain their occurrence in CPs and their failure to coincide with root infinitives. It is interesting that at least one of the two children with pro-drop L1s behaved more like the other children (without pro-drop L1s) than like the adults; null subjects appear to be null constants rather than *pro*.

To summarize so far, two main differences were uncovered between the child and adult L2 learners in the usage of null subjects. The children rarely produced null subjects in CPs and the occurrence of null subjects in their utterances was found to parallel that of root infinitives. When root infinitives disappeared from the data, so did subjectless finite declaratives. These facts are consistent with the Truncation Hypothesis,

TABLE 8.4   Clitic subjects in L2 French declaratives

Age	Learners	Subject types	Nonfinite	Finite
Children	Kenny	− clitic	73	269
		+ clitic	3 (3.9%)	159 (37.1%)
	Greg	− clitic	45	180
		+ clitic	13 (22.4%)	411 (69.5%)
Adults	Abdelmalek	− clitic	104	121
		+ clitic	168 (61.8%)	532 (81.5%)
	Zahra	− clitic	116	208
		+ clitic	120 (50.8%)	392 (65.3%)

which proposes that null subjects are null constants and that the two phenomena are related. In contrast, adult root infinitives and null subjects did not pattern together. In addition, the adult learners used null subjects in CPs. These results are more consistent with the Missing Inflection Hypothesis (plus L1 influence).

5.2.2 Clitics
In this section we describe the use of subject clitics by the child and adult learners of French. (German lacks the relevant subject clitics.) The findings show considerable differences between the children and adults; while the children produced subject clitics only in finite contexts, as predicted by the Truncation Hypothesis, the adults produced clitic subjects in nonfinite roots as well, consistent with the Missing Inflection Hypothesis.

Examples of subject clitics produced by both children are given in (18); overall incidence of subject clitics in finite and nonfinite contexts (up to month 18) is reported in Table 8.4. The children used subject clitics from their early interviews onwards and clitics were in fact the most frequently occurring subjects for both of them, other subjects consisting of DPs, pronouns and null subjects (Grondin and White 1996; White 1996). Crucially, clitics were far more frequent as subjects of finite verbs than nonfinite verbs; only 3.9% of Kenny's nonfinite verbs had clitic subjects, whereas 37.1% of his finite verbs occurred with clitics. Somewhat problematically, 22.4% of Greg's nonfinite roots had clitic subjects but this is still much lower than clitics with finite verbs (69.5%). (However, only 3.2% of all the clitics used by Greg were found in nonfinite contexts.) It is not surprising, then, to find a very high contingency between finiteness and the occurrence of subject clitics (Kenny: $X^2 = 32.62$, p < .0001; Greg: $X^2 = 51.8$, p < .0001).

(18) a. j'ai   fait ça et ça (Greg, month 5)
         I have-1S done this and this
     b. le bébé i va   là (Greg, month 5)
         the baby he go-3S there
     c. je suis ton ami (Kenny, month 3)
         I am your friend
     d. i crie   hey! (Kenny, month 4)
         he yell-1/2/3S hey

Clitics were the also most common type of subject used by the adult
L2 French learners. The examples in (19) illustrate clitics occurring
with finite and nonfinite verbs. In contrast to the children, the incidence
of subject clitics with nonfinite verbs was high. More than 50% of
subjects of root infinitives were clitics, which is clearly contrary to the
Truncation Hypothesis. Nevertheless, the contingency between finiteness
and the occurrence of subject clitics is significant for the adults, in that
clitics occurred more often in finite contexts (Abdelmalek: $X^2 = 40.5$,
$p < .0001$; Zahra: $X^2 = 14.97$, $p < .0001$).

(19) a. il est parti l' Espagne, lui (Abdelmalek, month 14)
         he is gone the Spain   him
     b. tu boire (Abdelmalek, month 27)
         you drink-INF
     c. je reviens   pas (Zahra, month 24.5)
         I return-1/2/3S not
     d. tu couper tout (Zahra, month 24.5)
         you cut-INF everything

5.2.3 Case

We turn now to properties of lexical subjects, specifically case. The
Truncation Hypothesis predicts a contingency: DPs should be found as
subjects of finite clauses, strong pronouns (and bare NPs) with nonfinite.
The incidence of bare NP subjects proved to be rare or nonexistent;[7]
these will not therefore be reported. As far as French is concerned, DPs
or strong pronouns occurring together with clitics have been excluded
from the analyses below, since they were included under clitics in the
previous section (see example (18b) above).

In French, default case is objective, the case found in strong pronouns. Table 8.5 gives the overall incidence of DP and pronoun subjects
(up to month 18 for the French child learners). As far as the children
are concerned, DP subjects appeared in the earliest interviews and were
overwhelmingly used in finite contexts by both Kenny and Greg, in
accordance with the Truncation Hypothesis. Strong pronouns[8] were used
as subjects of root infinitives, consistent with truncation (see (20a) and
(20c)); 59.2% of Kenny's root infinitives had strong pronoun subjects,

TABLE 8.5   Lexical subjects in finite and nonfinite declaratives

Age	L2	Learners	Finiteness	Total declaratives	DPs	Pronouns
Children	French	Kenny	+ finite	428	115	65
			− finite	76	6	45
		Greg	+ finite	591	99	32
			− finite	58	0	15
	German	Concetta	+ finite	150	56	45
			− finite	23	7	3
		Luigina	+ finite	42	12	11
			− finite	8	4	3
Adults	French	Abdelmalek	+ finite	653	53	13
			− finite	272	15	19
		Zahra	+ finite	600	71	26
			− finite	236	32	23
	German	Zita	+ finite	587	196	208
			− finite	191	54	105
		Ana	+ finite	688	183	263
			− finite	74	23	27

as did 25.9% of Greg's. The contingency between subject type (DP, strong pronoun) and finiteness is significant (Kenny: $X^2 = 43.29$, $p < .0001$; Greg: $X^2 = 35.21$, $p < .0001$). Strong pronouns were proportionally much less common as subjects of finite verbs, again in accordance with the Truncation Hypothesis: 15.4% of Kenny's finite declaratives and 5.4% of Greg's had strong pronoun subjects.

(20) a. toi aller   à Guy's (Kenny, month 5)
       you go-INF to Guy's
    b. toi parle   français (Kenny, month 5)
       you speak-1/2/3S French
    c. moi jouer   avec le   train (Greg, month 9.5)
       me play-INF with the train
    d. moi fais   ici (Greg, month 5)
       me do-1/2/3S here

However, contrary to the predictions of both the Truncation Hypothesis and the Missing Inflection Hypothesis, 60% or more of the children's strong pronoun subjects occurred in finite contexts. Examples are shown in (20b) and (20d). As noted by White (1996), the majority of instances of strong pronouns with a finite verb consist of just two forms, namely *moi est* ('me is') and *moi fais* ('me do'), suggesting that strong pronouns with finite verbs are not fully productive.

The contingency between subject type and finiteness is not significant for the children learning German. Nominative is the default case in German; hence, nominative pronouns are expected in finite contexts due to structural case assignment and in nonfinite environments, as the default. Subject pronouns were indeed used in both finite and nonfinite clauses, as illustrated in (21), more often occurring in finite clauses (see Table 8.5). For DPs, the prediction is the same as for French, namely that they should not occur in root infinitives. While the majority of DPs were indeed found in finite clauses, Concetta and Luigina's root infinitives are just as likely to have DP subjects as pronoun subjects, which is contrary to the Truncation Hypothesis and different from the French L2 children. However, this may be an artifact of the low number of root infinitives produced overall.

(21) a. sie gehen arbeiten   Montag (Concetta, month 12.4)
         she go-INF work-INF Monday
     b. sie sagt (Concetta, month 12.4)
         she says-3S
     c. ich schreibe eine auch (Luigina, month 14.9)
         I   write-1S one too
     d. na Hause du schreiben Blume (Luigina,   month 19.8)
         to house you write-INF flower

The adult L2 data show DPs occuring more often in finite contexts than nonfinite; however DP subjects of root infinitives are also found (see (22e) below). Strong pronouns occur in both finite and nonfinite contexts. Root infinitives are just as likely to have DP subjects as pronoun subjects for three of the four adults. The contingency between subject type and finiteness is significant for Abdelmalek (X^2 = 13.5, p < .001), barely nonsignificant for Zahra (X^2 = 3.62, p = .057), significant for Zita (X^2 = 9.79, p < .01) but not for Ana.

To summarize, all learners used pronouns bearing default case in root infinitives, as predicted by the Truncation Hypothesis and not by the Missing Inflection Hypothesis. However, strong pronouns were found in finite clauses as well, which is problematic in the case of French and contrary to the predictions of both hypotheses. Subject DPs occur predominantly in finite contexts and were not found in root infinitives in the child data. However, DP subjects were found in both finite and nonfinite contexts in the adult data. Once again, then, the results suggest that root infinitives are genuinely nonfinite for the children but that they may in fact be finite for the adults, consistent with the Missing Inflection Hypothesis.

5.3 Word order in L2 German
According to the Truncation Hypothesis, word order in V2 languages should differ, depending on the nature of the root. Since VP is right-

TABLE 8.6   Verb placement in L2 German

Age	Learners	Finiteness	VX	XV
Children	Concetta	+ finite	80	0
		− finite	15	1
	Luigina	+ finite	28	1
		− finite	4	0
Adults	Zita	+ finite	409	4
		− finite	115	9
	Ana	+ finite	594	0
		− finite	52	3

headed in German, the nonfinite verb in a root infinitive should appear in sentence-final position. In fact, the reverse is obtained in the L2 German data (both child and adult): most nonfinite verbs were found to precede VP-material, the most common word order being SVO, as can be seen in Table 8.6 and the examples in (22c, e, f):

(22) a. die Mutter bringt   Banane (Concetta, month 5.6)
     the mother bring-3S banana
   b. meine Mutter putzen (Concetta, month 13.5)
     my   mother clean-INF
   c. ein Junge spielen   Ball (Luigina, month 6)
     a   boy   play-INF ball
   d. meine Mutter ist   krank (Luigina, month 14.9)
     my   mother is-3S ill
   e. ein Herr verkaufen Blumen (Ana, month 4)
     a   man sell-INF   flowers
   f. du kaufen   eine Banane (Zita, month 9)
     you buy-INF a   banana

The Truncation Hypothesis also predicts that different word orders should be found in finite clauses in L2 German, depending on whether the root is a CP or an IP. Specifically, a CP root should yield utterances with the verb in the second position, i.e. preceding other material in the VP, whereas an IP root should result in sentences with the finite verb in final position, since there is no C for the verb to move to. However, finite verbs in final position were practically nonexistent, as can be seen in Table 8.6. Instead, SVO was by far the most common word order (the appropriate order for CPs), as in (22a, d).

Table 8.6 shows that verbs systematically precede VP-material across sentence types throughout the child and adult corpora. Vainikka and Young-Scholten (1994, 1996) argue that VP headedness is transferred from the L1, on the basis of different word orders produced in L2

German by speakers of languages with SVO and SOV order. They argue that headedness of functional projections is not transferred. Our data are consistent with transfer of the headedness of both lexical and functional categories (Schwartz and Sprouse 1994, 1996), since VP and IP are left-headed in the learners' L1s. In the child data, there is no evidence for the eventual acquisition of the target headedness of VP and IP. The data are consistent with truncation applying to transferred structure. In the adult data, there is evidence for the eventual acquisition of the target headedness (see Prévost 1997) but word order remains VX in root infinitives produced after the acquisition of German head-final VP. This suggests that these are not in fact nonfinite verbs but sentences involving functional categories and verb movement, i.e. supporting the Missing Inflection Hypothesis. As for lack of verb-final finite declaratives, by the time IP headedness switches to the target value, the properties of verb movement to C have also been acquired (cf. du Plessis *et al.* 1987; Schwartz and Tomaselli 1990), thus preventing the projection of verb-final finite IP roots.

5.4 Negation
Since truncation can occur at any point in the representation, any projection may form a root, including NegP. If NegP is located above TP, as in (1) above, a root truncated at NegP should be finite; hence, no negative root infinitives should be observed. The L2 data reviewed here disconfirm this prediction. Negative root infinitives were found, as well as differences between children and adults with respect to verb placement and negation.

As far as the child L2 French learners were concerned, negated utterances appeared throughout the data collection period. The child L2 German speakers, on the other hand, produced hardly any negatives and will not be discussed further. Negative root infinitives were found in the French data from the beginning. Examples of nonfinite and finite negatives are given in (23).

(23) a. pas jouer   avec la   ferme (Greg, month 10)
        not play-INF with the farm
     b. pas ouvrir   ça (Kenny, month 5)
        not open-INF this
     c. moi je va   pas là (Greg, month 5)
        me I go-3S not there
     d. t'   as   pas d'aide (Kenny, month 9.5)
        you have-2S not of help

The distribution of negative markers and verbal forms was systematic for the children. Table 8.7 shows how word order relates to finiteness in negative declaratives (up to month 18 in the case of the children).

TABLE 8.7   Verb placement in negative root declaratives

Age	L2	Learners	Finiteness	Neg V	V Neg
Children	French	Kenny	+ finite	4	86
			− finite	18	0
		Greg	+ finite	2	118
			− finite	6	0
Adults	French	Abdelmalek	+ finite	8	88
			− finite	24	4
		Zahra	+ finite	0	129
			− finite	1	6
	German	Zita	+ finite	7	78
			− finite	15	12
		Ana	+ finite	3	94
			− finite	4	6

Where the negative occurred with a root infinitive, the verb, without exception, followed *pas*, as can be seen in (23a) and (23b), while in finite negatives, such as (23c) and (23d), the verb preceded *pas*. The contingency between negative placement and finiteness is significant (Kenny: $X^2 = 84.44$, p < .0001; Greg: $X^2 = 92.92$, p < .0001).

The distribution of negative placement and finiteness was less clear in the adults. The adult learners used negation in almost all interviews. Most negatives were finite but some negative root infinitives were found (see Table 8.7). While Abdelmalek, like the children, shows a systematic relationship between finiteness and negative placement ($X^2 = 67.79$, p < .0001), Zahra appears to have only one word order (V Neg) regardless of finiteness. The two learners of German use the appropriate order (V Neg) for finite verbs (see (24)).[9] However, they also use this order with nonfinite verbs as often as they use Neg V, as can be seen in (25). The contingency between negative placement and finiteness is significant (Zita: $X^2 = 29.07$, p < .0001; Ana: $X^2 = 20.2$, p < .0001).

(24) a. ich studiere   nicht (Zita, month 3.7)
        I   study-1S not
     b. ich spreche   nicht Deutsch (Ana, month 4.5)
        I   speak-1S not   German

(25) a. du   mich verstehn   nix (Zita, month 6.5)
        you me   understand-INF not
     b. ich sprechen   nich Deutsch (Zita, month 6.7)
        I   speak-INF not German

The systematic word order alternation between V Neg and Neg V in the child data, and in Abdelmalek's data, is contrary to the Missing

Inflection Hypothesis. If nonfinite forms are in fact finite, only V Neg order should have been found, regardless of the morphological form of the verb. These data are also problematic for the Truncation Hypothesis if Neg P is above TP. However, they can be explained on the assumption that NegP is located below TP (Meisel 1997; Ouhalla 1991; Zanuttini 1991), in which case no functional category is projected in a NegP root, explaining why the verb appears in the nonfinite form, with Neg V order. The V Neg order with finite verbs is due to verb movement past the negative to a higher functional projection. Zahra's data are consistent with the Missing Inflection Hypothesis: negated root infinitives show the same word order as finite negatives (however, there are few negative root infinitives). For the German adults, V Neg and Neg V are used equally often in root infinitives. If all nonfinite forms are in fact finite, they should have shown a pattern of usage closer to Zahra's.

6 Discussion

To summarize our findings, finite and nonfinite roots co-occurred in the child and adult L2 data, suggesting variability. The child L2 data are largely consistent with the Truncation Hypothesis: nonfinite verbs are found only in root declaratives and not in CPs; null subjects do not occur in CPs and they disappear when root infinitives do, suggesting that they are null constants; subject clitics occur solely with finite verbs, as do DPs; strong pronouns are found in nonfinite contexts (and in finite contexts as well, which is somewhat problematic for both hypotheses in the case of French); negators systematically precede nonfinite verbs and follow finite ones. These findings suggest that nonfinite forms are indeed different from finite forms and that the distribution of nonfinite verbs is structurally determined.

In contrast, truncation is not confirmed for the adult learners. Even though both finite and nonfinite declaratives occurred in early acquisition, the adult data were found to include nonfinite verbs in CPs, null subjects in CPs, subject clitics in root infinitives and nonfinite verbs preceding negative markers. Many more (apparently) nonfinite verbs were found in the adult corpora and the adults produced these forms throughout. The adult results are consistent with the Missing Inflection Hypothesis: the adults do not treat main verbs bearing the infinitival marker as nonfinite. Rather, they use the infinitival marker as a substitute for finite inflection, explaining the occurrence of finite and nonfinite forms in the same contexts.

One might also consider whether the issue is not just missing inflection but 'faulty' inflection. That is, do learners use inflection inappropriately (1st person morphology with 3rd person subjects, for example)? This is not a problem in L1 acquisition: when inflectional morphology occurs, it is largely correct (Borer and Rohrbacher 1997; Hoekstra *et al.*

1997). Grondin and White (1996) similarly show that when Kenny and Greg (the same children studied here) use agreement morphology, it is accurate. As for the adult L2 learners investigated here, this remains to be determined but preliminary analyses indicate that inaccurate use of morphology most commonly takes the form of missing inflection rather than faulty inflection. Inflection, then, is not random; either appropriate agreement is used or nonfinite forms are used.

For neither the children nor the adults does the use of nonfinite morphology indicate a stage systematically lacking functional categories, nor is variation between finite and nonfinite morphology an indication of moving from one stage of grammatical development to another, contra Vainikka and Young-Scholten (1994, 1996). Our results are also not consistent with proposals that features of functional categories (even L1 features) are permanently inaccessible in L2 grammars (Beck 1998; Meisel 1997); such theories predict random use of finite and nonfinite morphology, which is not what we found. For the children, we have suggested that the incidence of finite versus nonfinite morphology is structurally constrained and reflects properties of the root, depending on the level of truncation. For the adults, on the other hand, the data are more consistent with the Missing Inflection Hypothesis; adults resort to nonfinite forms when they are not certain of the appropriate finite morphology.

Thus, our findings appear to indicate an age effect in the usage of nonfinite verbs in L2 acquisition. This does not, however, support claims for a maturational account of root infinitives in general (Rizzi 1993/ 1994; Wexler 1994), since the child L2 learners studied here were older than L1 acquirers in the root infinitive stage (White 1996). Furthermore, in the case of Kenny and Greg, data from their L1 English show that all functional categories were present and consistently used, again suggesting that they are past any optional infinitive or truncation stage in the L1 (Grondin and White 1996).

We believe that the difference between child and adult L2 is largely quantitative rather qualitative (cf. Grimshaw 1994 for L1). It is quite possible that what we have observed reflects a difference in the degree of truncation permitted. Both truncation and missing inflection may be involved in adult grammars; that is, some of the nonfinite forms produced by the adults were finite (as per the Missing Inflection Hypothesis), whereas others were genuinely nonfinite, the consequence of the projection of a truncated VP. In the case of a number of the properties that we have described, while the adults showed significantly greater use than the children of nonfinite morphology in contexts prohibited by the Truncation Hypothesis, they nevertheless showed significant contingencies between finiteness and those properties (e.g. finiteness and clitic placement, finiteness and DP subjects), suggesting that some of their nonfinite forms must genuinely have been nonfinite, rather than being finite with missing inflection. How could one possibly tease these two situations apart? The negation data from the adult learners of German described here are at least suggestive (although insufficient to draw strong conclusions); if the Missing Inflection Hypothesis is correct, all nonfinite negatives should show V Neg order. If the Truncation Hypothesis is correct and Neg P is below TP, all nonfinite negatives should show Neg V order. But in fact both orders are found to an equal extent in the adult German L2 data, suggesting that both truncation and missing inflection may obtain. Nor is there any reason in principle not to assume that children also resort to nonfinite morphology when in doubt (Haznedar and Schwartz 1997).

If the difference between children and adults is only a matter of degree, one might ask what causes children to truncate more than adults and adults to make far greater use of nonfinite morphology than children. As far as truncation is concerned, one possibility is that adults have better control over the limited pragmatic conditions under which root infinitives can appear (Lasser 1998). Adult L2 learners may be able to draw on such pragmatic knowledge from the L1. As for adult use of nonfinite morphology, Lardiere (1998) reports results that are consistent with the Missing Inflection Hypothesis. She shows that an adult L2 learner of English who has lived in the L2 environment for 18 years fails to use inflection (tense marking) accurately, predominantly producing untensed forms, but at the same time showing perfect performance on case-marking, a syntactic reflex of tense. Lardiere concludes that the functional category Tense is present in the grammar and proposes that L2 learners have a problem mapping from abstract syntactic features to morphological form. We speculate that, for reasons as yet undetermined, there is less of a mapping problem for children.

There are certain shortcomings of this study that need to be addressed in future research in order to determine whether our findings of a significant degree of truncation in child L2 in contrast to adult, can generalize beyond the data examined here. Firstly, the child German data were far less extensive than the data from the other subjects and clearly need to be supplemented. Secondly, it would be highly advisable to look at learners where neither the L1 nor the L2 is a pro-drop language, in order to be able to investigate the issue of null constants more clearly. Thirdly, while we were successful in finding child and adult learners of the same L2s, it would obviously be preferable if they had the same L1s as well. Nevertheless, despite these shortcomings, we believe that the data examined here are suggestive of the possibility that variation in use of inflection in child L2 acquisition is somewhat different in nature from variation in adult acquisition, truncation predominantly accounting for the child performance and missing inflection for the adults.

Appendix

TABLE 8.8 Proportion of nonfinite declaratives in child L2

	French				German					
	Kenny		Greg		Concetta			Luigina		
Month	RI/total	% RI	RI/total	% RI	Month	RI/total	% RI	Month	RI/total	% RI
0.3	1/1	100			0.2	0/0	—	0.7	0/0	—
0.5	0/1	0			1	0/0	—	1.4	0/0	—
1	0/5	0			1.8	0/0	—	2.3	0/0	—
2	1/5	20			2.5	0/0	—	3	0/1	0
3	4/10	40			3.2	0/0	—	3.7	0/1	0
4	0/18	0			4	0/0	—	4.4	0/0	—
5	5/22	22.7	7/43	16.3	5	0/6	0	5.4	0/4	0
7	6/43	13.9			5.6	0/6	0	6	1/2	50
8	7/32	21.9			6.8	0/6	0	7	0/5	0
9	5/19	26.3			8.4	1/7	14.3	7.9	0/2	0
9.5	8/31	25.8	3/39	7.7	9.1	0/10	0	8.6	0/0	—
10	5/30	16.7	13/69	18.8	11	3/29	10.3	8.8	0/1	0
11	6/39	15.4	2/24	8.3	12.4	10/34	29.4	9.5	3/3	100
14	10/67	14.9	13/134	9.7	13.5	8/54	14.8	11.4	0/0	0
15	11/74	15.8	13/209	6.6	14.5	1/27	3.7	12.8	1/3	33.3
18	7/107	6.5	7/131	5.3				14	0/4	0
20	1/110	1.8	2/156	1.3				14.9	1/11	11.8
25	1/134	0.75	1/310	0.32				19.8	2/13	16.7
27	1/137	2.8	0/218	0						
29	0/146	0.68	1/227	0.44						
Totals	79/1031	7.6	62/1560	4		23/173	13.3		8/50	16
Up to month 18	76/504	15	58/649	8.9						
After month 18	3/527	0.56	4/911	0.44						

RI = root infinitive

TABLE 8.9 Proportion of nonfinite declaratives in adult L2

	French						German					
	Abdelmalek			Zahra			Zita			Ana		
	Month	RI/total	% RI	Month	RI/total	% RI	Month	RI/total	% RI	Month	RI/total	% RI
	14	0/4	0	12	0/2	0	3	0/3	0	3	0/0	—
	15	1/5	20	14	11/16	68.8	3.5	0/1	0	4	9/44	20.5
	16.7	1/11	9.1	15.5	1/4	25	3.7	2/12	16.7	4.5	4/44	9
	17.7	39/95	41.1	17	2/12	16.7	4	2/5	40	4.7	0/11	0
	18.7	8/18	44.4	18.5	6/29	20.7	5.6	5/7	71.4	5.2	2/13	15.4
	20.5	6/13	46.2	20	4/12	33.3	6.5	7/21	33.3	7.2	6/59	10.2
	21.5	17/37	45.9	21.7	5/17	29.4	6.7	9/12	75	7.4	8/37	21.6
	24	14/36	38.9	23.2	4/4	100	7.5	5/16	31.25	8.2	9/52	17.3
	25	36/79	45.6	23.7	4/16	25	8	2/12	16.6	11	6/76	7.9
	25.7	16/43	37.2	24.5	17/43	39.5	9	3/14	21.4	11.7	11/79	13.9
	27	12/51	23.5	25.5	7/22	31.8	9.5	9/13	69.2	13	0/39	0

27.7	2/16	12.5	26.7	11/63	17.5	10	8/25	32	13.5	8/98	8.2
30	19/60	31.7	27.7	9/28	32.1	11	7/23	30.4	14.2	1/48	2.1
30.7	12/55	21.8	28.2	2/11	18.2	11.7	20/36	55.6	23	1/42	2.4
31.7	13/29	44.8	29.2	11/40	27.5	13.7	8/51	15.7	23.5	1/10	10
32.5	1/7	14.3	33.7	11/38	28.9	15	19/63	30.2	24	5/68	7.4
33.5	8/32	25	34.4	17/59	28.8	16.5	3/8	37.5	24.7	3/42	7.1
34.5	33/126	26.2	36	22/91	24.2	19	0/7	0			
35.7	9/41	22	36.5	20/63	31.7	22	23/70	32.9			
36.7	2/9	22.2	38.5	16/81	19.8	22.7	7/86	8.1			
38.7	8/55	14.5	39.5	13/60	21.7	23.4	3/25	12			
43.5	2/13	15.4	40	5/10	50	24.4	16/91	17.6			
51.5	2/33	6.1	41	28/80	35	25.4	28/105	26.7			
52.5	6/21	28.6	42	2/5	40	25.6	5/31	16.1			
54.5	5/36	13.9	43.5	8/30	26.7	25.8	0/41	0			
Totals	272/925	29.4		236/836	28.2		191/778	24.6		74/762	9.7

RI = root infinitive

TABLE 8.10 Null subjects in child L2 root declaratives

French

Month	Kenny NS/+F	%	NS/-F	%	Greg NS/+F	%	NS/-F	%
0.3	0/0	—	1/1	100				
0.5	1/1	100	0/0	—				
1	0/5	0	0/0	—				
2	0/4	0	0/1	0				
3	1/6	16.7	2/4	50				
4	1/18	5.5	0/0	—				
5	3/17	17.7	4/5	80	2/36	5.5	3/7	42.9
7	11/37	29.7	1/6	16.7				
8	7/25	28	0/7	0				
9	4/14	28.6	0/5	0				
9.5	9/23	39.1	3/8	37.5	4/36	11.1	2/3	66.7
10	5/25	20	0/5	0	2/56	3.6	7/13	53.8
11	9/33	27.3	2/6	33.3	5/22	22.7	1/2	50
14	12/57	21	3/10	30	14/121	11.6	5/13	38.5
15	15/63	23.4	3/11	27.3	19/196	9.7	8/13	61.5
18	9/100	9	4/7	57.1	13/124	10.5	5/7	71.4
20	7/109	6.4	1/1	100	2/154	1.3	1/2	50
25	2/133	1.5	1/1	100	4/309	1.3	1/1	100
27	3/136	2.2	0/1	0	4/218	1.8	0/0	0
29	3/146	2			5/226	2.2	0/1	0
Totals	102/952	10.7	25/79	31.6	74/1498	4.9	33/62	53.2

German

Month	Concetta NS/+F	%	NS/-F	%	Month	Luigina NS/+F	%	NS/-F	%
0.2	0/0	—	0/0	—	0.7	0/0	—	0/0	—
1	0/0	—	0/0	—	1.4	0/0	—	0/0	—
1.8	0/0	—	0/0	—	2.3	0/0	—	0/0	—
2.5	0/0	—	0/0	—	3	1/1	100	0/0	—
3.2	0/0	—	0/0	—	3.7	0/1	0	0/0	—
4	0/0	—	0/0	—	4.4	0/0	—	0/0	—
5	0/0	—	0/0	—	5.4	3/5	60	0/0	—
5.6	0/6	0	0/0	—	6	1/1	100	0/1	0
6.8	0/6	0	0/0	—	7	1/6	16.7	0/0	—
8.4	2/6	33.3	1/1	100	7.9	0/5	0	0/0	—
9.1	1/10	10	0/0	—	8.6	0/0	—	0/0	—
11	7/26	26.9	1/3	33.3	8.8	1/1	100	0/0	—
12.4	5/24	20.8	5/10	50	9.5	0/1	0	0/3	0
13.5	6/46	13	3/8	37.5	11.4	0/1	0	0/0	—
14.5	2/26	7.7	1/1	100	12.8	2/4	50	0/1	0
					14	1/4	25	0/0	—
					14.9	1/15	6.7	0/1	0
					19.8	2/15	13.3	1/2	50
Totals	23/150	15.3	11/23	47.8		13/42	30.9	1/8	12.5

NS = null subject; +F = finite; -F = nonfinite

TABLE 8.11 Null subjects in adult L2 root declaratives

French										German									
Abdelmalek					Zahra					Zita					Ana				
Month	NS/+F	%	NS/-F	%	Month	NS/+F	%	NS/-F	%	Month	NS/+F	%	NS/-F	%	Month	NS/+F	%	NS/-F	%
14	1/4	25	0/0	—	12	1/2	50	0/0	—	3	1/3	33.3	0/0	—	3	0/0	—	0/0	—
15	1/4	25	0/1	0	14	1/5	20	5/11	45.5	3.5	0/1	0	0/0	—	4	2/35	5.7	0/9	0
16.7	1/10	10	1/1	100	15.5	1/3	33.3	0/1	0	3.7	1/10	10	0/2	0	4.7	2/11	18.2	0/0	—
17.7	3/56	5.4	25/39	64.1	17	3/10	30	0/2	0	4	2/3	66.7	0/2	0	4.5	5/40	12.5	0/4	0
18.7	2/10	20	5/8	62.5	18.5	3/23	13	0/6	0	5.6	0/2	0	1/5	20	5.2	3/11	27.3	1/2	50
20.5	3/7	42.9	5/6	83.3	20	3/8	37.5	3/4	75	6.5	1/14	7.1	1/7	14.3	7.2	19/53	35.8	2/6	33.3
21.5	1/20	5	5/17	29.4	21.7	3/12	25	0/5	0	6.7	0/3	0	0/9	0	7.4	14/29	48.3	3/8	37.5
24	5/22	22.7	3/14	21.4	23.2	0/0	—	0/4	0	7.5	2/11	18.2	2/5	40	8.2	10/43	23.3	5/9	55.6
25	12/43	27.9	6/36	16.7	23.7	0/12	0	0/4	0	8	3/10	30	0/2	0	11	34/70	48.6	2/6	33.3
25.7	0/27	0	1/16	6.2	24.5	5/26	19.2	0/17	0	9	2/11	18.2	1/3	33.3	11.7	25/68	36.8	4/11	36.4
27	2/39	5.1	0/12	0	25.5	3/15	20	4/7	57.1	9.5	2/4	50	2/9	22.2	13	23/39	59	0/0	—
27.7	1/14	7.1	0/2	0	26.7	12/52	23.1	4/11	36.4	10	7/17	41.2	3/8	37.5	13.5	38/90	42.2	3/8	37.5
30	4/41	9.8	3/19	15.8	27.7	1/19	5.3	0/9	0	11	4/16	25	2/7	28.6	14.2	10/47	21.3	1/1	100
30.7	3/43	7	1/12	8.3	28.2	5/9	55.6	2/2	100	11.7	5/16	31.2	4/20	20	23	16/41	39	0/1	0
31.7	1/16	6.2	1/13	7.7	29.2	6/29	20.7	5/11	45.5	13.7	22/43	51.2	1/8	12.5	23.5	2/9	22.2	0/1	0
32.5	1/6	16.7	0/1	0	33.7	10/27	37	3/11	27.3	15	9/44	20.5	0/19	0	24	24/63	38.1	1/5	20
33.5	0/24	0	1/8	12.5	34.4	5/42	11.9	5/17	29.4	16.6	2/5	40	1/3	33.3	24.7	21/39	53.8	1/3	33.3
34.5	5/93	5.4	1/33	3	36	14/69	20.3	6/20	22.7	19	0/7	0	0/0	—					
35.7	2/32	6.2	4/9	44.4	36.5	7/43	16.3	5/16	30	22	7/47	14.9	4/23	17.4					
36.7	0/7	0	0/2	0	38.5	5/65	7.7	5/16	31.2	22.7	22/79	27.8	1/7	14.3					
38.7	3/47	6.4	2/8	25	39.5	6/47	12.8	5/13	23.1	23.4	10/22	45.5	0/3	0					
43.5	0/11	0	0/2	0	40	1/5	20	3/13	60	24.4	22/75	29.3	3/16	18.7					
51.5	0/31	0	0/2	0	41	10/52	19.2	4/28	14.3	25.4	27/77	35.1	3/28	10.7					
52.5	0/15	0	2/6	33.3	42	1/3	33.3	2/2	100	25.6	5/26	19.2	3/5	60					
54.5	0/31	3.2	1/5	20	43.5	5/22	22.7	1/8	12.5	25.8	7/41	17.1	0/0	—					
Totals	52/653	8	67/272	24.6		111/600	18.5	60/236	25.4		163/587	27.8	32/191	16.7		248/688	36	23/74	31.1

NS = null subject; +F = finite; -F = nonfinite

Acknowledgments

We are most grateful to Patsy Lightbown and Manfred Pienemann for making their data available, to Jürgen Meisel for data from the ZISA Project and to Wolfgang Klein for permission to use data from the ESF project on L2 Acquisition by Adult Immigrants. We would also like to thank Roger Hawkins and audiences at the 1997 Second Language Research Forum, the 1997 Boston University Conference on Language Development, and at Indiana University, for comments and suggestions. This research was conducted with the support of SSHRCC Research Grant #410-95-0720 (to Lydia White and Nigel Duffield).

Notes

1 A similar argument is made for L1 acquisition by Borer and Rohrbacher (1997), Boser *et al.* (1992) and Phillips (1996).
2 Here we show NegP as higher than TP. We return to this point below. In (1) we include AgrP and TP but we will often collapse these as IP.
3 This differs from the claim that the child's grammar in the earliest stage will always be a VP (i.e. necessarily truncated) (e.g. Radford 1990) or that functional categories are gradually added, each representing a different acquisition stage (e.g. Clahsen *et al.* 1994).
4 These data were available on earlier versions of the CHILDES database (MacWhinney 1995).
5 There are some minor discrepancies between the data we report here on Kenny and Greg and what is reported in Grondin and White (1996) and White (1996); this is due to changes in how data were tabulated and analysed.
6 The number of finite CPs reported here is less than the number reported in Table 8.2 because subject relative clauses and subject wh-questions were excluded from the count.
7 This contrasts with L1 acquisition (e.g. Friedemann 1993/1994). We did not count proper names as instances of bare NPs.
8 The French 3rd person pronouns *lui*, *elle*, *eux* and *elles* are excluded from the analysis, since they can occur as subjects of finite verbs when they bear contrastive stress.
9 There are some discrepancies between our data and the data reported in Meisel (1997) from the same adult German L2 subjects due to the fact that we look at a more limited set of negatives (i.e. root declaratives containing negatives) than Meisel did. In addition, there are discrepancies between our French L2 negation data from Abdelmalek and the data reported in Eubank and Beck (1998) for the same subject, due to the fact that we only look at root negatives. Furthermore, we excluded from consideration cases where the transcription of *ne* was ambiguous between a form with a finite auxiliary (*n'ai*; *n'est*) and a negative particle without an auxiliary (*ne*).

References

AUGER, J. (1994) 'Pronominal Clitics in Québec Colloquial French: A Morphological Analysis'. PhD dissertation, University of Pennsylvania.

BECK, M. (1998) 'L2 Acquisition and Obligatory Head Movement: English-speaking Learners of German and the Local Impairment Hypothesis'. *Studies in Second Language Acquisition* **20**: 311–48.

BORER, H. and B. ROHRBACHER (1997) 'Features and Projections: Arguments for the Full Competence Hypothesis'. In E. Hughes, M. Hughes and A. Greenhill (eds), *Proceedings of the 21st Annual Boston University Conference on Language Development*, Somerville, MA: Cascadilla Press, 24–35.

BOSER, K., B. LUST, L. SANTELMANN and J. WHITMAN (1992) 'The Syntax of CP and V-2 in Early Child German: The Strong Continuity Hypothesis'. In K. Broderick (ed.), *Proceedings of NELS* **23**, 51–65.

CLAHSEN, H., S. EISENBEISS and A. VAINIKKA (1994) 'The Seeds of Structure: A Syntactic Analysis of the Acquisition of Case Marking'. In T. Hoekstra and B. Schwartz (eds), *Language Acquisition Studies in Generative Grammar*, Amsterdam: John Benjamins, 85–118.

CLAHSEN, H., J. MEISEL and M. PIENEMANN (1983) *Deutsch als Zweitsprache.* Tübingen: Gunther Narr Verlag.

DU PLESSIS, J., D. SOLIN, L. TRAVIS and L. WHITE (1987) 'UG or not UG, that is the Question: A Reply to Clahsen and Muysken'. *Second Language Research* **3**: 56–75.

EPSTEIN, S., S. FLYNN and G. MARTOHARDJONO (1996) 'Second Language Acquisition: Theoretical and Experimental Issues in Contemporary Research'. *Brain and Behavioral Sciences* **19**: 677–714.

EPSTEIN, S., S. FLYNN and G. MARTOHARDJONO (1998) 'The Strong Continuity Hypothesis: Some Evidence Concerning Functional Categories in Adult L2 Acquisition. In S. Flynn, G. Martohardjono and W. O'Neil (eds), *The Generative Study of Second Language Acquisition*, Mahweh, NJ: Lawrence Erlbaum, 35–59.

EUBANK, E. and M. BECK (1998). 'OI-like effects in adult L2 acquisition'. In A. Greenhill, M. Hughes, H. Littlefield and H. Walsh (eds), *Proceedings of the 22nd Annual Boston University Conference on Language Development.* Somerville, MA: Cascadilla Press.

FRIEDEMANN, M. A. (1993/1994) 'The Underlying Position of External Arguments in French: A Study in Adult and Child Grammar'. *Language Acquisition* **3**: 209–255.

GRIMSHAW, J. (1994) 'Minimal Projection and Clause Structure'. In B. Lust, M. Suner and J. Whitman (eds), *Syntactic Theory and First Language Acquisition: Cross-linguistic Perspectives. Volume 1: Heads, Projections and Learnability*, Hillsdale, NJ: Lawrence Erlbaum, 75–83.

GRIMSHAW, J. (1997) 'Projection, Heads, and Optimality'. *Linguistic Inquiry* **28**: 373–422.

GRONDIN, N. and L. WHITE (1996) 'Functional Categories in Child L2 Acquisition of French'. *Language Acquisition* **5**: 1–34.

GUILFOYLE, E. and M. NOONAN (1992) 'Functional Categories and Language Acquisition'. *Canadian Journal of Linguistics* **37**: 241–72.

HAEGEMAN, L. (1995) 'Root Infinitives, Tense and Truncated Structures'. *Language Acquisition* **4**: 205–55.

HAZNEDAR, B. and B. SCHWARTZ (1997) 'Are There Optional Infinitives in Child L2 Acquisition?' In E. Hughes, M. Hughes and A. Greenhill (eds),

Proceedings of the 21st Annual Boston University Conference on Language Development, Somerville, MA: Cascadilla Press, 257–68.

HOEKSTRA, T. and N. HYAMS (1995) 'The Syntax and Interpretation of Dropped Categories in Child Language: A Unified Account. *Proceedings of WCCFL XIV*. CSIL, Stanford University.

HOEKSTRA, T., N. HYAMS and M. BECKER (1997) 'The Underspecification of Number and the Licensing of Root Infinitives. In E. Hughes, M. Hughes and A. Greenhill (eds), *Proceedings of the 21st Annual Boston University Conference on Language Development*, Somerville, MA: Cascadilla Press, 293–306.

JAEGGLI, O. (1982) *Topics in Romance Syntax*. Dordrecht: Foris.

LARDIERE, D. (1998) 'Case and Tense in the "Fossilized" Steady State'. *Second Language Research* 14: 1–26.

LARDIERE, D. and B. D. SCHWARTZ (1997) 'Feature-Marking in the L2 Development of Deverbal Compounds'. *Journal of Linguistics* 33: 327–53.

LASSER, I. (1998) 'Getting Rid of Root Infinitives'. In A. Greenhill, M. Hughes, H. Littlefield and H. Walsh (eds), *Proceedings of the 22nd Annual Boston University Conference on Language Development*, Somerville, MA: Cascadilla Press, 465–76.

LIGHTBOWN, P. M. (1977) 'Consistency and Variation in the Acquisition of French'. PhD dissertation, Columbia University.

MACWHINNEY, B. (1995) *The CHILDES Project: Computational Tools for Analyzing Talk*. Hillsdale, NJ: Lawrence Erlbaum.

MEISEL, J. (1997) 'The Acquisition of the Syntax of Negation in French and German: Contrasting First and Second Language Development. *Second Language Research* 13: 227–63.

OUHALLA, J. (1991) *Functional Categories and Parametric Variation*. London: Routledge.

PARODI, T., B. SCHWARTZ and H. CLAHSEN (1997) 'On the L2 Acquisition of the Morphosyntax of German Nominals'. *Essex Research Reports in Linguistics* 15: 1–43.

PERDUE, C. (1984) *Second Language Acquisition by Adult Immigrants: A Field Manual*. Rowley, MA: Newbury House.

PERDUE, C. (ed.) (1993) *Adult Second Language Acquisition: Crosslinguistic Perspectives*. Cambridge: Cambridge University Press.

PHILLIPS, C. (1996) 'Root Infinitives are Finite'. In A. Stringfellow, D. Cahana-Amitay, E. Hughes and A. Zukowski (eds), *Proceedings of the 20th Annual Boston University Conference on Language Development*, Somerville, MA: Cascadilla Press, 588–99.

PIENEMANN, M. (1981) *Der Zweitspracherwerb ausländischer Arbeiterkinder*. Bonn: Verlag Grundmann.

PRÉVOST, P. (1997) 'Truncation in Second Language Acquisition'. PhD dissertation, McGill University.

RADFORD, A. (1990) *Syntactic Theory and the Acquisition of English Syntax*. Oxford: Basil Blackwell.

RIZZI, L. (1986) 'On the Status of Subject Clitics in Romance'. In O. Jaeggli and C. Silva-Corvalan (eds), *Studies in Romance Linguistics*. Dordrecht: Foris, 391–420.

RIZZI, L. (1993/1994) 'Some Notes on Linguistic Theory and Language Development: The Case of Root Infinitives'. *Language Acquisition* **3**: 371–93.

RIZZI, L. (1994) 'Early Null Subjects and Root Null Subjects'. In T. Hoekstra and B. Schwartz (eds), *Language Acquisition Studies in Generative Grammar*, Amsterdam: John Benjamins, 151–76.

ROBERGE, Y. (1990) *The Syntactic Recoverability of Null Arguments*. Kingston and Montreal: McGill-Queen's University Press.

SCHWARTZ, B. (1998) 'On Two Hypotheses of "Transfer" in L2A: Minimal Trees and Absolute L1 Influence'. In S. Flynn, G. Martohardjono and W. O'Neil (eds), *The Generative Study of Second Language Acquisition*, Mahweh, NJ: Lawrence Erlbaum, 35–59.

SCHWARTZ, B. and R. SPROUSE (1994) 'Word Order and Nominative Case in Nonnative Language Acquisition: A Longitudinal Study of (L1 Turkish) German Interlanguage'. In T. Hoekstra and B. Schwartz (eds), *Language Acquisition Studies in Generative Grammar*, Amsterdam: John Benjamins, 317–68.

SCHWARTZ, B. and R. SPROUSE (1996) 'L2 Cognitive States and the Full Transfer/Full Access Model'. *Second Language Research* **12**: 40–72.

SCHWARTZ, B. and A. TOMASELLI (1990) 'Some Implications from an Analysis of German Word Order'. In W. Abraham, W. Kosmeijer and E. Reuland (eds), *Issues in Germanic Syntax*, Berlin: Walter de Gruyter, 251–74.

SPEAS, M. (1994) 'Null Arguments in a Theory of Economy of Projection'. *University of Massachusetts Occasional Papers in Linguistics* **17**: 179–208.

VAINIKKA, A. and M. YOUNG-SCHOLTEN (1994) 'Direct Access to X'-theory: Evidence from Korean and Turkish Adults Learning German'. In T. Hoekstra and B. Schwartz (eds), *Language Acquisition Studies in Generative Grammar*, Amsterdam: John Benjamins, 265–316.

VAINIKKA, A. and M. YOUNG-SCHOLTEN (1996) 'Gradual Development of L2 Phrase Structure'. *Second Language Research* **12**: 7–39.

WEXLER, K. (1994) 'Optional Infinitives, Head Movement and the Economy of Derivations'. In D. Lightfoot and N. Hornstein (eds), *Verb Movement*, Cambridge: Cambridge University Press, 305–50.

WHITE, L. (1985) 'The Pro-drop Parameter in Adult Second Language Acquisition'. *Language Learning* **35**: 47–62.

WHITE, L. (1996) 'Clitics in L2 French'. In H. Clahsen (ed.), *Generative Perspectives on Language Acquisition: Empirical Findings, Theoretical Considerations, Crosslinguistic Comparisons*, Amsterdam: John Benjamins, 335–68.

ZANUTTINI, R. (1991) 'Syntactic Properties of Sentential Negation: A Comparative Study of Romance Languages'. PhD dissertation, University of Pennsylvania.

Chapter 9

Null subjects and root infinitives in the child grammar of French
Lucienne Rasetti

Introduction

Recent work on language acquisition has revealed that certain particularities of early speech are not independent or isolated manifestations of individual grammars. Apparently unrelated phenomena sometimes follow analogous developmental patterns, suggesting not only that there are links among them, but also that such phenomena might constitute different manifestations of the same underlying process and could thus be amenable to a more primitive property of the grammar in question. In this respect, a topic which has received considerable attention in the literature on acquisition is the relationship between the distribution of null subjects and matrix infinitive clauses in the grammar of two-year-olds.

As is well known, part of the spoken production of children learning non-null subject languages such as English or French consists of sentences in which the subject has been dropped. These null subjects are attested very early (usually around 20–22 months) and gradually disappear before the child reaches three years of age.

(1) a. want more Naomi 1;10;17 (Pierce 1989: 75)
    b. est pour Marc Nathalie 2;3;2 (Lightbown 1977)
       is for Marc

Another distinctive property of early speech is the use of non-finite verbs in contexts disallowed by the target grammar, i.e. matrix clauses. These structures are attested in several languages and are generally referred to as 'optional' or 'root' infinitives.[1] Like early null subjects, they tend to disappear sometime after the child's second birthday.

(2) fermer yeux Daniel 1;11;1 (Lightbown 1977)
    close-*inf* eyes

The general picture which emerges from the literature on these topics is that null subjects tend to cluster with root non-finite forms in early grammars. This has led some researchers (Sano and Hyams 1994; Bromberg and Wexler 1995, among others) to regard null subjects of optional infinitives as the central aspect of subject omission in child speech and to argue in favor of a direct cause–effect relationship between both phenomena. Other studies (Rizzi 1992, 1994a, 1994b; Haegeman 1995a, 1995b, 1995c, for example) adopt a wider perspective and derive both the null subject and the root infinitive phenomena from a more primitive property of the child's grammar, the possibility of truncating the structure at different levels of representation.

The aim of this chapter is to examine French data in the light of the proposals above. Using as a basis a detailed analysis of the distribution patterns of null subjects and root infinitives in the grammar of six children from a development perspective, I discuss the following points:

- Null subjects do tend to cluster with root infinitives; however, to what extent are they attested in finite structures? A survey of the data will confirm that, in French, null subjects are robustly attested with unquestionably finite verbs throughout the root infinitive stage, and that they cannot be regarded as a marginal phenomenon in comparison with subject drop in matrix infinitival clauses. Note that, contrary to Auger (1990), Roberge (1986), Zribi-Hertz (1994), Kaiser (1992, 1994) and Pierce (1992), among others, I do not assume French to be a null subject language in which clitics are Agreement markers which replace inflectional suffixes which have almost disappeared in modern spoken French. Instead, I adopt the more standard analysis according to which clitic forms preceding finite verbs are subjects in [Spec,AgrSP] in the syntactic component (Kayne 1984).
- The concomitant disappearance of matrix infinitives and null subjects in general (that is, of finite and non-finite clauses) is generally related to the fact that the majority of root infinitives have null subjects: when root infinitives become rare, null subjects will automatically vanish. But is there any special developmental pattern relating null subjects of finite clauses to root infinitives? Based on a file-by-file analysis of the data, I will argue that the two phenomena follow analogous developmental patterns in which null subjects licensed in finite clauses tend to disappear in parallel with root infinitives. These results suggest that null subjects and root infinitives may be indirectly connected and that the link between the two phenomena is not restricted to a direct cause–effect relationship in non-finite sentences.

- Null subjects of root infinitives are generally treated on a par
with the adult null subject of embedded clauses, PRO. However,
pre-verbal lexical subjects are apparently licensed in the same environment, which is unexpected given the inability of non-finite verbs
to assign Case. It will be shown that lexical DPs in pre-verbal
position are relatively rare in the corpus, and that they may be
compatible with the formal licensing mechanisms for PRO in root
infinitives.

The discussion is organized as follows: section 1 provides an overview
of the figures reported in the literature. Section 2 discusses some of the
proposals which claim the existence of a direct structural relationship
between subject drop and the availability of root infinitives. Section 3
concentrates on the clausal truncation approach. Section 4 introduces
the data and section 5 comments on the results. The main conclusions
are summarized in section 6.

1 Overview of the figures

It is a well-known fact that children around the age of two produce
a large number of matrix infinitive structures which very often lack an
overt subject. The examples in (3) are from French, German, Dutch and
Flemish.

(3) a. jouer au football Augustin 2;9;30 (Hamann *et al.* 1995)
       play-*inf* football
    b. hubsauber putzn Andreas 2;1 (Krämer 1993: 203)
       helicopter clean-*inf*
    c. eerst kleine boekje lezen Hein 2;6 (Haegeman 1995a: 33)
       first little book read-*inf*
    d. e tore make ((een) toren maken) Maarten 1;11;4
       (a) tower make-*inf*   (Krämer 1993: 204)

Significant correlation rates have been established for several languages
between null subjects and optional infinitives. The general conclusion
that may be drawn from the various studies conducted on these topics
is that, although null subjects do occur in finite clauses, they tend to
cluster with non-finite matrix structures in early grammars. Table 9.1
reproduces some of the figures reported in the literature.

In most of the languages for which data are available, there is a
discrepancy between the proportion of null subjects attested with inflected
verbs and the proportion of null subjects attested with non-inflected
verbs.[2] The figures in Table 9.1 have naturally led to the assumption
that null subjects and root infinitives are somehow connected, an assumption reinforced by the apparent similarity between root infinitives and

TABLE 9.1   Null subjects in finite and non-finite sentences

	NS finite	%	NS non-finite	%	Total
French (Pierce 1989)					
Daniel	150/273	54.9	166/205	81.0	478
Nathalie	90/304	29.6	131/295	44.4	599
Philippe	182/782	23.3	153/194	78.9	976
German (Behrens 1993; Krämer 1993)					
Simone	781/3699	21.1	2199/2477	88.8	6176
Andreas	34/263	12.9	69/101	68.3	364
Dutch (Krämer 1993; Haegeman 1995a)					
Thomas	165/596	27.7	246/267	92.1	863
Heinz	1199/3768	31.8	615/721	85.3	4489
Flemish (Krämer 1993)					
Maarten	23/92	25.0	89/100	89.0	192
Hebrew (Rhee & Wexler 1995)					
(26 children, -N cases[3])	252/779	32.3	85/88	96.6	867
Faroese (Jonas 1995)					
O.	8/52	15.4	67/161	41.6	213
Danish (Hamann & Plunkett 1998)					
Anne	366/3379	10.8	394/667	59.1	4046
Jens	742/3173	23.4	539/937	57.5	4110
English (Phillips 1995)					
Adam	34/113	30.1	47/242	19.4	355
Eve	8/86	9.3	17/155	11.0	241

adult (embedded) infinitives with respect to the licensing of null subjects. The next section deals with some of the proposals which argue for a direct relationship between null subjects and root infinitives, whereas section 3 is concerned with an alternative approach which claims the existence of an indirect link between these phenomena.

2 The optional infinitive stage: PRO

In recent work on the topic, the connection between null subjects and root infinitives is expressed in terms of a direct cause–effect structural relationship. For the most part based on important work by Wexler (1992, 1994), some proposals which have been recently put forward in the literature draw a parallel between the subjectless infinitives of child discourse and the adult infinitive structures in which the subject is generally analyzed as PRO. In this framework, null subjects of finite clauses are excluded from any association with root infinitives and must be accounted for independently.

2.1 The optional infinitive stage

Seminal research on child grammars of French (Weissenborn 1988; Pierce 1989, 1992; Déprez and Pierce 1993) shows that finite and non-finite forms are not in free variation in early speech. Finite forms have presumably moved to their correct position, that is, raised to the Agreement Projection, whereas non-finite forms have remained in their base VP position.[4] On the grounds of these observations, Wexler (1992, 1994) explains the use of matrix infinitives by suggesting that the child goes through an early 'optional infinitive' (OI) stage in which, although s/he is aware that movement is obligatory in finite contexts and that infinitival verbs do not raise, s/he does not know that non-finite verbs are ruled out as main verbs. Data from German, Dutch, Swedish, Danish and Norwegian concerning the placement of negation in finite and non-finite structures by children indicate that these languages conform to the pattern observed in French. In English, the 'optional drop' of the third singular present tense marker -s is taken as evidence for the existence of an optional infinitive stage: when children optionally drop the present tense morpheme, they are in fact producing a non-finite form consisting of a verbal stem plus a zero infinitival marker, rather than a bare stem only.[5] In Wexler's framework, the optionality of finiteness is related to the possibility of omitting Tense from the clause. It is an open question whether the Tense node, the entire projection, or simply Tense features are missing from the structure. Wexler (1995), for example, suggests that the whole TP is absent from optional infinitives. I do not discuss the issue here.

2.2 PRO as the subject of optional infinitives

Based on the analysis outlined above, Sano and Hyams (1994, henceforth S&H) relate subject omission to the availability of root infinitives: if uninflected verbs are in reality infinitival forms, the verb presumably remains in the VP and does not raise to IP (at LF) to incorporate Agreement and Tense markers. According to these authors, such a structure can license PRO in subject position under a version of the PRO theorem by which this category cannot be governed by a lexically specified head or, following Chomsky and Lasnik (1993), under the assumption that PRO requires null Case which must be checked by a 'minimal Infl', where minimal Infl is understood as being devoid of lexical content.[6] In sentences where morphological affixes are overtly realized, the verb has presumably raised at LF, thus disrupting the environment that might license PRO and requiring the subject to be

TABLE 9.2   Proportion of null subjects with verbs inflected with -s and -ed
(adapted from Sano and Hyams 1994)

Child	File	Age	-s	-ed
Eve	01–20	1;6 to 2;3	10.0% (5/50)	22.5% (9/40)
Adam	01–20	2;3 to 3;0	25.8% (16/62)	56.5% (13/23)
Nina	13–21	2;2 to 2;4	no figures available	18.8% (3/16)

overt. The reasons for raising (or lack of it) lie in the specification (or non-specification) of the features in Infl, but not in the absence of functional projections.

S&H's hypothesis relies on data suggesting a tendency amongst two-year-olds not to omit the subject in contexts which are intrinsically finite, that is, in sentences containing the verb *be* and in those containing modals. In the standard approach to verb movement (Pollock 1989; Chomsky 1991), the overt Agreement features of inflected *be* indicate that this verb has raised to Infl, disrupting the environment that would license PRO and therefore requiring a lexically realized subject. In fact, S&H find very few examples of null subjects with inflected forms of *be*. In sentences with the third person singular *is*, they counted 13/114 null subjects for Adam, 2/50 for Nina and 0/109 for Eve; in sentences with first person singular *am* (5 tokens) or plural *are* (126 tokens) no null subjects were attested for any of the three children.[7] Data from Valian (1991) confirms the prediction that null subjects should not occur with modals, which are inherently finite in English and presumably generated under Infl. In a cross-sectional study of 21 children, she finds that the rates of non-overt subjects in sentences containing modals vary from 1% to 6%, whereas the rates of null subjects overall for the same children in the same period are considerably higher.

S&H note, however, that there are null subjects in contexts in which a lexical verb bears finite inflection (-s or -ed morphemes). Table 9.2 is adapted from their Tables 4 and 6.

In order to maintain their hypothesis despite the relatively high rates of subject omission in tensed clauses, S&H suggest that these markers can be regarded as participial affixes which associate to the verb in an Aspectual Projection (AspP) below IP, allowing the [Spec,IP] position to remain available for PRO. I come back to this proposal in section 5, where I discuss its implications for French.

Bromberg and Wexler (1995, henceforth B&W) also base their account on Wexler (1992, 1994), and argue in favor of a deep structural relationship between the optional infinitive stage and the null subject stage. Given that non-finite verbs generally license null subjects in adult

grammars, it is expected that matrix infinitive verbs should also license empty subjects. Thus they suggest that the existence of root infinitives explains the presence of null subjects in early child language, specifically during the optional infinitive stage. They do not take a position concerning the appropriate licensing mechanism, nor do they argue for a specific grammatical characterization of the null subject of infinitives, but they assume that a representation without Tense is one in which the subject can be null.

Although they have not performed a precise count of null subjects given finite and non-finite verbs[8], B&W note that not every null subject is a result of the availability of tenseless clauses, and they assume that proposals in terms of topic or diary drop (Rizzi 1992, 1994a, 1994b; Haegeman 1995b, 1995c) can account for null subjects of finite sentences. Thus they conclude that there are two kinds of null subjects: one which is licensed by uninflected verbs, and the other which is licensed by inflected (and possibly uninflected) verbs.[9] If both can appear in uninflected contexts, it is natural that null subjects are attested at higher rates with root infinitives. Note that it is not clear why the second type of null subject should be licensed by both inflected and uninflected verbs. If null subjects of root infinitives are not always PRO-like, there are fewer reasons to believe in a strict cause–effect relationship between null subjects and root infinitives in the sense of B&W. Observe also that one would still have to define which non-finite environments are available for PRO, and which are available for a topic/diary drop type of subject omission. Finally, it remains to be seen if the null subject of a root infinitive can really be PRO, or PRO-like. Whereas formal licensing of PRO in such contexts is admissible, its interpretative properties are less straightforward.[10] Besides, the fact that lexical subjects may occur in the same environment as early null subjects, in finite clauses but perhaps also in root infinitives, also casts doubts on an analysis in terms of PRO, given that PRO and lexical subjects are usually in complementary distribution. These issues will be discussed in section 5.3 in connection with French.

According to B&W, then, the occurrence of null subjects with uninflected verbs is the result of the availability of root infinitives, but what is the source of null subjects of finite sentences, i.e. why does the child assume that such structures are a legitimate option in his/her grammar? B&W suggest that Dutch and German children drop topics because the adult languages also have a topic drop process.[11] As for English, although it does not exhibit a topic drop strategy, there are constructions such as (4) and (5) which suggest that the child could be dropping topics in finite sentences in a way allowed by the adult language, but in a larger number of contexts.[12] Both examples are taken from B&W (1995:243).

(4) ___ felt a joy yesterday, ___ soon clouded. S. Plath, *Journals*
                                                    (McCullough 1982)

(5) What happened to Mary?
    ___ went away for a while.

In summary, the clustering of early null subjects with matrix infinitives observed in Table 9.1 has led some researchers to assimilate the null subject of root infinitives to the PRO subject of adult infinitives and to regard the early null subject phenomenon as dependent upon the availability of root infinitives. Null subjects of finite clauses are excluded from the connection with root infinitives and must therefore be accounted for independently. These analyses have been proposed for English. I do not discuss the English data, but come back to the implications of this approach for French in section 5.

3 Truncation: null subjects and root infinitives

Rizzi (1994b) proposes that every well-formed utterance in the adult grammar has a CP as the top node.[13] The principle requiring that CP be the root of a clause may not be fully operative in early stages and the child will then select another category lower than CP as a legitimate starting point of the derivation. Such a category may be the bare VP, AgrOP (cf. Haegeman 1995a), or the maximal projection of the head corresponding to the infinitival morpheme, the Infinitive Phrase (IP) of Kayne (1991). A detailed analysis of these choices is not relevant here; the important point is that TP and higher projections are absent from the structure and the verb will appear in its infinitival form.[14] In addition, the child may also choose to truncate the structure at the AgrSP level, in which case s/he will create the appropriate environment for a null subject in the specifier of a finite root clause. The reader is referred to Rizzi (1992, 1994a; see also this volume) for a detailed account of these null subjects. I briefly summarize it below.

As an empty category, the null subject must comply with the identification and formal licensing requirements of the Empty Category Principle (ECP):[15] it must be chain-connected to an antecedent. However, it has been noted that the null subject appears to be limited to the specifier position of the root in child grammars of non-null subject languages: it is incompatible with *Wh*-movement and subordinate clauses.[16] Given that it occurs in the higher specifier position of the clause, it is not c-commanded by any maximal projection and therefore it is not bound by any potential antecedent in the structure. If we interpret the ECP as obligatory only if virtually satisfiable, that is, only if the empty category is actually c-commanded by a phrase, the null subject in the specifier of the root will be exempt from the identification requirement. In such an environment it is therefore licit. However, if a CP is projected, the null subject cannot survive in [Spec,AgrSP] since [Spec,CP] will be a potential antecedent position, but not a suitable one. Thus the absence of null subjects in [Spec,AgrSP] of *Wh*-questions and embedded clauses is expected.

If truncation can account for the availability of root infinitives and for the licensing of null subjects in finite sentences, both phenomena should follow similar developmental patterns: the principle requiring that CP be the root being inoperative in the early stages, the child can truncate the structure at either level, below TP or at AgrSP, possibly within the same given stage of his/her development, giving rise both to matrix infinitive clauses and to null subjects in finite contexts. Thus the relationship between root infinitives and null subjects should be manifested not only in non-finite clauses, as proposed by Sano and Hyams (1994) or Bromberg and Wexler (1995), but also, and most significantly, in finite clauses. A detailed study of these patterns in Dutch and Danish has been carried out by Haegeman (1995c) and Hamann and Plunkett (1998) respectively, who show that there is an interaction between root infinitives and null subjects of finite clauses in that both decrease simultaneously. Based on these findings, I provide an extensive analysis of a corpus of French language which suggests that a similar connection is attested in this language.

4 The data

4.1 The corpus

Spontaneous productions of six children are examined in this chapter: Augustin, Marie, Daniel, Nathalie, Philippe and Jean. The recordings and transcripts of Augustin's production (from 2;0;2 to 2;9;30) were carried out by two students of the *Faculté de Psychologie et Sciences de l'Education (FAPSE)* of the University of Geneva.[17] Marie's corpus consists of twelve files ranging from 1;8;26 to 2;3;3. The recordings were done on a fortnightly basis by Marie's parents in their home in Geneva.[18] Both children are studied in the framework of the interfaculty project *Language et Communication* conducted at the University of Geneva. Daniel's and Nathalie's corpora have kindly been made available by Patsy Lightbown.[19] They consist of five files for Daniel (from 1;8;1 to 1;11;1) and seven files for Nathalie (from 1;9;3 to 2;3;2). The Philippe corpus is available on the CHILDES database.[20] I have selected the first twelve files, from 2;1;19 to 2;6;20. Jean's corpus consists of four files of 45 minutes each, recorded and transcribed by myself. The small size of this corpus is due to the fact that the child was already leaving the null subject/root infinitive stage in the first two recording sessions, at ages 1;7;16 and 1;8;24. Additional sessions were therefore considered superfluous in the framework of the present study. The reader may refer to Tables 9.5–9.10 in the appendix to this chapter for details concerning ages and recording intervals for all children.

4.2 Methodology

The same criteria were used in the analysis of the six corpora. Only spontaneous utterances were taken into account, and partial or full repetitions of adult speech were ignored except when modified by the child. Immediate repetitions of the same utterance by the child were also eliminated.

Null subject utterances are those in which no subject is lexically realized, not even in post-verbal position.[21] Utterances in which any missing portion could be interpreted as the subject were discarded. Overt subjects include pronominals, so that null subject rates overall are calculated against all types of overt subjects. Constructions with bare participles were counted separately. Homophonous infinitival and participial forms have been distinguished according to discourse context: non-finite forms referring to an action or state 'non-completed' are regarded as infinitival, whereas forms referring to a completed action are taken as participial. Both infinitival and participial forms are very often preceded by a 'proto-syntactic device' (PSD),[22] a monosyllabic place-holder, usually a vowel, that presumably fills the position of an auxiliary or modal verb, of the subject, or perhaps both. Thus a sentence such as *[e] demand[e] à la dame* (Augustin 2;9;2) could mean either *(j')ai demandé* ('I have asked') or *(je) veux/vais demander* ('I want to/will ask'). Although the context might provide some indication of the interpretation intended by the child, I have chosen to eliminate these utterances from my counts.

Large portions of Nathalie's production consist of utterances containing the expression *nya-nya*, used to signify 'eat' or 'food' indistinctly. Pierce (1989, chapter 3, fn. 5) follows Lightbown (1977), who based her interpretation on the context and on translations offered by Nathalie's mother. I have discarded all the utterances containing this word so as to avoid ambiguity, even if this exclusion has entailed a considerable reduction of the corpus.[23] No similar phenomenon has been attested in the production of the five remaining children.

Some of the results presented in this chapter seem to differ rather heavily from those obtained by Pierce (1989) for Daniel, Nathalie and Philippe. Although part of Nathalie's production is discarded here and the figures for Philippe come from different files from those selected by Pierce (i.e. Phil 01–04, 07, 09 and 11), the discrepancies are not immediately accounted for. A detailed comparison of these figures is outside the scope of this chapter, but notice that, in her classification of types of subjects, Pierce (1989) appears to include bare participles in the non-finite category (e.g. *tout mangé Patsy*, 'ate all Patsy') whereas here only root infinitives are taken into account. Besides, the totals regarding utterances considered for Daniel for the same files, and also for Philippe where the files are identical, do not coincide. These observations show that the criteria used for the analysis of the data in Pierce (1989) are probably distinct from the one adopted in the present chapter.

5 Results

5.1 Null subjects in finite clauses

The results obtained from the analysis of the six children's production conform to the general picture presented in Table 9.1: subject drop in root infinitives is higher than in finite sentences. As shown in Table 9.3, 88.7% of all uninflected verbs have null subjects whereas finite verbs license null subjects in 26.4% of the cases. A breakdown among age ranges is presented in the appendix.

In spite of the discrepancy between finite and non-finite verbs with regard to the licensing of null subjects, these figures provide clear evidence that null subjects are not only possible, but attested in approximately a quarter of all finite clauses. Work by Pollock (1989) has shown that, in the adult grammar of French, all finite verbs raise to Agreement and Tense heads in order to incorporate (check) inflectional morphology. Child production seems to conform to this pattern, as it has been observed that children are able to distinguish finite from non-finite structures at a very early age by correctly placing the verb in relation to the negative marker *pas*.[24] The phrasal structure generally adopted for French in the literature is the one proposed by Belletti (1990) for Italian, in which the order of the relevant functional projections is AgrP/NegP/TP/AspP. This implies that an inflected verb followed by *pas* is necessarily in Agr^0, and therefore unlikely to have

TABLE 9.3 Null subjects in finite and non-finite declarative sentences (bare participles excluded)

	Finite null subjects	%	Non-finite null subjects	%	Total utterances
Augustin	157/585	26.8	66/71	93.0	656
Marie	154/560	27.5	130/134	97.0	694
Daniel	191/408	46.8	189/227	83.3	635
Nathalie	92/303	30.4	52/69	75.4	372
Philippe	322/1397	23.0	225/246	91.5	1643
Jean	22/303	7.3	8/8	100.0	311
Total	**938/3556**	**26.4**	**670/755**	**88.7**	**4311**

raised from the VP to an Aspectual Projection as suggested by Sano and Hyams (1994) for English. An AspP would have to be lower than TP, therefore also lower than NegP, and sentences in which the negation marker is preceded by a tensed verb (*mange pas*, 'eats not') would remain unaccounted for. Given that all inflected verbs in French raise to the highest inflectional projection, and since the rate of null subjects in such contexts is important, it is hardly the case that subject omission can only take place in non-finite structures in this language. Besides, assuming the projection of an AspP implies postulating a construction which would be specific to the early grammars of English at a certain stage, and which is not necessarily found either in the target language or in early grammars of other languages.

These empty subjects cannot of course be PRO because they occur in the same environment in which overt DPs are found, that is, finite contexts. Given that PRO and lexical DPs are usually in complementary distribution, we are led to conclude that subject omission in finite clauses cannot be assimilated to subject drop in non-finite contexts.

In addition, the results presented in Table 9.3 are not compatible with Bromberg and Wexler's (1995) suggestion of an exaggerated use by children of a topic drop process which is available in the adult language because French exhibits no such construction.[25] I have examined adult speech in six of the files which constitute the corpus[26] and it turned out that, of 2150 declarative sentences, only 14 had null subjects, 3 of which were repetitions of the child's utterance by the adult. Among the 11 cases left, 7 were instances of null subjects with the verb *falloir* ('be necessary'), a verb which has the idiosyncratic property of licensing expletive null subjects in colloquial French as well.[27] This leaves us with the insignificant rate of 4 null subjects for 2150 utterances.

5.2 Finite null subjects and root infinitives

Is there any particular developmental pattern connecting null subjects of finite clauses to root infinitives in French? The synchronous drop-off of null subjects and matrix infinitive structures is apparent from the various studies which have dealt with these and other related topics, but to what extent is this parallel decrease attested in the French corpus under analysis?

In trying to answer these questions, the distinction made between finite and non-finite clauses is essential. Given that most root infinitives show subject omission, the concomitant disappearance of null subjects and root infinitives could be an effect of the discrepancy between finite and non-finite structures with regard to the licensing of null subjects. If PRO (or whatever the grammatical characterization of the empty subject of infinitives is) does indeed result from the availability of root infinitives, the parallel decrease is not interesting in itself. Rather, it is expected as an immediate consequence of the fact that infinitive verbs

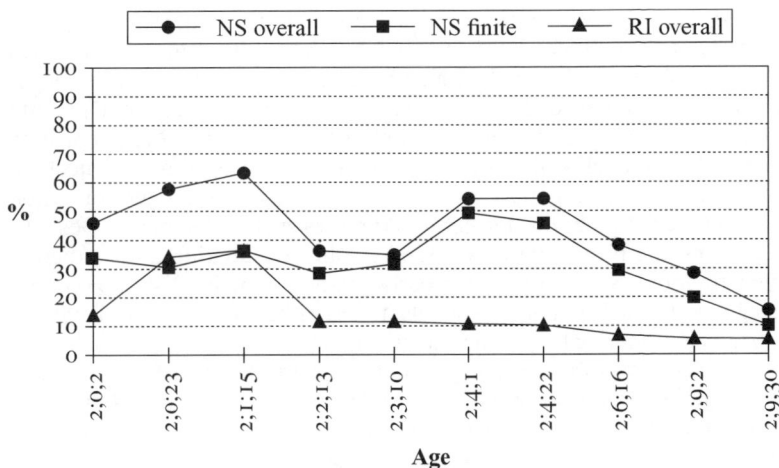

FIGURE 9.1   Null subjects and root infinitives in Augustin's production

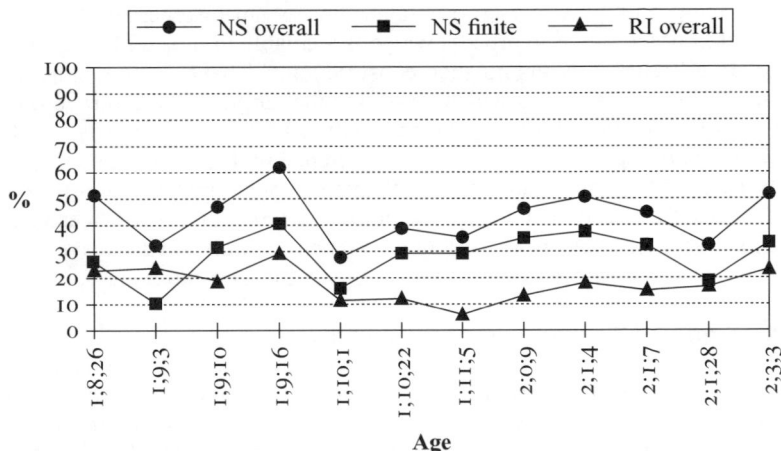

FIGURE 9.2   Null subjects and root infinitives in Marie's production

automatically license null subjects: when root infinitives become infrequent, null subjects will tend to disappear in parallel fashion. On the other hand, a similar correspondence observed in finite sentences considered separately will suggest the existence of a more complex pattern, since there is no apparent direct link between subject omission in tensed clauses and the availability of root infinitives.

Figures 9.1–9.6 show the development patterns of (a) null subjects overall, (b) null subjects in finite sentences and (c) root infinitives overall.

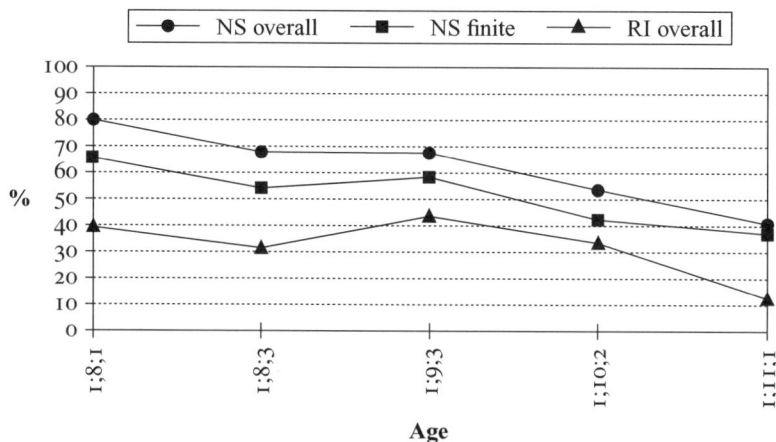

FIGURE 9.3   Null subjects and root infinitives in Daniel's production

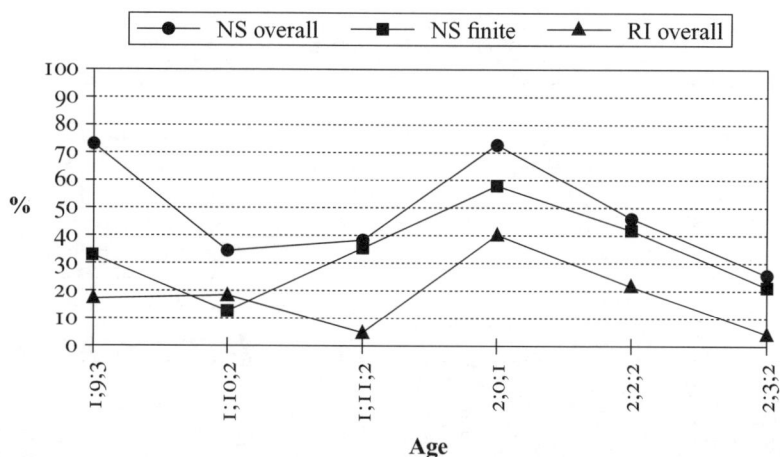

FIGURE 9.4   Null subjects and root infinitives in Nathalie's production

Raw figures and percentages for each child at each point of development are provided in the appendix.

Although the relatively small corpora hardly allow providing the charts above with a quantitative dimension, the property which is truly significant is the simultaneity in the stable drop-out of the phenomena.[28] The general picture which emerges from the graphs appears thus to be compatible with the truncation hypothesis as discussed in section 3.

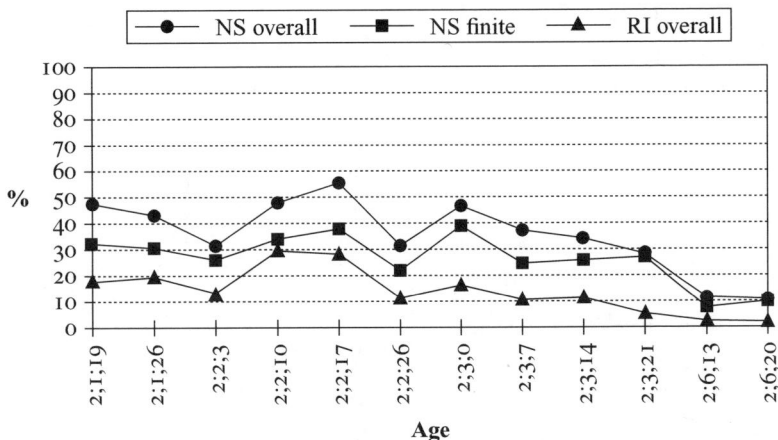

FIGURE 9.5   Null subjects and root infinitives in Philippe's production

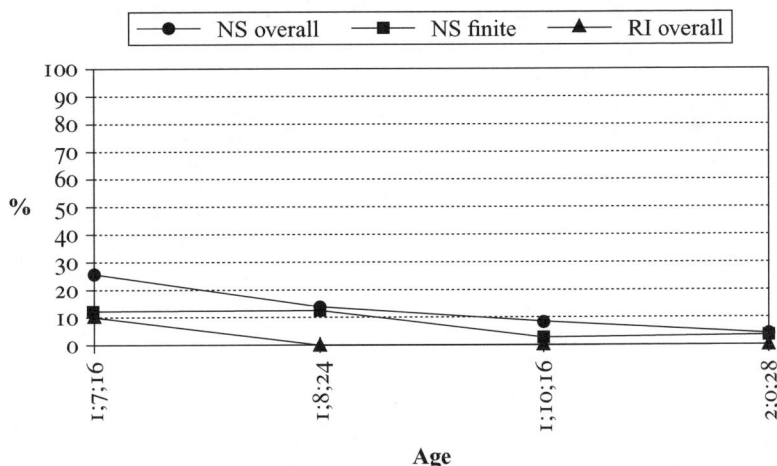

FIGURE 9.6   Null subjects and root infinitives in Jean's production

With some variation, subject drop in finite clauses and the use of matrix infinitival structures tend to disappear in parallel from the production of the six children under study. These findings also confirm evidence provided by Haegeman (1995c) and Hamann and Plunkett (1998) for Dutch and Danish respectively. Haegeman (1995c) examines the production of three Dutch children at the relevant stage, and finds a sharp parallel

TABLE 9.4   Root infinitives and finite null subjects in final stages

Child	Age (last file)	Root infinitives (%)	Finite null subjects (%)
Augustin	2;9;30	6.3	10.7
Marie	2;3;3	23.1	33.3
Daniel	1;11;1	13.2	37.2
Nathalie	2;3;2	4.5	21.9
Philippe	2;6;20	2.1	9.9
Jean	2;0;28	–	3.7

between the development of initial non-overt subjects and of root infinitives. Similar results are obtained by Hamann and Plunkett (1998) in their analysis of the use of null subjects by two Danish children. In fact, on the basis of large corpora, these authors establish that the profile of subject omission in finite utterances almost exactly matches that of root infinitives.

If null subjects of finite sentences and root infinitives derive from the non-operativeness of the principle requiring CP to be the root of a representation, it is expected that both phenomena will take place at the same period of development and that their evolution in time will be similar. The data examined above provide confirmation of this prediction. The existence of root infinitives in the spoken production of these children suggests that truncation is available at TP level and higher, hence subject drop in finite clauses is available as well. When root infinitives drop off, so do null subjects.

Note however that there is a one-way implication, since the availability of null subjects does not necessarily entail the availability of root infinitives. Indeed, null subjects of finite clauses appear to last a little longer than root infinitives.[29] In this respect, the six children display the same behavior: Jean, for example, who is practically out of the root infinitive stage from the beginning of the recordings, is still dropping a few subjects in subsequent files. The percentage of root infinitives decreases as low as 2.1% for Philippe in the last file, whereas subjects at the same stage are dropped up to 9.9%. Table 9.4 provides an overview of root infinitive and null subject rates in final stages. These figures suggest that, while truncation at TP level is practically no longer an option for the child, some form of CP truncation still remains possible. This means that when TP is projected, it is not necessarily the case that CP = root has become entirely operative, given that a structure can still be truncated at AgrSP level. As noticed by Haegeman (1995b), this is the situation in diaries, where null subjects, but not root infinitives, are attested. For a while, then, the child grammar appears to correspond to the adult one in that null subjects, but not root infinitives, are allowed. Some remarks concerning this apparent match between early and adult grammars are in order though. First, subject omission occurs in different contexts. Second, early null subjects, contrary to diary empty subjects, do not remain as a productive option and it is not clear why both grammars should converge only for a short period of time.

How could we explain, under a truncation approach and without any additional stipulations, that CP truncation lasts longer than TP truncation? Rizzi (this volume) suggests that our system of linguistic computation is constrained by an interplay between principles of structural economy and categorial uniformity. While a principle of structural economy limits the amount of structure to be used in a syntactic computation, a principle of categorial uniformity requires that a given semantic type be realized by a unique canonical structure. In early grammars, contrary to adult systems, structural economy prevails over categorial uniformity, whence the occurrence of truncated structures (assuming, as before, that the canonical realization of the proposition is CP). Once the child masters embedded declarative clauses, which are necessarily realized as CP, the issue of uniformity arises, leading to the adoption of CP as the root. Under these assumptions, there is no reason why matrix infinitives should disappear before root AgrSP clauses. It is not implausible, however, that the tension between the two principles mentioned above is resolved in successive steps. It could thus be the case that the principle of categorial uniformity is enforced in a progressive manner in early systems, gradually countering structural economy. The more 'economical' structures would be the first to disappear from the child's grammar, followed by the AgrSP root clauses, which are 'less economical' and closer to CP. The remaining null subjects of root AgrSP structures would then be accounted for.

5.3 Some notes on the subject of root infinitives

The data above reveal that subject drop in early French is attested in finite clauses, and that it is implausible that the null subject in such contexts could be assimilated to PRO. However, subjects are omitted in the majority of non-finite utterances in the corpus, namely 88.7%, a fact which may be compatible with an analysis of the empty subject of root infinitives in terms of PRO. Given that non-finite verbs license PRO subjects in adult French, and under the assumption that adult and child grammars differ minimally, a unified analysis should be welcome. However, a close investigation of the properties of PRO raises some points which warrant discussion.

Like any empty category, PRO needs to comply with specific requirements regarding its distribution and identification. For reasons of space, I will only deal here with some observations regarding its formal licensing, a detailed analysis of its interpretative properties being intended for future work. In the standard analysis (Chomsky 1981:124–131)[30] PRO must be ungoverned for theory-internal reasons and can only fill the subject position of an infinitival clause. More recently, Chomsky and Lasnik (1993) have proposed that PRO can bear null Case, assigned or checked by a minimal Inflection, that is, an inflectional head lacking Tense and Agreement features. In both cases, the position in which one or the other requirement may be satisfied is Spec of IP or AgrSP. Assuming similar structures for root infinitives and adult infinitives, a sentence such as (6a) would be represented as in (6b).

(6) a. aider maman (Augustin 2;4;22)
        help-*inf* mummy
    b. [$_{\text{AgrSP}}$ PRO [$_{\text{TP}}$ [$_{\text{VP}}$ aider maman]]]

The status of TP is unclear: it might be empty, underspecified or absent altogether. The issue will not be discussed here, but notice that under the truncation hypothesis, the licensing of PRO in [Spec,AgrSP] cannot take place. If the structure is indeed truncated below TP, PRO would have to sit under a lower Spec, presumably [Spec,VP]. A priori, nothing prevents this possibility, especially if we take into account the VP-internal subject hypothesis according to which subjects are base-generated in [Spec,VP] and then moved to [Spec,AgrSP] for Case reasons. Given that the child does not project the upper layers of the structure, PRO cannot raise and must remain in its base position. Since a verb which stays within the VP is necessarily uninflected, it might well be able to check the null Case required by PRO, although according to Chomsky and Lasnik's (1993) proposal it is a minimal Infl and not an uninflected verb which checks or licenses null Case. Now, if the [Spec,AgrSP] or, under the truncation approach, the [Spec,VP] position is one in which no Case or null Case is assigned, then sentences such as (7) need to be accounted for.

(7) a. maman manger (Daniel 1;8;1)
        mummy eat-*inf*
    b. on ôter[31] (Augustin 2;3;10)
        we-*Nom* remove-*inf*

Given the Case Filter and the Visibility Condition,[32] *maman* in (7a) is presumably Case-marked, but since Case is almost never visible in French (except in the pronominal system), we can only suppose that *maman*, as a subject, is marked Nominative. On the other hand, Case is visible in (7b), as subject clitics are overtly assigned Nominative. In both examples, given the inability of non-finite verbs to assign or check a Case other than null Case, it must be concluded that the infinitival verb is not the Case assigner and that Case in (7) is present independently of assignment by Inflection.[33] Alternatively, Case-assignment mechanisms may be partially or fully non-operative at this stage. These possibilities have already been raised in the literature; they are briefly summarized here, but the reader is referred to the work cited below for more detailed accounts.

It might be possible that overt subjects of matrix infinitives are not assigned Case in the syntax and that, instead, they are spelled out as the least-specified member of their paradigm. The existence of default or inherent Case mechanisms in child language has been suggested, among others, by Bromberg and Wexler (1995), Haegeman (1995a), Radford (1995), Rizzi (1994b) and Wexler (1995).[34] It has also been argued (Friedemann 1993/1994, Radford 1990) that the Case Filter is not fully operative in the early stages, and that overt subjects occur in Caseless positions. Assuming that the Case Filter applies to DPs and not directly to NPs, and supposing that children do not necessarily project the functional category DP, then bare NPs can do without Case. Alternatively, it could be that at least some of these subjects are dislocated or topicalized elements filling an A'-position (Friedemann 1993/1994) and bearing inherent Case.

Aside from the issues regarding the Case properties of overt subjects in infinitives, the utterances in (7) may seem incompatible with the truncation hypothesis (under the assumption that the subject should sit under [Spec,AgrSP], considering that under this approach no structure should be projected above the non-finite verb if the clause is truncated below TP level). On the other hand, if we assume the VP-internal subject hypothesis and some mechanism that does not require the standard specifier–head agreement relation for the assignment of Case, these subjects could remain in [Spec,VP], or in the specifier position of another projection relatively low in the structure (InfP or AspP), and the sentence would still be truncated at higher levels. At any rate, and as we shall see, quantitative considerations become crucial in this respect, and the problematic examples are rather rare. Therefore, before trying to account for pre-verbal subjects of root infinitives, let us examine their distribution more closely.

Sentences such as (7b) are seldom attested in French: in the entire corpus under analysis here, only 10 examples of the sort were found (5 for Augustin, 3 for Daniel and 2 for Philippe),[35] which corresponds to 1.3% of all root infinitives. Note that subject clitics are nevertheless used productively with inflected verbs: approximately one third of all finite sentences have subject clitics (see Table 9.12 in the appendix). Sentences such as (7a), in which a lexical DP surfaces pre-verbally, are less rare, but still unusual. I have counted 30 instances in the entire corpus, representing 4% of all root infinitives.

In addition to Nominative clitics and lexical DPs, we also find occurrences of non-Nominative pronouns such as (8).

(8) moi aller à la maison (Daniel 1;10;2)
    me go-*inf* home

Non-Nominative subjects are attested in only 1.7% of all root infinitives. It should be noted however that of the 13 tokens containing a non-Nominative pronoun such as *moi* ('me') or *toi* ('you'), 11 come from Daniel's corpus. This child resorts to a special strategy not attested in any of the other children with similar frequency. The other two examples come from Marie's corpus.

In sum, of 755 root infinitives, 30 (4%) have pre-verbal DP subjects which are supposedly Nominative, 10 (1.3%) have Nominative clitics, and 13 (1.7%) have non-Nominative pronouns. The majority of subjects are of course non-overt, as seen before (670 or 88.7%), and the remaining 32 are post-verbal (4.2%). The breakdown among children is provided in Table 9.11 in the appendix. The low percentages of pre-verbal subjects with root infinitives and their distribution in the corpus suggest that these strategies cannot be considered as true grammatical options for every child, especially if we take into account the following facts: (a) the majority of pre-verbal DP subjects come from Daniel's and Nathalie's files, 13 and 10 tokens respectively; besides, 9 out of Nathalie's 10 pre-verbal lexical subjects come from a single file (Nathalie-6), and (b) half (or maybe all) of the Nominative clitics may be reanalyzed as proto-syntactic devices. On the whole, then, these sentences appear to be isolated cases and suggest the existence of special strategies specific to one child or another at a certain stage of development. Their scarcity also makes plausible the hypothesis of performance errors or even transcript mistakes. Interpreted as such, they cannot be viewed as a serious challenge for an analysis in terms of PRO for the empty subject of root infinitives. On the other hand, if these utterances are indeed made available by the child's grammar and do not constitute performance errors, we can still admit truncation at higher levels with the subject remaining internal to the VP as discussed above.

Subjects are not the only kind of pre-verbal material present in early infinitives. We also find several examples of what have been called by Bottari *et al.* (1992) 'proto-syntactic devices' (PSD). These entities have been defined as monosyllabic place-holders which perform the role of rudimentary functional categories when appearing in front on nouns, past participles, adjectives or infinitives. A PSD preceding an infinitive is illustrated in (9a). They can also stand for true arguments and be treated on a par with projections of true lexical categories when filling the place of a clitic pronoun,[36] for example in (9b).

(9) a. [ə] chercher cabane (= vais? je vais?) (Marie 1;11;5)
      (will? I will?) get-*inf* hut
    b. [e] veux nounours (= je?) (Marie 2;0;9)
      (I?) want-*inf* teddy-bear

We do not exactly know what a PSD placed before an infinitive verb stands for. It might be that it fills the position of a modal verb which is normally required in this type of construction,[37] but it might also stand for the subject, or perhaps for both the modal and the subject.[38] Although the presence of a PSD necessarily implies the projection of additional structure, it is hard to tell at this stage how much structure is being projected and what the status of a null subject is in such an environment. At any rate, a PSD does not necessarily exclude PRO, especially if we assume that additional positions are available in the structure.

In sum, the structural environment of root infinitives appears to allow the occurrence of PRO. If the structure is truncated below TP level, PRO can remain under [Spec,VP] and have its null Case checked by the non-finite verb. Lexical subjects which eventually surface pre-verbally fill Caseless positions or are Case-marked independently and, as such, do not interfere with an environment which is suitable for PRO. Besides, they are extremely rare. Thus it might well be the case that children's infinitives are similar to adult's with respect to the syntactic licensing of a PRO subject, except for the fact that, under the truncation hypothesis, PRO does not raise to [Spec,AgrSP] for lack of a target position for movement. On the other hand, the fact that lexical subjects may appear in such environments (although very infrequently) might argue against such an analysis, given that PRO and lexical subjects are usually in complementary distribution. A careful analysis of the interpretative properties of null subjects in root infinitives as well as in finite clauses is expected to provide further arguments for or against the view that null subjects of root infinitives are indeed PRO.

6 Conclusion

This chapter has dealt with questions related to subject drop and the use of root infinitives by two-year-olds. A detailed analysis of the production of six French-speaking children has illustrated the following points. First, early subject drop is attested in approximately a quarter of all finite sentences comprised in the French corpus examined here, indicating that the phenomenon should by no means be considered a marginal one, nor be regarded as an overgeneralization of an adult option, given that adult French does not allow the phenomenon in any spoken register. Second, the distribution pattern of null subjects in finite sentences is analogous to that of root infinitives. The development of these phenomena across time is similar in that both tend to drop off simultaneously.

This tendency is attested in the production of the six children examined here and strongly suggests the existence of a specific link between the two phenomena which can reasonably be accounted for by a version of the clausal truncation hypothesis put forward by Rizzi (1992, 1994a, 1994b). Third, it seems to be the case that the structural environment of root infinitives actually allows PRO subjects. However, while licensing conditions for PRO might be fulfilled in root infinitives, a careful examination of the interpretative properties of these null subjects should provide additional arguments for or against this hypothesis.

Appendix

Distribution of subjects and root infinitives

TABLE 9.5   Null subjects and root infinitives in Augustin's spoken production

File	Age	NS overall	%	NS finite	%	NS RI	%	RI overall	%
Augustin-1	2;0;2	23/50	46.0	14/41	34.1	7/7	100	7/50	14.0
Augustin-2	2;0;23	15/26	57.7	5/16	31.3	9/9	100	9/26	34.6
Augustin-3	2;1;15	12/19	63.2	4/11	36.4	7/7	100	7/19	36.8
Augustin-4	2;2;13	15/41	36.6	10/35	28.6	5/5	100	5/41	12.2
Augustin-5	2;3;10	12/34	35.3	9/28	32.1	1/4	25	4/34	11.8
Augustin-6	2;4;1	34/62	54.8	26/53	49.1	6/7	85.7	7/62	11.3
Augustin-7	2;4;22	31/57	54.4	22/48	45.8	6/6	100	6/57	10.5
Augustin-8	2;6;16	40/106	37.7	27/91	29.7	8/8	100	8/106	7.5
Augustin-9	2;9;2	42/147	28.6	26/131	19.8	9/9	100	9/147	6.1
Augustin-10	2;9;30	23/142	16.2	14/131	10.7	8/9	88.9	9/142	6.3

TABLE 9.6   Null subjects and root infinitives in Marie's spoken production

File	Age	NS overall	%	NS finite	%	NS RI	%	RI overall	%
Marie-1	1;8;26	37/72	51.4	10/38	26.3	16/17	94.1	17/72	23.6
Marie-2	1;9;3	24/75	32.0	5/46	10.9	16/18	88.9	18/75	24.0
Marie-3	1;9;10	27/58	46.6	13/41	31.7	10/11	90.9	11/58	19.0
Marie-4	1;9;16	21/34	61.8	9/22	40.9	10/10	100	10/34	29.4
Marie-5	1;10;1	10/36	27.8	5/31	16.1	4/4	100	4/36	11.1
Marie-6	1;10;22	19/50	38.0	13/44	29.5	6/6	100	6/50	12.0
Marie-7	1;11;5	23/65	35.4	17/58	29.3	4/4	100	4/65	6.2
Marie-9	2;0;9	31/68	45.6	19/55	34.5	9/9	100	9/68	13.2
Marie-10	2;1;4	42/82	51.2	23/62	37.1	15/15	100	15/82	18.3
Marie-11	2;1;7	23/52	44.2	13/40	32.5	8/8	100	8/52	15.4
Marie-12	2;1;28	39/122	32.0	16/90	17.8	20/20	100	20/122	16.4
Marie-13	2;3;3	27/52	51.9	11/33	33.3	12/12	100	12/52	23.1

TABLE 9.7   Null subjects and root infinitives in Daniel's spoken production

File	Age	NS overall	%	NS finite	%	NS RI	%	RI overall	%
Daniel-1	1;8;1	88/110	80.0	31/47	66.0	40/44	90.9	44/110	40.0
Daniel-2	1;8;3	94/138	68.1	33/61	54.1	40/44	90.9	44/138	31.9
Daniel-3	1;9;3	78/115	67.8	24/41	58.5	45/51	88.2	51/115	44.3
Daniel-4	1;10;2	100/186	53.8	49/114	43.0	48/63	76.2	63/186	33.9
Daniel-5	1;11;1	79/190	41.6	54/145	37.2	16/25	64.0	25/190	13.2

TABLE 9.8   Null subjects and root infinitives in Nathalie's spoken production

File	Age	NS overall	%	NS finite	%	NS RI	%	RI overall	%
Nathalie-1	1;9;3	16/22	72.7	3/9	33.3	4/4	100	4/22	18.2
Nathalie-2	1;10;2	11/32	34.4	3/23	13.0	5/6	83.3	6/32	18.8
Nathalie-3	1;11;2	8/21	38.1	7/20	35.0	1/1	100	1/21	4.8
Nathalie-4	2;0;1	40/55	72.7	15/26	57.7	19/22	86.4	22/55	40.0
Nathalie-5	2;1;1	7/17	41.2	1/6	16.7	3/5	60.0	5/17	29.4
Nathalie-6	2;2;2	50/108	46.3	31/73	42.5	13/24	54.2	24/108	22.2
Nathalie-7	2;3;2	40/155	25.8	32/146	21.9	7/7	100	7/155	4.5

TABLE 9.9   Null subjects and root infinitives in Philippe's spoken production

File	Age	NS overall	%	NS finite	%	NS RI	%	RI overall	%
Philippe-1	2;1;19	58/123	47.2	25/78	32.1	19/22	86.4	22/123	17.9
Philippe-2	2;1;26	68/158	43.0	34/111	30.6	27/31	87.1	31/158	19.6
Philippe-3	2;2;3	57/184	31.0	36/143	25.2	19/23	82.6	23/184	12.5
Philippe-4	2;2;10	81/168	48.2	30/90	33.3	46/51	90.2	51/168	30.4
Philippe-5	2;2;17	53/96	55.2	22/58	37.9	26/27	96.3	27/96	28.1
Philippe-6	2;2;26	53/168	31.5	25/113	22.1	18/19	94.7	19/168	11.3
Philippe-7	2;3;0	70/151	46.4	38/98	38.8	25/25	100	25/151	16.6
Philippe-8	2;3;7	28/76	36.8	13/54	24.1	8/8	100	8/76	10.5
Philippe-9	2;3;14	55/161	34.2	28/108	25.9	18/18	100	18/161	11.2
Philippe-10	2;3;21	44/150	29.3	34/126	27.0	9/9	100	9/150	6.0
Philippe-11	2;6;13	31/277	11.2	20/247	8.1	7/9	77.8	9/277	3.2
Philippe-12	2;6;20	21/193	9.9	17/171	9.9	3/4	75.0	4/193	2.1

TABLE 9.10   Null subjects and root infinitives in Jean's spoken production

File	Age	NS overall	%	NS finite	%	NS RI	%	RII overal	%
Jean-1	1;7;16	20/78	25.6	8/65	12.3	8/8	100	8/78	10.3
Jean-2	1;8;24	9/64	14.1	8/63	12.7	–	–	0/64	–
Jean-3	1;10;16	6/70	8.6	2/66	3.0	–	–	0/70	–
Jean-4	2;0;28	5/110	4.5	4/109	3.7	–	–	0/110	–

Distribution of subjects in root infinitives

TABLE 9.11 Distribution of subjects in root infinitives

Child	Total root infinitives	Pre-verbal DP	Non-Nominative pronouns	Nominative clitics	Null subjects	Post-verbal DP
Augustin	71	0	0	5	66	0
Marie	134	1	2	0	130	1
Daniel	227	13	11	3	189	11
Nathalie	69	10	0	0	52	7
Philippe	246	6	0	2	225	13
Jean	8	0	0	0	8	0
Total	**755**	**30**	**13**	**10**	**670**	**32**
% of RI		**4.0**	**1.7**	**1.3**	**88.7**	**4.2**

Distribution of subjects clitics in finite clauses

TABLE 9.12   Distribution of subject clitics in finite clauses

Child	Clitics	Finite clauses
Augustin	207	585
Marie	169	560
Daniel	42	408
Nathalie	68	303
Philippe	586	1397
Jean	70	303
Total	**1230**	**3556**
% of finite clauses	**34.6**	

Acknowledgements

I wish to thank Marc-Ariel Friedemann, Liliane Haegeman, Cornelia Hamann, Christopher Laenzlinger, Luigi Rizzi and Michal Starke for helpful comments and suggestions. Errors are of course my own. An earlier version of this chapter appeared in the *Geneva Generative Papers* (1996). This work was partially supported by a grant from the *Département d'instruction publique du Valais*, Switzerland (No. 0126.780) and was conducted in the framework of the *Projet Interfacultaire Langage et Communication* at the University of Geneva.

Notes

1 Terminology proposed by Wexler (1992, 1994) and Rizzi (1994b) respectively. I use both terms indistinctively here.
2 According to Phillips (1995), the generalization does not extend to English. Notice also that in Faroese and Danish the discrepancy is less important than in the other languages.
3 Hebrew is partially *pro*-drop, i.e. the personal pronoun is obligatorily dropped only in 1st and 2nd persons, non-present tense. In all the other contexts, the subject must be phonetically realized. Rhee and Wexler refer to the 1st and 2nd person morphology as bearing +N features which can license null subjects, and to the remaining ones as being -N and therefore unable to license an empty subject. The figures in Table 9.1 refer to the -N cases, that is, illegitimate instances of subject drop.
4 Inflected verbs precede the negative marker *pas* (*mange pas*, 'eat(s) not') whereas non-inflected verbs follow *pas* (*pas manger*, 'not eat-*inf*'). See Weissenborn (1988), Pierce (1989, 1992) and Déprez and Pierce (1993).
5 I do not discuss the evidence for the assumption that English represents the OI stage (see also Harris and Wexler 1996; Rice *et al.*, 1995). This analysis of uninflected sentences in English raises some problems, though. As noted

by L. Rizzi (class lectures 1996), English 'root infinitives' seem to differ from root infinitives of other languages in many respects:

- they are compatible with preposed *Wh*-elements (see Bromberg and Wexler 1995; Roeper and Rohrbacher 1995)
- they license overt subjects in a proportion comparable to inflected clauses (see data from Phillips 1995 in Table 9.1)
- they are still attested when subjects are no longer omitted
- when the subject is overt, it may bear both default or non-default case (see Schütze and Wexler 1996a,b).

6 Note that in Chomsky and Lasnik (1993), a minimal Infl checks null Case when it lacks Tense and Agreement features. The idea that a minimal Infl might be viewed as lacking lexical content is suggested by S&H.

7 Adam and Eve, see Brown (1973); Nina, see Suppes (1973).

8 But see Phillips (1995).

9 This distinction is also proposed by Krämer (1993), although in different terms: true *pro*-drop (finite sentences) vs. apparent *pro*-drop (non-finite sentences).

10 Cf. L. Rizzi, class lectures 1996.

11 But Haegeman (1995c) shows that in Dutch the empty subject of early speech is structurally different from the adult one.

12 As a matter of fact, the distribution of the null subject in diaries, exemplified in (4), suggests that this element should be assimilated to the early null subject phenomenon rather than to a topic drop strategy: like early null subjects, null subjects in diaries are limited to root contexts and, contrary to null topics, they can be expletives and quasi-arguments. Moreover, there are no null objects (which could be analyzed as instances of topic drop) in diary registers. In addition, the null subject allowed in informal speech in English (5) also appears to be similar to the null subject in diaries. Therefore, if both (4) and (5) can be assimilated to the early null subject phenomenon, the child will not be 'dropping topics'. The reader is referred to Haegeman (1995b, 1995c, this volume) for a detailed discussion of null subjects in written and spoken registers.

13 See Rizzi (1994b, this volume) and Haegeman (1995b, 1995c) for discussion.

14 Observe that Rizzi's (1994b) truncated approach to root infinitives converges with Wexler's (1994) proposal in admitting tenseless clausal representations in early grammars. For Wexler, though, the properties of the optional infinitive stage are derived from the primitive assumption that the child can omit Tense from the representation. For Rizzi, these tenseless representations are not a primitive property of these grammars, but arise from the non-operativeness of the principle requiring the CP to be the root.

15 See Rizzi (1990) for the relevant version of the ECP.

16 Rizzi (1992, 1994a, 1994b), Crisma (1992) and Levow (1995) for French. Roeper and Rohrbacher (1995) and Bromberg and Wexler (1995) obtain different results for English *Wh*-questions, but not if the finite/non-finite distinction is taken into account. In finite structures the results are clearly the same (see Rizzi this volume for a brief discussion).

17 Christelle Girod and Isabelle Schindeholz. They were subsequently checked by three students of the *Faculté des Lettres*, Nathalie Martinez, Daniela Renggli and myself. See Hamann *et al.* (1995) for details.

18 Transcripts were also carried out by five students of the *FAPSE*, Nathalie
    Bernoud, Angela Cicoira, Joëlle Cretton, Emanuelle Lehr and Sylvie
    Mayoraz, and subsequently checked by myself.
19 Lightbown (1977).
20 Suppes *et al.* (1973).
21 Post-verbal subject structures in French can be analyzed as instances of
    right-dislocation (Labelle and Valois 1996), or as a construction in which
    the verb has raised to an Inflectional Projection (in finite clauses) or to a
    Inf(initive) Projection (in root infinitives), leaving the subject behind in a
    left- or right-branching [Spec,VP] (Pierce 1989, 1992). Post-verbal subjects
    can also be accounted for as filling a right-branching [Spec,VP] in a struc-
    ture where the verb raises to IP if inflected, or remains in the VP if uninflected
    (Friedemann (1993/1994). All these analyses require an empty element in
    the specifier position of AgrSP in compliance with the Extended Projection
    Principle (EPP). While the empty (pre-verbal) subject of an utterance con-
    taining a post-verbal subject may well be a null constant, its identification is
    perhaps different from the null constant of a null subject utterance. In the
    first case, the subject can be identified clause-internally, perhaps through a
    chain, whereas in the second the subject is discourse-identified. This is the
    reason why the two types of structure are treated separately. It should be
    noted however, that clause-internal identification is not guaranteed, since
    the post-verbal subject presumably does not c-command the empty subject
    (see Friedemann, this volume).
22 Cf. Bottari *et al.* (1992).
23 If we consider *nya-nya* as a verb in all the cases in which the context allows
    it, we have the following percentage of *nya-nya* utterances in each file:
    67.6% (N1), 46.0% (N2), 52.9% (N3), 8.8% (N4), 26.1% (N5), 13.4%
    (N6) and 9.7% (N7) of all verbal utterances selected for analysis.
24 See note 4.
25 French does have constructions like the English examples (4) and (5) in
    special written registers such as diaries, notices on commercial products
    and informal notes (examples from Haegeman 1995b):

    (i)   Me donne son nom, son adresse et les (Paul Léautaud, *Journal*
          heures de train pour venir chez elle   *particulier*, p. 44: 6.2.1933)
          me gives her name, her address and the hours of the train to come to her
    (ii) Se boit très frais (Coca-Cola tin)
          se-reflexive drinks very fresh
    (iii) Préparons les copies (e-mail message, 1993)
          prepare (1pl) the copies

    The observations mentioned in note 12 carry over to French.
26 Daniel-1, Daniel-5, Nathalie-1, Nathalie-7, Augustin-2, Augustin-9.
27 It is possible that expletive *il* in general may be non-overt in colloquial
    speech (M.-A. Friedemann, p.c.). Note however that, according to the
    native-speakers consulted on the matter, null subjects with the verb *falloir*
    are preferred to the examples in (i) and (ii), which are more marked.

    (i)   ?Paraît qu'il est parti
          seems that he has left

(ii) ?M'est arrivé une chose bizarre
me arrived a thing strange
Something strange happened to me

28 Marie at age 2;3;3 is an exception, although in the preceding files her behavior corresponds to that of the other children. The subsequent transcripts (as well as file number 8 at age 1;11;18) were unfortunately unavailable at the time of printing. Note also that Nathalie-05 contained an extremely small amount of data and has not been included in the chart (see Table 9.8 in the appendix).

29 Some types of root infinitives such as answers to questions and jussives are also expected to last; however, the use of a matrix infinitive in such contexts is adult-like and is therefore not taken into account in the present discussion.

30 On PRO, see also Bouchard (1984:165–210), Bresnan (1982), Chomsky (1986:119–131), Koster (1984), Manzini (1983), Mohanan (1985) and Williams (1980).

31 It will be seen that utterances such as (7b), in which a weak subject pronoun occurs with an infinitive, are rarely attested. They are cited here for the sake of completeness.

32 The Case Filter states that every phonetically realized NP must be assigned (abstract) Case. The Visibility Condition requires that a chain is visible for theta marking if it contains a Case position (see Chomsky and Lasnik 1993 for a brief explanation).

33 It is a well-known fact that infinitives can have lexical (Nominative) subjects in some languages. European Portuguese is the classic example (from Raposo 1987):

(i) Eles aprovarem a proposta será dificil
They-*Nom* to-approve-*Agr* the proposal will be difficult
'It will be difficult for them to approve the proposal'

Note that the non-finite verb is inflected for person, and that Case assignment is arguably associated to the presence of the agreement morpheme on the verb. This kind of structure is absent from adult French, and it is implausible that children have access to such a strategy. Besides, if this mechanism were available in early French, we would have to explain why only a few root infinitives have overt subjects in pre-verbal position.

34 On default Case, see for example Halle and Marantz (1993).

35 As noted by Hamann *et al.* (1995) in their detailed study of Augustin's acquisition of the French pronominal system, all the cases involve the impersonal subject clitic *on* ('people', 'we'). They suggest that some or even all the cases could be reanalyzed as being instances of the proto-syntactic device [o], found elsewhere in the corpus, rather than a genuine occurrence of the subject clitic.

(i) on ôter (three times) (2;3;10)
'we' take-*inf* out

(ii) on jouer aux (pe)tites autos (2;4;1)
'we' play-*inf* with small cars

(iii)   on mettre sur ça (2;9;30)
        'we' put-*inf* on this

Philippe's utterances also involve the pronoun *on*:

(iv)   on en mettre là (2;6;13)
        'we' of-this put-*inf* there
(v)   des animaux on tuer (2;6;20)
        some animals 'we' kill-*inf*

Daniel, on the other hand, uses the personal pronoun *elle* ('she') and *je* ('I'). One of the examples is unclear, although it has been analyzed as an instance of *je* ('I').

(vi)   moi [jə] prendre ə petit joujou (1;10;2)
        me I take-*inf* small . . .
(vii)   elle tenir celui-là (1;11;1)
        she hold-*inf* that one there
(viii) moi je mettre (1;11;1)
        me I put-*inf*

36 Bottari *et al.* note that these elements could also be considered as functional categories, although they do not discuss the issue any further. This is the case, for instance, of subject clitics treated in terms of agreement markers.
37 *Aller* ('go'), *devoir* ('must') *falloir* ('be necessary'), *pouvoir* ('can'), *vouloir* ('want'). These are lexical verbs which can nevertheless function as modals.
38 This is certainly a phenomenon which deserves further study, as suggested by its frequency. For example, Marie and Augustin produce respectively 56 and 65 PSDs with infinitival forms.

References

ALDRIDGE, M. (1989) 'The Acquisition of INFL'. IULC, Bloomington.
AUGER, J. (1990) 'Colloquial French Argument-markers: Independent Words, Clitics or Prefixes?' Ms., University of Pennsylvania at Philadelphia.
BEHRENS, H. (1993) 'Temporal Reference in German Child Language. Ph.D. dissertation, University of Amsterdam.
BELLETTI, A. (1990) *Generalized Verb Movement*. Turin: Rosenberg & Sellier.
BORER, H. and K. WEXLER (1987) 'The Maturation of Syntax'. In T. Roeper and E. Williams (eds), *Parameter Setting*. Dordrecht: Reidel.
BOSER, K., E. LUST, L. SANTELMANN and J. WHITMAN (1992) 'The Syntax of CP and V-2 in Early Child German (ECG): The Strong Continuity Hypothesis. In K. Broderick (ed.), *Papers From the Tenth Annual Meeting, NELS*, GLSA, University of Massachusetts, Amherst.
BOTTARI, P., P. CIPRIANI and A. M. CHILOSI (1992) 'Proto-syntactic Devices in the Acquisition of Italian Free Morphology'. *Geneva Generative Papers* 0.1–2: 83–101.
BOUCHARD, D. (1984) *On the Content of Empty Categories*. Dordrecht: Foris.
BRESNAN, J. (1982) 'Control and Complementation'. *Linguistic Inquiry* **13** (3): 343–434.

BROMBERG, H. S. and K. WEXLER (1995) Null Subjects in Wh-questions. *MIT Working Papers in Linguistics* **26**: 221–48.

BROWN, R. (1973) *A First Language.* Cambridge, MA: Harvard University Press.

CHOMSKY, N. (1981) *Lectures on Government and Binding.* Dordrecht: Foris.

CHOMSKY, N. (1986) *Knowledge of Language, its Nature, Origin, and Use.* New York: Praeger.

CHOMSKY, N. (1991) 'Some Notes on the Economy of Derivation. In R. Freidin (ed.), *Principles and Parameters in Comparative Grammar.* Cambridge, MA: MIT Press: 417–54.

CHOMSKY, N. and H. LASNIK (1993) 'Principles and Parameters Theory'. In J. Jacobs, A. Von Stechow, W. Sternefeld and T. Vannemann (eds), *Syntax: An International Handbook of Contemporary Research.* Berlin: de Gruyter.

CRISMA, P. (1992) 'On the Acquisition of *Wh*-questions in French. *Geneva Generative Papers* 0.1–2: 115–22.

DÉPREZ, V. and A. PIERCE (1993) 'A Cross-linguistic Study of Negation and Functional Projections in Early Grammar'. *Linguistic Inquiry* **24**: 25–67.

FRIEDEMANN, M.-A. (1993/1994) 'The Underlying Position of External Arguments in French: A Study in Adult and Child Grammar'. *Language Acquisition* **2** (3): 209–55.

GRUBER, J. S. (1967) Topicalization in child language. *Foundations of Language* **3**: 37–65.

GUASTI, M.-T. (1994) 'Verb Syntax in Italian Child Grammar: Finite and Non-finite Verbs'. *Language Acquisition* **3** (1): 1–40.

HAEGEMAN, L. (1990a) 'Non-overt Subjects in Diary Contexts'. In J. Mascaro and M. Nespor (eds), *Grammar in Progress.* Dordrecht: Foris.

HAEGEMAN, L. (1990b) 'Understood Subjects in English Diaries'. *Multilingua* **9**: 157–99.

HAEGEMAN, L. (1995a) 'Root Infinitives, Tense, and Truncated Structures in Dutch'. *Language Acquisition* **4** (3): 205–55.

HAEGEMAN, L. (1995b) 'Null Subjects in the Non *Pro*-drop Languages'. Ms., University of Geneva.

HAEGEMAN, L. (1995c) 'Root Infinitives and Initial Root Null Subjects in Early Dutch'. In C. Koster and F. Wijnen (eds), *Proceedings of the Groningen Assembly on Language Acquisition.* Groningen University: 239–50.

HAEGEMAN, L. (1996) 'Root Infinitives, Clitics and Truncated Structures'. In H. Clahsen (ed.), *Generative Perspectives on Language Acquisition.* Amsterdam: Benjamins: 271–308.

HALLE, M. and A. MARANTZ (1993) 'Distributed Morphology and the Pieces of Inflection'. In K. L. Hale and S. J. Keyser (eds), *The View from Building 20: Essays in Linguistics in Honor of Sylvain Bromberger.* Cambridge, MA: MIT Press: 111–67.

HAMANN, C. and K. PLUNKETT (1998) 'Subjectless Sentences in Child Danish'. *Cognition* **69**: 35–72.

HAMANN, C., L. RIZZI and U. FRAUENFELDER (1995) 'On the Acquisition of the Pronominal System in French'. *Recherches Linguistiques* **24**: 83–101.

HARRIS, A. and K. WEXLER (1996) 'The Optional Infinitive Stage in Child English: Evidence from Negation'. In H. Clahsen (ed.), *Generative Perspectives on Language Acquisition.* Amsterdam: John Benjamins: 1–42.

266   THE ACQUISITION OF SYNTAX

HULK, A. (1991) 'Les pronoms clitiques sujets et la théorie linguistique'. *Actes du XVIIIè congrès international de linguistique et philologie romanes. Université de Trèves (Trier) 1986. Tome 2: Linguistique théorique et linguistique synchronique*. Tübingen: Niemeyer: 504–13.

HYAMS, N. (1986) *Language Acquisition and the Theory of Parameters*. Dordrecht: Reidel.

HYAMS, N. and K. WEXLER (1993) 'On the Grammatical Basis of Null Subjects in Child Language'. *Linguistic Inquiry* 24: 241–59.

JAEGGLI, O. and K. SAFIR (1989) *The Null Subject Parameter*. Dordrecht: Kluwer.

JONAS, D. (1995) On the Acquisition of Verb Syntax in Child Faroese. *MIT Working Papers in Linguistics* 26: 265–80.

KAISER, G. (1992) *Die klitischen Personalpronomina im Französischen und Portugiesischen. Eine synchronische und diachronische Analyse* (*Editionen der Ibero-americana*, Reihe III, 44). Frankfurt am Main: Vervuert.

KAISER, G. (1994) More about INFL-ection and agreement: The acquisition of clitic pronouns in French. In J. Meisel (ed.), *Bilingual First Language Acquisition: French and German Grammatical Development*. Amsterdam: John Benjamins: 131–59.

KAISER, G. and J. MEISEL (1991) 'Subjekte und Null-Subjekte im Französischen'. In S. Olsen and G. Fanselow (eds), *DET, COMP und INFL. Zur Syntax funktionaler Kategorien und grammatischer Funktionen* (*Linguistische Arbeiten* 263). Tübingen: Niemeyer.

KAYNE, R. (1984) *Connectedness and Binary Branching*. Dordrecht: Foris.

KAYNE, R. (1991) 'Romance Clitics, Verb Movement and PRO'. *Linguistic Inquiry* 22: 647–86.

KOSTER, J. (1984). 'On Binding and Control'. *Linguistic Inquiry* 15 (3): 417–59.

KRÄMER, I. (1993) 'The Licensing of Subjects in Early Child Language'. *MIT Working Papers* 19: 197–212.

LABELLE, M. and D. VALOIS (1996) 'The Status of Post-verbal Subjects in French Child Language'. *Probus* 8: 53–80.

LASNIK, H. and T. STOWELL (1991) 'Weakest Crossover'. *Linguistic Inquiry* 22: 687–720.

LEVOW, G.-A. (1995) 'Tense and Subject Position in Interrogatives and Negatives in Child French: Evidence for and against Truncated Structures'. *MIT Working Papers in Linguistics* 26: 281–304.

LIGHTBOWN, P. (1977) 'Consistency and Variation in the Acquisition of French'. Ph.D. dissertation, Columbia University, NY.

MACWHINNEY, B. and C. SNOW (1985) 'The Child Language Data Exchange System'. *Journal of Child Language* 12.

MANZINI, R. (1983) 'On Control and Control Theory'. *Linguistic Inquiry* 14 (3): 421–46.

MCCULLOUGH, F. (1982) *The Journals of Sylvia Plath*. New York: Dial Press.

MOHANAN, K. P. (1985) 'Remarks on Control and Control Theory'. *Linguistic Inquiry* 16: 637–48.

PHILLIPS, C. (1995) 'Syntax at Age Two: Cross-linguistic Differences'. *MIT Working Papers in Linguistics* 26: 325–82.

PIERCE, A. (1989) 'On the Emergence of Syntax: A Cross-linguistic Study'. Ph.D. dissertation, MIT.

PIERCE, A. (1992) *Language Acquisition and Syntactic Theory: A Comparative Analysis of French and English Child Grammars*. Dordrecht: Kluwer.

POEPPEL, D. and K. WEXLER (1993) 'The Full Competence Hypothesis of Clause Structure in Early German'. *Language* **69**: 1–33.

POLLOCK, J.-Y. (1989) 'Verb Movement, Universal Grammar and the Structure of IP'. *Linguistic Inquiry* **20**: 365–424.

RADFORD, A. (1990) *Syntactic Theory and the Acquisition of English Syntax*. Oxford: Basil Blackwell.

RADFORD, A. (1995) 'Children – architects or brickies?' In D. MacLaughlin and S. McEwen (eds), *Proceedings of the 19th Annual Boston University Conference on Language Development*. Somerville: Cascadilla Press: 1–19.

RAPOSO, E. (1987) 'Case Theory and Infl-to-Comp: The Inflected Infinitive in European Portuguese'. *Linguistic Inquiry* **18**, 85–109.

RHEE, J. and K. WEXLER (1995) 'Optional Infinitives in Hebrew. *MIT Working Papers in Linguistics* **26**: 383–402.

RICE, M., k. WEXLER and P. CLEAVE (1995) 'Specific Language Impairment as a Period of Extended Optional Infinitive'. *Journal of Speech and Hearing Research* **38**: 850–63.

RIZZI, L. (1986) 'Null Objects in Italian and the Theory of *pro*'. *Linguistic Inquiry* **17**: 501–59.

RIZZI, L. (1990) 'Relativized Minimality'. Cambridge, MA: MIT Press.

RIZZI, L. (1992) 'Early Null Subjects and Root Null Subjects'. *Geneva Generative Papers* 0.1–2: 102–14.

RIZZI, L. (1994a) 'Early Null Subjects and Root Null Subjects'. In T. Hoekstra and B. Schwartz (eds), *Language Acquisition Studies in Generative Grammar*. Amsterdam: John Benjamins.

RIZZI, L. (1994b) 'Some Notes on Linguistic Theory and Language Development: The Case of Root Infinitives'. *Language Acquisition* **3** (4): 371–93.

RIZZI, L. (1995) 'The Fine Structure of the Left Periphery'. Ms., University of Geneva.

ROBERGE, Y. (1986) 'Subject Doubling, Free Inversion, and Null Argument Languages'. *Canadian Journal of Linguistics* **31**: 55–79.

ROBERGE, Y. (1990) *The Syntactic Recoverability of Null Arguments*. Montréal: McGill-Queen's University Press.

ROEPER, T. and B. ROHRBACHER (1995) 'Null Subjects in Early Child English and the Theory of Economy of Projections'. Ms., University of Massachusetts at Amherst and University of Pennsylvania.

SANO, T. and N. HYAMS (1994) Agreement, finiteness and the development of null arguments. *Proceedings of NELS* **24**: 543–58.

SCHÜTZE, C. and K. WEXLER (1996a) 'Subject Case Licensing and English Root Infinitives'. In A. Stringfellow, D. Cahana-Amitay, E. Hughes and A. Zukowski (eds), *Proceedings of the 20th Annual Boston University Conference on Language Development*. Somerville, MA: Cascadilla Press: 670–81.

SCHÜTZE, C. and K. WEXLER (1996b) 'What Case Acquisition Data Have to Say about the Components of Infl'. Paper presented at WCHTSALT, OTS, Utrecht University, June 1996.

SUPPES, P. (1973) 'The Semantics of Children's Language'. *American Psychologist* **88**: 103–14.

SUPPES, P., R. SMITH and M. LÉVEILLÉ (1973) 'The French Syntax of a Child's Noun Phrase'. *Archives de Psychologie* **42**: 207–69.

VALIAN, V. (1991) 'Syntactic Subjects in the Early Speech of American and Italian Children'. *Cognition* **40**: 21–81.

VERRIPS, M. and J. WEISSENBORN (1992) 'Routes to Verb Placement in Early German and French: The Independence of Finiteness and Agreement'. In J. M. Meisel (ed.), *The Acquisition of Verb Placement*. Dordrecht: Kluwer: 283–331.

WEISSENBORN, J. (1988) 'The Acquisition of Clitic Object Pronouns and Word Order in French: Syntax or Morphology?' Ms., Nijmegen, The Netherlands, Max-Planck-Institut.

WEISSENBORN, J. (1992) 'Null Subjects in Early Grammars: Implications for Parameter Setting Theory'. In J. Weissenborn, H. Goodluck and T. Roeper (eds), *Theoretical Issues in Language Acquisition*. Hillsdale, NJ: Lawrence Erlbaum.

WEVERINK, M. (1990) 'The Subject in Relation to Inflection in Child Language. MA thesis, University of Utrecht.

WEXLER, K. (1992) 'Optional Infinitives, Head Movement and the Economy of Derivation in Child Grammar'. Occasional paper no. 45, Center for Cognitive Science, MIT, Cambridge, MA.

WEXLER, K. (1994) 'Optional Infinitives, Head Movement and the Economy of Derivations'. In D. Lightfoot and N. Hornstein (eds), *Verb Movement*. Cambridge: Cambridge University Press.

WEXLER, K. (1995) 'Feature Interpretability and Optimality in Early Child Grammar'. Paper presented at the workshop on optionality, Utrecht.

WIJNEN, F. (1994) 'Incremental Acquisition of Phrase Structure: A Longitudinal Analysis of Verb Placement in Dutch Child Language'. Ms., University of Groningen.

WILLIAMS, E. (1980) 'Predication'. *Linguistic Inquiry* **11** (1): 203–38.

ZRIBI-HERTZ, A. (1994) 'La syntaxe des clitiques nominatifs en français standard et en français avancé'. G. Kleiber and G. Roques (eds), *Travaux de linguistique et de philologie*. Strasbourg-Nancy: Klincksiek: 131–47.

Chapter 10

Remarks on early null subjects
Luigi Rizzi

1 Introduction

In recent years, an increasing number of theoretical linguists has started to pay serious attention to language development. Why is this? Decades of pioneering work by theoretically oriented psycholinguists have conclusively shown that language development presents a highly structured mix of elements of continuity and discontinuity with respect to adult systems. This mix is extremely attractive for the theoretical linguist. Continuity, which clearly is the prevailing factor, makes sure that developmental evidence will bear on the object of inquiry that the linguist cares about, the study of systems constrained and made possible by the human language faculty. Discontinuity is what makes development interesting for us: we can reasonably hope that development will allow us to see properties that are not immediately accessible to observation in adult systems, thus allowing us to identify and explore neglected areas of the grammatical space defined by Universal Grammar.

It is not surprising that this growth of interest coincided with the consolidation of the principles and parameters models of UG in the mid eighties. Parametric models introduced a theoretical language well adapted for the comparisons of systems fundamentally cast in the same mold, but diverging on some structurally well-defined points. On top of making available certain technical tools for comparing languages, they renewed an interest in and a taste for comparison by showing that not only language invariance but also language variation was amenable to rigorous, theory-guided study. It was only natural to try these models out on development, another domain showing limited variation within fundamental boundaries of uniformity. The same methodology used for the comparison of adult languages was successfully extended to developing systems. It proved useful to extend the ordinary tools of adult comparative syntax to compare early systems with each other, early systems with the corresponding adult target systems, and even early systems with developmentally unrelated adult systems, say Child English and Adult Italian, thus adding entirely new dimensions to the empirical basis of comparative work.

In this chapter I would like to review an area of comparative acquisition studies which has been extensively investigated over the last decade, and in which constant and significant progress has been made.

2 Early null subjects in the development of non-Null Subject Languages

Around the age of two, children typically produce sentences with null subjects even if their target language is not a Null Subject Language:

(1) *English*
   a. ____ was a green one (Eve 1;10: Brown 1973)
   b. ____ have to drink grape juice first (Eve 1;10)
   c. ____ goin(g) use the box (Eve 1;10)
   d. ____ falled in the briefcase (Eve 1;10)

(2) *French*
   a. ____ a tout tout tout mangé (Augustin 2;0:
   '____ has all all all eaten'   Hamann *et al.* 1996)
   b. ____ ôter tout ta (Augustin 2;0)
   '____ empty all that'

(3) *Danish*
   a. ____ er ikke synd (Jens 2;1, from Hamann and Plunkett 1997)
   '____ is not a pity'
   b. ____ ikke køre traktor   (Jens 2;0, from Hamann and
   '____ not drive tractor' Plunkett 1997)

The first natural move was to explore whether the phenomenon was related to the option of subject omission that many adult languages possess, one of the topics of intensive investigation in the early years of the parametric approach under the heading of the Null Subject Parameter (Rizzi 1982, etc.). Much research has been devoted to this question, starting from the pioneering work of Hyams (1986), with the goal of identifying the fine-grained structural properties of early subject omission. Ten years of intensive investigations have strongly substantiated a negative answer: early subject omission is not like the option found in adult Null Subject Languages.

3 Early null subjects as root null subjects

Let me focus on a difference which seems to me to be particularly significant. The post Wh subject position strongly disfavors early null subjects while it is a perfectly natural environment for null subjects in adult Null Subject Languages. In other words (restricting our attention to finite environments in English for reasons that will become clear in a moment), we typically do not find examples such as (4b) alternating with (4a) in natural production corpora, while equivalent structures such as (5) are perfectly natural in Adult Italian, Spanish, etc.:

(4) a.   Where dis goes? (Adam 2;8)
    b. (*) Where ___ goes?

(5) Dove va?
    'Where goes?'

This constraint was hinted at in Valian (1991), but the observation was not used in her analysis. On the basis of Valian's hint, and of her observation that null subjects did not occur in the first subordinate clauses in her corpus of Early English, the following conjecture was made:

(6) *The Root Null Subject Conjecture*
    Early null subjects are restricted to the specifier of the root
    (Rizzi 1992)

and the attempt was made to develop a formal approach expressing this generalization, which I will come back to.

Conjecture (6) was substantiated for the first time in a systematic way in Crisma's (1992) work on Early French. She found that, while null subjects freely alternate with overt subjects in declaratives, overt subjects are by and large the only option in post Wh environments in Philippe's corpus (Suppes *et al.* 1973), i.e. the pronoun does not alternate with zero in the (b) examples:

(7) a. ___ est perdu xxx celui-la (Philippe 2;2)
    '___ is lost that one'
    b. Où il est le fil? (Philippe 2;1)
    'Where it is the wire?'

(8) a. ___ va sous le tabouret (Philippe 2;3)
    '___ goes under the stool'
    b. Où elle va maman? (Philippe 2;6)
    'Where she goes mummy?'

Crisma (1992) observed a sharp quantitative difference strongly supporting conjecture (6):

(9)   *Tot*   *NS*
    Philippe (2;1–2;3)   Decl   1002   406
                          WhQ   114   1

Phillips (1995:369) raised doubts about the relevance of Crisma's
observation for conjecture (6) on the basis of the observation that most
of the Wh questions in Philippe's corpus involve a functional verb.
He pointed out that since it had been noticed that English children
are reluctant to license null subjects with functional verbs (auxiliaries
and copulas: Hyams and Sano 1994), it could be that the virtual non-
occurrence of null subjects in post Wh environments is a function of
this independent constraint, rather than of the non-root position of the
subject. But after more careful observation, Phillips' objection turns out
not to be valid: on the one hand, even in Early English the reluctance to
license null subjects with functional verbs is only a tendency, not a
categorical effect like the one found by Crisma; moreover, Rasetti (1995)
observed subject drop with functional verbs ranging from 24% to 33%
in the corpus of Early French natural production she looked at (Daniel
1–5, Nathalie 6–7, see Lightbown 1977, and Augustin 1–10); even
though some of the children drop subjects less with functional verbs
than with inflected lexical verbs, this is a weak tendency in Early French,
so that the occurrence of functional verbs in questions could not be
deemed responsible for the sharp effect in (9).

Another possible objection to Crisma's findings, related to Phillips'
but independent of it, could be that her 1002 declarative environments
lumped together finite and infinitival declaratives; now it is known that
root infinitives licence a higher proportion of null subjects than finite
declaratives (see the discussion below); on the other hand, Wh questions always involve a finite verb in Early French (for reasons related
to the structural constraints on the distribution of root infinitives, on
which see Rizzi 1993/1994), so that the disproportion between the two
columns of (9) could be a function of the non-occurrence of non-finite
clauses in Wh environments. Again, Rasetti's work counters this
objection: finite clauses in Early French admit subject drop to a very
substantive degree, so that even if we look only at finite structures in
corpora such as Crisma's, we continue to observe a very strong effect.

Crisma's findings were replicated on a different French corpus:

(10) Levow (1995) based on Grégoire 1;9–2;3, Nathalie 1;9–2;3,
     Daniel 1;8–1;11: 55% of null subjects in declaratives (779/1412)
     vs only 5% of null subjects in post Wh environment (2/39).

The result was replicated for Early Dutch by Haegeman in different
papers. Haegeman (1996a) found the following percentages of subject
drop in the initial position of finite declaratives:

(11)

		Tot	NS
Thomas (2;3–2;11)	Decl (S) V O	2334	570 (24.4%)
Hein (2;4–3;1)	Decl (S) V O	1920	443 (23.1%)
Niek (2;8–3;10)	Decl (S) V O	2148	495 (23%)

In Haegeman (1996a, 1996b) she observed that the same children in the same periods produce a negligible number of structures with null subjects in post Wh environments:

(12)

		Tot	NS
Thomas	Wh V (S) O	321	9 (2.8%)
Hein	Wh V (S) O	152	2 (1.3%)
Niek	Wh V (S) O	209	4 (1.9%)

(Haegeman also observed that non-initial null subjects in post topic V-2 constructions are somewhat more frequent than in post Wh position, while still being much less frequent than in initial position, a fact which she explained through a natural extension of the system discussed here.)

A clear reluctance to produce structures with null subjects in post Wh environments is also documented for Early German in Clahsen *et al.* (1995). From their Table 3 it is possible to determine that from the very large data base of this study (134 recordings from 9 children 1;7–3;8) only 4% of post Wh subjects were null. It is not possible to determine from this study the number and proportion of initial null subjects in the same corpus. On the other hand, initial null subjects are a robust phenomenon in Early German (e.g. Duffield (1993) reports over 2000 null subjects in Simone's files 3–22, i.e. over a quarter of the subject environments), so that it is very likely that Early German will reproduce the sharp asymmetry that Haegeman found in Early Dutch.

Once it was established that generalization (6) held in the Null Subject phase of the acquisition of non-Null Subject Languages, it was natural to ask whether it was valid for the early phases of Null Subject Languages as well. It was quickly determined (Rizzi 1992) that the answer is negative: learners of Italian clearly license null subjects in non-initial post Wh environments, as the following sample from Cipriani *et al.* (1993) shows:

(13) a. Ov'è? (1;8)
   'Where is?'
   b. Cos'è (1;10)
   'What is?'
   c. Che voi? (2;3)
   'What (you) want?'
   d. Pecché piangi? (2;3)
   'Why (you) cry?'
   e. Quetto cosa fa? (2;5)
   'This what does?'

Guasti (1995) gave a quantitative dimension to this observation:

(14) Guasti (1995): (corpus: Martina 1;8–2;7, Diana 1;10–2;6, Guglielmo 2;2–2;11): out of 171 non-subject questions, 104 have null subject (60%).

The conclusions supported by the previous findings are the following: the Null Subject Parameter is correctly fixed early on, as is shown by the sharp difference between Early Italian and Early English, French, Dutch and German in the non-initial (post Wh) context. Learners of Italian drop subjects in the same environments as adult Italian speakers. Learners of non-Null Subject Languages have fixed the NS Parameter on the negative value, but have the independent option of dropping the subject in the Spec of the Root. Once this option is factored out, the Null Subject Parameter appears to involve an early fixation, on a par with the other major parameters investigated in the recent literature.

4 Two kinds of early null subjects

Roeper and Rohrbacher (1994) made an inportant observation which at first sight seemed to challenge the validity of conjecture (6) for Early English. They looked at post Wh environments in Adam's corpus and found plenty of null subjects, except that they were restricted to uninflected contexts. In other words, null subjects appear to be freely possible in context (15b), but not in context (15a):

(15) a. (*) Where ____ goes/went/is going?

b. Where ____ go(ing)

Here is their count:

(16) Roeper and Rohrbacher (1994) compared null and pronominal subjects in contexts (15) in Adam 1–18 (2;3–2;11):
+Inflected: 6/113 null subjects (5%)
−Inflected: 99/204 null subjects (49%)

NB: these authors included inflected functional verbs as well as inflected lexical verbs in the count, and calculated the ratio of null subjects against the total number of null subjects and overt *pronominal* subjects rather than against the total number of null subjects and overt subjects (lexical and pronominal) as other comparable counts have done.

This result was then replicated by Bromberg and Wexler (1995). On the basis of these observations, these and other researchers were led to resurrect an old idea, which in its common-sense, pretheoretical, characterization goes as follows: it is generally accepted that the early null subject phase basically coincides with another remarkable phenomenon of child language, the fact that the child can use uninflected verbal forms also in main clauses. In adult grammars, uninflected verbal forms generally can or must cooccur with null subjects, so the early null subject could just be a direct, in fact rather trivial, consequence of the more widespread use of uninflected forms in early grammars (see Guilfoyle (1984), O'Grady *et al.* (1989), Kraemer (1993) for different proposals along these lines). The most straightforward theoretical implementation of this hypothesis is that PRO can occur in early uninflected clauses, as Hyams and Sano (1994) and Wexler and Bromberg (1995) have proposed (Roeper and Rohrbacher (1994) suggested that the relevant empty category could be pro, if its licensing conditions were defined as in Speas (1994)). This analysis is very plausible in accommodating the Roeper and Rohrbacher effect. On the basis of this evidence, the inevitable conclusion is that the uninflected environment can license null subjects, quite independently from generalization (6). Taking the PRO strand for concreteness, the following licensing condition is at work in the relevant cases (either as a consequence of Binding Theory, as in Chomsky (1981), or as a stipulation on PRO's case requirements, as in Chomsky (1995)):

(17) PRO is licensed in uninflected clauses.

On the other hand, it is equally clear that this can't be the whole story about early null subjects. It is a well-established fact that null subjects can occur in robust proportions also in inflected environments, in Early English and in the other early systems which have been submitted to analysis (French, German, Dutch, Danish, etc.).

As for Early English, it can be determined from Hyams and Sano's (1994) tables that Adam 1–20 (2;3–3;0) has 34% subject drop in declaratives with inflected lexical verbs (subject drop with inflected functional verbs is more reduced, a point which we will come back to in a moment). Moreover, Valsecchi (1997) has observed that throughout the whole Eve corpus, subject drop with inflected lexical verbs is even slightly higher than with uninflected verbs (13.6% vs 11.3%), while in Sarah's corpus, subject drop with uninflected verbs is slightly higher (25.4%), but with inflected verbs it is still substantial (19.3%). There is good evidence that such inflected lexical verbs count as finite, inflected forms for the child (contra Hyams and Sano's suggestion that they be analyzed as non-finite participial forms): in joint work with Teresa Guasti, we have looked at the same corpus studied by Hyams and Sano searching for post Wh environments with inflected lexical verbs, i.e. Roeper and Rohrbacher's context (15a) without the functional verbs, and have observed a drop in subject omission comparable with the one they found:

(18) Adam 1–20 (2;3–3;0) has 4.6% (2/43) subject drop with inflected lexical verbs in post Wh contexts.

This result is now immediately comparable with Hyams and Sano's:

(19) a. ____ goes/went
     b. Where ____ goes/went?

Adam drops subjets one third of the times in context (19a), and less than 5% in the post Wh position (19b), a state of affairs which strongly supports the substantial role of subject drop in early finite clauses and the validity of conjecture (6) for finite environments.

The possibility of dropping subjects in finite environments is also clearly shown in the early phases of other non-Null Subject Languages. Remember that the Dutch corpus studied by Haegeman (1996a, 1996b), with results summarized in (11), shows subject drop in initial position in about a quarter of finite sentences. As for Early French, Rasetti (1995) found a substantial number of null subjects in inflected clauses, about one third of the cases in the corpus she looked at, with a markedly stronger proportion of null subjects in non-finite clauses:

(20) Daniel 1–5, Nathalie 1–7, Augustin 1–10

	Tot	NS
+infl	1229	416 (33.8%)
−infl	565	457 (80.9%)

Kraemer (1993) has observed comparable asymmetries in Dutch, Flemish, German, and in a partly different French corpus. This cross-linguistic evidence uniformly points to the robustness of subject drop in inflected environments – it is not at all a marginal phenomenon in language development. Thus the idea, sometimes expressed in the recent literature, that early null subjects are by and large restricted to non-inflected clauses seems to be empirically unjustified. At the same time, the observed asymmetries between inflected and uninflected environments suggest that two different kinds of null subjects are to be postulated.

The conclusion which strongly suggests itself then is that both conjecture (6) and Roeper and Rohrbacher's proposal (however it is implemented, say through principle (17)) are correct in that they both point to the existence of genuine environments for early null subjects. In fact, there are two kinds of null subjects in Early English, one licensed in the specifier of the root and insensitive to the finiteness of the clause, the other licensed in uninflected clauses and insensitive to the root/non-root distinction. Assuming that the null subject licensed in uninflected clauses is PRO and calling the one in the specifier of the root *ec* for the time being, we have the following four potential environments:

(21)   *ec*   *PRO*

+infl +root	'____ goes/went'		+	−
−infl +root	'____ go(ing)'		+	+
−infl −root	'Where ____ go(ing)'		−	+
+infl −root	'Where ____ goes/went'		−	−

So, at least one null subject is licensed with all combinations (with uninflected root clauses both kinds are licit), except in inflected non-root environments. Whence the virtual non-occurrence of sentences such as (15a) in early production corpora.

5 Against pragmatic and performance accounts

The observed patterns of null subject licensing provide significant evidence against certain accounts of early null subjects as an extra-grammatical phenomenon. Let us consider this aspect before coming back to more technical questions about the types of empty categories involved. Different extragrammatical accounts have in common the plausible idea that early systems operate under severe processing constraints (related, e.g., to limitations in working memory) which determine a production which is not fully consistent with the grammatical knowledge already developed by the child. In this view, the dropping of certain elements in early production may be governed by the interaction between the grammar and the processor, rather than being a genuine grammatical option.

An approach of this sort to early subject drop is the so-called pragmatic account: under the pressure of some constraint in the performance system, the child is led to drop, or leave unpronounced, some elements in production; she or he basically chooses to drop old information material and tends to limits overt production to new information, or focus. As grammatical subjects are often old information, they are more frequently dropped than other parts of the structure (Greenfield and Smith 1976). However, the virtual absence of subject drop in post Wh environments provides strong evidence against this view: in non-subject (main) Wh questions the focus is always taken up by the Wh element, so the subject is always (not just frequently) defocalized; the pragmatic approach would then predict that this should be an even more favorable environment for subject drop than the subject position of declaratives, contrary to fact.

A different extragrammatical account implies a theory of processing according to which processing load is maximal initially, then it progressively decreases as one gets close to the end of the structure (see Bloom (1990) and the discussion in Hyams and Wexler (1993)); elements tend to be dropped in production to alleviate processing load; as subjects are generally initial, they tend to be dropped more than other elements. As far as I can tell, such a theory would expect the likelihood of an element being dropped to decrease gradually from the beginning to the end of the clause, rather than there being a categorical distinction between first position and everything else. But the virtual absence of subject drop in post Wh environment shows precisely such a categorical effect, not predicted under the processing account. Moreover, as Schuetze (1997) pointed out, the Roeper and Rohrbacher effect is particularly damaging for a processing approach to this kind of early null subjects: on the one hand, subject drop in post Wh environments is clearly structurally governed, as it depends on the lack of inflection; moreover, uninflected clauses are morphologically simpler than inflected ones (minimally the latter contain an extra morpheme), so if subject drop was demanded by some processing overload, one would expect it to be more likely to occur in the more complex inflected clauses, contrary to fact.

One result that is often mentioned in favor of a performance account of early subject drop is that null subject sentences in Early English tend to have longer VPs than sentences with overt subjects (Bloom 1990). The planned production of a sentence with long VP involves a higher processing load, whence the likelihood of subject drop, so the reasoning goes. The VP-length effect is significant, and appealing to a processing component to explain it looks plausible (but this is not the only plausible possibility: see Hyams and Wexler (1993) for an alternative). On the other hand, I doubt that it should be interpreted in terms of a model in which performance can directly override competence: the clear structurally governed nature of the early subject drop would be missed. An interpretation more consistent with the whole array of relevant evidence seems to me to be that early systems have the grammatical option of licensing null subjects in certain environments, and that this grammatical option may well be used to circumvent processing limitations, if the processing interpretation of the effect on VP length is correct. There are plenty of obvious cases, in adult systems as well, in which grammatical options may have the effect of alleviating processing constraints. Consider for instance the well-known center embedding problem (Miller and Chomsky 1963) illustrated by an example such as (22), virtually unprocessable in Italian, like its English equivalent. On the other hand, the processing problem can be alleviated in Italian by leaving one of the subjects containing a relative in postverbal position, as in (23), which is much more easily processed:

(22) Il libro che l'editore che il governo ha finanziato ha pubblicato ha vinto un premio
'The book that the publisher that the government funded published won a prize'

(23) Il libro che _____ ha pubblicato [l'editore che il governo ha
finanziato] ha vinto un premio
'The book that published the publisher that the government
funded won a prize'

Nobody would presumably want to argue that in (23) a performance
factor overrides competence. Rather, here Italian has a grammatical
option (leaving the subject in VP-final position) which can be used to
circumvent a performance limitation, while other systems, for instance
Adult English, do not have it. I believed that the putative processing
consequences of early null subjects, if correct, should be interpreted
along similar lines.

6 Types of *ec* involved

I will continue to assume that the kind of early null subject occurring in
uninflected environments is PRO, as in adult grammars, except that
early grammars have the special option of licensing uninflected clauses
in root environments more liberally than adult grammars. There are
some interesting questions that arise concerning the interpretation of
this kind of early null subject, which, under continuity assumptions,
one would expect to be interpreted as adult PRO, all things being equal
(does this kind of early null subject share all the interpretative properties of uncontrolled PRO in adult systems?), but I will not be able to
address this point here. I'll just assume the following licensing condition to be operative, and leave it at that:

(24) PRO is licensed in uninflected environments

What about the null subject licensed under generalization (6)? The
question of the nature of the empty category involved here goes hand
in hand with the question of how such a special licensing condition is
to be formally expressed. The idea developed in Rizzi (1992) was the
following: empty categories generally require identification, an unidentified gap is not licit in a structural representation. One identification
principle, traditionally seen as a component of the Empty Category
Principle (ECP), requires identification of a certain type of null element
through connection to an antecendent in a chain:

(25) *ec* must be chain-connected to an antecedent.

Suppose that this principle is interpreted, much along the lines of
Chomsky's (1986) Binding Theory, as enforced up to virtual satisfiability:
the principle is obligatory if virtually satisfiable, i.e. if there is a phrase
c-commanding the *ec*, thus acting as a potential antecedent. This has
the effect of freeing up from the identification requirement the specifier

of the root, the position which is not c-commanded by any other category in the structure. Consider, then, two representations such as (26)
and (27), corresponding to examples (7a)–(7b) in Early French:

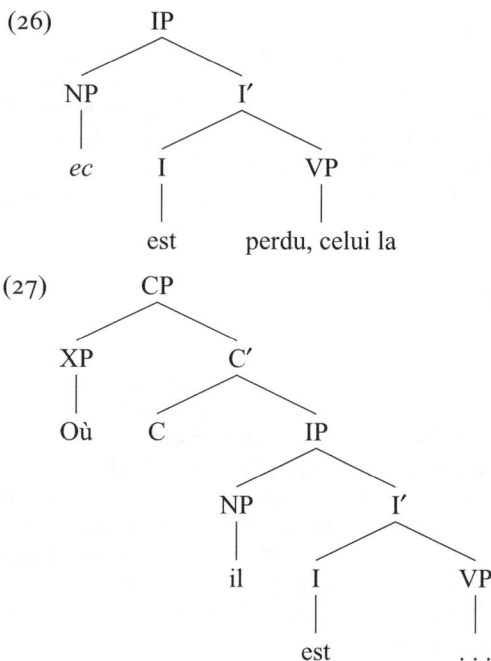

(26)

```
                    IP
            ┌────────┴────────┐
           NP                 I′
            │          ┌──────┴──────┐
           ec          I            VP
                       │             │
                      est      perdu, celui la
```

(27)

```
                CP
        ┌───────┴───────┐
       XP               C′
        │        ┌──────┴──────┐
       Où        C            IP
                        ┌──────┴──────┐
                       NP             I′
                        │      ┌──────┴──────┐
                       il      I            VP
                               │             │
                              est           . . .
```

In (26) the subject is the specifier of the root, the identification principle does not apply to it, under the proposed interpretation, and so it
can be structurally realized as an unidentified empty position. In (27)
the subject position is not the specifier of the root, as the higher CP
layer must be represented in the structure to accommodate the preposed
Wh element, so the identification principle is fully operative on the
subject position, which cannot be represented as an unidentified empty
element. The privileged status of the specifier of the root thus receives
a simple formal account.

What about Adult Standard English, French, etc. in which subject
drop is disallowed even in declaratives (i.e. (26) is ungrammatical in
Adult French)? In Rizzi (1992) the assumption is made that the following principle is operative in adult grammars:

(28) CP = Root

If all clausal types are uniformly CPs in adult grammars, then the
subject position will never be the specifier of the root in such systems,

due to the systematic presence of a higher CP layer, hence root null subjects will be generally excluded. On the other hand, according to this approach, early systems freely allow for truncated root clauses, root constructions categorially different and smaller than CPs; when such truncated structures are bare IPs, as in (26), the root null subject is allowed. I will come back to the developmental presuppositions and implications of this analysis, and focus for a moment on the formal status of the empty category involved.

As the ECP is the identification principle relevant for traces, this approach formally assimilates a root null subject to a trace. Does this make sense? In Rizzi (1992) an attempt was made to formally pursue this possibility in terms of the standard 'Principles and Parameters' typology of *ecs* induced by features +/−a(naphoric), +/−p(ronominal).

The kind of trace which was identified as a close interpretative analogue of a null pronoun was the trace A′ bound by an anaphoric (non-quantificational) operator in constructions such as the following (the trace in question being dubbed 'null constant', *nc*, in opposition to the variable bound by a genuinely quantificational operator):

(29) a. John is too clever [$_{Op}$ [$_{PRO}$ to catch *nc*]]
     b. John, whom I met *nc* yesterday, . . .

Such traces are interpreted as picking up a referential value from an antecedent, and as such are interpretatively akin to pronominals.

A difficulty with this view is that null constants of the type involved in (29) appear to be restricted to referential arguments, as the following near minimal pair, originally pointed out by Barry Schein, suggests (see Rizzi 1986: 528 fn. for discussion), with the quasi-argumental weather *it* unable to identify the null constant:

(30) a. ?The train was running too fast [$_{Op}$ [$_{PRO}$ to consider [*nc* likely to stop]]]
     b. *It was raining too heavily [$_{Op}$ [$_{PRO}$ to consider [*nc* likely to stop]]]

The difficulty is that early null subjects can be expletives of various kinds (non-arguments and quasi-arguments: Hyams 1986, Wang *et al.* 1992, Haegeman 1995).

A rather different angle on the problem is offered by the new typology of null elements emerging from Chomsky's (1995) theory. According to this typology, traces have a completely different status from inherently pronominal *ecs* (PRO and pro) in that they fully reproduce the structure of their antecedents, except that they are not pronounced (we conventionally write trace material within angled brackets). This approach is strongly motivated by so-called reconstruction effects, illustrated by examples such as (31b), in which the anaphor is interpreted in the position within the trace of the Wh phrase:

(31) a. John seems [<John> to have been arrested <John>]
     b. Which picture of himself do you think John likes <which picture of himself>?

In Chomsky's system, the fact that traces are not pronounced is somehow built into the movement algorithm, but there are obvious formal alternatives. Suppose that we now dissociate the option of leaving a position unpronounced, formally expressed by the assignment of angled brackets, from the creation of a trace via movement, and we consider it an independent grammatical option constrained by the identification principle (25) (a move which may be of particular interest in view of identifying a common core between traces and other unpronounced material in ellipsis).

(32) Assign $< \ldots >$

If we continue to interpret the identification principle as obligatory up to virtual satisfiability, we obtain the desired result that (32) can freely apply to the Spec of the root. So we can have well-formed representations such as the following in early systems:

(33) <il> va sous le tabouret

Nothing now excludes the possibility of leaving an expletive unpronounced in the Spec of the root, as desired.

7 Some adult analogues

The study of early systems has led us to postulate a formal device which assigns a privileged status to the specifier of the root, as the only position in which an *ec* can survive even if it is not identified clause-internally. Under continuity assumptions, we have attributed this device to UG; if this is correct, we expect to find reflexes of the privilege of the root in adult systems as well. This illustrates another significant effect of acquisition and development studies on syntactic theory and comparative syntax: the search for adult analogues of early phenomena, prompted by continuity assumptions, may focus or reactivate research into unexplored or neglected areas of adult syntax, leading to new discoveries and analyses.

The closest adult analogue to the generalizations observed in early systems is the subject drop possible in diaries and other abbreviated registers first discussed by Haegeman (1990), and then explicitly analyzed by Haegeman (this volume) in the context of the theoretical debate on early null subjects:

(34) A very sensible day yesterday. ____ saw no-one. ____ took
      the bus to Southwark Bridge.
      ____ walked along. . . .
                        (Virginia Woolf, *Diary*, from Haegeman 1990)

(35) ____ m'accompagne au Mercure, puis à la gare . . .
      (he) takes me to Mercure, then to the station . . .
      ____ me demande si . . . je lui eus montré les notes . . .
      (I) ask myself if . . . I would have shown him the notes . . .
                        (Paul Léautaud, *Le Fléau, Journal Particulier,*
                        1917–1930, pp. 60–70, from Haegeman 1990)

This special register can be described as allowing truncation of the CP
layer, an option obviously related to its abbreviated character. While
certain informal registers of spoken English seem to allow this option,
drop of the root subject is apparently confined to written registers of other
languages, such as French, which strictly disallow root subject drop in
oral registers (see below for discussion).

Another case is topic drop – drop of an argument limited to the left
peripheral position, a property manifested by some Germanic languages,
such as spoken German and Dutch.

(36) a. (Ich) habe es gestern gekauft
          '(I) have it yesterday bought'
      b. Wann hat *(er) angerufen?
          'When has he telephoned?'
      c. Hans glaubt *(ich) habe es gestern gekauft
          'Hans believes I have it yesterday bought'
      d. Hans glaubt dass *(ich) es gestern gekauft habe
          'Hans believes that I it yesterday bought have'

Of particular significance here is that the pronominal subject can be
dropped in the Spec of C in the main V-2 construction, but not in the
embedded V-2 of (36c), a clear manifestation of what we have called
'the privilege of the root'.

As a first approximation, one could think that this option is offered
for free in initial position in V-2 languages: whatever constituent is in
Spec of C should meet the requirement for escaping the effects of the
identification principle. In fact there are at least two problems with this
view: one is that topic drop is not automatically licensed by V-2: some
V-2 languages such as Flemish (and at least some varieties of Danish)
do not allow this option (as pointed out by Haegeman (1995); the
reciprocal of this problem is that V-2 is not even a necessary condition
for topic drop: some topic drop languages, such as Chinese and Portuguese are not V-2). The second problem is that, while expletives can

fulfill the V-2 requirement, some languages allowing topic drop don't allow expletive drop, such as the variety of German described by Cardinaletti (1990), and at least some varieties of Dutch:

(37) a. *(Es) wurde viel getanzt
        'It was a lot danced'
     b. *(Es) ist ein Mann da
        'There is a man there'
     c. *(Es) hat viel geregnet
        '(It) has a lot rained'

While other V-2 languages such as spoken Swedish allow topic drop (as in (38c)), and also drop of expletive root subjects (as in (38a); (38b) is excluded because an expletive, overt or null, cannot be topicalized from an embedded clause):

(38) a. (Det) verkar som om . . .
        '(It) seems as if. . . .'
     b. *(Det) vet jag [t verkar som om . . .]
        '(It) know I seems as if . . .'
     c. (Det) visste jag [t skulle haenda]
        '(It) knew I [t should happen]

Clearly these options of dropping initial topics or expletives cannot come for free with V-2, some independent parametrization must be involved.

I think the key to the problem is that postulating a simple CP layer is clearly inadequate as a theory of the left periphery, much as postulating a simple inflectional head is grossly inadequate as a theory of the clause. In recent years, detailed studies on the clause and its left periphery are bringing to light a very complex cartography, which is nevertheless very simple in that its atomic component is always the same, the basic X-bar schema (or the even more rudimentary structural schemata assumed in Kayne (1994) and Chomsky (1995)). I have proposed in recent work that a theory of the left periphery must specify at least the following positions, illustrated through Italian examples (see Rizzi 1997):

(39) Credo che a Gianni, QUESTO domani   i tuoi amici gli
            Force Top   Foc   Top Fin
     dovranno dire
     'I believe that to Gianni THIS tomorrow your friends will have to say to him'

(40) Ho deciso, a Gianni, di parlargli domani
                Top   Fin
     'I decided, to Gianni,   to talk to him tomorrow'

The finite complementizer *che* manifests the Force position in (39), the position which expresses the clausal type and closes the CP system upwards, while the infinitival complementizer *di* manifests the Finiteness head, which closes the C system downwards, agreeing with the IP system in finiteness. The Topic-Focus field is sandwiched in between these two positions.

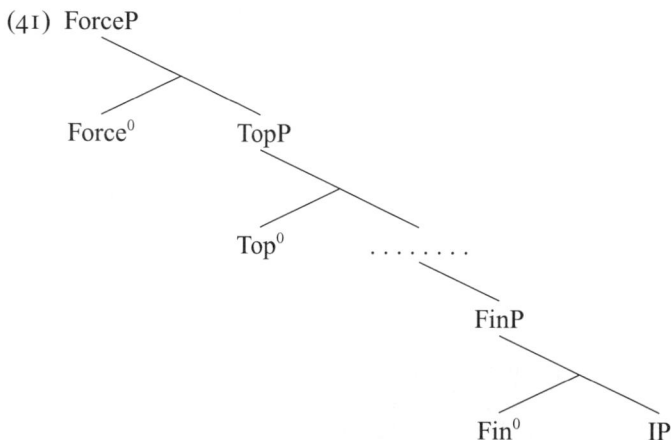

(41) ForceP

```
ForceP
   /\
  /  \
Force⁰  TopP
         /\
        /  \
      Top⁰  ........
               \
                \
                FinP
                 /\
                /  \
              Fin⁰   IP
```

Now, if we adapt this approach to the analysis of V-2 languages, as in Haegeman (1996b), for example, it is clear that the null topic option will not come for free for V-2 or any other languages, because the topic is not the highest position. On the other hand, there is also a simple way to express the relevant parametrization: Topic Drop Languages are those in which the topic can reach the Spec of the root. For example, TopP can be the root in such languages. Along similar lines, it is possible to express the parametrization differentiating root expletive drop languages from the others, basically by allowing the A-chain of the local expletive subject to be extended to reach the Spec of the root in the C system, in a way that I will not develop formally here.

8 Development

Why is the early null subject option lost, very roughly around the end of the third year of life? As for the kind of early null subject which is restricted to uninflected clauses, things are clear: it disappears when the licensing environment, the root infinitive construction, ceases to be available to the child. The fact that root infinitives disappear is far from being a trivial problem in itself, but whatever solution is adopted, it will automatically extend to explain the loss of null subjects in uninflected environments. Things are less straightforward for the kind of early null subject that is restricted to the specifier of the root. It is sometimes suggested in the literature that the problem may not be of primary importance in the development of English: after all, there are colloquial registers in which some kind of root null subject option remains available, so maybe the development does not involve a real loss of the formal option, but rather some kind of fine-tuning of the pragmatic conditions in which the option can be used. However, I do not think this is an adequate way to address the problem in general, and not even for English. First of all, there are adult registers of English that do not allow root null subjects, and these registers must be acquired sooner or later. Moreover, the pragmatic fine-tuning idea is straightforwardly inadequate for languages in which no oral register allows root null subjects (and the option is restricted to explicitly abbreviated registers, such as the written register of diaries). One case in point is French. Even in question/answer pairs such as the following, which provide the most favorable pragmatic environment, subject drop is just ungrammatical in French:

(42) a. Jean, qu'est-ce qu'il fait?
         'John, what is he doing?'
     b. *____ viendra demain
        '____ will come tomorrow'

In order to substantiate this observation by making it directly comparable to the quantitative results on early productions, Rasetti (1995) looked at adults' utterances in 6 files of the corpus she considered (Daniel 1, Daniel 5, Nathalie 1, Nathalie 7, Augustin 2, Augustin 9). Out of 2130 declaratives, she found only 14 cases of null subjects (0.6%); of these, 7 examples involved the impersonal verb *falloir*, which has the idiosyncratic property of allowing a null expletive subject in colloquial registers (*faut partir*, etc.), 3 cases were repetitions of null subject utterances produced by the child, 1 case was quite unclear, which leaves us with 3–4 cases of subject omission out of over 2000 examples, a proportion which is well within the limits that anyone would probably be prepared to admit for genuine performance errors. So, in French, root subject drop is restricted to the written diary register, which is explicitly felt to be abbreviated. Therefore, there can simply be no doubt, in this case, that between the third and the fourth year of life the learner loses a grammatical option; so, whatever its merits for (certain varieties of) English, the pragmatic fine-tuning hypothesis is not general enough. The same conclusions reached by Rasetti for French were arrived at for Danish by Hamann and Plunkett (1997).

Our original proposal was to relate the unavailability of root null subjects in (most) adult systems to principle (43), requiring all kinds of root clauses to be CPs:

(43) Root = CP

If adult declaratives are always introduced by an invisible CP layer, the subject position is never the specifier of the root, hence the root null subject option is not available.

Development was then accounted for by assuming that principle (43) is not operative initially, which makes possible the free generation of truncated root clauses; (43) becomes operative around the end of the third year of life, thus triggering a number of changes in the early grammatical system, the most significant being the loss of early null subjects and root infinitives (Rizzi 1992). This approach raised questions about the nature of principle (43) and the plausibility of the developmental assumptions connected to it.

Starting from the latter point, given the implausibility of data-driven learning of an abstract principle of this sort, the assumption was that (43) somehow matures in the mind around the third year of life. Now, maturation is a very plausible mechanism triggering language development (Wexler 1996); nevertheless, there are some arguments against a maturational approach in this specific case, at least if we interpret 'property P matures in the mind' as meaning 'the capacity to compute P comes about at some point of development for endogenous causes'. One problem is that some adult systems, written registers and sometimes also oral registers, allow root null subjects, as we have seen. It would not make much sense to consider such adult systems as immature: once the relevant computational capacity has developed, it is there, available for use. Moreover, Prévost and White (this volume) have shown that early second language learners acquiring a non-Null Subject Language (French) around the age of 5–6 go through a stage of subject omission with the structural characteristics of first language acquisition (while, interestingly, adult L2ers drop subjects but not under the same structural constraints). Again, reference to maturation to express this effect raises doubts, since these children presumably are well out the null subject stage in their first language (these facts are problematic unless we are prepared to take the position that certain computational capacities may mature in connection with the acquisition of specific grammars in childhood, rather than once and for all grammars). In view of such considerations, it is desirable to explore the possibility of alternative developmental mechanisms for this case.

Let's then address the problem from a different angle, and look at the nature of statement (43). Is it empirically justified, apart from the consequences we drew from it? A reasonable independent empirical motivation for this statement comes from a simple inspection of embedded clauses: the CP system is by and large obligatory, since it must be there not only in questions, where it is needed to accommodate the operator, but also in embedded declaratives (this is clearly shown in languages such as French, in which the overt C *que* is obligatory in finite embedded declaratives; as for English, the structurally selective nature of *that* omission (with trace-like characteristics, as observed by Stowell (1981), Kayne (1983)) also argues for the stystematic presence of a CP layer). So, the null assumption is that clauses are categorially uniform throughout, including root clauses (the C of root declaratives being null most of the time for reasons discussed in Rizzi 1992). In the refined approach to the C system sketched out in the previous section, the assumption of categorial uniformity amounts to saying that root clauses are ForcePs.

On the other hand, uniformity cannot be an absolute requirement on clausal structures. By looking again at embedded clauses we see that UG must allow for exceptions: there are ECM clauses and small clauses that are interpreted as declaratives even though they lack the C system altogether.

(44) a. I consider [that [John is sick]]
      b. I consider [John to be sick]
      c. I consider [John sick]

Given the existence of such cases, it must be possible in special cases to assign declarative force by default to a structure, even in the absence of a structural locus specifying a force feature, the head of ForceP. So, the requirement of starting from a ForceP is not a categorical demand on the semantic type 'proposition', rather it represents the unmarked structural realization of this semantic type. How can we express these informal considerations more precisely, in a way useful to an understanding of the developmental course?

Let me speculate along the following lines. I will assume the following two principles to limit our system of linguistic computation:

(45) *Structural Economy*
      Use the minimum of structure consistent with well-formedness constraints.

(46) *Categorial Uniformity*
      Assume a unique canonical structural realization for a given semantic type.

The first is more or less transparent, even though not easy to implement formally (for different implementations see Safir (1992), Speas (1994), Crisma (1992), Cardinaletti and Starke (1994), Giorgi and Pianesi (1997), etc.). The second can also be seen as an economy principle, but one acting upon the inventories of elements that enter the syntactic computation, rather than on the syntactic computation itself. Under categorial uniformity, the inventory of categories to be used for the syntactic computation will be maximally simple and transparent for the translation to semantics.

There is an obvious tension between the two economy principles in certain cases, which clearly arises for the analysis of root declarative clauses. Take any root declarative, such as (47a):

(47) a. He is sick
     b. I think that he is sick

Structural economy would push for the minimal analysis integrating the overt material of (47a), hence a bare IP analysis; categorial uniformity, taking into account the overt CP status of embedded declaratives such as (47b), would push for a uniform CP analysis of all propositions, root and embedded, with the postulation of a phonetically null CP layer in the representation of (47a). Interpreting this state of affairs in the light of the previous discussion on the licensing of root null subjects, we are led to the conclusion that in a standard adult system, categorial uniformity prevails over structural economy in the unmarked case, with the effect of proscribing root null subjects.

As for development, it is conceivable that the issue of categorial uniformity does not arise in the initial period, when the child's system deals only with root declaratives: in that phase, structural economy is not countered by any problem of categorial uniformity for the semantic type proposition, so it prevails and makes the IP analysis possible (and perhaps compulsory) for declaratives. The issue of uniformity only arises when the child has mastered embedded declaratives, which lead to a revision of the root IP hypothesis to meet uniformity. The root null subject option is then lost. On the other hand, the victory of uniformity over economy is not overwhelming (remember that uniformity represents the unmarked case, leaving room for exceptional cases of clausal reduction illustrated by ECM, small clauses, etc.), so it is not surprising that on special registers, particularly registers explicitly connoted as abbreviated, structural economy may prevail again, with the structural consequences that we know.

This interplay between structural economy and categorial uniformity may well be involved in other cases of development such as the apparent initial optionality of determiners in the acquisition of languages with obligatory determiner, which may involve an initial alternation of DP and NP to express arguments, later abandoned in favor of a categorially uniform DP analysis as the canonical realization of arguments. I will not be able to seriously explore this possibility here.

9 Conclusions

Intensive research over the last ten years has conclusively shown that early null subjects reflect a grammatical option distinct from the licensing of adult null subjects under the Null Subject Parameter. In fact, two formally distinct types of early null subjects must be separated: null

subjects licensed in root infinitives and null subjects licensed in the
Spec of the root, the latter being possible in inflected environments as
well. Performance-based accounts seem to be unable to express the fact
that selective subject omission in early productions is governed by fine
structural properties, which strongly suggests that genuine grammatical
options are involved. Both kinds of early null subjects have (close or
identical) grammatical equivalents in some adult systems, as we are led
to expect by continuity assumptions. Current syntactic theory offers
plausible candidates for the formal status of both kinds of early null
subjects. We have concluded with some speculations on the factors
determining development in this area, identifying one possible factor in
the tension and interplay between two economy principles.

Note

This chapter was presented as a plenary lecture at the Boston University Conference on Language Development 97 and was published in the proceedings,
Cascadilla Press, Somerville, MA, 1998.

References

BLOOM, P. (1990) 'Subjectless Sentences in Child Language', *Linguistic Inquiry*
    21, 491–504.
BROMBERG, H. and K. WEXLER (1995) 'Null Subjects in Wh Questions', *MITWP* **26**.
BROWN, R. (1973) *A First Language. The Early Stages*, Harvard University
    Press, Cambridge, MA.
CARDINALETTI, A. (1990) 'Pronomi nulli e pleonastici nelle lingue germaniche e
    romanze', PhD diss ertation, University of Venice.
CARDINALETTI, A. and M. STARKE (1994) 'The Typology of Structural Defi-
    ciency', ms., University of Geneva, University of Venice.
CHOMSKY, N. (1981) *Lectures on Government and Binding*, Foris Publications,
    Reidel.
CHOMSKY, N. (1986) *Knowledge of Language*, Praeger, New York.
CHOMSKY, N. (1995) *The Minimalist Program*, MIT Press, Cambridge, MA.
CIPRIANI, P., A. M. CHILOSI, P. BOTTARI and L. PFANNER (1993) *L'acquisizione
    della morfosintassi in italiano: fasi e processi*, Unipress, Padova.
CLAHSEN, H., KURSAWE, C. and PENKE, M. (1995) 'Introducing CP', GALA
    Proceedings, 1995, 5–22.
CRISMA, P. (1992) 'On the Acquisition of Wh Questions in French', *GenGenP*
    0, 115–22.
DUFFIELD, N. (1993) 'Roots and Rogues: Null Subjects in German Child Lan-
    guage', ms., University of Düsseldorf.
GIORGI, A. and F. PIANESI (1997) *Tense and Aspect: From Semantics to
    Morphosyntax*, Oxford University Press, New York/Oxford.
GREENFIELD, P. and J. SMITH (1976) *The Structure of Communication in Early
    Language Development*, Academic Press, New York.

GUASTI, T. (1996) 'The Acquisition of Italian Interrogatives', in H. Clahsen, (ed.), *Generative Perspectives on Language Acquisition*, Benjamins, Amsterdam/Philadelphia.

GUASTI, T. and L. RIZZI (1998) 'Agr and T as distinct Syntactic Positions: Evidence from Acquisition', ms., University of Siena.

GUILFOYLE, E. (1984) 'The Acquisition of Tense and the Emergence of Lexical Subjects in Child Grammars of English', *McGill Working Papers in Linguistics*.

HAEGEMAN, L. (1990) 'Non Overt Subjects in Diary Contexts', in J. Mascaro and M. Nespor (eds), *Grammar in Progress*, Foris, Dordrecht.

HAEGEMAN, L. (1995) 'Root Inifinitives, Tense and Truncated Structures in Dutch', *Language Acquisition* 4.

HAEGEMAN (1996a) 'Root Infinitives and Initial Null Subjects in Early Dutch', *GALA Proceedings*, 1996, 239–50.

HAEGEMAN, L. (1996b) 'Verb Second, the Split CP and Null Subjects in Early Dutch Finite Clauses', *GenGenP* 4, 133–75.

HAEGEMAN, L. (1997) 'Adult Null Subjects in non-Pro Drop Languages', to appear in Friedemann & Rizzi (eds.)

HAMANN, C. and K. PLUNKETT (1997) 'Subject Omission in Child Danish', *Boston University Conference on Language Development* 21, 220–31.

HAMANN, C., L. RIZZI and U. FRAUENFELDER (1996) 'On the Acquisition of Subject and Object Clitics in French', in H. Clahsen (ed.), *Generative Perspectives on Language Acquisition*, Benjamins, Amsterdam/Philadelphia.

HYAMS, N. (1986) *Language Acquisition and the Theory of Parameters*, Reidel, Dordrecht.

HYAMS, N. and T. SANO (1994) 'Agreement, Finiteness and the Development of Null Arguments', *NELS* 24.

HYAMS, N. and K. WEXLER (1993) 'On the Grammatical Basis of Null Subjects in Child Language', *Linguistic Inquiry* 24, 421–59.

INGHAM (1992) 'The Optional Subject Phenomenon in Young Children's English: A Case Study', *Journal of Child Language* 19, 133–51.

KAYNE, R. (1983) *Connectedness and Binary Branching*, Foris, Dordrecht.

KAYNE, R. (1994) *The Antisymmetry of Syntax*, MIT Press, Cambridge, MA.

KRAEMER (1993) 'The Licensing of Subjects in Early Child Language', *MITWP* 19, 197–212.

LEVOW, G. (1995) 'Tense and Subject Position in Interrogatives and Negatives in Child French', *MITWP* 26.

LIGHTBOWN, P. (1977) 'Constituency and Variation in the Acquisition of French', PhD dissertation, Columbia University.

MACWHINNEY, B. and C. SNOW (1985) 'The Child Language Data Exchange System', *Journal of Child Language* 17, 457–72.

MILLER, G. and N. CHOMSKY (1963) 'Finitary Models of Language Users', in R. Luce, R. Bush and E. Galanter (eds), *Handbook of Mathematical Psychology*, Vol. II, Whiley, New York, 419–92.

O'GRADY, W., PETERS, A. M. and MASTERSON, O. (1989) 'The Transition from Optional to Required Subjects', *Journal of Child Language* 16.

PHILLIPS, C. (1995) 'Syntax at Age Two: Cross-linguistic Differences', *MITWP* 26, 325–82.

PIERCE, A. (1992) *Language Acquisition and Syntactic Theory*, Kluwer, Dordrecht.

RADFORD, A. (1990) *The Acquisition of Syntactic Structures*, Basil Blackwell, London.

RASETTI, L. (1995) 'La distribution du sujet nul dans la grammaire enfantine du français', mémoire de licence, University of Geneva.

RIZZI, L. (1982) *Issues in Italian Syntax*, Foris, Dordrecht.

RIZZI, L. (1986) 'Null Subjects in Italian and the Theory of *pro*', *Linguistic Inquiry* **17**, 501–57.

RIZZI, L. (1990) *Relativized Minimality*, The MIT Press, Cambridge, MA.

RIZZI, L. (1992) 'Early Null Subjects and Root Null Subjects', *GenGenP* 1992, published in in T. Hoekstra and B. Schwartz (eds), *Language Acquisition Studies in Generative Grammar*, John Benjamins, Amsterdam/Philadelphia.

RIZZI, L. (1993/1994) 'Some Notes on Linguistic Theory and Language Development: The Case of Root Infinitives', *Language Acquisition* **3**.

RIZZI, L. (1997) 'The Fine Structure of the Left Periphery', in L. Haegeman (ed.), *Elements of Grammar*, Kluwer, Dordrecht.

ROEPER, T. and B. ROHRBACHER (1994) 'True Pro-drop in Child English and the Principle of Economy of Projection', ms., University of Massachusetts, Amherst.

SAFIR, K. (1992) 'Structural Economy', ms., Rutgers University.

SCHUETZE, K. (1997) 'Infl in Child and Adult Language', MIT dissertation.

SCHUETZE, K. and K. WEXLER (1996) 'Subject Case Licensing and English Root Infinitives', *Boston University Conference on Language Development* 20.

SPEAS, P. (1994) 'Null Arguments in a Theory of Economy of Projections', *University of Massachusetts Occasional Papers in Linguistics* **17**, 179–209.

STOWELL, T. (1981) 'Origins of Phrase Structure', PhD dissertation, MIT.

SUPPES, P., R. SMITH and M. LEVEILLÉ (1973) 'The French Syntax of a Child's Noun Phrases', *Archives de Psychologie* **42**, 207–69.

VALIAN, V. (1991) 'Syntactic Subjects in the Early Speech of American and Italian Children', *Cognition* **40**.

VALSECCHI, D. (1997) 'L'omissione del soggetto nel linguaggio dei bambini inglesi', Tesi di Laurea, Università di Bergamo.

WANG, Q., D. LILLO-MARTIN, C. BEST and A. LEVITT (1992) 'Null Subjects vs. Null Objects': Some Evidence from the Acquisition of Chinese and English', *Language Acquisition* **2**, 221–254.

WEXLER, K. (1994) 'Optional Infinitives, Head Movement and the Economy of Derivations in Child Grammar', in O. Lightfoot and N. Horstein (eds), *Verb Movement*, Cambridge University Press, Cambridge.

WEXLER, K. (1996) 'Maturation and Growth of Grammar', ms., MIT.

Chapter 11

The acquisition of verb placement in Lucernese Swiss German
Manuela Schönenberger

1 Introduction

This chapter focuses on the acquisition of verb placement in Swiss German and is based on data spontaneously produced by two children as they acquire the Lucernese variant of Swiss German. Swiss German, like German, is a Verb-Second (V2) language which generally displays the verb-final pattern in embedded clauses. The consensus in the literature is that children master verb placement early in their linguistic development, and accordingly the parameter regulating verb placement is set very early (see Wexler 1996, and in press). The data presented here conflict strongly with this widely held view: the striking fact about these data is that both children move the verb in any type of embedded clause, even in the presence of a complementizer, leading to a large number of verb placements which are not compatible with the adult grammar.

Although the children produce many verb-placement errors in embedded clauses, I argue that their underlying grammar is in fact minimally different from that of the adult. In the adult grammar, the presence of a complementizer blocks verb movement but I suggest that the children misanalyse certain complementizers as maximal projections, so that in their grammar C° is empty, which allows verb movement in embedded clauses. Once the complementizers are properly linked to the C-position around age 5;0, the verb-final pattern arises, and clauses displaying verb movement gradually disappear.

This chapter is organized as follows: section 2 describes the general verb-placement patterns in Swiss German, which basically coincide with those in German. Section 3 briefly reviews the literature on the acquisition of verb placement in German and Swiss German. The emerging result is that while German children do not seem to have any problems in placing the verb correctly in embedded clauses, Swiss-German children sometimes produce errors in this context. Section 4 summarizes the data of the two Lucernese children who, before age 5;0, productively make verb-placement errors in embedded but not main clauses. I concentrate on the embedded clauses introduced by a complementizer; these are discussed in section 4.1. In section 5, an account of the Lucernese acquisition data is given. Section 6 presents my conclusions.

2 Verb placement in Swiss German

2.1 Verb-placement patterns

Swiss German displays the V2-phenomenon in matrix clauses: the finite verb surfaces in the second position of the sentence and is preceded by one and only one maximal projection, illustrated in (1). Crucially, the maximal projection preceding the finite verb does not need to be the subject. It is an object in (1b) and a sentential adverb in (1c).

(1) a. De Rochus bacht hüt zwei chlini Rüeblitorte.
       the Rochus bakes today two small carrot-cakes
       'Rochus bakes two small carrot-cakes today.'
    b. Zwei chlini Rüeblitorte bacht hüt de Rochus.
       two small carrot-cakes bakes today the Rochus
    c. Hüt bacht de Rochus zwei chlini Rüeblitorte.
       today bakes the Rochus two small carrot-cakes

The verb typically occupies the clause-final position in embedded clauses.[1] It always occurs clause-finally in clauses introduced by a complementizer other than <u>wil</u> 'because' (2) and in restrictive relative clauses (3), which are introduced by the relative complementizer <u>wo</u>. For clarity of exposition I mark the embedded clauses by brackets and underline the finite verb form.

(2) a. T' Rahel freut sich [dass de Rochus eren Geburtstag nöd
       vergässe <u>hät</u>].
       the Rahel pleases self that the Rochus her birthday not forgotten has
       'Rahel is pleased that Rochus did not forget her birthday.'
    b. [Wenn de Rochus Schoggi öber<u>chunt</u>] isch er ganz seelig.
       when/if the Rochus chocolate gets is he totally blissful
       'When/if Rochus gets chocolate, he is very happy.'

(3) a. T' Rahel [wo de Rochus guet <u>mag</u>] überhüft en mit chline
       Gschenkli.
       the Rahel who the Rochus dear has heaps him with little presents
       'Rahel, who likes Rochus, heaps little presents on him.'

b. [Wo t'Rahel Geburtstag gha <u>hät</u>] sind alli iiglade worde.
when the Rahel birthday had has are all invited been
'When Rahel had her birthday, everybody was invited.'

Although embedded clauses usually show the verb-final pattern, verb movement in this context is sometimes possible in Swiss German (and German). In the absence of the complementizer <u>wenn</u> 'if', verb movement is possible in hypotheticals (and conditionals), as in (4a). It is also possible in the complement clauses of emotive-factive predicates (4b) if the complementizer <u>dass</u> 'that' is absent.

(4) a. [<u>Wär</u> de Rochus au as Fescht cho] heet t' Rahel schaurig Freud gha.
were the Rochus also to-the party come had the Rahel extremely pleasure had
'If Rochus had come to the party too, Rahel would have been very happy.'

b. De Rochus isch froh [<u>cha</u>-n-er so guet choche].
the Rochus is pleased can he so well cook
'Rochus is pleased that he can cook so well.'

Although the unmarked pattern of embedded questions is verb-final (5a), verb movement in this context is possible (5b). There is a subtle difference in meaning. (5b) is more directly linked to the discourse: rather than making a statement, as in (5a), in (5b) the speaker expects an answer from the addressee. In other words, (5b) is close in meaning to a direct question.

(5) a. I weiss nöd [wo-n-er häre <u>isch</u>].
I know not where he away is
'I don't know where he went.'

b. ?I weiss nöd [wo <u>isch</u> er häre].
I know not where is he away

Verb movement is possible in the complement clause of bridge verbs if these clauses are not introduced by <u>dass</u> (6a).

(6) a. Er hät gseit [er <u>hig</u> si gern].
he has said he have (subj) her dear
'He said he liked her.'

b. Er hät gseit [dass er si gern <u>hät</u>].
he has said that he her dear has
'He said that he liked her.'

Verb movement is also possible in clauses introduced by the complementizer <u>wil</u> 'because', which besides the verb-final pattern (7a) can also show the V2-pattern (7b), again entailing a difference in meaning.

Penner and Bader (1995) refer to wil-clauses with the verb-final pattern (7a) as *causal*, and to wil-clauses with the V2-pattern (7b) as *diagnostic*. While the flat bicycle tyre in (7a) is the reason for his not coming, in (7b) one can only deduce from the fact that his bicycle has a flat tyre that he is not coming. The diagnostic reading is most transparent in epistemic sentences, as in (7c), where the lit lights are not the cause of the dark, but rather serve as an indicator that it is dark.

(7) a. Er chunt hüt nüme [wil sis Velo en Platte hät].
    he comes today no more because his bike a flat one has
    'He won't come today because his bike has a flat tyre.'
   b. Er chunt hüt nüme [wil sis Velo hät en Platte].
    he comes today no more because his bike has a flat one
   c. Es mues tunkel gsi si [wil überall händ t'Liechter brennt].
    it must dark been be because everywhere have the lights burned
    'It must have been dark because the lights were on everywhere.'

2.2 Various analyses of verb movement

In this section three different analyses are outlined which can be used to account for verb placement in Swiss German.

The first analysis, which I shall refer to as 'the traditional analysis', traces its origins to the pioneering work by Koster (1975) and Den Besten (1977). The traditional analysis is based on the assumption that Swiss German and related languages have an underlying Subject Object Verb (SOV) order, and that there is a unique functional projection dominating IP. On the assumption that the underlying structure of Swiss German is SOV, it is generally claimed that in V2-clauses the CP-level is involved, independent of whether the subject or a non-subject precedes the finite verb. Thus in (8a) the subject, and in (8b) the direct object, has moved into [Spec,CP] and the finite verb has been raised to C°, giving rise to the V2-pattern.

(8) a. De Rochus ässt hüt en Oschtereier.
    the Rochus eats today an Easter egg
    'Rochus eats an Easter egg today.'
   b. Das Oschtereier ässt de Rochus hüt.
    this Easter egg eats the Rochus today
    'This Easter egg, Rochus eats today.'

Embedded clauses introduced by a complementizer, in which the finite verb occupies the clause-final position, as in (9), are analysed as involving string-vacuous movement of the verb to the head of a head-final IP. The C-position is occupied by a base-generated complementizer (dass), which blocks movement of the finite verb into C°. From this viewpoint the finite verb and the complementizer are in complementary distribution (cf. Den Besten 1977).

(9) I weiss [dass de Rochus en Oschtereier ässt].
    I know that the Rochus an Easter egg eats
    'I know that Rochus eats an Easter egg.'

To sum up, in an SOV(I) analysis the finite verb uniformly moves to C° in V2-clauses and to I° in head-final structures. The complementizer in C° and the finite verb are in complementary distribution.

In his analysis of verb movement in Dutch, which is based on the hypothesis that all languages are underlyingly Subject Verb Object (SVO), Zwart (1993, 1997) proposes that subject-initial clauses are to be distinguished from non-subject-initial clauses. This insight originated with Travis (1984, 1991), who observed a crucial contrast between the distribution of subject clitics and object clitics in German. While subject clitics can occur in clause-initial position in German, object clitics cannot. The same contrast obtains in Dutch (and Swiss German).[2]

In Zwart's analysis, the verb moves to I° in the subject-initial sentence (8a), and to C° in the non-subject-initial sentence (8b). The subject has moved to [Spec,IP] in both (8a) and (8b), while the object has moved to [Spec,AgrOP] in (8a) and to [Spec,CP] in (8b).

The finite verb does not raise to I° in embedded clauses introduced by a complementizer. To block verb movement to I°, Zwart suggests that there is abstract movement of I-to-C, the overt reflex of which can be found in complementizer-agreeing languages, shown in (10):

(10) a. [datst (do) jûn komst] (Frisian)
       that-2sg you tonight come-2sg
       'that you come tonight'
    b. [ob s du wëlls] (Luxemburgish)
       whether-2sg you want-2sg
       'if you want'

(Zwart 1997:138)

If verb movement to I° were not blocked in Zwart's system, the ungrammatical word-order in (11) would be derived:

(11) *[dass de Rochus ässt morn en Oschtereier]
     that the Rochus eats tomorrow an Easter egg

In an S(I)VO approach, the finite verb thus moves either to I° or to C° in matrix clauses, depending on whether the first constituent is a subject or a non-subject. In embedded clauses the finite verb remains *in situ*. There is no complementary distribution between the complementizer and the finite verb. The presence of the complementizer in C° does not block leftward movement of the verb to I°.

Based on data from Italian, French and English, Rizzi (1997, and this volume) suggests that the CP-layer consists of a number of discrete functional projections (cf. also Müller and Sternefeld 1993, Shlonsky 1994, Zwart 1997, among others). Force Phrase (ForceP) serves as a mediator between the matrix clause and the embedded clause and contains information about the illocutionary force, while Finite Phrase (FinP) serves as the link between ForceP and IP and contains information about the finiteness of the clause. Other functional projections below ForceP and above FinP can be activated, such as Focus Phrase (FocP), which hosts focused constituents as well as interrogative constituents, and Topic Phrase (TopP), which hosts topics.

Given a richer CP-system, the phenomenon of V2 need no longer receive a uniform analysis – in which the verb targets C° and a maximal projection targets [Spec,CP] – but becomes a cover term for verb movement to some head-position in the CP-domain, and movement of an XP to a specifier-position c-commanding that head-position (cf. Haegeman 1996). Note that the split-CP hypothesis is independent of the question of the underlying order of German and Swiss German.

The children of my study produce many examples of embedded V2 introduced by a complementizer in which the constituent intervening between the complementizer and the finite verb is generally the subject, as in (12) and (13). These word-orders are child-language-specific – indicated by the symbol % – and are excluded in the adult grammar. The crucial question to address is to what position the finite verb has moved, which is intertwined with the question of what position the subject occupies. In this chapter I argue that these subject-initial V2-clauses cannot be analysed as involving CP-recursion, an analysis which can be used to account for V2-clauses introduced by wil (section 4.1.1). Based on the assumption that pronominal subjects (12) do not necessarily occupy the same position as non-pronominal subjects (13), I propose that subject-initial embedded V2-clauses do not unambiguously show that IP in Swiss German is head-initial (section 4.1.2).

(12) %[Wenn s lütet no einisch] denn isch denn grad Pause. (M:4;11)
     when it rings still once then is DENN just break
     'When it rings once more then the break starts.'

(13) %Weisch du [dass t'Rahel hät drü Chind]? (M:5;0)
     know you that the Rahel has three children
     'Do you know that Rahel has three children?'

What I wish to show is that the verb does not target the same position in (12) and (13), although in both cases the subject intervenes between the complementizer and the finite verb. I shall argue instead that the verb targets the same position in (12) and (14) despite the difference in word-order. I try to account for this difference in word-order in terms of optional piggybacking of a pronominal subject on verb movement to C°.

(14) %[Wenn hät er Buchweh] cha-n-er nüt mache bim (E:3;11)
      Elefant.
      when has he bellyache can he nothing make for-the elephant
      'When he has a bellyache, he can't do anything for the elephant.'

A consequence of my analysis is that there is no stage during which the children systematically move the verb to a head-position of a head-initial IP, which would provide evidence for a Zwart-type analysis, but that before age 5;0 they consistently move the verb to C° in an embedded context. After age 5;0 the children start producing verb-final sentences much more frequently and sentences with verb movement become rare.

3 Review of the acquisition literature on verb placement

3.1 German acquisition literature on subordination
This section briefly reviews the literature on the acquisition of verb placement in German. The general claim is that German children place the verb correctly in embedded contexts, which is reflected in the following quote from Clahsen and Smolka (1985:150): 'Stage IV is characterized by the use of embedded clauses. It is most significant that we could not find any word-order error in subordinate clauses. Rather, the children always place the finite verbal element correctly in sentence-final position. . . . It has become evident that the children have no problems using verb-final patterns in embedded clauses'.

This claim is widespread in the German acquisition literature (Clahsen 1982, 1989, Mills 1985, Roeper 1973, Rothweiler 1993). Based on the production of 12 embedded sentences, all of which are verb-final, Clahsen (1982:68) concludes that children make no errors in embedded sentences. Mills (1985) contains a summary of the results from other studies, but does not contain new data. To the best of my knowledge, the only detailed study is Rothweiler (1993), who analysed some eight hundred embedded clauses produced by several monolingual German children.[3]

Only in 12 embedded clauses does the verb not occupy the clause-final position in an embedded clause which is not the complement of a bridge verb. In 9 of these the verb occurs in the second position after weil 'because', which is acceptable in certain varieties of German (cf. also (7b/c)). And in one instance, the verb occurs in the second position

TABLE 11.1   German (adapted from Rothweiler 1993)

Position of the finite verb	TOTAL	V2	V2 with _weil_	V-final
Relative clauses	85	1	0	84
Complementizer clauses	508	1	9	498
W-complements	207	1	0	206
Bridge-verb complements	28	28	0	0
Total	**828**	**31**	**9**	**788**

of a relative clause, which is also allowed in the target grammar (15). Note that German relative clauses generally display the verb-final pattern. The two instances where verb placement seems not to coincide with the adult grammar are shown in (16):

(15) Es gibt Menschen [die werfen einfach Dreck ausm (XI:5;06) me aufm Fenster].
there are people who throw simply dirt out of the on-the window
'There are people who simply throw garbage out of the window.'

(16) a. (%) sach ich se – [was sing ich]
say I sing (pause) what sing I
'I say what I sing.'
b.   % [weil möcht ich doch]
because want I really
'because I really want to'

(Rothweiler 1993:42)

Rothweiler's findings confirm Clahsen's original claim that German children do not produce verb-placement errors and that they use the verb-final pattern.

The number of utterances per embedded clause-type in Rothweiler's study are summarized in Table 11.1.

Gawlitzek-Maiwald *et al.* (1992) provide counter-evidence against the general claim that children place the verb correctly in embedded clauses. They observe that there is some significant variation among children. Their study is based on two monolingual children called Paul and Benny. While Paul performs as 'expected', Benny sometimes places the finite verb incorrectly. There seem to be two different patterns of mistakes: either Benny places the finite verb immediately after the complementizer (17a) or the W-word (17b), or there is a constituent between the complementizer and the finite verb, as in (18):

(17) a. %[wenn <u>hav</u> i au mal Burtstag habt] (3;1)
  when have I too once birthday had
  'when I had a birthday too'
 b. %Da war hoffentlich kein Ding da drauf [wo <u>tut</u> man (3;9)
  bügeln].
  there was hopefully no thing there upon which does one iron
  'Hopefully there was no such thing on it that one irons.'

(18) %Will die Meerjungfrau habe [dass du <u>has</u> net die (3;0)
  Meerjungfrau].
  want the mermaid have that you have not the mermaid
  'I want to have the mermaid so that you won't get the
  mermaid.'

(Gawlitzek *et al.* 1992: 146–7)

In summary, the standard claim is that monolingual German children place the verb correctly in embedded clauses. There seem to be a few counter-examples, but no quantitative analysis has been published.

3.2 Swiss-German literature on subordination

Given that verb placement in Swiss German essentially coincides with verb placement in German, one would expect young Swiss Germans to perform like their German peers. My data on two Swiss-German children acquiring Lucernese do not at all confirm this (see Schönenberger 1995, 1996, 1998). These children's verb placement in main clauses is entirely target-consistent (see Schönenberger 1998), but their verb placement in embedded clauses is not. Before discussing these data in section 4, I first turn to earlier studies of the acquisition of verb placement in Swiss German.

There are two studies on the acquisition of one of the Swiss-German dialects (Bernese), both by Penner (1990, 1996). Penner (1990) contains a study of some production data from four children; Penner (1996) is a longitudinal study of one child.

Two of the four children in Penner (1990) always place the verb correctly in embedded contexts, a third (Michael) makes only one verb-placement error, and the fourth (Simone) makes several errors.

The one error Michael produces occurs in a relative clause (19a). In his remaining relative clauses the verb is correctly placed. In the same environment, Simone incorrectly places the verb a number of times, as in (19b). In the grammatical cases, as in (20), it is unclear whether the surface position of the verb is due to verb movement to the left or to Verb-Projection Raising (VPR). Only the latter would be the target-consistent derivation.

(19) a. %dr Buur [wo <u>he</u> mer es Huus gmacht da] (M:2;10)
the farmer who have we a house made here
'the farmer for whom we built a house here'
   b. %O, lue das isch ds Bebe [wo <u>ha</u>-n-i usgschnitte]. (S:2;10)
o look here is the baby who have I cut out
'O look that is the baby that I have cut out.'

(20) nume die [wo <u>tüe</u> Töff fahre] (S:2;8)
only those who do motorbike drive
'only those who ride a motorbike'

(Penner 1990:177–8)

From my own examination of the part of the corpora reproduced
in Penner's article, it seems that the only context in which Simone
systematically moves the verb is in relative clauses. Thus her verb-
placement errors seem to be limited to a specific environment.

Penner's (1996) study of child J. is based on diary data and elicitation data and covers the entire acquisition of subordination, from the
emergence of the very first embedded clauses without an overt complementizer up to the productive use of doubly-filled COMPs. What
becomes clear in the case of child J. is that an item-by-item acquisition
of the complementizers proceeds in parallel with the U-shape of her
grammatical verb placement.

Embedded clauses which lack a complementizer first appear a few
days before J.'s 2nd birthday and show the verb-final pattern:

(21) a. mau luege [chaut <u>isch</u>] (J:2;01,12)
want look cold is
'let's look (whether) it is cold'
   b. grosse Schnägg [Pfüseli <u>het</u>] (J:2;01,18)
big snail feelers has
'big snail (which) has feelers'

The gradual onset of complementizer-insertion at age 2;04 coincides
with the acquisition of generalized V2 in matrix clauses. The first utterance containing a complementizer is produced at the same time as the
first target-consistent W-questions and topicalizations in matrix clauses.
Besides a few clauses which lack a complementizer, there are several
instances of relative clauses introduced by <u>wo</u>. The clauses which are
not introduced by a complementizer disappear within a month and the
number of complementizers increases:

(22) a. e Schnägg [wo Pfüseli <u>isch</u>] (J:2;03,30)
a snail which feelers is
   b. so [wi de Luca <u>het</u>] (J:2;08,15)
so (the same) as the Luca has

   c. [wen i use <u>wöu</u>] (J:2;08,10)
     if/when I outside want
   d. tue warte [bis d'Ima <u>chunt</u>] (J:2;10,11)
     do wait until the mummy comes

Around age 3;2 the predominant verb-final pattern is given up. For several months – 3;02–3;05,15 – the child vacillates between using the verb-final pattern and the V2-pattern. The latter is only attested in W-complements and <u>wo</u>-relatives, illustrated in (23). W-complements are sometimes compatible with verb movement in the target grammar (cf. example (5b)), while restrictive relative clauses are not:

(23) a. %lueg do [wi <u>chunt</u>'s nid] (J:3;04,09)
     look there how comes it not
   b. %dr Peter [wo <u>het</u> es Seili] (J:3;04,25)
     the Peter who has a rope

This ungrammatical verb-placement pattern is gradually replaced by a verb-copying pattern, shown in (24). J. uses verb copying for several months (3;04,24–3;11).

(24) a. %so eine Traktor [wo <u>hei</u> mir nid gfunde <u>hei</u>] (J:3;05,07)
     such a tractor which have we not found have
   b. %[wenn i <u>ha</u> d'Schuttbaue <u>ha</u>] (J:3;06,09)
     if/when I have the football have

The first embedded declarative V2-structures emerge around the age of 3;6, shown in (25a). The acquisition of these V2-structures is assumed to be a prerequisite for CP-recursion in clauses introduced by <u>wöu</u> 'because', as in (25b), which involve a degree-2 embedding of V2.

(25) a. I ha gmeint [das <u>sig</u> Chueche]. (J:3;05,15)
     I have thought this be (subj.) cake
   b. [wöu i <u>cha</u> nid alleini schribe] (J:3;09,04)
     because I cannot alone write

The final stage of the acquisition process is marked by the emergence of <u>dass</u> in complement clauses (26a) just before J.'s fourth birthday and the use of doubly-filled COMPs (26b) 11 months later:

(26) a. I ha wöuue [dass si ou <u>lüchte</u>]. (J:3;11,12)
     I have wanted that they also shine
   b. Lue mau [wi längi Finger dass i <u>ha</u>]. (J:4;10,12)
     look once how long fingers that I have

A summary of the various verb-placement patterns is contained in Table 11.2.

TABLE 11.2   Verb placement in embedded clauses (child J.)

Clauses without a complementizer	18
Ungrammatical verb placement	21
Grammatical V2 (bridge-verbs)	53
Grammatical V2 (with <u>wöu</u>)	10
Verb copying	34
Verb-final	900
Total	**1036**

4 The Lucernese acquisition data

My acquisition data on Lucernese comprise the embedded sentences
of two children (Moira and Eliza) who have been recorded for more
than two years. Moira's corpus contains 3980 embedded sentences, in
which the verb placement is unambiguous, i.e. does not coincide with a
derivation involving VPR, and Eliza's contains 492 embedded sentences. From age 3;10 – the beginning of the recordings – to age 4;11,
these embedded sentences look quite uniform: the vast majority of these
sentences display verb movement (27–29), and only very few display
the verb-final pattern (30), or verb copying (31):

(27) a. %Det hät s no es Eili [wo <u>chamm</u>ǝr ned uftue]. (E:4;11)
there has it still a little egg which can-one not open
'There is still a little egg which one cannot open.'
   b. %[Wo <u>händ</u>'s gsunge] händ's gsunge 'ich bin (M:4;6)
doch au schwarz'.
when have – they sung have – they sung I am DOCH also black
'When they (the ravens) sang, they sang "I am also black".'

(28) a. %[Wenn <u>hät</u> er Buchweh] cha-n-er nüt mache bim (E:3;11)
Elefant.
when has he bellyache can he nothing make for-the elephant
'When he has a bellyache, he can't do anything for the
elephant.'
   b. %Weiss si [dass ich <u>go</u> hüt nomitag furt]? (E:5;0)
knows she that I go today afternoon away
'Does she know that I am going away this afternoon?'
   c. Du chasch mit de Tanja schpile [wil morn z'obig (M:4;3)
<u>chum</u> ich zu dir].
you can with the Tanja play because tomorrow evening
come I to you
'You can play with Tanja because I am going to come to
your place tomorrow evening.'

(29) a. %Ich weiss nur [wo tuetmər abschtelle]. (M:4;4)
    I know only where does-one off-turn
    'I only know where one turns (it) off.'
  b. %De weiss si [wie tüend t'Chind lere rede]. (E:4;0)
    then knows she how do the children learn speak
    'Then she knows how the children learn to speak.'

(30) a. [Wenn ich es Autöli mache] mues ich . . . (M:3;11)
    when/if I a little car make must I
    'When/if I make a little car, I have to . . .'
  b. [wenn ich die aalegge] (E:4;4)
    when/if I this one on put
    'when/if I put on this one'

(31) a. %nochether [wo hät s fertig gschlofe hät] (M:4;4)
    afterwards when has it finish sleep has
    'afterwards when it finished sleeping'
  b. %Ich ha gern Eier [wo sind ehm no t'Schale dra (M:4;11)
    sind].
    I have dear eggs which are e still the shell on are
    'I like eggs which still have their shell.'

Around age 5;0, a transition occurs in Moira's linguistic development (and slightly later in Eliza's case) which is reflected in the onset of verb-final sentences and the drastic increase in verb copying. The onset of verb-final sentences is accompanied by a decrease in verb-movement constructions, but these only gradually disappear.

There are two properties which are particularly striking in these data. (i) The children almost exclusively move the verb in embedded clauses for an extended period of time and do not use the verb-final pattern. (ii) Before the onset of the verb-final pattern, clauses introduced by complementizers other than wil 'because' (mainly wenn 'when, if' and dass 'that') sometimes show the V1-pattern (28a) and sometimes the V2-pattern (28b), while restrictive relative clauses show only the V1-pattern (27) and clauses introduced by wil show only the V2-pattern (28c). W-complements display the V2-pattern (29) before the gradual onset of the verb-final pattern.

The observation that before the onset of the verb-final constructions two different verb-placement patterns can be found in clauses introduced by complementizers other than wil, while in all other contexts the children opt for just one verb-placement pattern, is puzzling, and will be examined in section 4.1. Only the data of one of the children (Moira) will be taken into account, since this child has been recorded much more regularly than Eliza and her corpus is much more extensive.

4.1 A closer examination of Moira's complementizer-introduced sentences

In this section I concentrate solely on clauses which are introduced by a complementizer, because they are the only type of clauses which display the V1-pattern as well as the V2-pattern.

I assume that in all the clauses listed in (32), which do not show any alternative pattern with verb movement in the child data, the verb has moved to C°.[4]

(32) a. W-word V_{fin} . . .
    b. relative complementizer wo V_{fin} . . .[5]
    c. bridge-verb . . . [XP V_{fin} . . .

The finding that the verb surfaces in two seemingly different positions in clauses introduced by a complementizer is surprising. In (33) the verb precedes the subject, whereas in (34) it follows the subject, suggesting that the verb does not move to C° in the latter. I shall show (i) that examples of type (34) cannot be analysed as involving CP-recursion, and (ii) that examples of type (34a) and type (34b) should not be analysed along similar lines. In particular, I want to show that (34a) – like (33) – involves verb movement to C°, whereas (34b) involves verb movement to a head-position below C° if a non-split CP system is adopted.

(33) complementizer V_{fin} Subject$_{pronominal/non-pronominal}$ · · · V1

(34) a. complementizer Subject$_{pronominal}$ V_{fin} · · ·   V2
    b. complementizer Subject$_{non-pronominal}$ V_{fin} · · ·   V2

4.1.1 A comparison between V2-clauses introduced by wil and by other complementizers

In this section I shall compare Moira's V2-sentences introduced by wil with her V2-sentences introduced by other complementizers. I shall focus on what kind of constituent intervenes between the complementizer and the finite verb, i.e. Z in (35):

(35) complementizer Z V_{fin} . . . .

It will be shown that Moira's clauses introduced by wil show properties which are typical of matrix clauses in the adult grammar, whereas her clauses introduced by a complementizer other than wil have properties which are typical of embedded clauses in the adult grammar.

There is a further difference between these two types of embedded V2-clauses relating to the occurrence of a non-pronominal subject.

Pronominal subjects are attested in any type of V2-clause introduced by a complementizer, but non-pronominal subjects are not. While non-pronominal subjects are attested in the initial position of V2-clauses introduced by <u>wil</u> from the beginning of the recordings, they are absent from this position in V2-clauses introduced by other complementizers until around the age of 5;0. This difference plays a minor role in the present section, but is at the heart of the discussion in section 4.1.2.

4.1.1.1 Topicalization Moira quite frequently uses topicalization in V2-clauses introduced by <u>wil</u>. 60 of 342 (18%) V2-clauses introduced by <u>wil</u> involve topicalization:

(36) a. ja [wil döt <u>hät</u> s ä schwarzes Gitter] (M:4;1)
yes because there has it a black fence
'yes, because there is a black fence there'
b. Die muesch do lo [wil die <u>wott</u> ich ned]. (M:5;4)
these must-2sg there leave because these want I not
'You must leave these here because I don't want them.'

Moira rarely uses topicalization in V2-clauses introduced by other complementizers. There are only 4 such examples (2%) in a total of 181 V2-clauses, illustrated in (37):

(37) a. % . . . [wenn etz <u>wär</u> ein abkeit] (M:5;7)
if now were one down-fallen
'if now one had fallen down'
b. % . . . [bis einisch amene Tag <u>isch</u> de Wolf zum (M:6;0)
Strohhüsli cho]
until once on-a day is the wolf to-the straw-hut come
'until one day the wolf came to the straw-hut'

Although superficially Moira's V2-clauses introduced by a complementizer look alike, there is a difference with respect to topicalization, which is attested much more frequently in clauses introduced by <u>wil</u> than in clauses introduced by other complementizers.

4.1.1.2 The distribution of pronominal subjects[6] Pronominal subjects (e.g. <u>ich</u> 'I') which can occur either preverbally (<u>ich</u> V_{fin} . . .) or post-verbally (V_{fin}/complementizer <u>ich</u> . . .), can be found in any V2-clause introduced by a complementizer in the child data, shown in (38):

(38) a. Etz cha-n-i halt ned rede [wil ich <u>han</u> s Muul (M:4;9)
voll].
now can I HALT nod speak because I have the mouth full
'I cannot speak now because my mouth is full.'
b. %Jo [wenn ich <u>weiss</u> ned wo] (M:4;6)
JO when I know not where
'but I don't know where'

    c. %Ich bin so fröhlich [dass ich <u>bin</u> so froh]. (M:4;6)
        I am so glad that I am so happy
    d. %. . . hät gseit [öb ich <u>well</u> die] (M:4;7)
        has said if I want these

Pronominal subjects which are restricted to the preverbal position,
however, are found only in V2-clauses introduced by <u>wil</u> (39), but not
in V2-clauses introduced by other complementizers.

(39) a.   Weisch worum? [wil es <u>isch</u> Winter]. (M:4;3)
           know 2sg why because it is winter
           'Do you know why – because it is winter.'
     b.   . . . [wil me lueget immer Aladin] (M:4;7)
           because we watch always Aladdin
           'because we always watch Aladdin'
     c.   . . . [wil si <u>wend</u> ned [dass t'Chind mitenand (M:5;2)
           schpilet]]
           because they want not that the children with each other
           play
           'because they do not want the children to play with each
           other'

On the other hand, pronominal subjects which are restricted to the
postverbal position are attested in the V2-clauses introduced by the
complementizers <u>dass</u> 'that' and <u>wenn</u> 'when, if', shown in (40). There
is only one case in which such a pronominal subject occurs in a V2-
clause introduced by <u>wil</u> (41).

(40) a. %ersch [wenn't <u>häsch</u> es eis] . . . (M:4;9)
         only when-you have a one [when throwing a dice]
     b. %De muesmər lang schlofe [wemmər <u>isch</u> früe is (M:4;7)
         Bett gange].
         then must-one long sleep when/if-one is early in-the bed
         gone
         'One has to sleep for a long time when/if one goes to bed
         early.'
     c. %[dass-mər <u>gönd</u> abe] (M:5;9)
         that-we go verbal particle
         'that we go downstairs'
     d. %[wenn's <u>hetet</u> ebe no s'Papier] (M:5;11)
         if-they had EBE still the paper
         'if they still had the paper'

(41) % . . . [wil's <u>sind</u> rund] (M:5;5)
      because-they are round

To sum up, pronominal subjects which are restricted to the preverbal position are only attested in V2-clauses introduced by <u>wil</u> (32 cases), whereas those restricted to a postverbal position are only attested in V2-clauses introduced by complementizers other than <u>wil</u> (19 cases). There is just one exception to this generalization (example (41)).

4.1.1.3 The distribution of non-pronominal subjects An unexpected difference between V2-clauses introduced by <u>wil</u> and V2-clauses introduced by other complementizers appears when looking at the distribution of non-pronominal subjects. I draw a distinction between pronominal subjects which are weak pronouns (e.g. <u>me(r)</u> 'we') or clitics (e.g. <u>mər</u> 'we'), and non-pronominal subjects which are nominal expressions (e.g. <u>t'Chue</u> 'the cow'), strong pronouns (e.g. <u>mir</u> 'we') or demonstrative pronouns (e.g. <u>die</u> 'that one'). While pronominal as well as non-pronominal subjects are found in clause-initial position of <u>wil</u>-clauses from the beginning of the recordings at age 3;10, pronominal subjects occur a year before non-pronominal subjects in V2-clauses introduced by complementizers other than <u>wil</u>.

The first occurrence of a non-pronominal subject in a V2-clause introduced by each type of complementizer is shown in (42) and (43):

(42) . . . [wil dä <u>hät</u> nur ein Fuess] (M:3;10)
      because that one has only one foot

(43) a. %Vorher hät s usgsee [wie das <u>wär</u> de Chopf]. (M:4;11)
        before has it out-looked as (if) this were the head
        'Beforehand it looked as if this were the head.'
   b. %Weisch du [dass t'Rahel <u>hät</u> drü Chind]? (M:5;0)
        know you that the Rahel has three children
        'Do you know that Rahel has three children?'
   c. %Ich weiss ned [öb de Schleier <u>goot</u> bis det abe]. (M:5;4)
        I know not whether the veil goes until there down
        'I do not know whether the veil reaches down to here.'
   d. %Am beschte isch [wenn die <u>sind</u> z'vorderscht (M:5;4)
        [wo wüsset de Weg]].
        to-the best is if those are at-the front who know the way
        'It's best if those are at the front who know the way.'

To sum up, in the child data V2 is found both in clauses introduced by <u>wil</u> and in clauses introduced by other complementizers. An examination of the V2-patterns found in Moira's corpus reveals that two types of sentences must be distinguished, although both are superficially of the type (44):

(44) complementizer Z V_{fin} . . .

The differences between the two types of embedded V2-patterns emerge when we consider the nature of Z, the constituent intervening between the complementizer and the finite verb. Two contrasts are shown to obtain: (i) <u>wil</u>-sentences allow for Z to be a topic, sentences introduced by other complementizers do not; (ii) in sentences introduced by a complementizer other than <u>wil</u>, Z can be an enclitic on C°; Z is not an enclitic on <u>wil</u>.

V2-clauses introduced by <u>wil</u> share properties with matrix clauses. I therefore suggest that they can be analysed as instances of CP-recursion:

(45) [$_{CP}$ [$_{C'}$ wil [$_{CP}$ XP V$_{fin}$ . . .

V2-clauses which are introduced by complementizers other than <u>wil</u> do not share properties with matrix clauses. They cannot therefore be analysed as involving CP-recursion.

4.1.2 A comparison between V1-and V2-clauses introduced by complementizers other than wil

The observation that until the age of 4;11 there are no non-pronominal subjects in V2-clauses introduced by complementizers other than <u>wil</u> merits further scrutiny. Based on the distribution of pronominal and non-pronominal subjects, I propose that 'early' V2-clauses (47a) are V1-clauses in disguise (46), while 'late' V2-clauses (47b) are not. I claim that in 'early' V2-clauses the verb moves to the same position as in V1-clauses, and that the verb moves to a different position in 'late' V2-clauses, which arise at the same age as verb-final constructions.

(46) complementizer V$_{fin}$ Subject . . .   V1

(47) a. complementizer Subject$_{pronominal}$ V$_{fin}$ · · ·   'early' V2
      b. complementizer Subject$_{non-pronominal/pronominal}$ V$_{fin}$ · · ·   'late' V2

Figure 11.1 shows the distribution of pronominal subjects.[7] Pronominal subjects are attested in embedded V1-clauses as well as in V2-clauses. They are also found in verb-final clauses, which are very rare before age 4;11.

Figure 11.2 below shows the distribution of non-pronominal subjects. In contrast to pronominal subjects, non-pronominal subjects occur only in V1-constructions before age 4;11. After age 4;11 non-pronominal subjects are mainly found in verb-final constructions. They also occur in V2-constructions, but very rarely in V1-constructions.

I take the appearance of non-pronominal subjects in V2-constructions after age 4;11 to reflect a major change in the underlying child grammar. If non-pronominal subjects occupy [Spec,IP] in these V2-constructions then the verb cannot have moved to C°, but must have moved to a lower functional head:

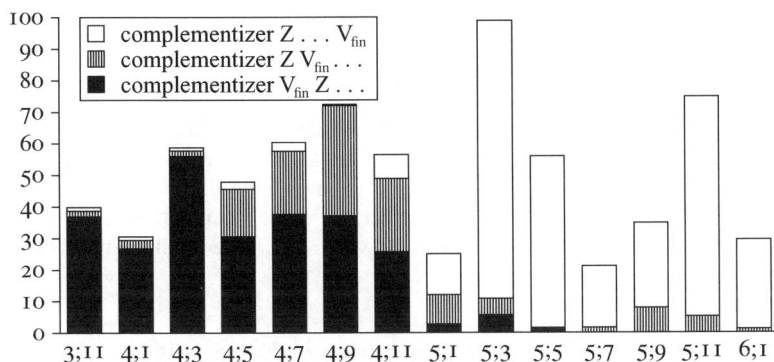

	weak subject pronoun	subject enclitic
complementizer V_{fin} Z . . .	176	87
complementizer Z V_{fin} . . .	112	19
complementizer Z . . . V_{fin}	255	63

FIGURE 11.1 Distribution of pronominal subjects in embedded clauses (Moira)

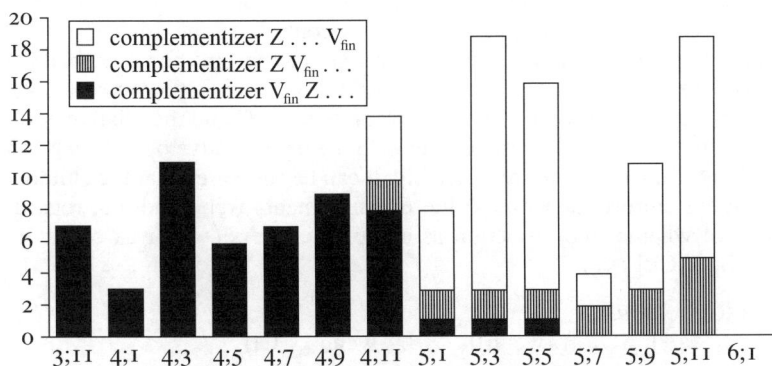

	non-pronominal subject
complementizer V_{fin} Z . . .	54
complementizer Z V_{fin} . . .	18
complementizer Z . . . V_{fin}	62

FIGURE 11.2 Distribution of non-pronominal subjects in embedded clauses (Moira)

(48) %Und do hät s gschpilt [$_{CP}$ dass [$_{IP}$ s Ross <u>goot</u> (M:5;0)
     zum Zauberer]].
     and then has it played that the horse goes to-the magician

In section 5, I shall suggest that in all 'early' V2-clauses the verb has
moved to C°, and that in 'late' V2-clauses the verb has moved to a
lower functional head, for example I°. I make the division into 'early'
and 'late' V2-clauses dependent on the first occurrence of a non-
pronominal subject, in which the verb has clearly not undergone
movement to C°, as in example (48) above.

5 An account of the Lucernese acquisition data

Consider example (49) in which the verb <u>schterbt</u> 'dies' precedes the
non-pronominal subject <u>s Schneewittli</u> 'Snow White' and follows the
complementizer <u>dass</u> 'that'. If the non-pronominal subject occupies
[Spec,IP], then the verb cannot be in I°, but must be in a higher functional head:

(49) %Aber si wott [dass <u>schterbt</u> s Schneewittli]. (M:4;5)
     but she wants that dies the Snow White
     'But she wants Snow White to die.'

The crucial question to address is what position the finite verb occupies given that the complementizer is associated with the C-position
in the adult grammar. I suggest that in contrast to the adult grammar
the complementizer does not occupy C° in the children's embedded
V1-clauses, but [Spec,CP]. At first sight, this seems rather implausible,
but given that the complementizer <u>wenn</u> 'when, if' and the relative complementizer <u>wo</u> are homophonous with the interrogative operators <u>wenn</u>
'when' and <u>wo</u> 'where' respectively, it can be suggested that the children
assign a uniform analysis to the overt elements <u>wenn</u> and <u>wo</u>, regardless of whether they function as complementizers (50) or as operators
in [Spec,CP] (51):

(50) *adult*   *child*
    a. [$_{CP}$ OP [$_{C'}$ wenn]]   [$_{CP}$ wenn [$_{C'}$ C]]
    b. [$_{CP}$ OP [$_{C'}$ wo]]   [$_{CP}$ wo [$_{C'}$ C]]

(51) *adult*   *child*
    a. [$_{CP}$ wenn [$_{C'}$ C]]   [$_{CP}$ wenn [$_{C'}$ C]]
    b. [$_{CP}$ wo [$_{C'}$ C]]   [$_{CP}$ wo [$_{C'}$ C]]

<u>Wil</u> 'because', on the other hand, seems to be treated as a head in the
child grammar. <u>Wil</u> might be correctly analysed as a head by the children either because <u>wil</u> does not have a homophonous counterpart which

is a maximal projection in the target grammar, or because wil can also function as a conjunction rather than a complementizer. Conjunctive wil translates into German denn, and is compatible with the V2-pattern in the adult grammar.

Moira uses wenn, wo and wil from the beginning of the recorded period. Other complementizers, such as dass 'that', öb 'whether if' and wie 'as' are acquired a couple of months later. I suggest that once new complementizers are added to the class of complementizers they are all assigned the same X-bar status as the original two members of that class (wenn and wo): they are misanalysed as maximal projections in [Spec,CP] rather than as heads in C°.

If the children do indeed misanalyse the complementizers as maximal projections, then the C-position is not filled and the verb can move into it, giving rise to embedded V-to-C movement.[8]

The analysis proposed here allows us to account for the postverbal position of non-pronominal subjects in embedded V1-sentences, which I assume to occupy the subject position, i.e. [Spec,IP]:

(52) $[_{CP}$ complementizer $[_{C'}$ V_{fin} $[_{IP}$ non-pronominal subject . . .

Besides the V1-pattern, for which I assume that the verb moves to C°, Moira also produces the V2-pattern in clauses introduced by a complementizer other than wil. In these embedded V2-clauses the constituent which intervenes between the complementizer and the finite verb is generally the subject. Crucially, this subject is always pronominal before age 4;11. I suggest that in these embedded V2-constructions the verb also moves to C° and that the pronominal subject can piggyback on verb movement to C°, giving rise to a superficial V2-pattern. It is essential for me to assume that pronominal subjects are treated as heads in child grammar.[9]

The non-occurrence of non-pronominal subjects between the complementizer and the finite verb before age 4;11 can be explained straightforwardly. Non-pronominal subjects are maximal projections which cannot piggyback on verb movement to C°. Therefore all non-pronominal subjects, which I assume to occupy [Spec,IP], follow the verb, resulting in the V1-pattern.

The advantage of such an analysis is that in all the embedded clauses displaying verb movement the verb targets the same position, i.e. C°, before age 4;11.

At some stage in their linguistic development the children must learn that all complementizers are heads. I suggest that the distribution of doubly-filled COMPs is the trigger for the reanalysis of the complementizers. In the target grammar, doubly-filled COMPs occur in W-complements (53a) and certain free relative clauses (53b). Doubly-filled COMPs are frequently used in W-complements in the target grammar.

(53) a. I weiss nöd [worum dass de Beowulf de Grendel aagriffe hät].
I know not why that the Beowulf the Grendel attacked has
'I don't know why Beowulf attacked Grendel.'
b. Si tanzt [mit wem dass si wott].
she dances with whom that she wants
'She dances with whomever she pleases.'

Since the children know that the interrogative constituent worum
'why' in (53a) is a maximal projection, which can be deduced from
their forming correct matrix-constituent questions, the co-occurrence of
dass with an interrogative constituent in the CP-domain will lead them
to abandon the assumption that dass is a maximal projection once they
become aware of the doubly-filled COMPs in the input data. I suggest
that the reanalysis of dass as a head entails a reanalysis of all lexical
items with the same function, i.e. the whole class of complementizers
(i.e. wenn, öb, wie, etc.).

As a result of this reanalysis, the majority of clauses introduced by
complementizers start to show the verb-final pattern. While in clauses
introduced by these complementizers there is a sudden increase in the
production of embedded verb-final clauses and a rapid decrease in
verb-movement constructions around age 5;0, this development is less
pronounced in relative clauses (and W-complements).

I suggest that the relative complementizer wo is not reanalysed as a
head at the same time as the other complementizers. To link the relative
complementizer wo to C° the child might need access to a doubly-filled
COMP of the type in (54a), which rarely occurs in the input. Although
these doubly-filled COMPs are possible in certain Swiss-German dialects, including certain varieties of Lucernese, there is a preference
to use a relative construction involving a resumptive pronoun, as in
(54b):

(54) a. Das isch de Bueb [mit dem wo 'Miriam tanzet hät].
this is the boy with this one that the Miriam danced has
'This is the boy with whom Miriam danced.'
b. Das isch de Bueb [wo 'Miriam mit em tanzet hät].
this is the boy that the Miriam with him danced has

In the vast majority of cases the verb is spelled out in the base-
position in embedded clauses after age 5;0, in agreement with the target
grammer. However, occasionally it is spelled out in functional head-
positions below C°, which sometimes yields V2-constructions in which
the initial constituent is a non-pronominal subject. These late verb-
movement examples could ultimately be used to argue for the existence
of head-initial functional projections below CP.

6 Conclusions

This chapter has focused on the natural production data of two Lucernese children. A striking fact of these data is that the children produce many verb-placement errors in embedded clauses, while their matrix clauses are adult-like. Before age 4;11, they consistently move the verb in embedded clauses and very rarely use the verb-final pattern. They move the verb in any type of embedded clause, even in clauses introduced by a complementizer (55a/b). Verb movement in clauses introduced by a complementizer is non-target-consistent, except in those introduced by the complementizer wil 'because', which are compatible with verb movement in the adult grammar (56).

(55) a. complementizer V_{fin} Z ... V1
     b. complementizer Z V_{fin} ... V2

(56) wil Z V_{fin} ...   V2

The children produce many sentences of type (55a) at the same time as they produce those of type (55b). They also produce many wil-clauses (56).

A detailed examination of the constituent Z in these constructions revealed that:

(57) a. Z is generally the subject in (55), while it can be a subject or a topic in (56).
     b. Z in (55a) is either a pronominal or a non-pronominal subject, while before age 4;11 Z is always a pronominal subject in (55b).

Based on the observation in (57a), I argued that superficial V2-constructions cannot be analysed along similar lines: while V2-clauses introduced by wil can be analysed as involving CP-recursion, V2-clauses introduced by other complementizers cannot. Moreover, I interpreted the difference relating to the realization of the subject in (57b) as highly significant. I argued that the complementizer-introduced V2-sentences in (55b), in which Z is generally the subject, contrary to appearances, do not unambiguously support an analysis of Swiss German involving head-initial IP and verb movement to I°.

Based on the assumptions in (58), I proposed instead that the verb moves to C° in both (55a) and (55b):

(58) a. The children misanalyse the complementizers as maximal projections.
     b. Pronominal subjects (i.e. weak pronouns/clitics) are heads in child grammar.

316 THE ACQUISITION OF SYNTAX

I accounted for the difference in word-order between (55a) and (55b) in terms of optional piggybacking of the pronominal subject on verb movement to C°.

After age 5;0 the verb-final pattern arises, and constructions of type (55) gradually disappear. I suggested that the acquisition of doubly-filled COMPs around age 5;0 triggers a reanalysis of the complementizers as heads. Once these are linked to the C-position, verb movement to C° is no longer an option in the child grammar. The reanalysis of the complementizers thus leads to a drastic increase in verb-final constructions and sometimes to verb movement to a head-position below C°. This in turn occasionally gives rise to 'V2-constructions' in which Z can also be a non-pronominal subject.

One of the questions which I have not addressed here is why the Lucernese children productively make verb-placement errors whereas neither the German children nor the Bernese children seem to do so. My account of the Lucernese acquisition data is based on a lexical miscategorization of the class of complementizers as maximal projections due to homophony with certain interrogative constituents. I tentatively suggest that in German and Bernese no such confusion arises. In German the interrogative constituent wann 'when' is not homophonous with the complementizer wenn, and relative clauses are generally introduced by der, die, das, which do not occupy C°. Whatever blocks verb movement in these relative clauses (but see example (15)) has nothing to do with an overt element in C°. In the case of Bernese, the complementizer wenn can also sometimes be pronounced as we, whereas the interrogative constituent is always wenn (cf. Penner 1996). Zvi Penner (p.c.) informs me that there is a difference in vowel-length between the relative complementizer wo and interrogative wo in Bernese. These features are consistent with my tentative suggestion.

Notes

1 Due to Verb-Projection Raising (VPR), which is preponderant in Swiss German, the verb-final character of this language is often masked, as in (i), where the finite verb wöt 'wants' of the embedded clause does not surface in the clause-final position (cf. Haegeman and Van Riemsdijk 1986).

(i) T' Rahel hofft [dass hüt de Rochus wöt mindeschtens zwei Rüeblitorte bache].
the Rahel hopes that today the Rochus wants at least two carrot-cakes bake
'Rahel hopes that Rochus wants to bake at least two carrot-cakes today.'

Based on the underlying structure in (iia), the word-order in (i) can be accounted for by assuming that the complement of wöle has undergone rightward adjunction to the maximal projection headed by wöt, sketched in (iib) (cf. Haegeman 1992).

(ii) a. . . . dass hüt de Rochus mindeschtens zwei Rüeblitorte bache wöle
that today the Rochus at least two carrot-cakes bake wants
b. . . . dass hüt de Rochus t$_i$ wöt [mindeschtens zwei Rüeblitorte bache]$_i$

2 For arguments against an analysis which makes a structural distinction between subject-initial clauses and non-subject-initial clauses, see Schwartz and Vikner (1996).

3 The children's age-range is given in (i):

(i)
Carsten	(CA)	3;06
Daniel	(DA)	3;02–3;06
Marianne	(MA)	3;03–3;10
Martin	(MT)	2;09–3;08
Oliver	(OL)	4;00–4;10
Simone	(SI)	4;01–4;03
Xilla	(XI)	5;03–5;06

4 If a split-CP system is embraced, the verb has moved to a functional head of the C-domain.

5 As pointed out in the introduction, I assume that the children initially misanalyse certain complementizers, including the relative complementizer wo, as maximal projections in [Spec,CP] (see section 5). This assumption is not necessary in a split-CP framework (see notes 8 and 9).

6 The distribution of certain pronominal subjects is unrestricted, while the distribution of other pronominal subjects is restricted. The former can either occur preverbally (i) or postverbally (iia) in the adult as well as the child grammar. The postverbal position (iia) is often compared with the post-complementizer position (iib):

(i) Ich gang morn is Dorf.
I go tomorrow in-the village
(ii) a. Morn gang ich is Dorf.
tomorrow go I in-the village
b. [dass ich morn is Dorf gang]
that I tomorrow in-the village go

Pronominal subjects whose distribution is restricted cannot freely occur in either preverbal or postverbal position. Some of these pronominal subjects are restricted to the preverbal position (e.g. the weak pronoun me 'we'), while others are restricted to the postverbal (or post-complementizer) position (e.g. the clitic mər 'we'):

(iv) Me/*mər gönd morn is Dorf.
we$_{weak pronoun}$ we$_{clitic}$ go tomorrow in-the village
(v) a. Morn gömmər/*me is Dorf.
tomorrow go we$_{clitic}$ we$_{weak pronoun}$ in-the village
b. [dassmər/*me morn is Dorf gönd]
that we$_{clitic}$ we$_{weak pronoun}$ tomorrow in-the village go

7 The labels on the abscissa refer to the mean age of the child: e.g. 3;11 (3 years 11 months) covers the period from 3;10 to 4;0, etc., and the labels on the ordinate refer to the number of times the sentence in question is produced.

8 Although the homophony hypothesis does work, it may not be the only analysis possible. If a split-CP system is embraced, the finite verb in the children's V1-clauses (and 'early' V2-clauses) can move to a head-position in the C-domain which is different from the head-position occupied by the complementizer (see also note 9).

9 The assumption that all pronominal subjects are treated as heads in child grammar is not necessary in a split-CP system. In such a system one could suggest that pronominal subjects as opposed to non-pronominal subjects can occupy either [Spec,IP] or a specifier-position in the C-domain, for instance [Spec,FinP]. The finite verb could then be assumed to target Fin° rather than C° before age 5;0 in clauses introduced by a complementizer:

(i) a. $[_{ForceP} [_{Force'}$ complementizer $[_{FinP} [_{Fin'} V_{fin} [_{IP}$ pronominal   V1
        subject . . .

    b. $[_{ForceP} [_{Force'}$ complementizer $[_{FinP}$ pronominal subject 'early' V2
        $[_{Fin'} V_{fin} [_{IP} . . .$

(ii) $[_{ForceP} [_{Force'}$ complementizer $[_{FinP} [_{Fin'} V_{fin} [_{IP}$ non-pronominal V1
        subject . . .

References

CLAHSEN, H. (1982) *Spracherwerb in der Kindheit. Eine Untersuchung zur Entwicklung der Syntax bei Kleinkindern*, Narr, Tübingen.

CLAHSEN, H. (1989) 'Bedingungen der Parameterfixierungen: Zur Analyse einiger Erscheinungen aus der Kindersprache im Rahmen der GB-Theorie', Paper presented at the University of Hamburg.

CLAHSEN, H. and K.-D. SMOLKA (1985) 'Psycholinguistic Evidence and the Description of V2 Phenomena in German' in H. Haider and M. Prinzhorn (eds), *Verb Second Phenomena in Germanic Languages*, Foris, Dordrecht.

DEN BESTEN, H. (1977) 'On the Interaction of Root Transformations and Lexical Deletive Verbs', Ms. MIT and University of Amsterdam. Also published in Den Besten (1989), 14–88.

DEN BESTEN, H. (1989) 'Studies in West Germanic Syntax', Ph.D. dissertation, University of Tilburg.

GAWLITZEK-MAIWALD, I., R. TRACY and A. FRITZENSCHAFT (1992) 'Language Acquisition and Competing Linguistic Representations: The Child as Arbiter' in J. Meisel (ed.), *The Acquisition of Verb Placement. Functional Categories and V2 Phenomena in Language Acquisition*, Kluwer, Dordrecht, 139–80.

HAEGEMAN, L. (1992) *Theory and Description in Generative Syntax. A Case Study in West Flemish*, Cambridge University Press, Cambridge.

HAEGEMAN, L. (1996) 'Verb Second, the Split CP and Null Subjects in Early Dutch Finite Clauses', *GenGenP* 4.2, 133–75.

HAEGEMAN, L. and H. VAN RIEMSDIJK (1986) 'Verb Projection Raising, Scope and the Typology of Verb Movement Rules', *Linguistic Inquiry* 17, 417–66.

KOSTER, J. (1975) 'Dutch as an SOV Language', *Linguistic Analysis* 1, 111–36.

MILLS, A. E. (1985) 'Acquisition of German' in D. I. Slobin (ed.), *The Cross-linguistic Study of Language Acquisition, Vol. 1: The Data*, N. J. Erlbaum, Hillsdale, 141–254.

MÜLLER, G. and W. STERNEFELD (1993) 'Improper Movement and Unambiguous Binding', *Linguistic Inquiry* **24**, 461–507.

PENNER, Z. (1990) 'On the Acquisition of Verb Placement and Verb Projection Raising in Bernese Swiss German', in M. Rothweiler (ed.), S*pracherwerb und Grammatik. Linguistische Untersuchungen zum Erwerb von Syntax und Morphologie.* Linguistische Berichte Sonderheft 3, 166–89.

PENNER, Z. (1996) 'From Empty to Doubly-Filled Complementizers. A Case Study in the Acquisition of Subordination in Bernese Swiss German', Fachgruppe Sprachwissenschaft der Universität Konstanz, *Arbeitspapier* Nr. **77**.

PENNER, Z. and T. BADER (1995) 'Issues in the Syntax of Subordination: A Comparative Study of the Complementizer System in Germanic, Romance, and Semitic Languages with Special Reference to Bernese Swiss German' in Z. Penner (ed.), *Topics in Swiss German Syntax*, Peter Lang, Bern, 73–290.

RIZZI, L. (1997) 'The Fine Structure of the Left Periphery' in L. Haegeman (ed.), *Elements of Grammar. A Handbook of Generative Syntax*, Kluwer, Dordrecht.

ROEPER, T. (1973) 'Approaches to a Theory of Language Acquisition with Examples from German Children', Ph.D. dissertation, Harvard University.

ROTHWEILER, M. (1993) *Der Erwerb von Nebensätzen im Deutschen*, Niemeyer, Tübingen.

SCHÖNENBERGER, M. (1995) 'Embedded V-to-C in Early Swiss German', *MITWPL* **26**, 403–50.

SCHÖNENBERGER, M. (1996) 'Why Do Swiss German Children Like Verb Movement So Much?'*Proceedings of the 20th Boston University Conference on Language Development*, Cascadilla Press, Somerville, MA.

SCHÖNENBERGER, M. (1998) 'The Acquisition of Verb Placement in Swiss German', Ph.D. dissertation, University of Geneva.

SCHWARTZ, B. and S. VIKNER (1996) 'All Verb Second Clauses are CPs' in A. Belletti and R. Rizzi (eds), *Parameters and Functional Heads*, Oxford University Press, Oxford, 11–62.

SHLONSKY, U. (1994) 'Agreement in Comp', *The Linguistic Review* **11**, 351–75.

TRAVIS, L. (1984) 'Parameters and Effects of Word Order Variation', Ph.D. dissertation, MIT.

TRAVIS, L. (1991) 'Parameters of Phrase Structure and V2 Phenomena' in R. Freidin (ed.), *Principles and Parameters in Comparative Grammar*, MIT Press, Cambridge, MA.

WEXLER, K. (1996) 'The Development of Inflection in a Biologically Based Theory of Language Acquisition' in M. L. Rice (ed.), *Toward a Genetics of Language*, Lawrence Erlbaum, Mahwah, NJ.

WEXLER, K. (1999) 'Maturation and Growth of Grammar' in W. C. Ritchie and T. K. Bhatia (eds), *The Handbook of Language Acquisition*, Academic Press, San Diego.

ZWART, J. W. C. (1993) 'Dutch Syntax. A Minimalist Approach', Ph.D. dissertation, University of Groningen.

ZWART, J. W. C. (1997) *Morphosyntax of Verb Movement. A Minimalist Approach to the Syntax of Dutch*, Studies in Natural Language and Linguistic Theory, Kluwer, Dordrecht.

Index

164n29, 172–4, 184, 186–92,
202–4, 206, 225, 237, 242–3,
252, 254, 257, 260–1,
270–3, 279–81, 284, 287–8,
298
Roberge, 206
Roberts, 79n2, 145
Roeper, 6, 12, 59, 59n4, 125n7,
162n19, 173, 197n2, 261,
274–5, 277–8, 299
Rohrbacher, 12, 99, 162n19, 197n2,
224, 261, 274–5, 277–8
Ronat, 76
de Roo, 96
root
   infinitives, 6–7, 9–11, 15, 66–7,
73–5, 79, 174, 179–83, 187,
194, 206–7, 216–18, 220, 222,
224–6, 236–40, 242–4,
246–58, 261, 263, 272, 285,
287
   phenomenon, 138
   principle, 202, 204
   specifier of, 6–7, 12, 14, 71, 73,
271, 276, 279–83, 285
Ross, 142
Rothstein, 100
Rothweiler, 18, 299, 300
Rowlett, 157

Safir, 136–7, 288
Saito, 150
Sano, 11–12, 181, 185, 237, 240–1,
244, 247, 272, 275
Sasanuma, 97
Schaeffer, 10
Schein, 281
Schmerling, 133–4
Schönenberger, x, 18–19, 301
Schuetze, 173, 185, 261, 278
Schwartz, 14, 203, 206, 222, 226,
317n2
scope
   assignment, 177, 187
   marking, 171, 176, 178, 187
   position, 176–7
   relation, 171–3
Scupin, 36

second language (L2), 14–15, 20,
202–32, 287
   child vs adult, 225–6, 287
Shapiro, 95
Shields, 134
Shlonsky, x, 100, 298
Siloni, x, 17, 28, 79
Smart, 134–5
Smith, 11, 63–4, 77, 157, 277
Smolka, 299
Snow, 5, 11, 77, 79n1, 107, 110
Sonnenstuhl-Henning, 59
Spanish, 10, 271
Speas, 205, 275, 288
Sprouse, 222
Starke, 146, 162n18, 260, 288
Sternefeld, 143, 298
Stowell, 98, 136, 288
Stromswold, 106, 109–11, 114, 118,
120, 122–3, 124n4
stylistic inversion, 65–7, 76, 80n7
subject (*see also* null subject)
   clitics, 10, 14–15, 206, 217–18,
224
   non-referential: *see* expletive
   postverbal, 12, 63–81, 137, 145,
161n13
   pronoun, 4, 67, 75, 91
   VP-internal, 12, 63–7, 70–1,
73–4, 76–8, 79n3
subject-auxiliary inversion (SAI),
105–6, 109–10, 121–2
subordination, 6, 18–19, 95–7, 271,
293–318
Suppes, 11, 63–4, 77, 107, 261–2,
271
Swedish, 3, 65, 73, 284
Symons, 132–4
Szabolcsi, 17, 28

tense
   anchoring in C, 98
   impairment, 19, 85–100
   inflection, 9, 84–9, 202–3, 224–6
   node, 10, 20, 98–9, 206
   underspecification, 202
that-trace, 138
Thompson, 95

QUEEN MARY &
WESTFIELD
COLLEGE LIBRARY